The publisher and the University of California Press Foundation gratefully acknowledge the generous support of the Roth Family Foundation Imprint in Music, established by a major gift from Sukey and Gil Garcetti and Michael P. Roth.

The publisher also gratefully acknowledges the generous support of the AMS 75 PAYS Fund of the American Musicological Society, supported in part by the National Endowment for the Humanities and the Andrew W. Mellon Foundation, in making this book possible.

Freedom Moves

HIP HOP STUDIES

H. Samy Alim and Jeff Chang, Series Editors

1. *Women Rapping Revolution: Hip Hop and Community Building in Detroit,* by Rebekah Farrugia and Kellie D. Hay
2. *Rebel Speak: A Justice Movement Mixtape,* by Bryonn Rolly Bain
3. *Freedom Moves: Hip Hop Knowledges, Pedagogies, and Futures,* edited by H. Samy Alim, Jeff Chang, and Casey Philip Wong

Freedom Moves

HIP HOP KNOWLEDGES,
PEDAGOGIES,
AND FUTURES

Edited by
H. Samy Alim, Jeff Chang,
and Casey Philip Wong

UNIVERSITY OF CALIFORNIA PRESS

University of California Press
Oakland, California

© 2023 by The Regents of the University of California

Cover art by Maxwell Southgate, better known by his artist name MAK1ONE, a legendary street artist and muralist in Cape Town, South Africa. This piece was painted in real time during the African Hip Hop Indaba Lecture Series at the University of the Western Cape in August of 2014.

Library of Congress Cataloging-in-Publication Data

Names: Alim, H. Samy, editor. | Chang, Jeff, editor. | Wong, Casey Philip, editor.
Title: Freedom moves : hip hop knowledges, pedagogies, and futures / edited by H. Samy Alim, Jeff Chang, Casey Philip Wong.
Other titles: California series in hip hop studies ; 3.
Description: Oakland, California : University of California Press, [2023] | Includes bibliographical references and index.
Identifiers: LCCN 2022000544 (print) | LCCN 2022000545 (ebook) | ISBN 9780520382787 (cloth) | ISBN 9780520382800 (paperback) | ISBN 9780520382817 (ebook)
Subjects: LCSH: Rap (Music)—Political aspects. | Rap (Music)—Social aspects. | Rap musicians—Political activity. | Hip-hop—Influence.
Classification: LCC ML3918.R37 F74 2022 (print) | LCC ML3918.R37 (ebook) | DDC 306.4/84249—dc23
LC record available at https://lccn.loc.gov/2022000544
LC ebook record available at https://lccn.loc.gov/2022000545

32 31 30 29 28 27 26 25 24 23
10 9 8 7 6 5 4 3 2 1

H. SAMY ALIM dedicates this book to James G. Spady, "a Free Black Man,"
who taught so many of us how to be Hip Hop scholars,
and continues, even beyond his transition,
to be our conscience and our guide
as we keep pushing to make
freedom move(s).

JEFF CHANG dedicates this book to
Timothy "Gift of Gab" Parker and Greg Tate,
peerless conjurers of the soaring,
inciting, living word.

CASEY PHILIP WONG dedicates this book to the memory of his fierce and fearless mother,
Geraldine "Geri" Daffron-Wong, and her hopeful vision
of a world defined by just peace, inescapable joy,
and transformative love.

Hip Hop is a huge hero for me. I love it. I love its vitality. I love the fact that it speaks to young people the way it spoke to me. It recognized my talent, it recognized that I was beautiful, it recognized that I was lonely, it recognized my despair and it told me, "Don't cry, don't despair. I understand you. I got something for you to do with all your energy. I got something for you to do with the hopefulness in you. I got something for you to do with the anger inside of you, with the sadness inside of you. I got a way for you to turn that around."

Mos Def (Yasiin Bey)
Cape Town, South Africa
2014

I write impossible worlds into existence because visioning is a collective act, one that invites new ways of being in relationship, one that acts as a useful tool toward collective liberation.

A-lan Holt, poet, playwright, filmmaker
San Francisco Bay Area
2020

Hip Hop was a way to say, "I am somebody"; it acted as some kind of medicine. It was about reconnecting [to Africa]. It was also about ghettocentrism . . . thinking of the ghetto as a repository of energy, livelihood, community and not just this racial, spatial presence that symbolized abandonment and containment. It was also about hypermasculinity, which was really a sign of powerlessness, and it reified heteronormativity, and I think it is important to mention that. It was a lot of things we needed to unlearn as well. As I mentioned earlier, medicine often has some serious side effects.

Shaheen Ariefdien, Prophets of da City
Palo Alto, California
2014

To me, that's what Hip Hop is, sharing wisdom, sharing our way of living, and helping people just exist on this earth while at the same time giving them joy and beauty and connection to their heart and their heartbeat . . . And what I think what we see as Dream Warriors, among many other things, is our youth are safe. Our youth love themselves. Our youth feel empowered and our youth have the older sisters and brothers they need to not just survive, but truly thrive and be the people they were born to be, whatever that is, whatever they choose that to be.

Lyla June, Diné Hip Hop artist, Dream Warriors
Taos, New Mexico
2020

Contents

Preface	xiii
Shout Outs	xvii
Making Freedom Move(s): Hip Hop Knowledges, Pedagogies, and Futures	1
H. Samy Alim, Casey Philip Wong, and Jeff Chang	

PART I: BLACK, INDIGENOUS, AND DIASPORIC KNOWLEDGES — 27

1. Sweat the Technique: The Politics and Poetics of Hip Hop — 29
    Rakim, Chuck D, and Talib Kweli

2. Know the Ledge(s): The Meanings of Knowledge of Self in "Post"-Apartheid South Africa — 53
    Shaheen Ariefdien and Emile YX?

3. "Al-shaab yurid isqat al-nitham!": Sustaining Revolution in Palestine and Syria through Hip Hop — 83
    DAM (Tamer Nafar, Suhell Nafar, and Mahmoud Jreri), Omar Offendum, and Ramzi Salti

4. "The Revolution Will Be Indigenous": Collective Liberation, Healing, and Resistance to Settler Colonialism through Hip Hop   103

Jessa Calderon, Gunner Jules, Lyla June, Tall Paul, and Tanaya Winder, with Casey Philip Wong

5. "Luchando Derechos" in Neoliberal Spain: Hip Hop Visions beyond Racism, Xenophobia, Islamophobia, and the Gentrification of El Raval, Barcelona   131

La Llama Rap Colectivo with H. Samy Alim

PART II: HIP HOP ORGANIZING FOR ABOLITION, REPARATIONS, HEALING, AND GROWTH   157

6. 1Hood: Hip Hop Art, Activism, and Media Creation in Pittsburgh   159

Jasiri X

7. "Protection from Police Who Hinder Respiratory Airways": Hip Hop Theatre and Activism with Kuumba Lynx in Chicago   180

Jacinda Bullie, Jaquanda Saulter-Villegas, and Leyda "Lady Sol" Garcia

8. Ripples of Hope and Healing: Sustaining Community by Creating a Social Justice Arts Ecosystem   193

Sonya Clark-Herrera, with Measha Ferguson Smith, hodari blue fka Adorie Howard, Reagan Ross, and Casey Philip Wong

9. Beyond Trauma: Storytelling as Cultural Shift and Collective Healing   213

Bryonn Bain, Mark Gonzales, A-lan Holt, and Michelle Lee

PART III: HIP HOP AS CRITICAL, CULTURALLY RELEVANT, AND CULTURALLY SUSTAINING PEDAGOGY   243

10. "Where the Beat Drops": Culturally Relevant and Culturally Sustaining Hip Hop Pedagogies   245

Gloria Ladson-Billings, Django Paris, and H. Samy Alim

11.	How Hip Hop Means: Retrospect for Beats, Rhymes, and Classroom Life	269
	Marc Lamont Hill	
12.	The Magic behind Science Genius: How Hip Hop Can Transform Science Education	298
	Christopher Emdin and The GZA, with Bryan Brown	
13.	Hip Hop, Whiteness, and Critical Pedagogies in the Context of Black Lives Matter	322
	A. J. Robinson	
PART IV:	QUEER, FEMINIST, AND DIS/ABILITY JUSTICE HIP HOP FUTURES	347
14.	The Pleasure Principle: Articulating a Post–Hip Hop Feminist Politics of Pleasure	349
	Joan Morgan, Brittney Cooper, Treva Lindsey, Kaila Adia Story, and Esther Armah	
15.	"When Can Black Disabled Folks Come Home?": The Krip-Hop Movement, Race, and Disability Justice	376
	Leroy F. Moore Jr. and Stephanie Keeney Parks	
16.	Queering Hip Hop Feminist Pedagogies in the New South	396
	Bettina Love, Regina N. Bradley, and Mark Anthony Neal	
17.	"These Are Not Sonnet Times": Building toward Liberatory Futures	413
	Maisha T. Winn	
	Contributor Bios	423
	Index	435

Preface

Moving through over a dozen cities across four continents, *Freedom Moves: Hip Hop Knowledges, Pedagogies, and Futures* represents a cutting-edge, field-defining moment in Hip Hop Studies. As we celebrate 50 years of Hip Hop cultural history, and 30 years of Hip Hop scholarship, Hip Hop continues to be one of the most profound and transformative social, cultural, and political movements of the late twentieth and early twenty-first centuries. In this book, H. Samy Alim, Jeff Chang, and Casey Philip Wong invite us to engage dialogically with some of the world's most innovative and provocative Hip Hop artists and intellectuals as they collectively rethink the relationships between Hip Hop knowledges, pedagogies, and futures.

Rooting Hip Hop in Black freedom culture, this state-of-the-art collection presents a globally diverse group of Black, Indigenous, Latinx, Asian American, Arab, European, North African, and South Asian artists, activists, and thinkers who view Hip Hop as a means to move freedom forward for all of us.

Contributors do so by taking stock of the politics of Hip Hop culture at this critical juncture of renewed racial justice movements in the United States and globally (Chuck D, Rakim, and Talib Kweli); resisting oppressive policing and reimagining community safety, healing, and growth in US urban centers like New York (Bryonn Bain), Pittsburgh (Jasiri X), Chicago (Kuumba Lynx), Atlanta and "the New South" (Bettina Love, Regina Bradley, and Mark Anthony Neal), and the San Francisco Bay Area (Mark Gonzales, A-lan Holt, Michelle Lee, and the Mural Music and Arts Project); and recovering traditional, Indigenous knowledges and ways of being in the world at the same time that they create new ones (Dream Warriors).

Leading thinkers take seriously the act of forging new languages for new articulations of Black / feminist / queer / disabled futures within and beyond Hip Hop (Joan Morgan, Brittney Cooper, Treva Lindsey, Kaila Adia Story, Esther Armah, Leroy F. Moore Jr., and Stephanie Keeney Parks); theorizing pedagogies that sustain the voices and visions of our youth in our collective movements toward freedom (Marc Lamont Hill, Christopher Emdin and The GZA, Gloria Ladson-Billings, Django Paris, and Maisha Winn); creating independent institutions within the White settler capitalist context of a "post"-apartheid South Africa (Prophets of da City's Shaheen Ariefdien and Black Noise's Emile YX?); envisioning life beyond "occupation" and the crushing (neo)colonial geopolitics of Palestine (DAM) and Syria (Omar Offendum); and organizing against suffocating, neoliberal austerity measures while fighting for a world free of racism, xenophobia, Islamophobia, and political repression (La Llama Rap Colectivo in Spain).

This volume is a testament to Hip Hop's power in that it functions as an art "form / forum," as James G. Spady wrote 30 years ago, and as such, it stands positioned to offer us new futures and new ways to imagine *freedoms*. This book, this forum, was birthed within the broader context of nearly a decade of interaction with some of the world's leading thinkers on freedom. More specifically, these contributions grow out of a forward-looking, public-facing Hip Hop course, which was free and open to the public, taught by the three of us under the auspices of Stanford University's Institute for Diversity in the Arts (IDA). Beyond this course, we organized dozens of panel discussions, lectures, performances, readings, jam sessions, ciphers, and held dialogues that occurred well into 2020. Not only did we enjoy building with each other, but we also enjoyed building a Hip Hop "beloved community" together.

Contributors weave narratives, tell tales, teach, drop a verse or two, laugh, share, and sometimes even cry together, and in the process, create a familiar / familial text that breathes life into studies of Hip Hop culture. It is through this critical and celebratory engagement with Hip Hop—rooted in the very same Hip Hop sensibilities that have captivated the world—that we invite you to consider how you can join in the project of making freedom move(s).

Shout Outs

Bismillah Al-Rahman Al-Rahim. In the Name of Allah, the Beneficent, the Merciful. Deep breath. For anyone who knows both the joy and the labor of putting a book out into the universe, you know that the acknowledgments section is often the hardest part to write. This book was written over the span of a decade, the last few years of which saw us right in the middle of the dual pandemic of COVID-19 and the ongoing police violence that continues to ravage many of the Communities of Color where Hip Hop is, as Jeff Chang has written repeatedly, "a *lived* culture." Deep breath. I've been writing about Hip Hop for a quarter century now, and each time as I take these deep breaths—these moments to reflect—I grasp anew the depth of what Hip Hop culture has meant to so many of us.

Shout out to everybody who loves / lives this culture. Shout out to the UMUM Crew and all those who understand, as Black Arts Movement poet Sista Sonia Sanchez would say, the "deeply deep" thing that's going on with Hip Hop. Samir Meghelli knows. Shout out to the DJ who mixed in the record, "Last night a DJ saved my life," and provoked a collective exhale from the crowd that night. Robin Kelley knows. Deep breath. Shout out to the culture that educated so many of us and shored up our commitment to resistance, justice, disruption, and transformation. Shout out to the NOI, No. 26 on 3rd & Revere, and the legions of artists who taught us how to speak up and out. You have breathed life into all of us over the years and transformed us with your vision. If anything, this book stands as a testament to the power of what late, great Hip Hop historian James G. Spady called "the Hip Hop vision" and its continued evolution as it is (re)created by youth around the globe, and by those who refuse to give up on the culture by reinventing it through feminist, queer, and disability justice lenses. Deep breath.

Shout out to the FAM speaking through the pages of this book. Rakim Allah. Chuck D. Talib Kweli. Shaheen Ariefdien. Emile YX?. DAM. Omar Offendum. Ramzi Salti. Jessica Calderon. Gunner Jules. Lyla June. Tall Paul. Tanaya Winder. La Llama Rap Colectivo. Jasiri X. Jacinda Bullie. Jaquanda Saulter-Villegas. Leyda "Lady Sol" Garcia. The MMAP Family. Sonya Clark-Herrera. Hodari fka Dorien Blue fka Adorie Howard. Measha Ferguson Smith. Reagan Ross. Bryonn Bain. Mark Gonzales. The entire IDA Family. A-lan Holt. Michelle Lee. The Notorious GLB (Gloria Ladson-Billings). Django Paris. Marc Lamont Hill. Christopher Emdin. The GZA. Bryan Brown. A. J. Robinson. The Pleasure Ninjas Fam. Joan Morgan. Brittney Cooper. Treva Lindsey. Kaila Adia Story. Esther Armah. Leroy F. Moore Jr. and Stephanie Keeney Parks (both UCLA Anthropology doctoral students!). Bettina Love. Regina Bradley. Mark Anthony Neal. Maisha Winn. When I look back over this list of beautiful people I see a global family, spanning at least two decades and four continents. One Love.

Shout out to my two brothers from another mother, Jeff Chang and Casey Wong. Words can't even express how deeply I care about and appreciate you both. As I write this, my heart warms as I think about all of the many good times we had over the years, the conversations, the delicious dinners (yes!), the courses and conferences that we organized around Hip Hop, the intellectual debates and exchanges, the long afternoon book sessions in Jeff's office (with the poster board and post-its flying left and right!), and of course, the love. It's always an honor to work with you and to count you among my dearest friends and fam. I look forward to building with you for many years to come, insha'Allah. The academy can often be a cold, lonely place, and sometimes we gotta do our work in the belly of the beast (y'all know what I'm talking about). So thank you for moving through the world with honesty, integrity, and I want to underscore this one, humility, and for constantly restoring my faith in the work. Respect.

Shout out to Raina Polivka, UC Press Acquisitions Editor. Raina, you already know how wonderful it has been to work with you on this project and on the Hip Hop Studies Book Series. It is safe to say that you are, in large part, responsible for the success of both. It is not often in this game that Scholars of Color encounter editors who truly "get" their projects. Thank you not only for your brilliant editorial advice and intellectual insights, but for your *deep* listening, your continued encouragement, your ability to understand the heart and soul of our project, and for pushing us, always gently, when necessary. For all of that, I am deeply grateful. But even more than that, I am grateful for our friendship and our many meetings that sometimes turned into mutual therapy sessions where we helped each other through. We're also grateful to UC Press Production Editor, Francisco Reinking. Thank you for your passion, commitment, and attention to detail in helping us close out this project.

Speaking of getting each other through, shout out to the Hip Hop Studies Working Group and the broader Hip Hop Initiative (HHI) at UCLA, including co-organizers Tabia Shawel and Samuel Lamontagne, and Kelly Lytle Hernández and Gaye Theresa Johnson, and the entire family at the Ralph J. Bunche Center for African American Studies. Respect to the one and only Chuck D of Public Enemy for serving as the HHI inaugural Artist in Residence and tearing the roof off of Haines Hall in the Spring of 2022. Much love to dream hampton, Davey D, and Ben Caldwell. Stephanie Keeney Parks. Leroy F. Moore Jr. Mercedes Douglass. Natalie Marshall. MiRi Park. Joaquin Noguera. Erick Matus. Dexter Story. Lucas Avidan. Ife Jie. Bella Stenvall. Jasmine Jackson. Kayla Boyden. Khyla Horton. Alexander Williams. Casey Wong. Wade Fulton Dean. And all of the faculty at UCLA who have engaged the Hip Hop Studies Working Group. Cheryl L. Keyes. Robin D. G. Kelley. Bryonn Bain. Adam Bradley. Shana Redmond. Kyle Mays. Scot Brown. Shout out of course to all of my colleagues in the Department of Anthropology and the Discourse Lab community, who have supported this work from jump. Shout out to my Cape Town brothers, Adam Haupt, Quentin Williams, and Emile Jansen, for their friendship and their brilliance in *Neva Again: Hip Hop Art, Activism, and Education in Post-Apartheid South Africa*. Love to Dee. And Dr. G. Always.

We also acknowledge the research reported in this volume was made possible in part by a Lyle Spencer Research Grant and the generosity of the Spencer Foundation, "A Cross-Cultural Study of Culturally Sustaining Pedagogy in Global Perspective" (#202000135). The views expressed are our own, and do not necessarily reflect the view of the Spencer Foundation. We would also like to acknowledge Elizabeth Mendez Berry, Judilee Reed, and Jessica Garz of the Surdna Foundation for their generous support that helped us to launch this project in East Palo Alto in 2014.

I need to say this before I pass the mic to Casey. These past two years have seen so much loss, so much death. In my darkest hours of the pandemic, after the loss of James G. Spady (may Allah rest his soul) and so many others near and dear to my heart, I clung to this book for life. In the moments where we all question the value and purpose of what we do as academics with respect to movements for racial justice, this book gave me clarity. When I was immobilized, with writing deadlines for other projects piling up on my desk, I was somehow able to pour hours into this one. And so I end where I began—Hip Hop, like D-Nice's Club Quarantine parties on Instagram, once again saved my life. Shout out to all the Hip Hop heads, activists, artists, thinkers, and educators who blessed this project with their contributions—your words and actions are helping all of us make freedom move(s).

To pick up the mic, and carry on where Alim left off, I have to start off my shout outs by pouring out a few more words for loved ones, chosen kin, freedom fighters, and Hip Hop luminaries who passed during the past few years as we worked on this book... In thinking about our collective freedom, I have to pour out words for the freedom fighters, activists, and intellectuals Bob Moses, John Lewis, Juan Gómez-Quiñones, Gloria Richardson, Martha White, Miriam Jiménez Román, among so many who left us—we remember you. In the Hip Hop world, we lost Biz Markie, DMX, MF Doom, Shock G, and so many more, including Timothy "Gift of Gab" Parker, to whom Jeff dedicated this book—we remember you.

I have to offer a special remembrance of the Bay Area Hip Hop legend, Stephen "Zumbi" Gaines. As we closed editing of this book we got word that you left us. Zumbi, I remember the first time I heard your music (and Alim remembers interviewing you and building with your brilliance right after Mind Over Matter dropped over twenty years ago!). I was cratedigging with my fam Husam (Shout out to you, Steph, and Nahla livin up on Shaolin Mountain!). I scanned and listened to your album *True & Livin'* on those old headphones at the Berkeley *Rasputin*—I'll never forget the first time I heard that opening trumpet sequence on "Doin My Thang"! I kept that album on repeat for weeks! All those shows that you did at UC Berkeley, and across the Bay, I couldn't imagine Bay Area Hip Hop without you, and your banger, "The Bay." Imagine my surprise when years later the Bay Area Hip Hop Ed legend, Adisa "the Bishop" Banjoko, invited me to participate on a panel on martial arts, and you were in the front row! You came up after, we exchanged numbers and texts, and planned to break bread—little did I know we'd never get the chance. I briefly got a chance to witness your humility, bars, and graciousness, which I know is legendary, iconic, and felt by so many, rest in power . . .

And speaking of Adisa the Bishop, I'm grateful that you're still with us after your close call! Shout out to all that you've done and will continue to do for Hip Hop, martial arts, and chess (check the bishopchronicles.com, if you don't know, now you know!)—I'll never forget how you came out for the love at Berkley Maynard Academy for the FRESH! kids, you're loved!

Alongside acknowledgments of those special lives that we lost, I have to recognize the peoples and lands I am in relation with—the US nation-state is a White settler colonial-capitalist cisheteropatriarchal ableist monolingual project. It continues to exist based upon the continuing erasure of Indigenous peoples (i.e., I am currently on lands stained with the blood and sweat of Tongva peoples, and upon lands that continue to be dishonored as "property"). Our collective freedom won't be achieved without returning power to Tongva peoples and giving land back (i.e., for more see landback.org), and entering into just relations with the lands, and the peoples who have lived upon these lands. Just relations will mean acknowledging and acting upon the knowledge that intersecting and overlapping African, Latinx, Asian, and Pacific Islander communities have continued to face racial terror and processes of colonialism upon these lands. Just relations will mean engaging in decolonization and abolition—we won't be free until we're all free, and freedom is a process, not an event.

I wouldn't have these worldviews without my parents, Geraldine Daffron-Wong and Leland Wong, and my grandmother, Garth Greene, and all the love and wisdom you left me. This is especially the case for my

xxii SHOUT OUTS

mother—I have dedicated this book to you—who sustained my participation in Hip Hop because she knew its power and possibilities. I still fondly remember the car ride we took down to Playa Del Rey, and the stories about your upbringing that you told me as we listened to Pac and Eminem! You were the GOAT storyteller—I've never heard anyone who can top you, Mom!—and I know we shared so much joy listening to Hip Hop because you saw between, within, beneath, and over every line. You taught me how to bear witness. I miss listening to music with you.

This book definitely wouldn't have been possible without the ongoing love and support and laughter with my sister, Rachael! Our daily chats in our family apartment have been everything, we've been through so much, and I know we have so many diapers, jokes on Pablo, and adventures left—even though, no more trips while you're pregnant! #StairsInRome lol. I'm so glad we've come together in our common vision of transforming the world through education! Shout out to my brother-in-law, Pablo Tagliavacche, who was my "co-worker" through the pandemic. Your humor has kept us afloat, and so glad Luca is returning the favor with jokes on you! And speaking of Luca, shout out to you my baby nephew, Luca! I look forward to the day that I'll get a chance to share what I was doing behind closed doors over the past few months—thanks for reminding me to keep my water bottles filled and to stay hydrated! Also shout out to you, my new baby nephew, Thiago! You were born right as we finished edits on this volume, your presence has been such a beautiful addition to our family!

Shout out to my brother, Travis, and sister-in-law, Maura! Maura, your generosity of heart and spirit has been such a great addition to our family! And Trav, editing and writing in this volume took me all the way back to those long commutes between Colton and Berkeley in our 94' Sentra, listening to my latest finds from Rasputin and Amoeba, which in so many ways fueled knowledges that led to my work in Hip Hop Education! A Tribe Called Question. Lauryn Hill. Mos Def (now Yasiin Bey). Talib Kweli. Erykah Badu. De La Soul. Pharcyde. Da Brat. Nas. I know your fav is Gang Starr! So many tracks flew by on our humble sound system that we barely managed to wire and install! Those were the good ol' days, right?! In the words of that seminal Wu-Tang Clan track, *Can It All Be So Simple* . . .

This project would have DEF not happened without all the IDA family! Shout out to the OG Adam Banks and the whole Arts and Education

Project researcher squad and fam: Kareem Alston, Anjana Bala, Ali Barajas, Tyler Brooks, hodari blue fka Adorie Howard, Janei Maynard, Measha Ferguson Smith, Yeji Jung, Ari Marcus, Natasha Mmonatau, Thomas Plank, Reagan Ross, Chris Russ, Elliot Williams, and so many more! And a mile-long special shout out to Ellen Oh and A-lan Holt, who held us together! You did so much behind-the-scenes work to make all this happen, that no words could really do justice! Appreciate you so much!

A HUGE shout out to all my incredible mentees and students across space and time (forgive me once again if I miss you here!)—who still teach me and continue to impact my life, who I miss and have moved on to transform the world, and those who have passed on and stay in my heart... Surabhi Balachander, Melodyanne Cheng, Dontae "Don Da Menace" Cochran, Emma Coleman, Justean Delacruz, Alexis Demery, Alysia Demery, Mercedes Douglass, Joshua Feliz, Simon Fung, Julissa "Julie" Gaytan, Laura "Lala" Gaytan, Omar "Tlatoani JIGP" Gaytan, Alexandrea "Ally" Gulley, Lajae "Laee" Harmon, Jaquelin Henriquez, Courtney Heredia, Josue Hernandez, David Hidalgo, Torian Hughes, Celina Jackson, Jahnae "JayJay," Jo Lee, Vy Luu, Francesca Mendez, Jeremy Navarro, Ashley Negron, Tsadiku Obolu, Jose Banderas Padilla, Enrique Maldonado Peraza, Tamius "Silent-T" Perez, Neil Prakash, Betty Qiu, Miguel Padilla Quintero, John Rafael, Trinity Rogan, Kayla Smith, Kevin Trimpin, and Jiazheng "James" Wu.

I have to give another special shout out to my academic "Quaranteam"! I wouldn't have made it through the global panorama without you—Shena Sanchez, Joya Hampton-Anderson, Maria Jones, and Derek Novacek! I'm so grateful to call each of you some of my closest friends and colleagues, it's been one of the most beautiful things in my adult life getting to know, work, and laugh with you! And of course, I know you're gonna hate it, but I have to give a special embarrassing shout out to you, Shena! I'm so glad that you came and sat by me at the MTSS retreat—I didn't think it was possible to form such a close and defining friendship with someone who I'd meet so late in life! It's not an overexaggeration that you've changed my life—you went out of your way to re-teach me how to live, like *really* live, and practice joy—beyond the theory! Lol I look forward to all our trips, adventures, retreats, and collaborations to come—even if I have to drag you to the writing ones!

And as long as I'm speaking of comrades, friends, mentors, and chosen kin who have supported me through this work, there's too many to name (forgive me if I miss naming you here!), but I have to give a special shout out to Mercy Agyepong, e alexander, Julio Alicea, Nivay Anandarajah, Mysia Anderson, Derek Ang, Jose Arias, Erica Atwood, Renée Blake, Vince Brown, Tanja Burkhard, Miguel Casar, Marco Chavez, Channa Mae Cook, Alejandro Cisneros, Keith Cross, Vicken Donikian, Darlene Edouard, Kareem Edouard, Kaya Edouard, Venus "Empress Dr. Mam" Evans-Winters, Eli Jacobs-Fantauzzi, Kahlil Jacobs-Fantauzzi, Amanda Frye, Emmanuel "Manny" Garcia, Lorena Camargo Gonzalez, Samra Ghermay, Rose Ann Gutierrez, Denae Hannah, Jamelia Harris, Adam Haupt, Awad Ibrahim, Stan Johnson, Malia Jones, Torin Jones, Renata Love Jones, Sharese King, Valerie Kinloch, Sonja Lanehart, Brian Lau, Annie Le, Greglon Yimm Lee, Ian Levy, Charmaine Mangram, Brenda Giselle Martinez, Danny Martinez, Kai Monet Mathews, Tameka McCullough, Koritha Mitchell, Peter Muller, Ashley Newby, Joaquín Noguera, Tsadiku Obolu, Penny Pasque, Timothy San Pedro, Courtney Peña, Krysada Binly "Lance La Rock" Panusith Phounsiri, Kathleen "Chefleen" O'Brien Price, Denise Resendez, Angela "Angie" Reyes, Elaine "Docta E" Richardson, Gary Segura, Jaspal Singh, Kendra Sobo, Remi Sobo, Tunde Sobo, Shirley Steinberg, Shayna Sullivan, Amanda Tachine, Francis Tongpalad, Shirin Vossoughi, Vajra Watson, Quentin Williams, and Husam Zakharia. Also special shout out to my chosen kin at Youth United for Community Action (YUCA): Ofelia Bello, Tameeka Bennett, Cristal Montes, Kenia Najar, Karely Nunez, and my young co-conspirators Cristina, Fili, Hailey, Julian, Julissa, Raquel, and the whole YUCA crew! And Alim already shouted out our Hip Hop working group and folks appearing in this book, but grateful to also call so many of you comrades, friends, mentors, and chosen kin!

These shout outs would also be remiss without going back to my roots and giving a shout out to my Hip Hop big sister, Martha Diaz! Working with you at the Hip Hop Education Center on the Hip Hop education think tanks was defining to my understandings of the game! And the Hip Hop Education Center wouldn't have been possible without my mentor and elder, Pedro Noguera! Thanks for always looking out for me and guiding me—I can't say enough about how you've always given me the benefit of the doubt and sustained me amidst everything else going on in your world! I'm forever grateful! During my journey as an intellectual, educator, and organizer, I was also beyond blessed to have had Kimberlé Crenshaw, Dawn-Elissa Fisher, Ericka Huggins, Joan Morgan, and Yolanda Sealey-Ruiz enter my life, and support me and my Hip Hop education and justice work with the youth! And this seems as good a time as any to give another special shout out to—Django Paris! I'm so overwhelmingly thankful that Samy introduced us! You've been much more than a guide in this academic game. You've been a moral and political guide, always supporting me to find ways to do CSP, follow my spirit, and intellectualize on my own terms! Also special shout out to my dissertation committee for their ongoing friendship, mentorship, and guidance: Bryan Brown, John Rickford, Treva Lindsey, Jonathan Rosa, Ramón Antonio Martínez, Adam Banks, and of course H. Samy Alim, and my informal committee member, Jeff Chang!

And on that tip, I have to give the ultimate shout out to my older brothers, elders, kale-mojito-sippin-comrades, roti-prata-and-prawn-eating-co-conspirators, SAMY and JEFF!! I'm beyond grateful that we came together like Voltron, and to have learned infinite lessons from y'all on writing, editing, publishing, organizing, facilitating, teaching, and how to just survive and not get knocked TF out in these cold academic and publication streets! You've guided me and given me all the grace as I navigated the 36 chambers! You've always looked out for me, given me love and the benefit of the doubt! So many good laughs, shade, and sh*t-talkin! Samy, can't believe it's been almost 15 years since we met at that Hip Hop conference at UC Berkeley, and how we've co-conspired and eaten ILL food from Palo Alto, to NYC, to Barcelona, to Cadiz! So many text chains on how to live, sustain, and get free! You've pushed my thinking forward from Day 1, on anything from racialization and indexicality, pedagogical foundations and taking the perfect selfie, to learning how to edit a chapter that honors a contributor's vision! And I still remember the first time you introduced me to Jeff back in 2012, you walked me over to the Harmony House, and Jeff yelled out from that top window, and I was like, *who TF is that?*! lol Jeff, so appreciative of all your patience with me, from sitting in your office trying to justify Lyft receipts, to teaching me fundamentals of what it means to write a strong sentence, and that unforgettable lesson on argument as structure, and structure as argument, and to have confidence in myself and my purpose! It's been such a gift to know y'all, my fam and friends for life! I'm looking forward to ALL the collabs, projects, organizing, and good work to come—of course, only as it feels right, on our time, because we're on that #HealthyLiving sh*t! And relatedly, HUGE shout out to my mentor, Dr. Na'ilah Suad Nasir, who changed my life, and set this all into motion as she introduced me to Samy, as she encouraged me to follow my heart and pursue educational justice and Hip Hop work! Forever grateful to you!

Sending lots of love to everyone who gave this a read, we appreciate you, and hope this inspires freedom moves!

And now we must bring this to a close, so that's what I (Jeff) will try to do. Hip Hop is nothing if not an African-activated space to build community and relations in the ways Black people and Indigenous peoples have done for millennia. So it's no surprise that we would conclude this offering by presenting genealogies of our relations. These webs of chosen family also become maps for us to guide us forward individually and collectively. There is no way to repay our forebears, inspirations, and peers the ample gifts that they have given us; it is simply our *kuleana* (*'ōlelo Hawai'i* meaning "inheritance, privilege, and responsibility") to share it forward with the best of our heart, our intellect, and our spirit. It's yours, as well. Each one, teach one.

H. Samy Alim, Casey Philip Wong, and Jeff Chang
Palm Springs, Los Angeles, and Berkeley, February 2022

Making Freedom Move(s)

HIP HOP KNOWLEDGES, PEDAGOGIES, AND FUTURES

H. Samy Alim, Casey Philip Wong, and Jeff Chang

On February 16, 2021, just outside of Barcelona, dozens of Spanish police in riot gear stormed the Universitat de Lleida, where Catalonia's anti-capitalist, anti-fascist rapper, Pablo Hasél, and dozens of his supporters were barricading themselves.[1] Dramatic images and videos of the Mossos d'Esquadra detaining Hasél outside of the university building, with his fist up, shouting, "They will never silence us! Death to the fascist state!" circulated rapidly on social media. What followed were weeks of protests where thousands of young people clashed with police across several major cities in Spain, including Madrid, Valencia, Girona, Bilbao, Barcelona, and of course, Lleida, Hasél's hometown. Hasél was arrested by the state and is, at the time of writing, serving a nine-month prison sentence for insulting the King of Spain and "inciting violence" and "glorifying terrorism" with his tweets and lyrics. The case recalled rapper Valtònyc's arrest in 2012, when he was just 18 years old, and his exile to Belgium where he fled to avoid his three-year jail sentence for similar "crimes."[2]

Ironically, the Spanish state's repression of Valtònyc, Hasél, and others only served to strengthen their arguments that El Franquismo was alive and well in Spain nearly half a century after the end of Franco's dictatorship. The Spanish king Juan Carlos I, who left Spain for the United Arab Emirates after multiple corruption allegations, has been roundly criticized in Spanish media.[3] From Hip Hop heads, and the youth of Spain more generally, the critiques have been particularly vehement because Pablo Hasél's case has become a symbol of not only state repression but also of the resistance to the severe, neoliberal economic austerity measures and the threat of fascism spreading across Europe.

Many continue to march in the streets, pushing for an overturning of the government's "la ley mordaza,"[4] which Mr. Michael, a Spanish Moroccan member of La Llama Rap Colectivo (see chapter 5), described as "a bandage over your mouth ... to keep us quiet." Waqar, a Pakistani member of La Llama Rap Colectivo, added, "That's why in the song, 'Luchando Derechos,' I wanted to send the message that the police mistreats us because of how we look and also, more in general, for the system, it seems like they complain about us, but the system does nothing for us either." Turning specifically to the Spanish state's repression of Hip Hop artists, he reflected upon the power of Hip Hop in Spain: "They want to scare us, if you want to know the truth. Because I think Hip Hop in Spain has grown a lot ... There's like a united struggle also, in Hip Hop, in favor of freedom of expression. And I think that scares them ... We use Hip Hop as a tool for change, because we believe that we can change the way people think, right ... I think that music is freedom."

Beyond the systemic oppression of the state's politics of abandonment and containment,[5] Communities of Color within Spain, as elsewhere, have been suffering under the debilitating weight of capitalism as well as the daily indignities of racism, xenophobia, and Islamophobia, all of which are manipulated to serve the state's repressive agenda. In Catalonia, the irony is that Communities of Color—who are routinely excluded from definitions of "who counts as Catalan" because of the regional identity's ideological links to Whiteness—are holding Spain's feet to the fire by insisting it live up to its democratic ideals. La Llama Rap Colectivo, like many artists within the pages of this book, make use of Hip Hop as a way to envision expansive futures beyond the narrow possibilities offered to them by the state.

FREEDOM MOVES: BLACK, INDIGENOUS, AND DIASPORIC KNOWLEDGES

Speaking in front of an audience of approximately five hundred people in Los Angeles's California African American Museum on March 11, 2020—the last event before the COVID shutdown—Chuck D explained how Hip Hop, as a continuation of Black freedom culture, or in his words, the next iteration of "Black creativity for survival," has always imagined new futures even within the most brutal of contexts: "The Black culture had to speak loud because we had to be in code because we just couldn't say, 'Slavemaster, put your fucking whip away!' We had all kinds of code in our music and our music was everything emitted from us. We spoke it even when we didn't speak it. We hummed it to say so many things when we didn't want to have to say it in words" (see chapter 1).

With Rakim co-signing, Talib Kweli explained: "Because it's folk language, Hip Hop was speaking in the language that everybody could relate to. It's like Dr. [Martin Luther] King called a riot 'the language of the unheard.' Chuck D talked about 'a riot going on' just like Sly and the Family Stone did. And so when you talk about the language of the unheard, what you're talking about is Hip Hop music." Then Kweli historicized Hip Hop even further, rooting it in African traditions: "You're talking about something that goes back before us, before the Last Poets and Gil Scott Heron, before the Negro spirituals and gospel songs that slaves sang to get them through the day. You're talking about things that go way back before, all the way to the African griot tradition. Banging on a drum and telling our story."

In "Part 1: Black, Indigenous, and Diasporic Knowledges," Rakim, Chuck D, and Talib Kweli are joined by Black, Indigenous, Arab, European, North African, and South Asian[6] artists who continue to bang that drum, who continue to tell their stories. Collectively, they are recovering and rethinking traditional knowledges and ways of being at the same time that they are creating new ones; building worlds where the voices and visions of our youth are taken seriously in the futures of collective movements for freedom, sovereignty, and self-determination; imagining new ways of moving in the world within and beyond the "White settler capitalist" contexts of a "post"-apartheid South Africa and the United States; envisioning life beyond "occupation" and the crushing (neo)colonial geopolitics of the

Middle East (Palestine and Syria); and organizing against the suffocating, neoliberal austerity measures spreading throughout Europe and globally, as well as fighting for a world free of racism, xenophobia, Islamophobia, and political repression (Spain).

Organizing. Fighting. Recovering. Forging. Rethinking. Building. Imagining. Envisioning. Creating. From the rich and diverse narratives in this section, we learn that these are the actions necessary for making freedom move(s). They are both the engine that makes freedom move *and* the actions that facilitate freedom moves by young people creating art in contexts where just merely existing can seem like "a miracle," as South Africa's Prophets of da City once put it. Hip Hop, as conceived by many artists in this book, is necessarily an antiracist, decolonial framework that refuses[7] and seeks to abolish[8] White settler capitalist and global neoliberal systems, and increasingly, the ableist, cisheteropatriarchal, and other oppressive systems that have long haunted Hip Hop from within.

These artists, however, urge us to refuse being locked into languages and modes of resistance, and when we do think about resistance, to complicate the damage-centered narratives[9] and all-too-often joyless depictions of our struggles.[10] As Emile YX? shared, his music video for the haunting "Butterflies Fly By" recalled a moment in time in 1985 when "staring down the gun barrel of apartheid" was not just a metaphor for Hip Hop in South Africa (chapter 2). "The whole song explains me going to the rally, and for the first time in my life, a guy pointed his gun at me. And as the gun passed me, it slowed down, and I thought, 'Damn, when is this passing me?' Because it's focused on me, right. And in that moment, my self-worth, in my own mind, was tested because all the time I was shouting, 'Freedom or death, victory is certain.'" As he locked eyes with the apartheid regime's soldier, he recalled others at the rally who were tired of waiting for the speaker to begin, asking him to "entertain" them:

> So, in my own mind, I'm in this conflict. "We're fighting a revolution and you want me to dance?" "Oh, okay, just clap your hands, everyone, let's do it!" So constantly, for me, this period of time, when people speak about the struggle, it was a combination of picking up a brick and throwing it at whoever is pointing a gun at you, picking up teargas canisters and throwing them back at them. And, on the weekend, I go play soccer, and practice Kung Fu and go to a club and dance to Aretha Franklin, whatever. [*Laughter*]

As Lyla June, a Diné member of one of the most prominent collectives of Indigenous Hip Hop artists in North America known as the Dream Warriors (chapter 4), explained, Hip Hop doesn't have to be framed solely as resistance: "To me, that's what Hip Hop is, sharing wisdom, sharing our way of living, and helping people just exist on this earth while at the same time giving them joy and beauty and connection to their heart and their heartbeat." Further, Muslim Mexican American spoken word poet Mark Gonzales argued (chapter 9) that abandoning postures of resistance, even temporarily, opens up new ways of thinking about our futures:

> I don't like this language of what they call resistance and fighting back. I've been rooted and lived a lot of my life in that language, and I realized [that] even the best we were thinking about was like, "What's an alternative look like?" And I'm like, "No, I want to *center* what's important to me." I want to create my own universe and my own galaxy. What's in there, and who's in there, and what are my values, and what are my dreams, and what are my hopes, and how do I just stay alive long enough to figure it out?

What happens when we center what's important to us, rather than the value systems that have been imposed upon us? What happens when we are bold enough to consider the radical proposition: "What does it look like when we've won?" Recalling workshops by the NDN Collective, an Indigenous-led organization dedicated to building Indigenous power by decolonizing and transforming systems through radical imagination, Lyla June reflected upon the first time she confronted the possibility of freedom on Indigenous terms:

> I started crying because as Indigenous peoples, we don't often get to even think that way. We're too busy fighting off today's onslaught, everything from our kids need food, to our water's getting poisoned, to our women are going missing, to our language is going extinct . . . It's fucking hard to just wake up and be Indigenous, generally speaking. I think that for him to ask us that question of what does it look like after we've won, there's an aching in my heart, a good kind of aching that says, wow, no one's ever asked me that. I grieve for that fact that I've never been able to think about that. And then after that grieving, immediately there's celebration because now I'm thinking about that for the first time. And what I think what we see as Dream Warriors, among many other things, one of the things we see is our youth are safe. Our youth love themselves. Our youth feel empowered and

our youth have the older sisters and brothers they need to not just survive, but truly thrive and be the people they were born to be, whatever that is, whatever they choose that to be.

Casey Philip Wong's conversation with the Dream Warriors highlights why contemplating futures, and even presents, from the Indigenous perspective can be profoundly political. The Dream Warriors' artistic production forces viewers to think about how White settlers imagine Indigenous peoples as inescapably locked in the past, as if Indigenous people are already eliminated, do not exist, and have not continued to live, resist, and thrive. Because if Indigenous folks have a present and future, then it questions the legitimacy of White settler nation-states like the United States, their permanence, their history and future. In the case of the Dream Warriors' Hip Hop production, Indigenous presence and futurity exposes the immoral foundations of the US because the very fact of *being* throws into stark relief the connection between the violent, White imperial project and the accompanying ideologies of erasure that uphold and maintain it.

"FREEDOM MOVES AT A WACK PACE": BUILDING AZANIA, A NEW WORLD, FOR THE SAKE OF OUR CHILDREN

The same issues are thrown into sharp relief for artists in the White settler neocolonial-capitalist context of South Africa. Shaheen Ariefdien, of the legendary South African Hip Hop group Prophets of da City (POC), shared the lyrics to their now classic single, "Never Again," which the group performed at the 1994 inauguration of then recently freed president Nelson Mandela (chapter 2). To put this performance in perspective, it took place less than one year after their classic album, *Age of Truth*, was banned by the repressive apartheid regime.[11] Amidst all of the excitement and national fervor around the ushering in of a "post"-apartheid and "post"-racial democratic "rainbow nation," POC sampled the most memorable line of Mandela's inauguration speech, "Never, and never again, shall it be that this beautiful land will again experience the oppression of one by another," to which Shaheen rapped:

> So I dedicate this to those who are down with the revolution,
> all over the world and never snoozing

I dedicate this to those who are down with a struggle, G
even when things got ugly.
'Cause the Black race always had a slapped face.
'Cause freedom moves at a wack pace.
It sometimes takes a miracle to see my people free,
'Cause it's not done e-e-e-as-i-i-ly.
So I dedicate this to those who don't turn the other cheek,
and to those who would rather speak.
Against colonialism, imperialism and racism.
So I'm bringing it back to the basics and I—
know that those who supported the struggle locally,
I support your struggle globally.

Notably, Shaheen described that "freedom moves at a wack pace," which can be read broadly as a reference to centuries of living under brutal White settler colonial rule, or even specifically as a reference to Mandela's nearly three seemingly endless decades in prison. Critically, POC is also speaking directly to those who are "down with the revolution" and fighting "against colonialism, imperialism, and racism" by "rejecting calls for reconciliation that are not accompanied with a clear plan for distributive and restorative justice in post-apartheid South Africa."[12] As Adam Haupt has argued, the policies of the African National Congress have "done very little to reverse the racialized, class inequalities that legislated apartheid produced largely because they place a low premium on public spending and adopt a laissez-faire approach to state regulation of markets."[13] Today, over more than a quarter of a century after the legal fall of apartheid—talk about "a wack pace"—Hip Hop artists and activists are not only calling for a transformational racial politics that moves beyond the rainbow politics of reconciliation and toward the radical politics of redistribution, but they are also challenging White settler capitalist logics of privatization and ownership. As Shaheen explained: "People say 'post'-apartheid, but it was a reality of neoliberalism. The apartheid racial framework was and is still, to some degree, very much in place ... And with neoliberalism globally, people are feeling more and more under pressure, feeling more and more under siege. The conditions that we saw that gave birth to the South Bronx, and the Cape Flats, are being spread globally. And in the South Bronx and the Cape Flats, it's even more intensified" (see chapter 2).

If freedom moves at a wack pace, then POC's DJ Ready D rhymes about the need to make freedom moves by acquiring "knowledge of self" in preparation for a movement to "build Azania, the new world, for the sake of our children." This hopefulness—this imagining of a precolonial, yet renewed Azania[14]—captures much of the ethos behind the freedom moves that many Hip Hop artists and organizations in this book are trying to make from Pittsburgh to Palestine to Mitchells Plain.

MAKING FREEDOM MOVE(S) UNDER OCCUPATION, WAR, AND REVOLUTION IN PALESTINE AND SYRIA

Moving from "post"-apartheid South Africa, what does freedom look like under the current military occupation of Palestine or the devastating geopolitical warfare of Syria's forgotten revolution? Critically acclaimed Syrian American rapper Omar Offendum and the groundbreaking Palestinian group DAM, much like Prophets of da City and Black Noise in the South African apartheid context, are recognized internationally for their rhymes against the Israeli occupation of Palestine. Importantly, to them, they are also recognized *locally* by the people they are trying to reach (see chapter 3). DAM's Mahmoud Jreri explained:

> We come from a place that is very hard. There's a big poverty problem, big drug problem, and of course, a huge political problem ... When I speak about my neighborhood, when I speak about my poverty, when I speak about police violence on Arabs, or military violence on Palestinians, or against Arabs, when I speak about the right of return for Palestinian refugees, then of course, I will affect many people that feel or live the same thing that I live, because they feel connected to my message ... I also was affected in the beginning by Tupac and I was affected by him and from his images, 'cause I only saw the images. I didn't understand English back then, but I saw the neighborhood. I saw the poverty. I saw that he talked about political problems.

Omar Offendum, a Syrian American Muslim born in Saudi Arabia who broke through in 2011 with "#Jan25" (featuring Freeway, Amir Sulaiman, Narcy, and Ayah)—a song that both inspired, and was inspired by, the Arab Spring uprisings—explained that underneath the complexities of post–Arab Spring politics there is a humanitarian crisis to which he remains committed:

> Beneath all the political posturing, all the proxy wars, and all the conspiracy theories, there's very real human suffering taking place. It's half a million refugees outside of Syria, millions internally displaced, 70,000 killed, hundreds of thousands imprisoned... And for me, as a Syrian, and more importantly as a humanitarian, that's kind of what I feel like I want to focus on, because if you get sucked into the political argument, you'll end up losing sight of the fact that at the end of the day, there will be no Syria to come back to, you know? If nobody's taking care of these kids, who've been out of school for 2–3 years, who are now in these camps, then you know, what are we really fighting for?

As he continued, toggling between moments of despair and moments of hope, he echoed Rakim (see chapter 1) and drew powerful connections between Hip Hop's imperative to gain knowledge of self and his Islamic faith, given "the important status that the pursuit of knowledge holds in Islam." He explained: "We are taught that the Prophet Muhammad ﷺ said 'When a person dies, his deeds are cut off except for three: Continuing charity, knowledge that others benefited from, and a righteous son who supplicates for him'... This important reminder puts so much in perspective for me in terms of how fame and material success are not at all the end goal when it comes to this sort of cultural production." Reflecting back on his childhood, Offendum finds hope in a future his children will inherit: "I started rapping as a teenager and always felt the need to honor the great emcees who came before me by doing my best to not only entertain, but educate and inspire the way artists like Rakim and Nas did for me. Now that I'm a father I understand just how crucial this approach has been in terms of helping to shape the cultural spaces that my children will inherit in the not too distant future, insha'Allah."

HIP HOP ORGANIZING FOR ABOLITION, REPARATIONS, HEALING, AND GROWTH

In Part II, "Hip Hop Organizing for Abolition, Reparations, Healing, and Growth," we turn our focus squarely on the systemic injustices faced by

Black folks, as well as Indigenous, Latinx, and other Communities of Color, and the Hip Hop activists and organizers who are carrying forward freedom movements.[15] Whether it's large, predominantly Black and Brown communities in New York, Pittsburgh, and Chicago or the smaller, multiracial (Latinx, Black, Asian, and Pacific Islander) suburbs of the San Francisco Bay Area like East Palo Alto, Communities of Color are faced with the silent and sweeping forces of gentrification, White settler capitalist exploitation, and multiple forms of state repression and police violence that continue to constrain and contain communities through dehumanization, displacement, and death.

In the face of all of this, artists and activists involved in the Hip Hop movement continue to organize a generation of young people to make freedom move(s) by seeking justice, looking beyond justice to healing, and moving beyond healing to growth. These Hip Hop organizations join a reinvigorated movement of racial justice working toward the abolition of prisons and policing, reparations for victims of police violence, and finding creative, community-rooted solutions that invest in the futures of Communities of Color.

In Pittsburgh, Jasiri X and the 1Hood family (chapter 6) have continued to speak up and out for "the invisibles" about the consistent police murders in that city, which have vanished far too many Black lives, as they have across nearly every major city in the US. Describing what he called the "glaring contradiction of being Black in America," Jasiri X explained the impetus behind his song, "America's Most Livable City":[16]

> According to *Forbes* magazine, this is the place, of all cities in the United States, this is the most livable place ... When you come to Pittsburgh, if you ever come, when you get off in the airport it says, "America's most livable city." The same year Pittsburgh was named the most livable city, according to the United States Census, we were told we had the poorest Black community in the country. Poorer than Detroit, poorer than Cleveland, poorer than Chicago. The poorest inner-city Black people live in Pittsburgh. "Most livable" for who?

In Chicago, we hear an overlapping narrative from Jacinda Bullie, Jaquanda Villegas, and Lady Sol, the founders of the community-rooted Hip Hop organization Kuumba Lynx (see chapter 7). Modeled after the Mississippi Freedom Schools, they have for over two decades made use of the Hip Hop arts to engage youth in practices of "liberation through artistic expression." In their seeking "protection from police who hinder respiratory airways," Kuumba Lynx joined Project NIA and others working toward passing what became known as "the Reparations Ordinance," an ordinance to condemn and collectively heal from the violence committed by former Chicago police superintendent Jon Burge, who was convicted of obstruction of justice, perjury, and torturing hundreds of innocent men over a span of two decades in order to obtain confessions.[17] Through the creation of a $5.5 million city fund, Chicago became the first city to offer compensation to victims of police torture. Importantly, part of the reparations ordinance included the mandating of curriculum on police torture in Chicago public schools so that the children of these communities would learn all about the racist legacy of the Chicago police department.

Reflecting on the importance of this work to youth and Communities of Color, Jacinda Bullie explained:

> We talk about reparations and we talk a lot about reimagining a more just world, right . . . but what does that really mean? Because we often talk about this pain narrative, but we don't talk about the joy narrative, about what we accomplish through our coming together, through community. We don't talk about defining what our joy looks like in this work or what our reimagined world will be composed of. And this is that, in real time, young people witnessing what a reimagined world looks like, and can look like as we organize. How we heal. How we move forward.

Speaking from his experiences in New York City, Bryonn Bain imagines futures without mass incarceration, and ultimately without prisons. Describing his time working in Rikers Island, which he refers to as "the largest penal colony in the world" holding approximately 13,000 incarcerated men and women, he explained: "During any given year, there's four to five thousand teenagers, 16–19 years old, incarcerated at Rikers. They spend $167,000 per year per person at Rikers Island . . . And the New York state public schools spend less than $15,000 per student per year. They spend over 10 times the resources to actually incarcerate young folks in New York City as they do to actually fuel their education." Bringing the point home, he concluded, "So when I hear folks talk about, 'The system is broken, we gotta fix it,' I'm like, 'No, actually, the system is working exactly as it was designed to work.' Right? To make Black and Brown folks slaves and hard workers for White folks, and to make White folks—unless you come from the upper echelons of the socioeconomic ladder—a cog in the wheel." If we want to move from thinking about reforming and defunding, to abolishing, for Bain, "It's also about rethinking and reimagining where resources and where power is located in this society."

From New York, we move to East Palo Alto (EPA), a small, 2.5-square-mile suburb of the San Francisco Bay Area, that is a rapidly gentrifying and resegregating community of Latinx, Black, Asian and Pacific Islander, Indigenous, and other interconnected and overlapping Communities of Color. Flanked by some of the US's most affluent White suburbs on one side, the tech industry's billionaire behemoths like Amazon and Facebook on another, and one of the wealthiest, Whitest elite, private universities in the nation, EPA is surrounded by centers of global White supremacist wealth accumulation and knowledge production. And despite this, or more accurately *because* of this, EPA suffers from many of the same symptoms of systemic oppression faced by larger cities like Pittsburgh and Chicago, where these Hip Hop–centered arts organizations are helping youth to heal from the trauma and suffering caused by continued racial capitalist exploitation and to imagine new and more just futures.

Founded two decades ago, the Mural Music and Arts Project (MMAP, see chapter 8), like Pittsburgh's 1Hood and Chicago's Kuumba Lynx, has created "ripples of hope and healing" that sustain community by creating a youth-centered, social justice arts ecosystem where youth feel loved and cared for as part of an ever-expanding family—what Youth Speaks's Michelle Lee referred to as an "ethic of radical love" (see chapter 9). Beyond the metaphor of family, through youths' participation in the Hip Hop arts, MMAP's transformative power is manifested through how it links together and sustains families, neighborhoods, and the larger community of East Palo Alto. As Measha Ferguson Smith explained, *relationships* of love and care are key to MMAP's success because they allow youth "to make critical reflections on their own lives and critical connections with the people around them." MMAP engages the Hip Hop arts not just in the interest of honoring, fostering, and perpetuating the power of Hip Hop, but with a direct focus on sustaining young people *themselves* as they confront racial capitalist-contrived poverty and exploitation, hyperpolicing and mass incarceration, gentrification and resegregation, toxic masculinities and gendered violence, and other forms of systemic violence and injustice.

As Mark Gonzales shared, youth are not "checked out" or "numb," as they are often described; they are shellshocked:

> And how do the people begin to heal from this shellshock, and move beyond healing to growth? If we are only talking about healing then literally we are saying the best that we can do as humans is to restore ourselves to the baseline that we came out of the womb. We are not here to heal; we are here to grow. How do we center a discourse around growth, a discourse around not just surviving but living and not just living but thriving? What does it mean to thrive? How many of us are engaging with one another on *that* story? (see chapter 9)

Youth continue to survive oppressive circumstances, but moving beyond healing toward flourishing and thriving requires that youth feel safe enough to share and "surrender experiences to the collective, to the community, to be held by beats and harmonies, footwork, sacred ciphers—instead of in your body." For Ferguson-Smith, "The young artists at MMAP are coming into the sacred knowledge of how they can help themselves to do more than just survive, but to return to wholeness" and grow.[18]

"THE INSURRECTION OF SUBJUGATED KNOWLEDGES": HIP HOP AS CRITICAL, CULTURALLY RELEVANT, AND CULTURALLY SUSTAINING PEDAGOGIES

If we want to talk about subjugated knowledges, it's important to state at the outset that Hip Hop scholarship precedes the writings of scholars and journalists. It begins with the cultural movement itself. When the Herculords, the Furious Five, and the Cold Crush Brothers were trading and writing rhythms, they were creating a body of knowledge. When DJ Kool Herc, Grandmaster Flash, Charlie Chase, DJ Disco Wiz, and so many others were loading up their crates and refining their DJ techniques, they were building a body of knowledge. Every crate of records is a treasure trove of knowledge. What b-boys and b-girls were doing in terms of bringing movements together from across the diaspora was building knowledge. The dances are reminiscent of other corporeal movements throughout the centuries. This persistence of cultural memory, literally embodied—in people's bones, limbs, muscles, joints—and these reenactments of fluid forms of expression, of attack, of evasion, of illusion, of ecstasy on the dance floor, were forms of remembering, forms of knowledge production, forms of pedagogical innovation.

Despite pushes for standardization in education, the most effective pedagogies are profoundly local, profoundly personal. All of the Hip Hop artists and organizations in this book—from 1Hood in Pittsburgh and Heal the Hood in South Africa to Kuumba Lynx in Chicago and La Llama Rap Colectivo in Barcelona—move freedom forward by viewing Hip Hop as critical, culturally relevant, and cultural sustaining pedagogy. From paradigm-shifting theoretical interventions by Gloria Ladson-Billings, Django Paris, and Marc Lamont Hill, to the powerful collaborations between the Wu-Tang Clan's GZA and Christopher Emdin, and the protest pedagogies of White teacher A. J. Robinson, Part III brings together artists, activists, and leading pedagogical theorists to rethink the relationships between Hip Hop knowledges, pedagogies, and futures. These pedagogical moves toward freedom center and sustain Communities of Color in the face of the myriad ways that White settler capitalist terror manifests—culturally, racially, linguistically, politically, geographically, economically, epistemically, ontologically, and otherwise. These pedagogies are, at their core, what Django Paris[19] and H. Samy Alim[20] describe as *culturally sustaining pedagogies* (CSPs).

First and foremost, these pedagogies explicitly name Whiteness as the problem, and thus, decentering Whiteness and recentering communities is their point of departure. In the context of the US and other nation-states living out the legacies and contemporary realities of genocide, enslavement, apartheid, occupation, and various colonialisms, CSP recognizes that the purpose of state-sanctioned schooling has always been to forward the largely assimilationist and often violent White imperial project. As such, Django Paris further reflected as events unfolded in 2020, "That age-old question, 'What is the purpose of schooling?' has been thrown, for this generation, into existential relief. How can education be reclaimed, imagined anew, transformed to be a part of a possible future?"[21] In this way, CSP is necessarily and fundamentally a critical, antiracist, anticolonial framework that rejects the capitalist White settler gaze and its kindred cisheteropatriarchal, English-monolingual, ableist, classist, xenophobic, and other hegemonic gazes.[22] In many ways, as all of the narratives in this book demonstrate, Hip Hop functions as what Alim and Haupt referred to as an *organic form of CSP*.[23] This formulation requires us to theorize from the "ground-up" and from the "past-forward" by recovering and reworking suppressed pedagogies in the project of moving freedom forward.

Hip Hop's political project requires centering questions of pedagogy. As Marc Lamont Hill argues, drawing on the intellectual traditions of cultural studies, culture itself needs to be understood as a site of pedagogy, and popular culture in particular "is a vigorously contested terrain on which we come to understand what we're supposed to value" (chapter 11). So, even as we discuss the burgeoning field of Hip Hop education, contributors focus on the cultural work that people have been doing in the communities around Hip Hop for over four decades. As Jeff Chang has explained, "Hip Hop is part of a continuity that goes back long before the rise of the practices we now call Hip Hop. Hip Hop rises out of Black freedom culture, out of the Black freedom movement . . . The work does not originate from the Ivory Tower; the work is happening out in the communities. We want to center community in this work and we want to talk about its roots and foundation in Blackness."[24]

As Gloria Ladson-Billings and Django Paris shared, pedagogies must begin by asking critical questions about the construction of knowledge as well as the racialized political economy of knowledge (see chapter 10). Paris began, "I've been thinking about the 5th Element and about *knowledge*. Whose counts where, for what purposes?" And then pointing out the glaring irony that the very same people who subjugate Hip Hop culture are also the ones profiting off of its popularity and utility, he added:

> It's clear for instance that the knowledges and the practices and bodies of Black and Brown and Native people count quite a bit in the domestic and global marketplace. Think Hip Hop and Black music more generally. Think college and professional athletics. Think the prison industrial complex. But once we get into pre-K-12 through university classrooms they often count quite less, if they count at all. And the knowledges and practices of People of Color only do count if they can be assimilated into certain American stories

of progress, of opportunity, of meritocracy, of dominant norms of cultural practice. And so we continue the battle to make spaces for fully realized and complex engagements with the knowledges and practices of many of our communities.

Ladson-Billings offered additional insights by reminding us that, while certain knowledges are indeed suppressed, it is youth that often bear the brunt of state repression. "The overall agenda has figured out that the 18- to 25-year-olds are the most dangerous people in the society. So you either have to neutralize them through narcotics, lock them up, or convince them to go along with your program." Hip Hop pedagogical theory requires us to think critically about what we want to produce. "I think I have a pretty good idea what the neoliberal agenda wants to produce—workers. Workers that don't ask any questions, that don't challenge, and they certainly don't organize," Ladson-Billings noted. In this current neoliberal moment with "the privatization of everything," the erosion of labor unions, the suppression of voting rights for People of Color, Hip Hop, for many, functions as what Marc Lamont Hill, citing Foucault, referred to as "the insurrection of subjugated knowledges."[25]

But if we follow the critical reflexivity modeled by Hip Hop feminist Joan Morgan[26] and queer Hip Hop artist and theorist Tim'm T. West,[27] among others, we must also ask: Who is freed as a result of these insurrections and who remains oppressed under these new arrangements of power? Why is it that Hip Hop, not unlike many radical political and religious institutions, for example, so relentlessly critiques and unsettles the dominance of whiteness, but also just as frequently exploits and further subjugates already marginalized gendered, sexualized, and dis/abled bodies? As Hill pointed out in his already classic *Beats, Rhymes, and Classroom Life*, Hip Hop, like any popular cultural form, "inevitably creates spaces of both voice and silence, centering and marginalization, empowerment and domination."[28] Emdin, speaking about young women and queer youth who are marginalized within Hip Hop spaces, added:

> See, Hip Hop becomes a tool that oppresses these populations, but it becomes the only tool that can heal them. There are folks who love Hip Hop so much and are so hurt by what Hip Hop tells them they could become. And they're just looking for an opportunity to reclaim what speaks to them in their own voice . . . reforming and recreating what Hip Hop becomes.

"CREATING A LIBERATORY THING FOR MYSELF": A NEW LANGUAGE FOR NEW ARTICULATIONS OF BLACK / QUEER / DISABLED FUTURES

Many of the artists, scholars, and activists in the final section of the book not only raise queer, feminist, and disability justice-oriented critiques of Hip Hop but also theorize ways that Hip Hop might, and in some ways has already begun to, liberate itself in order to move freedom forward for all of us. Integral to all of their methodologies, as Joan Morgan argued, is the "creation of language" that shifts the terrains of these conversations (see chapter 14). In these final narratives, we witness artists and thinkers creating new language to navigate between the crushing weight of White supremacist, capitalist, ableist, cisheteropatriarchal systems, on the one hand, and the painful exclusion from both Hip Hop and the broader Black communities within which they participate, on the other. Oftentimes, this new language requires centering the body, and thinking through how Black / queer / disabled folks move through the world in revolutionary and intentional ways in order to "create a liberatory thing," as Kaila Adia Story put it, by "using the body as a revolting weapon to make folks uncomfortable with ideas of what is normative."

Joan Morgan, Brittney Cooper, Treva Lindsey, Kaila Adia Story, and Esther Armah—affectionately know to us as "The Pleasure Ninjas"—provide new language for articulating a "politics of pleasure" that lovingly critiques Hip Hop's sexism and misogyny, reductive views of Black women's bodies as no more than sites of the intersecting oppressions of racism, sexism, and classism, as well as both Hip Hop's and Black Feminist Theory's lack of engagement with Black queer identities. Bettina Love, in conversation with Regina Bradley and Mark Anthony Neal, explores how young Black girls in Atlanta, Georgia, critically engage Hip Hop to make sense of these politics as well as their social worlds in the contexts of police violence, neoliberal capitalism, and the sweeping gentrification of "the New South" (see chapter 16).

Leroy F. Moore Jr., in conversation with Stephanie Keeney Parks, describes not just the reclamation of ableist language by Krip-Hop Movement artists, but how these artists employ Hip Hop to critique the rampant ableism within it, the overwhelming Whiteness of the disability movement, and the broader intersecting systems of ableism and racism that alternatingly view Black disabled bodies as both "weak" *and* as threats deserving of police violence and brutality. And finally, and perhaps most painfully, he critiques forms of "Black ableism" that erase Black disabled bodies, at worst, or seek to "cure," merely provide services for, or pray away the "crippled" among them, at best. As the Krip-Hop Movement found inspiration and allyship in the Homohop Movement in the San Francisco Bay Area, they have also continued to produce music and events with gender nonconforming, trans, and queer women like GenderKrip, once again reinventing Hip Hop as it moves freedom forward. As an international collective of hundreds of artists, Krip-Hop is creating futures where Black and other disabled people can finally "come home" (see chapter 15).

What all of these artists and thinkers have in common is their sense that there are very few spaces outside of Hip Hop for Black / queer / disabled girls, boys, and nonbinary youth to think through how to navigate these complex and fraught cultural politics and the oppressive systems that seek to circumscribe their activity and mobility. Winn, citing Angela Davis, and thinking about youth who are not engaged with these critical, creative art forms, argued "that one of the consequences of racism [and all of these oppressive ideologies and systems], particularly in schooling, is that it has rendered a whole generation of people who do not see their future" (see chapter 17). Winn's "pedagogies of possibility" draw on Black artistic and literary traditions to ask what are arguably the most pressing questions within the pages of this book:

> How are we going to do the work of not only helping them see their future, but supporting them to really generate and think about a collective and expansive freedom? These are the questions that I hope we all carry with us as we continue to think about the intersection of Hip Hop knowledges, pedagogies, and futures, particularly in this moment where youth are leading a new racial justice movement... How will we be ready to think about liberatory futures, not just *for* our youth but *with* them? How will *you* show up for them? How will all of us show up for them?

These questions serve as both a challenge and a reminder to all of us to redouble our commitment to youth and to revisit and extend the most oft-used verbs in this book. Organize. Fight. Recover. Forge. Rethink. Reframe.

Reclaim. Build. Imagine. Envision. Create. Care. Love. Make freedom move(s). Whether we are dealing with freedom of expression; freedom to define ourselves beyond[29] White supremacist, cisheteropatriarchal, colonial identities, ideas, and borders; freedom of mobility beyond the constrictions of neoliberal capitalist systems; freedom "from police who hinder respiratory airways"; freedom to heal and grow beyond the wounds—internal and external—that once held us back; freedom from a miseducation that has us hating ourselves and each other; freedom to think beyond modes of resistance; freedom to seek, in the words of Treva Lindsey, "a pleasure that ain't got nothing to do with anybody else" and as Brittney Cooper put it, to "have great politics" *and* "want to fuck, too, sometimes"; and finally, freedom to think, feel, reflect, love,[30] or just to *be*. Still.

AN INVITATION TO RETHINK AND REMAKE THE WORLD

Within the pages of this book, contributors weave narratives, tell tales, teach, sometimes preach, drop a verse or two, laugh, share, and sometimes even cry together, and in the process, create a familiar / familial text that breathes life into studies of Hip Hop culture. We have done our best to take seriously the centrality and ceremony of story within Hip Hop. These stories are our methodology—a methodology that goes back centuries—as well as a primary means of theorizing. In short, every story is an invitation to rethink and remake the world. As Mark Gonzales put it, story is not only "a medium"; it is "an engine for new possibilities and realities" (chapter 9).

It's only appropriate, then, that we conclude by sharing the story of this book and how it came to be. It is not an exaggeration to say that our lives have been forever changed in the process of organizing and editing this book. The stories themselves are transformational and transformative. But this book wasn't "work" for us. In fact, it wasn't even a book. The process itself was a labor of love, a series of family gatherings, a continuation of a journey that we have been on, well, since falling in love with Hip Hop culture. Over the span of nearly a decade, we sent out invitations to like-minded folks to come to Stanford University's Institute for Diversity in the Arts (IDA) and build something beautiful with us, something that would

Figure 0.1 (Top) Chris Emdin engages crowd after lecture. Photo by Abdul Alim.

Figure 0.2 (Bottom) *Left to right*, Jeff Chang, Emile YX?, and H. Samy Alim. Photo by John Liau.

Figure 0.3 Left to right, Kaila Adia Story, Joan Morgan, and Treva Lindsey feeling the love. Photo by Abdul Alim.

help us imagine the kind of world we wanted to live in—and leave behind—for those who come after us.

In fact, that same motivation of building sustainable futures is the *very* reason why IDA itself exists. Over half a century ago, in 1969, it was a group of Black students who banded together to form the Committee on Black Performing Arts in response to a campus administration that showed little interest (to put it mildly) in Black art, Black culture, Black history, Black knowledge systems, the neighboring and then-unincorporated Black community of East Palo Alto, and one could argue, Black people, generally speaking. Within that historical context, those students saw the arts as a necessary site for Black cultural and political expression. Further, within the national context of the Black Arts Movement, they viewed the arts as part and parcel of the Black freedom movement and sought to leverage their position at Stanford to build with the local Black communities of East

Palo Alto. These students were creating art in ways that quite literally made freedom move(s).

Similarly, when we write about Hip Hop, we theorize it as a *local, lived culture.* Hip Hop didn't begin as a global commodity. It began as a movement of young Black people creating a culture, in one sense "out of nothing," and in a larger sense out of a Blackness that spans millennia. Art and cultural movements all come from a context; they don't descend upon us from on high. They're made by people who are living their lives. While art is something that's often thought of as transcendent, Hip Hop has taught us time and again that art comes from people and the culture they make amid social conditions. Like Black Stanford students in the late '60s, young people in the Bronx, when they were putting this culture together at that same moment, weren't trying to create a global commodity. They were just trying to have fun. They were not looking to put a political movement into place. They were not looking to transform education. They were looking for a way to pass the time. But their art was also a reaction to the oppressive conditions that they were living through. As well as the joy.

That joy and creativity came to continue the work of the Civil Rights Movement. At its best, Hip Hop advanced—as the great historian Robin D. G. Kelley would say—Black freedom dreams. It culturally desegregated the US, and it's doing the work of continuing to culturally desegregate other spaces as well. It gave us the idea that there could be a new culture, a new politics, a new approach to the social problems that we confront. Our work very much sought to honor these students' and these young people's profound legacy.

Over the years, we partnered with the Mural Music and Arts Program and East Palo Alto Academy in East Palo Alto to launch a multiyear Surdna Foundation grant of support and study related to the Hip Hop arts, and later the Spencer Foundation multiyear project on culturally sustaining pedagogies that expanded our scope globally to include Spain (La Llama Rap Colectivo), South Africa (Heal the Hood), and other sites. To help us continue the work of transforming the campus, we also invited some of the world's leading artists and thinkers on freedom, including Angela Davis and Robin D. G. Kelley, dream hampton and Joan Morgan, Emile YX? and Mark Gonzales, A-lan Holt, Aleta Hayes, and Cherríe Moraga, all of whom taught with us over 10-week quarters. We also built with dozens of creative icons and activists like Amiri Baraka, Sonia Sanchez, Grace Lee Boggs, Ericka Huggins, Harry Belafonte, Marc Lamont Hill, Patrisse Cullors, Alicia Garza, Boots Riley, Ryan Coogler, Favianna Rodriguez, Issa Rae, David Banner, Chuck D, Tef Poe, Linda Sarsour, Greg Tate, Omar Offendum, Gaye Theresa Johnson, Samir Meghelli, Dawn-Elissa Fischer, Martha Diaz, Davey D, Talib Kweli, and many more. We organized dozens of panel discussions, lectures, performances, readings, jam sessions, ciphers, and other events in order to build out that 1969 legacy—"to educate, activate, and transform."

It was within this broader context that we organized a course on Hip Hop culture (led by H. Samy Alim and Jeff Chang, with Casey Philip Wong as Teaching Assistant, along with Keith Cross, James Estrella, and Diane Lee) called "The 5th Element: Hip Hop Knowledge, Pedagogy, and Social Justice" in 2014, the accompanying conference "The 5th Element: The Future and Promise of Hip Hop Pedagogy" in 2017, and continuing dialogues that occurred well into 2020.[31] Each night of the course, we packed CERAS 100 beyond capacity to hear some of the most innovative and provocative artists, activists, and thinkers on these issues. The audience ranged from undergraduate and graduate students, local high school students, teachers, and administrators from East Palo Alto, community members and artists from around the Bay Area, and Hip Hop music industry folks and entrepreneurs. All in the same room. Building. Challenging. Debating. Learning. Laughing. Sneaking food in. And simply enjoying being in each other's presence. We all knew it was special.

For us, the course became an extended instance of one of those magical moments that both good pedagogues and improvisational artists recognize as irreplicable. The sessions felt more like reunions, as they became one of the few spaces on campus where Students of Color could come as they are, where they didn't have to perform twisted, distorted versions of themselves in order to be seen as intelligent, or even nonthreatening, and where they could bring their full, multidimensional beings to the table and be *seen* in all of their brilliance.

We invite you, now, into this room, so that we can share these special moments in time with you. But more importantly, we invite you to continue Hip Hop's cultural, political, pedagogical and intellectual legacy of moving freedom forward together. In the words of current IDA Director

A-lan Holt, the Hip Hop arts will continue to "write impossible worlds into existence because visioning is a collective act, one that invites new ways of being in relationship, one that acts as a useful tool toward collective liberation."

NOTES

1. For more on Pablo Hasél and the protests, see https://www.cnn.com/2021/02/21/europe/rapper-pablo-hasel-protests-continue-intl/index.html.
2. For context on Valtònyc's arrest, see http://opiniojuris.org/2020/11/13/the-spanish-rapper-extradition-case-before-a-belgian-court-fires-up-the-legal-discussion-on-freedom-of-expression-and-other-fundamental-rights/.
3. For more on one of the most significant corruption charges, see https://english.elpais.com/spanish_news/2020-06-08/supreme-court-prosecutors-to-investigate-spains-emeritus-king-over-kickback-scheme.html.
4. For more on "la ley mordaza," the gag law, see https://hrj.leeds.ac.uk/2019/12/08/la-ley-mordaza-the-gag-law/.
5. For more on the racialized politics of governmental and economic divestment in the communities that gave birth to Hip Hop, see Jeff Chang, *Can't Stop Won't Stop: A History of the Hip-Hop Generation* (St. Martin's Press, 2005).
6. These identity categories should not be seen as enclosing mutually exclusive groupings of people, but rather as entangled, intersecting and overlapping, and dependent on place, time, and context.
7. For more on "refusal" as a concept, see Audra Simpson, "The Ruse of Consent and the Anatomy of 'Refusal': Cases from Indigenous North America and Australia," *Postcolonial Studies* 20, no. 1 (2017): 18–33.
8. To learn more about abolition as a concept and movement, see Angela Y. Davis, *Abolition Democracy: Beyond Empire, Prisons, and Torture* (Seven Stories Press, 2011).
9. For a larger meditation on "damage-centered narratives," see Eve Tuck's open letter to communities, researchers, and educators: "Suspending Damage: A Letter to Communities," *Harvard Educational Review* 79, no. 3 (2009): 409–28.
10. For more on a Black feminist politics, which centers joy and pleasure, see Joan Morgan, "Why We Get Off: Moving towards a Black Feminist Politics of Pleasure," *Black Scholar* 45, no. 4 (2015): 36–46.
11. For more, see the following sources: Adam Haupt, "Rap and the Articulation of Resistance: An Exploration of Subversive Cultural Production during the Early 90s, with Particular Reference to Prophets of da City," unpublished MA thesis, University of the Western Cape, 1995; Adam Haupt, "Black Thing: Hip-Hop

Nationalism, 'Race' and Gender in Prophets of da City and Brasse Vannie Kaap," in *Coloured by History, Shaped by Place: New Perspectives on Coloured Identities in Cape Town*, ed. Z. Erasmus (Kwela Books, 2001), 172-94.

12. Quentin Williams, Adam Haupt, H. Samy Alim, and Emile Jansen, "Introduction," in *Neva Again: Hip Hop Art, Activism, and Education*, ed. Q. Williams, A. Haupt, H. S. Alim, and E. Jansen (HSRC Press, 2019), 1-17. For more on the disruption of White settler colonial logics, see H. Samy Alim, Quentin Williams, Adam Haupt, and E. Jansen, "'Kom Khoi San, kry trug jou land': Disrupting White Settler Colonial Logics of Language, Race, and Land with Afrikaaps," *Journal of Linguistic Anthropology*, 31, no. 2 (2021): 194-217.

13. Adam Haupt, *Static: Race and Representation in Post-apartheid Music, Media and Film* (HSRC Press, 2012).

14. This is a move that is outside of the construct of the "nation-state," and beyond White settler capitalist logics of ownership and privatization of territory, and toward thinking about collective spaces that honor what it means to be in just relation to human and nonhuman relatives, and waters and lands.

15. Here, we are thinking about the context of the Ferguson rebellions in 2014-15, the uprisings at US airports to protest the Muslim Travel Ban, the rise of the Movement for Black Lives, the Mni Wiconi ("Water is Life") movement at Standing Rock, the movement to protect the sacred lands of Mauna Kea, and the continuing racial justice movement of 2020-21.

16. Jasiri X, *America's Most Livable City* (video), June 6, 2011, YouTube, https://www.youtube.com/watch?v=0uP-5FjoKvs.

17. For more, see https://www.chicagotribune.com/news/ct-jon-burge-chicago-police-torture-timeline-20180919-htmlstory.html.

18. For more, see Bettina L. Love, *We Want to Do More Than Survive: Abolitionist Teaching and the Pursuit of Educational Freedom* (Beacon Press, 2019).

19. Django Paris, "Culturally Sustaining Pedagogy: A Needed Change in Stance, Terminology, and Practice," *Educational Researcher* 41, no. 3 (2012): 93-97.

20. For more on CSP, see the following article and edited volume: Django Paris and H. Samy Alim, "What Are We Seeking to Sustain through Culturally Sustaining Pedagogy? A Loving Critique Forward," *Harvard Educational Review*, 84, no. 1 (2014): 85-100; Django Paris and H. Samy Alim, eds., *Culturally Sustaining Pedagogies: Teaching and Learning for Justice in a Changing World* (Teachers College Press, 2017).

21. Django Paris, "Culturally Sustaining Pedagogies and Our Futures," *Educational Forum* 85, no. 4 (2021): 364-76.

22. H. Samy Alim, Django Paris, and Casey Philip Wong, "Culturally Sustaining Pedagogy: A Critical Framework for Centering Communities," in *Handbook of the Cultural Foundations of Learning*, ed. Na'ilah Suad Nasir, Carol D. Lee, Roy Pea, and Maxine McKinney de Royston, 261-76 (Routledge, 2020).

23. H. Samy Alim and Adam Haupt, "Reviving Soul(s) with Afrikaaps," in *Culturally Sustaining Pedagogies: Teaching and Learning for Justice in a Changing World*, ed. Django Paris and H. Samy Alim (Teacher's College Press, 2017), 157.

24. Jeff Chang, "The 5th Element of Hip-Hop: Know the Ledge" (lecture, spring 2014).

25. Michel Foucault, "Lecture: 7 January 1976," in *"Society Must Be Defended": Lectures at the Collège de France, 1975-1976*, vol. 1, ed. Michel Foucault and François Ewald (Macmillan, 2003).

26. Joan Morgan, *When Chickenheads Come Home to Roost: A Hip-Hop Feminist Breaks It Down* (Simon and Schuster, 2017).

27. Tim'm T. West, "Disidentification and Its Discontents," in *Black Cultural Traffic: Crossroads in Global Performance and Popular Culture*, ed. Harry J. Elam, Jr. and Kennell Jackson (University of Michigan Press, 2005).

28. Marc Lamont Hill, *Beats, Rhymes, and Classroom Life: Hip-Hop Pedagogy and the Politics of Identity* (Teachers College Press, 2009).

29. For more on the context of how scholars, activists, educators, and artists have thought about building "beyond," see Casey Philip Wong, "The Wretched of the Research: Disenchanting Man2-as-Educational Researcher and Entering the 36th Chamber of Education Research," *Review of Research in Education* 45, no. 1 (2021).

30. For more on the pedagogy and politics of love, see Casey Philip Wong, "Pray You Catch Me: A Critical Feminist and Ethnographic Study of Love as Pedagogy and Politics for Social Justice," unpublished doctoral dissertation, Stanford University, 2019.

31. For more on the 5th Element, and its transformations since the beginnings of Hip Hop, see Jeff Chang, ed., *Total Chaos: The Art and Aesthetics of Hip-Hop* (Civitas Books, 2006).

PART I Black, Indigenous, and Diasporic Knowledges

1 Sweat the Technique

THE POLITICS AND POETICS OF HIP HOP

Rakim, Chuck D, and Talib Kweli

ALEXSANDRA MITCHELL: Good evening and welcome to the California African American Museum. My name is Alexsandra Mitchell. I'm the Manager of Education and Public Programs here at CAAM. We are so delighted, thrilled, and honored that you chose to spend your evening with us, for what is sure to be a very special program. I want to begin by thanking our program partners, who helped make this evening possible. The Los Angeles Philharmonic, who's been partnering with us in a series of programs for the Power to the People! Festival. Julia Ward, Director of Humanities, and Tyree Boyd-Pates, the festival's humanities curator. I also would like to send a very deep thank you to our partners, friends, and colleagues at UCLA's Ralph J. Bunche Center for African American Studies, Ms. Tabia Shawel, Assistant Director, and Dr. Gaye Theresa Johnson, who've been really integral in making tonight happen. I'd like to send a very special thank you to our staff and our volunteers, who've been very hard at work to make tonight possible. Your efforts don't go unnoticed and we appreciate it.

I now have the privilege of introducing another integral person to tonight's program, Dr. H. Samy Alim. H. Samy Alim is author of *Roc the Mic Right: The Language of Hip Hop Culture,* and co-editor of the new

Figure 1.1 Left to right, Chuck D, Rakim, Talib Kweli, and Tyree Boyd-Pates at the California African American Museum, Los Angeles. Photo by HRDWRKER.

book, *Neva Again: Hip Hop Art, Activism, and Education in Post-Apartheid South Africa*. He has also co-authored, with the great James G. Spady, two oral histories of Hip Hop culture, *Street Conscious Rap* and *Tha Global Cipha: Hip Hop Culture and Consciousness*, in which they interviewed many artists, including Grandmaster Flash, Kool Herc, Queen Latifah, Scarface, Trina, Ice Cube, Kurupt, Snoop, Eve, Bahamadia, Common, Mos Def, Pharoahe Monch, Chuck D, and other legendary artists. Currently he's the co-editor of the groundbreaking Hip Hop Studies Series for University of California Press and teaches at the Department of Anthropology at UCLA, where he holds the David O. Sears Presidential Endowed Chair in the Social Sciences. So please help me in welcoming Samy to the stage.

H. SAMY ALIM: It's wonderful to be here tonight and to see all you beautiful people. When Bakari Kitwana first contacted me and he said, "Samy, do you think there'd be any interest in Rakim at UCLA or in LA?" I said, "Bakari, we're on the phone, but if you could look at my face!" [*Excited expression*] So I turned to Kelly Lytle Hernández at the Bunche Center, and I said, "Kelly, you know Rakim, right?" And she looked at me with that same look on her face. And then we turned to Tabia Shawel, same look! So this is a very special evening for us tonight, welcoming Rakim.

And I just want to take an extra second to thank Tabia Shawel, Assistant Director of the Bunche Center, who's put in her time, energy, heart, spirit, mind, creativity, and talent to make this happen. She's worked very diligently over a long span of time. Those of you who know how long it takes to make things happen, we're very, very thankful, Tabia. And also of course, to Alexsandra and to Cameron at CAAM, the LA Phil and Power to the People! Festival, big up to everybody.

When Hip Hop scholar and Princeton professor Imani Perry wrote *Prophets of the Hood* in 2004, one of the most profound pieces of Hip Hop scholarship to date, she focused on both the politics and the poetics of Hip Hop, but she didn't do this as if the art of Hip Hop was something that could be separated from its politics. The art, the poetics, the aesthetics themselves are political. Those of you who know sister Sonia Sanchez, a brilliant poet of the Black Arts Movement, we just recently attended the funeral of the late great Hip Hop historian, James G. Spady, and she told us that Hip Hop was both the beauty of the music and the message. It was both saying what needed to be said and saying it in a style that was unforgettable. She said that Hip Hop artists understood the connection between words, thoughts, and action.

And this is why we are discussing both the politics and poetics of Hip Hop, what James G. Spady referred to as the most profound, lyrical, linguistic, musical, cultural, political movement of the late twentieth century. We're discussing both the art and the activism tonight as we celebrate the release of a beautiful new book, *Sweat the Technique: Revelations on Creativity from the Lyrical Genius*, written by Rakim himself in collaboration with Bakari Kitwana.

We have an incredible lineup tonight. For those of us who grew up on Hip Hop, tonight is what Hip Hop dreams are made of. Let's get straight to introducing tonight's all-star panel. We'll begin, of course, with Rakim. Rakim reigns as one of Hip Hop's most transformative artists. Along with his partner Eric B, he recorded *Paid in Full* in 1987, a landmark recording. MTV named it the greatest Hip Hop album of all time. Rakim's brilliant, inimitable lyrical style, adding layers, depth, complexity, musicality, and soul to elevate the art of emceeing has drawn comparisons to jazz icons, like Thelonious Monk and John Coltrane, and has been cited as an influence on a wide range of top-selling musicians, including Jay-Z, Nas, Eminem, Tupac, 50 Cent, the Notorious B.I.G., and many more. Rakim is the recipient of the 2012 I Am Hip Hop Trophy, the 2013 BET Hip Hop Lifetime Achievement Award, as well as many others. But beyond all these major awards, he's got the love of the Hip Hop community. I've interviewed dozens of Hip Hop artists and I can say without a doubt that Rakim is "your favorite emcee's favorite emcee." The polysyllabic rhymes, the internal rhymes, the bridge rhymes, the true songwriting skill. He has stamped his imprint on Hip Hop globally and across generations. And even though he told us not to, we all sweat the technique. Rakim Allah, the God MC. Here he is, give it up. Rakim! [*Applause*]

Next, and I can't even believe I'm saying this, but I'd like to introduce Chuck D. Chuck D, rapper, producer, graphic artist, and political activist, rose to prominence through his groundbreaking, mic shattering, politically conscious Hip Hop recordings and performances. Chuck D assembled DJ Terminator X, Professor Griff, and Flava Flav, along with Hank Shocklee and Bill Stephney, and formed one of the most prominent and powerful Hip Hop groups of all time, Public Enemy, who was inducted into the Rock and Roll Hall of Fame in 2013. From *Yo! Bumrush the Show* to *It Takes a Nation of Millions* to *Fear of a Black Planet*, Chuck's booming voice urged us not to believe the hype and always fight the power. He has done remarkable things, both inside and outside the industry, and serves as an inspiration to so many of us. Chuck D! [*Applause*]

And I'm still pinching myself because next up is Talib Kweli. Talib Kweli earned his stripes as one of the most lyrically gifted, socially aware, and politically insightful Hip Hop artists known around the world for his artistry and his support of activism from his projects against police brutality with *41 Shots* about Amadou Diallo in New York to the Ferguson movement in more recent years. After 20 years of releasing mesmerizing music, whether working with Mos Def as one half of Blackstar, partnering with Hi-Tek for Reflection Eternal, his solo work and his impressive Twitter game, Talib Kweli stands as one of the world's most talented, accomplished artists and one of Hip Hop's most important voices today. Please, welcome Talib Kweli! [*Applause*]

Tyree Boyd-Pates is the Humanities Curator for the Power to the People! Festival. The former Curator of History at the California African American Museum, Boyd-Pates now serves as the Associate Curator of Western History at the Autry Museum of the American West. In 2016, Boyd-Pates was named the Herb Carter and Yvonne Brathwaite-Burke distinguished lecturer in African American Studies at CSU Dominguez Hills. He has also been honored by the Empowerment Congress as one of Los Angeles's 40 Emerging Civic Leaders. He has received the MLK Jr. Unsung Hero Award from the California Legislative Black Caucus among many others. I can't tell you what a thrill it is to introduce him and this amazing panel, your moderator for the evening, Tyree! [*Applause*]

TYREE BOYD-PATES: Peace, peace, y'all. This is arguably Hip Hop Mount Rushmore up here. Let's just get straight into the conversation. So for you, Rakim, and everybody on the panel, when did you fall in love with Hip Hop? When was that moment?

RAKIM: The first rap song that I heard was "King Tim III," the Fatback Band. Shortly before that, Hip Hop was buzzing in the neighborhood, I was always into music so, as soon as when any kind of music came through the hood, I was on it, you know what I mean? But when Hip Hop came through, man, it was like we could tell there was something different about it. Every little kid, every teenager in the neighborhood wanted to be a part of it. You could tell by the way people dress, by the way they talk, by the way they dance. The expression was always loud and clear, man. So being a little kid, coming up in the neighborhood, man, getting my first knowledge of Hip Hop, man, I think I was like eight years old, man, seven years old.

CHUCK D: Well, before there was records, and I think Ra could remember back to that. Before there was records when somebody came up to me and said, "There's going to be a Hip Hop record in a couple of years," I was like, "How the fuck can that happen?" Because I was like, Hip Hop was like this occurring circumstance. You went to an event and it was about five hours, so that's what rap and Hip Hop was. So when they said it was going to be a Hip Hop record and nobody knew when it was or how it was going to be, it

Figure 1.2 Rakim Allah blesses the mic. Photo by HRDWRKER.

was like, "Yo man, how could this happen? We know what rapping is and we know what the party is like." But when the record finally happened with "King Tim III," that was the first sign. It was like, "Yo, that's almost it." And then with "Rapper's Delight" came out as a record, and that record was about 15 minutes long. But the irony in it, y'all, was not how long that 15 minutes was; it was like, how could they get six hours knocked into 15 minutes. They gave you a whole party in 15 minutes. And I would say my first love of rap records was right there at those two records, because all they had to do back in the day is put that record on and play it twice, and you already had a half an hour of the party going on. And it'd be like all the way to "and the chicken tastes like wood!" [*Laughter*] I'm like, "Yo, what the fuck?"

And here's a short story I want to give you. I was going to college when "Rapper's Delight" came out. And I was pretty nice as a 19-year-old. And I grabbed the mic and everybody would get on the microphone and rock songs, like "Love Is the Message" and "Good Times" and stuff like that. And I wanted to get my dance on, so there was a lot of wack emcees fucking up my dance because you dancing with somebody and all of a sudden they shaking their heads because the emcee is wack and messing up the record. So I would get on the mic to sit wack emcees down. Like Rakim, he talk about "Emcees put them in a line," that was like what I did at my college. And then I'm getting down to "Good Times," right, and everybody is, "Yeah, go Chuck!" And now I'm hearing words come behind me so what do y'all think I did? I let the words happen and I lip-sync'd like a muthafucka. And then when the party was over and everybody giving me props, I went to the DJ, his name was Larry T. It's 1979, October. And I looked, and it was a red label and I was like, "'Rapper's Delight,' oh, they finally did it. What the fuck?" And everybody gave me props. But when the next week we had a DJ named Frankie Crocker and he broke the record. Frankie Crocker said, "Ladies and gentlemen, a new record, 'Rapper's Delight,' Sugarhill Gang." And my shit was busted from that point on! I went back, they're like, "Boy, you nice but you're changing voices and shit like that, you ain't that nice." [*Laughter*]

TALIB KWELI: These two gentlemen raised me when it comes to Hip Hop, but when you say "fall in love with Hip Hop," I was born and raised in New York City so Hip Hop for me was always a part of the fabric of the city. Me being a child, I wasn't listening to Hip Hop records, but I was seeing b-boying and I was seeing graffiti and Hip Hop was just a part of it. But when I fell in love with Hip Hop, it was because of "Don't Believe the Hype" and because of "I Ain't No Joke" and because of "Follow the Leader" and records like that that I heard on Kiss FM or WBLS with Marley Marl and Red Alert on Kiss FM. That's the era for me when I was in junior high school and I fell in love with Hip Hop.

TYREE: Now, Rakim, can you share the story of how you and Eric B met, and how you were really initially just supposed to be a quarterback? Tell us that story.

RAKIM: Yo, coming up, man, I had a great love for sports. I played football, basketball, baseball, but I loved football though, man. I was pretty good at quarterback, getting myself together, trying to go to college, but a funny thing happened along the way. Quarterbacks went from 6'5" to 6'7", 240 pounds, you know what I mean? [*Laughter*] So Hip Hop kind of knocked on the door for me, you know what I mean? So, one of my close friends actually that I played football with named Alvin Toney, knocked on the door one day. And I always told my friends, "If you come to the house, come by yourself. Don't bring nobody, especially don't bring nobody I don't know to the house." So there was a knock on the door, go to the door, open up the shade. I look, I see Alvin Toney, but then I see a big cat standing behind him with a fur coat on. I give Alvin the eye like, "What the fuck is you doing?"

He was like, "Yo, Ra, man, open up the door, man. Yo, I gotta introduce you to this kid, man. His name is Eric, he lookin for a rapper, he know Magic and Marley Marl." That was his let-him-in code word and shit, "Magic and Marley Marl," and shit. So I said, "Alright, come on in." So Eric B, you know, my man introduced me to him, he was like, "Yeah, peace, Ra," you know, "I know Magic, Marley. I work at the station and I'm out here lookin for an emcee." Long story short, I had made a cassette tape, if anybody know what cassette tapes are. [*Laughter*] Back in the day a cassette tape was like a Grammy Award. If you could go somewhere and record your voice on a cassette tape, it was like gold in the hood. That was like our first sign of any kind of studio, a cassette tape, you know what I mean? But I had this cassette tape that I rhymed on in case I made it to college to play football—this the tape I was going to put in when emcees started talking crap. But I managed to let Eric B hear that tape, man, and the rest is history. I was able to sign as a guest on the first record, still thinking I was going to play football. I held on to that thought as long as possible, man, but signed up with Eric B—well, he signed the contract, and I just got on the record and the rest was history. And the way it was embraced, it was better that I signed the contract after that, you know what I mean?

[*Laughter*] I'll be straight. But it was definitely an awkward situation in the beginning because I was screwfacing Eric B the whole time like, "Who the fuck... You better know Marley Marl, man. You better know Marley, man." But it worked out good, man. Word up.

TYREE: You were effectively a prodigy. From my research you wrote "I Ain't No Joke" at 18. Can you share with us what space you were in when you wrote it, because that's a classic record and 18-year-olds don't be droppin classic records every day.

RAKIM: Coming up, I seen a lot, but I was always very knowledgeable, man. I used to ear hustle when I was a little kid. That ear hustling turned into just trying to find out what's going on and curious of what's going on. But coming up at that time I had my hands in a little bit of everything. And music was taking off, the golden era was coming into play, man. And it was a lot of emcees—Chuck D was killin them, Big Daddy Kane was killin them, Kool G Rap was killin them, KRS was killin them. And then here come Lil Ra from Long Island. So it's like, "I gotta let them know I ain't playin with them." So just to let them know how I felt and how I felt about my music. Another thing I always wanted to do was try to speak for the audience. And I think something that anybody would want to say is, "I Ain't No Joke," so it was just something that I felt fit the mold and what needed to be said.

TYREE: To both Chuck and Talib, can you tell us all what Rakim has done for the genre that has made him so effective and legendary? From your heart to his ears, what about what he's contributed has been so impactful?

CHUCK D: Well, I'll tell you quite succinctly, when you asked the question about what made us fall in love with Hip Hop, there's moments that we fall in love with Hip Hop that are significant. It's like, you fall in love and then you fall in love again and again with the genre. Rakim has about three of those moments. His first moment, as everybody was doing one particular wave, and as Run and D and Jay brought the styles in, Rakim in 1986 changed the style with one big swoop. "Eric B Is President." And then "My Melody," where he was the first emcee—and also a credit goes to

KRS-One because they both came at the same time on poetry—but Ra was the first emcee that didn't rhyme to the beat, the beat rhymed to him. *The beat rhymed to him.*

Look, a lot of times, emcees make a mistake to try to look for the perfect beat. That's why Bambaataa and them ain't looking for the perfect beat. The beat is the emcee and Rakim was significant. He's our Miles Davis. I mean, really serious. He made the beat go to *him*, because back before that, you'd have a beat go on. It was East, West, North, and South and cats had to catch up and ride the beat. When they get thrown off the beat, it was called "getting thrown off the pony" in 1985. So either you was on beat or you was off beat. You got thrown off the beat, if you wasn't on the beat, especially out here, back when you all had Electro. Muthafuckas couldn't fuck with that, the LA Dream Team and all that. Cats wasn't ridin that fuckin beat! [*Laughter*]

Ra had the audacity—the beat walked and followed him. And it opened me, because I did my first album, *Yo! Bumrush the Show*, and I was on another beat trying to catch up with the beat and nailing the beat. But when I heard Ra on those two records, I was like, "Yo! This is a whole way to . . . " Rakim is like Louis Armstrong to jazz phrasing. He changed the phrasing of Hip Hop and we went from there. And if those two records wasn't enough . . . As competitors, there's love, and you're like, "Damn! Yeah, go bro!", but at the same time, when they came out with, "I Know You Got Soul," it made you want to quit, cry, or lock yourself in the lab to try to get that shit back. And I locked myself in the lab. We came up with "Rebel without a Pause," with the whole team trying to figure it out.

There was a DJ at a local college, Stony Brook, Old Westbury, it's a state college. And this DJ, I swear to God, the first time I ever seen this done at a party, college party, he played "I Know You Got Soul" nine times in a row. And as happy as me and Hank Shocklee was, we was fucking deflated as fuck. I was like, "How the *hell* could something be this good?!" And that was the spirit that was going on about Hip Hop. And you loved the competition because it raised your bar. The bar was raised as you had to come with the bars. And Ra changed it overnight. So 1986 was a significant year, where not only am I changing the phrasing, but the words were magnificent, like, "Oh my God, it's poetry, but it's—yo, man, this dude is a problem!"

RAKIM: Thank you. Thank you, bro. Thank you. Word up. [*Applause*]

CHUCK D: Hey, listen, we traveled together. The first tour we traveled on in '87, we was on the first tour. Eric B and Rakim went on *after* us. We gettin this head to head every day, man! I mean, we only got 10 minutes on stage, but every *day* I get a chance to peep, you know. And let's not underrate Eric B either. Because a lot of times people come up like, "Ra, we gotta see if you get better beats." It ain't about the better beats. That combination is what worked there, so we had to pay respect and look at that. That was a barometer for us.

TALIB KWELI: Rakim for us, if you really participate in Hip Hop, is known as the God MC. And I know for Rakim it come from representing the Gods and the Earths, but it's also representing what Rakim is in the emcee space. And I don't care what your faith is, what your belief system is, what you know or what you don't know. I don't care whether you pray to a mystery God or pray to a head of lettuce like Rerun. If you listen to Hip Hop, you acknowledge Rakim as the God MC, that's just how it go, you know what I'm saying? And the reason he's able to transcend that, because to be clear, some people have a spiritual belief where they feel uncomfortable calling a man God, you know what I'm saying? But when it come to *you*, it don't feel like that. And I think the reason is because, I used to play little league baseball and there was this thing called the ringer and the ringer is the dude, for where I was at, it was a Dominican or Puerto Rican kid with like a full mustache. And he doin a hundred mile an hour fastballs and you like, "He doesn't count in the conversation." When you talk about the top five, Rakim is a part of the top five, but really he's not, because he's a ringer—he's above the conversation. And for me as a fan, as an emcee, as a writer, to me, there's not a better Hip Hop song written than "Follow the Leader" by Rakim.

If you listen to people like Alice Coltrane, they talk about astro-traveling and going to visit the planets and the moons and the stars, but you don't have to leave the ground. You are still grounded right here on earth, but your mind is that powerful that you could leave your body and really go visit the stars. And Rakim took us up there to the stars, "Planets as small as balls of clay / Astray into the Milky Way / Far as the eye can see . . . not even a satellite." That's like the Tribe of Dogon type of shit. And he was givin us those bars, but not taking it away from the realm of the party. The beats, like Chuck D said, and the vibe, those were party records. "I Ain't No Joke," "Follow the Leader," "Eric B Is President," those are party records. And then on top of that, Rakim is the rare MC that, for as far as I can remember, don't really curse. Because the impact of the words, he don't need to curse.

And at the time when Chuck D and Public Enemy, and Eric B and Rakim was out, crack addiction was very prominent in our neighborhoods. And what Chuck D did with "Night of the Living Baseheads," I feel like Rakim and Eric B did with "Microphone Fiend," because that record wasn't about drug addiction, but for me in an era where crack was so prevalent, it was good to hear a record that was like, "I'm fienin for this microphone." "Feed me Hip Hop and I start trembling." That's how I felt. It felt like we were fienin for that. In an era where crack was takin over, for us to be like, "No, we fiend for these rhymes and these beats," was very important for the culture.

CHUCK D: Space is very important, space and phrasing. Other emcees in other places don't get a chance to shine on their beats and music because, if you're racing the beat, you don't get a chance to have your accent stand out. Because Rakim spaced it out, it gives a chance from the West and the South, you could hear the accent a little bit more. You hear Cube in the beginning, you hear the accent stretching out a word. So Ra is revolutionary for opening up the gates for people with their own tonality to live in Hip Hop and Rap. And a lot of this is underexplored because, well, hell it ain't no goddamn class that goes deep like it is. It's crazy because I was on Talib's show yesterday, as he was interviewing me, and I interviewed Ra last week in New Mexico. And we all talk about this telepathy we have as emcees that we kind of feel and talk about all the time. This is why the book is so important because Ra is putting things in the book that like, "Yeah, damn, I never seen that in words." And like I said, the phrasing. Like, who would connect Rakim to Tha Pharcyde when you hear an accent come across or Del the Funky Homosapien? It comes because Rakim opened up the floodgates to allow you to breathe with your accent and still spit.

TYREE: What's the inspiration behind the book? How did this all begin?

RAKIM: It actually took a while for it to actually happen. Throughout my career, people used to always ask me to do a book. I never thought I was interesting enough to do a book. What am I going to talk about? Ra, what do you like to do? Chill. What's your favorite thing to do? Chill. So what are you doing when you off tour? Chill. [*Laughter*] To me, I've been touring since I was 17, 18. And so when I get home, that's what I like to do. And that's my peace, being able to sit back, relax, and just enjoy life.

But finally I figured out how I can do the book and make it somewhat entertaining. And I wouldn't feel like I was shorting you, you know what I mean? But it was the fact that I can inspire more than tell you my life story. So that was the way that I said, "Okay, I can do book." If I can just inspire people—rap artists, DJs, paint artists, dancers, people from all walks of life—if I can try to give some inspiration and people can get something, or just tell them about my creative process and maybe they can realize that the same thing they go through when they sit down to create, I go through too. It was therapeutic because I also got a chance to kind of go back through my history. And some of the things that we take for granted—you live so fast in the entertainment world. You want to look back and see some of the things that made you who you are. So, that was my chance to do that.

TYREE: Rakim, we all know how much heroes like Bruce Lee and Muhammad Ali meant to you, but I don't think people know much about the inspiration you got from Miss Bonaparte, your English teacher.

RAKIM: Yeah, my English teacher, Miss Bonaparte. Comin up in school I was kind of, how could I say? A little not interested. I used to cut class a lot. My main problem was lunch periods. You got fourth, fifth, and sixth period for lunch and for some reason I was down there four, fifth, *and* sixth period. But I used to cut class and I remember standing down in the hallway, and Miss Bonaparte, she was supposed to be teaching. But somehow she snuck right up on me and she called me by my government name. She said, "William, why ain't you in my class?" I was stuck. I was like, "Yeah, uh . . ." and just started walking with her. Yeah, I'm busted. Let's go to the classroom.

But along the way, she said, "I heard you like rap. You like rapping and all that?" I said, "Yeah." She said, "Well, this is English. Don't you think you should be in my class and learning?" I started walking a little slower, like, "Wow. She's deadass right!" What am I thinking? I'm down there clownin around. I need to be in there learning the four, five, six syllable words. Since that day, I went to her class. And I don't wanna say it was just because of rap, but sometimes it takes somebody to kind of wake you up and let you know what you're doing wrong. And I'm not that hard to convince when it comes to right and wrong. So I started excelling, which made it good for my schooling and it made it good for my rap. So I blame her, in large part, for making me a better emcee. Word up. Big time. So big up to Miss Bonaparte, wherever she at. I hope she's still alive and everything. Big up. Education. All the teachers, thanks for what you do.

TYREE: Let's big up the teachers. We appreciate you. [*Applause*] And it's a good segue because I want to bring Chuck D and Talib back in this conversation. Can you both just speak to how powerful Hip Hop is as an educational tool? We know it comes out of strife and struggle, and revolution, but how is it a good tool for political education?

TALIB KWELI: Well, these brothers started with, of course KRS-One, who called himself the teacher. And Chuck D was teaching and Rakim was teaching. This was my Mount Rushmore, as you said, and my Holy Trinity of conscious rappers. And just like you had gangsta rap, the first gangsta rap records was like Schoolly D and Boogie Down Productions back in the day, but gangsta rap got its foothold and really blew up out here in the West Coast. And the original gangsta rap is super conscious music. We talk about NWA, Ice Cube, and stuff like that. And there was a lot of influence going back and forth, but I mentioned that because there's the original gangsta rap shit and then there's a lot of copies. And the same thing goes for quote, unquote, conscious rap. There's the original and there's a lot of copies. And when you talk about the original conscious rap, you're talking about Eric B and Rakim, Public Enemy, KRS-One. I'll throw Big Daddy Kane in there as well. I come from educators. Both my parents are educators. My brother's an educator. My father now works at Adelphi and Chuck D went to Adelphi and worked with my father there. So this is all connected. I told Chuck yesterday that he's like my rap dad and my dad is my real dad. [*Laughter*]

But Hip Hop, because it's folk language, Hip Hop was speaking in the language that everybody could relate to. It's like Dr. King called a riot "the language of the unheard." Chuck D talked about a riot going on just like Sly and the Family Stone did. And so when you talk about the language of the unheard, what you're talking about is Hip Hop music. You're talking about something that goes back before us, before the Last Poets and Gil Scott-Heron, before the Negro spirituals and gospel songs that slaves sang to get them through the day. You're talking about things that go way back before, all the way to the African griot tradition. Banging on a drum and telling our story. And people get confused because the rapping part of Hip Hop is very easy to sell. So they removed the rapping part of Hip Hop and they put it in a nice box and a package. They make a product out of it and they sell it. And when you do that, imposters can get down with it. And you have people who are doing Hip Hop for the wrong reasons. Hip Hop is doing very well. I won't go as far as to say it's not Hip Hop, because of a lot of that corporate rap, I like a lot of it, you know what I'm saying? I like it if it's well-done songwriting. It doesn't mean just because something is a well-written song, that it pays tribute and honors the pillars of Hip Hop.

There's a lot of conversation around what a purist is. Shout out to my homegirl, MyVerse, who's a rapper, she's very good from Florida. I told her, "I don't consider myself a Hip Hop purist because that feels limiting. Too often Hip Hop purists limit the conversation to Hip Hop and don't allow no new sounds or inspiration in. I don't want to be a part of that." She said, "No, a Hip Hop purist is someone who does allow those new sounds in. A Hip Hop purist is someone who's not just stuck in one old-school mind frame. It's someone who can hear the new Hip Hop music and goes exploring and does the work of looking for the new music." She opened up my perspective and she allowed me to say I can own being a Hip Hop purist without being like an old fogy, "get off my lawn" type of dude. [*Laughter*]

CHUCK D: In terms of Hip Hop and education, it's simple. It has a use of words and the juxtaposition of words can make you actually move on top of whatever the beat of the music is. It necessarily doesn't have to come out and deliver you from evil. It's not actually scripture from a Bible book. And by the way, you acknowledge things in your cipher, like, we have the great Chali 2na over there, one of the greats. Worldwide greats! So it's a community inside of itself that also has this language.

When we first all came out, the whole job for Hip Hop was to be as panoramic as our music already was. You had Gladys Knight and the Pips and when you saw them on TV and all you were like, "Damn!" You couldn't help but look this way. So Hip Hop with its stage presentation has the emcee, the DJ who supplies the music, the movement which is with the dance, the style of dress and gear, that's the art. You have sight, sound, story, and style. Basically, emcee, DJ, graffiti, dance is the same thing as dance culture, vocalization, musicianship, and its art, the style of it. So, Hip Hop is just the terminology starting off in the '70s replacing the creativity of Black culture. The Black culture had to speak loud because we had to be in code because we just couldn't say, "Slavemaster, put your fucking whip away!" We had all kinds of code in our music and our music was everything emitted from us. We spoke it even when we didn't speak it. We hummed it to say so many things when we didn't want to have to say it in words. When the narrative changes from "Black creativity for survival" into something that's just a commodity and the narrative changes to the point, where right this minute, it's like Hip Hop, in order to get known, you got to have a bad look, and we got to figure out how dead rappers rise up the charts. That's something that we got to change in Hip Hop.

Pay attention to the good look. Be careful what you see in here (your mind). This man, Rakim, is always giving the good look. His last two albums are just as significant if not more than the first two albums that he did. The last album he had was *The Seventh Seal*. He had a cut on there, "Holy Are You." Fantastic cut. Don't depend on your radio stations or your TV networks, or even blogs to pay attention to it. That record is phenomenal. *The 18th Letter* before that. Don't wait on Talib Kweli's music. All the artists that are within your realm, Chali 2na, his solo work and the Jurassic Five. We don't have curation for the art form that we created that goes around the world that's in so many different languages. Pay attention when Hip Hop is on its good look. This book is a good look.

We just lost Pop Smoke and nobody knew who Pop Smoke was until he was dead and he's rising up the Billboard charts. We lost Nipsey Hussle last year at this time. Most of the Hip Hop world didn't know anything about Nipsey Hussle. The locals did and was looking at his rise to the top. They didn't kill themselves, they were murdered. But boom, these artists out there, they say, "If I'm doing a good thing to the art form, is my good look getting acknowledged? Or do I have to get something to get a bad look to get follows, social media attention, rising up the charts?" This art form belongs to the people and us and you can't talk about it slipping out of your hands. There's somebody that controls the narrative just for profit. Think about that.

Listen. I've known Rakim for—it's good in our art form to look at somebody and say, "I've known this man *for 35 years*." When he was a teenager. I was 27. I seen him on his first concert in an arena. I've never seen this man with a bad look. Never. I've never heard this man with a bad look. That man right there, Talib Kweli, came out in the '90s along with Yasiin Bey, formerly known as Mos Def, Blackstar. Never seen him with a bad look. Pay attention, y'all. Everything you see in here might be different when you keep watching and understanding what's coming at you. That's the code that emcees know. Chali know.

TYREE: Who are the female emcees that inspire you?

RAKIM: Oh, man. We're gonna take it back to Sha-Rock, Pebblee-Poo, some of the early emcees. Before I continue, what was so dope about females in the game like you see somebody break dance or see your homeboy break dance and that's dope but then when you see a female doing it, it just put like a whole new twist on it. It just made the culture look better. Big up to all the ladies out there that represent Hip Hop and made us look good. When females started to make their way and break into the Hip Hop game, it just completed the genre and it made people like me respect the genre more because women was involved.

TALIB KWELI: When I first started listening to Hip Hop, female emcees or women emcees that were dominant were MC Lyte, Queen Latifah, Monie Love, Nikki D was doing her thing at that time. Heather B was doing her thing at that time. But later on when my career started, I came in the game with one of my favorite emcees, Jean Grae. She's great. I'm proud and honored that I have a musical chemistry with her and I've known her since I was 13 years old. Like, she's in my personal top 5, top 10. It's a revolving door but Jean stays there along with Miss Hill. Jean stays there. And that's somebody else I came in the game with as well. Jean is the emcee that made me understand that I don't have to look at it as female emcee and male emcee. Jean is the emcee and she vocalized that and made that a part of her thing. She would make us aware of events that were being marketed and sold in that way, and be like, "Nah, it's just an emcee."

I also gotta big up dream hampton because me as a songwriter, one thing she said to me as a Hip Hop fan and a Hip Hop journalist was, I think all of us who make records are guilty of making a song for the ladies. You make a song for the club, you make a song for the ladies, you make a song for your boys. You know. But what dream helped me to understand is—and look, I'm proud of my love songs, but they *love* songs and not songs for the ladies, because men need love too. What dream said to me back in the days was like, "Don't try to make a song for the ladies, as if the ladies don't like the same hard shit that you like." She's like, "I like Wu-Tang too! Why you trying to make a song for me that sounds like some sappy sucker shit, when you could just make some hard shit and it'll be a song for the people?" Shout out to Rhapsody who was just on my show. Shout out to Lil' Kim, who was on my show as well. I like Noname a lot right now, too.

CHUCK D: As far as women are concerned, I had a crew called Crew Girl Order, they were three deep. Godessa from South Africa, they were one of the all-time favorites. So, when you hear women spit in harmony and their voice tones, there ain't a sound like that in the world, y'all, I'm trying to tell you. When they do the back and forth thing, it's something that has been abandoned by this country. There's a lot of things in Hip Hop when they're reintroduced with new people, new ideas, and new voices, you get new magic popping up that says, "Damn!" [*The forum opens up to questions from the audience.*]

QUESTION 1: One of the elements you talk about deeply in the book is spirituality. What spiritual practices have grown and become important at this stage in your life and career?

RAKIM: I study Islam. It's been my guide and it's been what's kept me grounded. It's also been like my A&R when it comes to me being in the studio and let me know what to say and what not to say. Let me know what's positive, what's not positive. Being able to have Knowledge of Self or just study literature or be passionate about culture, and being able to make sure it reflected in my work. So having Knowledge of Self and being able to study literature was very important in my career.

TALIB KWELI: I'm not someone who subscribes to any particular religion or anything, but I had good upbringing in my home. I was raised right, I believe, in my home, but also through artists like Rakim, Big Daddy Kane, KRS, Chuck D. These are the people I grew up listening to, so when Rakim talks about Knowledge of Self, I got a song called "Knowledge of Self" that's on the Blackstar record. And it's because I grew up listening to these brothers and that's something I take very seriously, having Knowledge of Self and understanding that. Just a connection to your past. For me, it's about, be connected to all living things. The trees put out oxygen and we take it in and push out the bad stuff that we don't need, the carbon dioxide. And then other things take it in and the trees take stuff in and grow. It's all a cycle. So to me, it's all about understanding your connection with living things and just being compassionate. If I had to say what my religion is, or my spiritual practice would be, it would be compassion.

CHUCK D: Words are powerful. They start wars and they can end them. The fact that the gift of words and language and the ability to have those words magnified in the arts and culture. Art is within us. A lot of this stuff that we have, we're all furnaces, so the creativity within us, sometimes some people could get and be heard and renowned with getting it out of them. And then when it resonates, if the word is good, people will actually follow that. If it's a portal, just for something on the negative side, it can actually be pouring gasoline on seeds as well. So, the Knowledge of Self is *definitely* something you have to be fortunate to have to your core, and it makes you go through life and understand some basics, like, "Treat others how you would like to be treated." These simple things that people kind of overlook in this century when the simple things really were laid out to a lot of people in the beginnings. It's not gonna come with a commercial or pop tune. These are basics.

And that was a beautiful thing, whenever I heard Rakim, back in his early records, I was like, "This dude, man. I know he's 17, but he's 58, man!" [*Laughter*] So that comes from another place, man, and the fact that we're gifted on that space, that he can actually make it happen in words. You share the words, this is what we can share. We share culture and the ability that it comes out of a furnace for good is a good thing, man. It's so many things in the world that have to protect you. And a good word is a great thing. It can start problems and it can end problems, and that's why they call it The Word.

QUESTION 2: How does Hip Hop today intersect with politics for impact?

CHUCK D: I want to tell y'all, separate yourself from the gadgets for a second. Is this the first time you've seen me in real life, talk to y'all? Person to person, like in a room instead of a gadget? Understand the difference, people. People today are relying so much on their gadgets, stuck in their gadgets, right. They call themselves wanting to get their word out on some kind of platform. "I'm on this platform, I'm going to use social media platforms." I did that Bernie Sanders shit right down the block, man, used the platform, and people didn't even hear a word I said. If the transcript came out based on what they saw and based off what they heard and based on what they connected, you get three different stories. So I told somebody, I said, "Well, I'm gon use the platform. I ain't going to use the social media shit. I'm going to use *his* platform to say what I got to say." But like I said, the points will come out as it unfolds. You use your platforms in political situations, *not* to change what you're going to do anyway. You don't follow nobody, but you follow your instinct. Ain't nobody in this particular government going to give any Messiah answers to its population. Sorry. I'm not relying on this system for anything. You should *use* the platform to communicate and people'll make a wise choice in your local area. This talk about presidential politics is bullshit. If you don't know who's running the school board for your child, that is a problem.

So the ability to talk and knock shit in Iran is the ability to truncate something in the world, into a rhyme, into a verse. I truncated the situation. For example, how many people believe in voting? Put your hand in the air. Now, Chuck D, as the emcee, how do you break down voting to a population? To me, I said, simple. Voting is like washing your ass. Now, listen. You don't have to wash. You *don't*. Even with the coronavirus, you ain't gotta wash. [*Laughter*] But then it does not behoove you, or grant you the right to walk around in your neighborhood telling somebody that something stinks!

You gotta figure out your crib and where your crib is at, like, "Who is that dude that's locking up all the people on the same block I live in?" Before you even get into an understanding or how big the picture is. How many of y'all got a passport, right? Less than half. Relying on the United States of America. And now this orange dude telling everybody your ass better not leave here. Just think about what's happening right now. So it doesn't mean go out, "I'm political now, we're going to get reparations from Joe Biden," and shit like that. [*Laughter*]

You better understand *you*, because they built cyberspace to purchase the remaining unused part of your fucking mind. That's the real estate and the mortgage. Now, are you mortgaging your mind? Do you own it, or are you paying rent to somebody? That's why you better understand what to vote for, you understand? So, I *used* that platform, and all you gotta do is stop looking at the images and look at the transcripts. That's all I got to say. And let me tell you, Flava Flav will be alright in April. And if you don't know me, these gentlemen know me. That's why you don't see me on TV. You don't see me. I'm heard but unseen. And when I'm going to be seen, I'm going to be seen and heard. So I'll leave you all with that. Thank you.

QUESTION 3: Who are your individual top five, top ten of all time, or your Mount Rushmore?

TALIB KWELI: For me, I feel I'm in a very unique space. I was interviewing Jadakiss yesterday and me and Jadakiss both born in 1975. And that means I'm old enough to remember some of the stuff that Chuck is talking about and Rakim was talking about where they talk about the rudiments of Hip Hop culture. I was a child. They maybe were teenagers or coming into their own at that time. But I'm also young enough to hear new styles and keep my ear closer to the street. It's about your region, your age, your perspective, your resources. It's about your level of privilege. But for me, more than anything it's about a mood. There's some days when I feel like MF Doom is the best emcee to ever do it. There's some days when I feel like Scarface is the best emcee to ever do it. There's some days when I feel like Jean Grae is the best emcee to ever do it. I mean, but these gentlemen—Chuck D and Rakim—they never leave my top five, you know what I'm saying, even as that door revolves. I really do think it's a mood. Some days I'm like, "Man, nobody's better than Mos Def." Some days, *most* days I'm like, "Nobody's better than Black Thought." Black Thought is the one that's most consistent to me.

CHUCK D: This is the shit that get people in trouble. [*Laughter*] I be watching the NBA on TNT and they be saying the top five NBA players, that shit is *impossible*, man. I have to back up what Talib said, because me, I'm going to go on the generation I came up in that I thought was unrepeatable. I mean, the atmosphere, the feeling in the air in the beginning of Hip Hop was only because it came outta somewhere and nobody saw it coming. And it was like, you could take the air and slice it, take a cut out of the air. I mean, it was automatically just amazing. And I was on some of the first tours. So when we traveled to every town, and Ra could back this up, it's like '87. You know, I was on the '87 leg, which was the second generation of touring groups. The first years were '84, the Fresh Fest and all that. But all I know is that as we're going around to every place, like the Wichitas and the Minneapolises, in the middle of the '80s, you're seeing people's faces like [*Shocked, excited expression*]—especially that gold chain *he* wore. [*Laughter*] So they were like, "Oh!" and then they get it. And then the styles start morphing and they manifest.

So, how many heads in the Mount Rushmore? If it's four, then you got to say significant points. He changed the game, right? Melle Mel, it was the largest distance between the number one emcee and number two was Kool Moe Dee, but he was *way* down at number two. So Melle Mel's like Wilt Chamberlain. When I first heard Melle Mel, I'm like, "How the . . . ?!" And he doesn't get talked about because it's so far in the beginnings. And then, particularly how the West was won, Ice Cube. I tell Cube all the time! Listen, Cube connected the West to the East, like boom! With *AmeriKKKa's Most Wanted*, bam, that was done! And Cube got like three brains in his head. I don't even see how he does it to this day. So, and me, my homie is Ice-T, and we're in the category of kind of looking at this talent and activity going on. LL Cool J. LL will walk in a place, if you got 10,000 dudes and 10,000 women, he got them both eatin' out his hand in the concert and I'm like, "Okay, he like, 'I Need Love,' 'Jack the Ripper.'" And we witnessing that. So there's some greats out there. And then the '90s brings on a whole different level of accents and styles and things like that. So is it a Mount Rushmore? There's a bunch of different mountains going on at the same time. It's a mountain range of Mount Rushmore.

And you know what? Sometimes people get so stupid that they leave Hip Hop when I give a favorite of mine, right. For example, I like Rick Ross's voice. I mean, people like, "Oh yeah, but what he's talking about is . . . " I ain't listening to that shit, I'm a grown goddamn man. I ain't gonna be influenced by Rick Ross. I just like the way he sound, you know, I'm listening, like, "Damn, I wanna snatch some of that style, man." I like the way Chali 2na rhyme, man, you know. Chali go into those roles, you know, rapping with Chali 2na's flow. I'm a 60-year old-man, man. So I want to hit some *man* rap. So I might not be open to listening to a 17-year-old dude from Chicago or some drill rapper. I'll wait for that to catch up to me. But I wanna listen to some shit that would make me bang the dashboard, like, "Yeah! Fuck that! *Yeah!*"

RAKIM: Mine kind of change, too, man. And I'm such a fan of Hip Hop that I can't pick five, you know what I mean? Like Chuck was saying, my favorite emcees back in the day was Melle Mel, Kool Moe, Grandmaster Caz, you know what I mean? So if you asked me who the best, I can't give you five without incorporating them. So, but again, I'm a big fan. I like Eminem, I like Jay Z, I like Talib. We know what Talib do, you know what I mean? And when you love conscious rap and then you hear other conscious emcees come out, it just make you feel better about what you're doing, man. And it almost makes it easier for you to do what you do, man. So this is one of the cats, when Talib came out and I was like, "Ahhhhhh!" I mean, it just make you feel good, man. So big up to Talib. And another one of my favorite emcees is Black Thought, the most underrated emcee in the game. To tell you a quick story, I remember sittin at the crib chillin, late night. I told you I be chillin. [*Laughter*]. Late night, chill, and watching a little TV, flashing through. I see The Roots and Black Thought rockin. Black Thought is singing Frank Sinatra, *killin* it. Sound a little bit

Figure 1.3 Left to right, Chuck D, Rakim, Talib Kweli, Tyree Boyd-Pates, and H. Samy Alim. Photo by HRDWRKER.

like Frank, too, you know what I mean? So, for me, that shows me this kid is the whole package. I mean, he can rap, he loves music. He sings. And if you know any rapper that can sing Frank Sinatra, it's different, you know what I mean? I can sing a *little* bit. I can front, you know what I mean, with some Frank Sinatra shit. But he *kilt* it. And to me, man, that's talent. And you know, it's brothers like that, that you got to take your hat off, man. And brothers like that make you a little better and make you appreciate what you're doing a little better. Big up to the emcees that just push the envelope, man, word up. Peace and love, peace and love.

2 Know the Ledge(s)

THE MEANINGS OF KNOWLEDGE OF SELF IN "POST"-APARTHEID SOUTH AFRICA

Shaheen Ariefdien and Emile YX?

H. SAMY ALIM: We got Cape Town Family in the house. Tonight, we're interested in Hip Hop *as* pedagogy, that is, not necessarily how the educational establishment has made use of Hip Hop culture to educate, but how Hip Hop *itself* is an arts movement that is inherently pedagogical. Our two guests are not only two of the most well-known pioneers of Hip Hop in South Africa, but they are also activists who've been putting it down for Hip Hop and educating, through Hip Hop, for over three decades. They are two humble brothers, with soaring, searing intellects, boundless energy, and a creativity that knows no limits.

Shaheen is an artist-activist-scholar who not only holds the mic as a radio DJ, as well as for Prophets of da City (POC), but holds a MA degree in anthropology from York University and has published on Hip Hop pedagogy and Hip Hop in South Africa. Shaheen and POC produced the first South African Hip Hop release in 1990, *Our World*. And while they were busy winning awards they also went on a huge 80-leg antidrug school tour, getting their message out there to the youth of South Africa. They would come to be censored left and right for their critiques of the apartheid regime, as they led voter education campaigns in the community. Then their most critically acclaimed album, *Age of Truth* (1993), was

Figure 2.1 Shaheen Ariefdien (*left*) and Emile YX? (*right*) at the Hip Hop Knowledge Cipha, Cape Town, South Africa. Photo by Ference Isaacs.

released, and damn near the whole thing was censored. This is an album that almost never made it out. The next year, the game changed for real, as POC performed "Never Again" with the opening line, "Excellent, finally a Black President," at the inauguration of Nelson Mandela. They have also performed all over Africa, Europe, and elsewhere. [*Applause*]

Emile YX? is a world-renowned b-boy, author, organizer, mentor, actor, producer, scholar—and teacher, certified teacher. He's a founding member of the legendary South African Hip Hop crew, Black Noise. He's best known for his developmental work in community outreach projects like Heal the Hood and hosting events like The African Hip Hop Indaba. I've seen Emile move in and about Cape Town as a leader in the Hip Hop community, constantly educating youth—and I mean, day and night—about each other, about themselves and their history as South Africans, their language and linguistic practices that connect them to Indigenous people, etc. I've also been honored to attend some of Emile's legendary Heal the Hood meetings, where representatives of at least 50 organizations from

Figure 2.2 Left to right, Dr. Geneva Smitherman, Shaheen Ariefdien, and H. Samy Alim, Cape Town, South Africa. Photo by Ference Isaacs.

media to industry types to community organizers to NGOs, teachers, and activists, everyone looking for ways to develop youth under extremely challenging and precarious circumstances for People of Color in Cape Town who face a deeply entrenched structural and economic apartheid in a "post"-apartheid South Africa.

On a personal note, both of these cats have been hugely inspirational. I've invited both of them to speak in my Hip Hop class in Cape Town on Hip Hop art, activism, and education in South Africa. And they blew us away! But more importantly, it was their generosity of spirit, their willingness to engage, to break bread, to have conversations with me and my students that really makes these two stand out, in my mind, as some of the most dedicated, committed, and inspirational Hip Hop heads on a global level. They embody the meaning of Hip Hop, to quote Shaheen Ariefdien and Nazli Abrahams, as "the resilience of the human spirit, that process of transforming yourself and your environment." Let us welcome, Shaheen Ariefdien and Emile YX?. [*Applause*]

Figure 2.3 Shaheen Ariefdien of Prophets of da City. Photo by Ference Isaacs.

SHAHEEN ARIEFDIEN: My name is Shaheen Ariefdien. My pronouns are he and him. I'd like to thank Samy and Jeff, and your whole team, for having us here. I want to give a big shout out to Dr. G., Geneva Smitherman—she's not here with us today, but she's definitely here with us in spirit. And especially to everyone who showed up here, and everyone who's watching the stream as well, thank you, very much. Also, important, I'd like to dedicate this to all our ancestors, and especially the fallen soldiers back home who have contributed to Hip Hop magnificently but are no longer here with us, so B-boy Mark, Mr. Fat, Devious, Hueman, Jo-Ann, Robo the Technician, B-boy Ice, to name a few. I think it's important to state from the bat that this is not a South African perspective, or even a Cape Town perspective on Hip Hop. This is a Shaheen and an Emile perspective on Hip Hop. I attended too many panels where they announce me and it's like, "Shaheen's going to give us an African perspective." No, none of that. [*Laughter*] And, for me, it's super important to state that people back home have different analyses, and stories that should all be acknowledged and we are just very fortunate to be here with you.

SO-CALLED "COLOURED" PEOPLE AND A BRIEF HISTORY OF SOUTH AFRICAN APARTHEID

Okay, so straight from South Africa, a country with a colonial name that is both self-descriptive, and a direction [*laughter*], and from the Cape Flats section of Cape Town. The Cape Flats is considered the birthplace of Hip Hop in South Africa and the socioeconomic conditions were similar to the South and West Bronx. It also has the largest, so-called, Coloured population, and that's significant for our talk. Cape Town is a port city, so like other port cities, it's quite prone to diverse cultural influences. For the purposes of our talk, I want to focus on apartheid, the structural conditions that made Hip Hop necessary for us and look at similarities and differences between the US and South Africa. Finally, I'll explore how we interpreted and reworked aspects of Hip Hop to suit our contexts, before I hand it over to Emile. We are going to aim to fit a courseload of information into this one session, which means massive gaps are inherent in attempting this. So we're just going to go briefly into a description of apartheid as described by BBC News' segment called *Apartheid 46 Years in 90 Seconds*:

> Apartheid in South Africa crumbled after Nelson Mandela walked to freedom. But Black people suffered decades of government-backed injustice before it did. Apartheid really began in 1948. But separating Black Africans from the white minority had long been a policy aim. Laws made white people officially superior. And the large Black majority faced discrimination in every aspect of their lives. Living, doing business, or owning land in White areas was banned. There were separate public facilities, transport and schools. Interracial marriage was banned. Many had no right to citizenship. And were regarded as aliens in major cities. Instead, they were made citizens of Bantustans, homelands scattered throughout South Africa. But resistance grew. In 1960, a huge peaceful protest against pass laws ended in a massacre at Sharpeville; 69 people were killed. The deaths galvanized opposition, radicalizing liberation movements like the ANC. "There are many people who feel that it is useless and very futile for us to continue talking peace and nonviolence." Open conflict erupted in the 1980s, with anti-apartheid activists frequently shot at, beaten, or arrested. Mass protests were firmly put down. But, little by little, the apartheid establishment crumbled. After gradual reform, Nelson Mandela, imprisoned since not long after Sharpeville, was set free in 1990. Four years later he was elected as South

Africa's first Black president. Apartheid had ended. (https://www.youtube.com/watch?v=2f2k6iDFCL4)

With that background, I'd like to briefly focus on Colouredness. So-called "Coloured" people are a diverse, exploited, and marginalized people. As Jeff Chang described, in terms of the people being on the receiving end of divestment and of racism, police brutality, etc., it's very similar. Colouredness, or Coloured people, is generally regarded as not White, and not Black African. It's a socially constructed category, and, at various moments of White supremacist rule in South Africa, the definition changed. Under Dutch rule, this heterogeneous group of enslaved peoples, from places as diverse as Indonesia to various areas along the southeast coast of Africa, came to be known as Coloured. The term was used for any person who was not considered of "purely" European descent. Under British rule, that definition shifted. And because the British feared the local Indigenous people banding together with enslaved communities against their enslavers, they created divide-and-rule strategies, as they've done elsewhere. Coloured then became not White and not Black, as a way to further separate and exploit people. These culturally and ethnically diverse groups of people who formed a community based on shared experiences of enslavement were further divided and oppressed. Later, the Afrikaner ruling class—Afrikaners are the descendants of the Dutch colonizers—took it a step further with apartheid, the intersection of Calvinism, Capitalism, White Supremacy, and Patriarchy on steroids. For them, Coloured meant inferior to White, and slightly superior to Black. The government passed a number of laws that banned sexual and marital relations between Whites and so called "non-Whites," laws that intensified land dispossession and laws that radically restricted the movement of the oppressed masses, especially Black Africans.

The psychological trauma Coloureds endured was brutal, because British colonial notions of "purity" added an additional layer to oppression. Since Coloureds were an already ethnically heterogeneous group who didn't fit into colonial notions of racial purity, typical tropes linked to impurity, whether they be promiscuity, shame, criminal, etc., were put on this group. Also, the Indigenous, First Peoples, the Khoi, the San, etc., were also now lumped into this group. And the apartheid regime had really bizarre ways of determining, or rather creating, group membership.

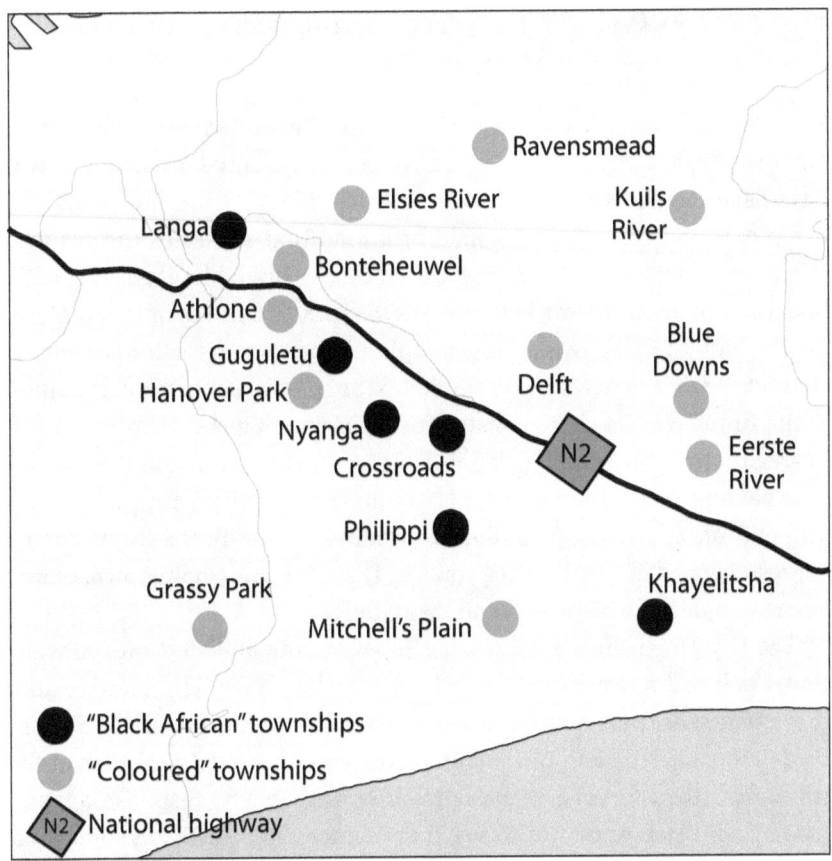

Figure 2.4 Map of the Cape Flats in Cape Town, South Africa.

One method was "the pencil test," where they put a pencil through your hair and depending on how smoothly it went through, you'd be given a particular racial designation. And it totally split up families and created all kinds of devastation. Many families, including our own, have been impacted by this. In terms of media depiction, so-called Coloured people were largely invisible or portrayed as alcoholics, coons, gangsters, drug addicts, etc. Coloureds were socialized to denounce any kind of identification with their African heritage. So that's important to keep in mind in terms of how Hip Hop knowledge played a role in our consciousness.

THE CAPE FLATS: SIMILARITIES AND DIFFERENCES WITH THE US HIP HOP CONTEXT

The Cape Flats is the home of Hip Hop. Places like Mitchells Plain, Hanover Park, Manenberg, etc. Those are all Coloured areas. Then you have Khayelitsha, Nyanga, that are so-called Black African areas. As you can see, sometimes it's just a field or a road that separates these areas. White areas would be nowhere close to this. A place like Ravensmead, I believe, is built on the world's biggest swamp, so instances of tuberculosis are the highest in the world, for example. As mentioned earlier, the conditions in the Cape Flats are very similar to the conditions that Jeff described in the Bronx. We also have a history of enslavement under British control. Segregation. In terms of Black political movements, we also suffered from internal tensions, co-optations, dangerous compromises, and/or imprisonment or assassinations. Forced removals, the Bronx–New Jersey expressway and in South Africa you had District 6 and Sophiatown, places where people were dispersed and displaced.

The Hip Hop community in Cape Town was not affiliated with conventional political movements, even though we had a few Hip Hop–related movements. At some point we even had local chapters of the Zulu Nation, the Nation of Islam, and Black Watch, that was connected to X-Clan at the time. And this, for me, is actually super important: response against trauma. Hip Hop was a way to say, "I am somebody"; it acted as some kind of medicine. As with most medicines, there are side effects, that's worth keeping in mind. [*Laughter*]

So now for the differences. In South Africa, we didn't have the "one drop" rule racial schema. South Africa had Black, Coloured, White, and later, Indian as categories. We didn't experience de-industrialization because the *bantustans*, the phony homelands, were kind of the satellite states where workers would come to work in South Africa "proper." There was no White flight because the way that the city was designed, including township areas, was around strict racial-spatial grids. In some cases it's the opposite of White flight—residents of District 6 were forcefully moved out of town so that Whites could move in.

Often it is said that Hip Hop in the US developed during a post–Civil Rights and post–Black Panther era. This meant that, to a large degree,

Hip Hop developed outside of the time frame and direct impact of mass progressive political movements. In South Africa, however, we actually had the United Democratic Front (UDF) and a number of other civil society groups. But there was this huge disconnect between the burgeoning Hip Hop community and mass progressive political movement. That's a story that will require its own talk.

The role of gangs in South Africa is very different. In the US, many gang members became part of a collective who created Hip Hop, like the Black Spades, etc. South Africa actually didn't have that. Many heads were not previously affiliated to gangs. Gangsters used to listen to Anita Baker [*laughter*], smooth jazz and Miles, and all of those kinds of things. They had an amazingly good collection. [*Laughter*]

Another huge difference is in South Africa we also had a more complicated relationship to US imperialism. In South Africa, there was an externally imposed BDS Campaign, the boycott, divestment, and sanction campaign, which meant that South Africa was ostracized from the global community to punish the apartheid regime. Inside South Africa there were also harsh censorship laws. So think of how tricky it was to gather information around Hip Hop when you had all these buffers.

ENCOUNTERING HIP HOP: NAVIGATING BDS AND
RAISING CONSCIOUSNESS

There were transformations in the US music industry with Michael Jackson's *Thriller* blowing up. US labels paid more attention to the global market, right? And so, because of the BDS campaign, the majority of music that we could purchase in South Africa didn't come from the US. It actually came from local subsidiaries in the UK or Europe that had totally different record label names. We accessed music and info from pen pals, friends, family, students who were abroad. Emile was amazing with the pen pal thing. He was in *Word Up!* magazine, like, "I'm from Africa, South Africa, send us music and information." [*Laughter*] Bootleg networks were crucial because we were able to get hold of information, music, etc. And technology played a role, in terms of double-deck tape recorders to be able to record the music, pass it on. That was key in terms of getting the music disseminated. So much so that the thousandth generation of a song, or a cassette or mix tape that circulated at the time, the recording was so bad that by the time people actually heard the original, it sounded funny. Like, "Nah, [*laughter*] we like the gritty version!"

The apartheid regime banned TV until, I think, 1976 because they were concerned about US cultural imperialism. You have a colonial, capitalist state that was anti-imperialist. And they were also concerned about depictions of White and Black people together. In the bantustans television and radio programming were more musically diverse, because they needed to perform sovereignty and appeal to local tastes for some legitimacy. That model was later transferred to South Africa "proper" with the advent of channels dedicated to Black African audiences. This was where we got some of our Hip Hop music videos from. Video machines, of course, served a very similar purpose to cassette decks. Later CDs, DVDs, the internet, and then software continued the tradition of dissemination.

However, keep in mind that because of the way the information flowed into South Africa via the UK and so on, British Hip Hop was as important as US Hip Hop for many of us. So, the crew that I was a part of lyrically were influenced by the US, but production-wise, we were more influenced by the UK. The music was more aggressive and up-tempo. Developing research skills with the BDS campaign and the censorship laws, we had to be very crafty in trying to find information. So, even for me, when I got to the university level some of my research skills had already developed in the early '80s, being a Hip Hop head. Critical thinking skills, as well, but with Hip Hop's fifth element, Knowledge of Self, or like I'd call it, Knowledges of Self. There's not just a singular framework that informs how we make a sense of self. It was also the identification with struggle elsewhere, like Grandmaster Flash and the Furious Five, "Broken glass everywhere, people pissin on the stairs, you know they just don't care," we totally related to that. There were similar stories from the UK, as well. So it was this identification with a global struggle, and we didn't feel as isolated, that hey, there's something else happening in the world and the US wasn't about just the Statue of Liberty, and Disney, and all of those things we often saw on television. There was some real shit happening there, as well.

Hip Hop was challenging societal sacred cows. And I think that was important because to question religion, to talk about certain institutions in ways that didn't reinforce the politics of respectability, Hip Hop helped push that, I think. It decentered Whiteness, and that was important, especially, in terms of the James Bonds that we saw in movies that it was now someone else who was the protagonist. Hip Hop provided tools to challenge the colonial classification of Colouredness, in terms of the way Blackness was constructed, through Hip Hop, and to reconnect with Africa. Remember one of apartheid's aims was to teach us to disconnect with Africa. So this was about reconnecting. It was also about ghettocentrism, with all the negative aspects that come from that, but it was also about thinking of the ghetto as a repository of energy, livelihood, community, and not just this racial, spatial presence that symbolized abandonment and containment. It was also about hypermasculinity, which was really a sign of powerlessness, and it reified heteronormativity, and I think it was important to mention that. It was a lot of things we needed to unlearn as well. As I mentioned earlier, medicine often has some serious side effects.

PROPHETS OF DA CITY: BLACK CONSCIOUSNESS AND THE POLITICS OF RACE

So the conditions that I described gave birth to groups like Prophets of da City. Given the political climate, Hip Hop's internal logic of making something out of what we were told is nothing, and the importance of defining ourselves outside of the state's hegemonic categories, motivated us to be on a conscious mission. We were known for being this Hip Hop group that was deeply involved in education and community. So we did a major drug awareness program tour because of the huge substance-abuse problems in our community, literacy campaigns, and we had a national voter education tour that took us to high schools and community centers. It was the first time our people had an opportunity to vote so it was Hip Hop's responsibility to teach people. We did in and out of school programs, workshops in prisons. We did all of this, while also spreading the gospel of Hip Hop since it was so new to most people. Abroad, we'd done conflict resolution work through Hip Hop in Northern Ireland with Protestant and Catholic youth, among other things. I've worked with refugee youth in

Figure 2.5 Left to right, DJ Ready D, Shaheen Ariefdien, and Ramone. Photo by Ference Isaacs.

Holland and ran numerous youth-related programs in South Africa. This focus on education, consciousness, and redefining ourselves were totally inspired by Hip Hop's fifth element, no doubt.

I'm going to share some lyrics with you from our song called "Black Thing" to look at Hip Hop's Knowledge of Self element in relation to Colouredness.

> I'm Black to the bone like a neckless victim.
> I attack your dome to perform an X-orcism.
> Freeing your mind from the demons, get the meaning, get the feeling, get the rhythm, because I'm not rhyming for no reason.
> Can you feel the effects of stolen history?
> Don't call me non-white, because that's implying that's what I wish to be.
> Calling me a Coloured is a diss to me.
> It's like victory for those who are twisting me.
> The term Coloured is a desperate case.
> Of how devils divided us by calling us a separate race.
> Calling me Coloured said my blood is impure, but see

I'm not yukking my insecurity.
So I respond to this.
And ventilate my mental state with Black consciousness.
I believe in, here it comes, each one teach one, reach one
from the heart because that's where the beats are from.
Just basing it on facts, placing it on tracks, my race is in a trap,
my nation seems to lack,
knowledge of self, and what it means, but it seems,
we are attracting anything but a Black thing.

So, the interesting thing about that, is that ideologically it's all over the place. The X-orcism—there was a line with devils, there was kind of like Nation of Islam influences and we had Afrocentricity influences, we had Biko influences. So it was a mishmash of Black-centered ideologies that were firmly against White supremacy, but that were, on their own, quite incompatible with some of the other thoughts displayed as well. Like here, immediately saying all these wonderful things and then talking about the race in a reified fashion. I was young. [*Laughter*] We lived, we learned.

But that was a crucial moment to make those kinds of statements in South Africa and a lot of people didn't respond well to that. I also wanted to mention this song because very often the way it's written about in terms of Knowledge of Self and consciousness in Hip Hop is that it's purely an East Coast influence. And the chorus of this song is from a Bay Area Hip Hop crew, Digital Underground, from a song called "No Nose Job." The line was, "Sometimes it feels like I'm not Black enough." So for us it was also the relationship to West Coast Hip Hop, as well.

And the same with this song. One of the POC members loved Casual of Hieroglyphics, and his song "that's how it was, and that's how it is." There's a line where it goes like, "E-e-e-e-easi-i-ily." And so, we loved saying that so it was like, "I've got to weave this somehow into the words." And so, this was also some indirect ode to Bay Area Hip Hop. This is a song called "Never Again." This was recorded the day after the inauguration of Nelson Mandela.

> [*Shaheen plays music, which begins with Nelson Mandela speaking*] "Never and never again, shall it be that this beautiful land will again experience the oppression of one by another."

The revolution was hard
Days were dark. We made our mark
So we better play our part
Yes, the revolution was hard
Days were dark. We made our mark
So we better play our part

Excellent, finally, a Black president.
To represent.
I know it so I speak it.
I sow it so I reap it
The poet will freak it
When I flow it with the beat, kid
So I dedicate this to those who are down with the revolution,
all over the world and never snoozing
I dedicate this to those who are down with a struggle, G,
even when things got ugly.
'Cause the Black race always had a slapped face.
'Cause freedom moves at a wack pace.
It sometimes takes a miracle to see my people free,
'Cause it's not done e-e-e-as-i-i-ly.
So I dedicate this to those who don't turn the other cheek,
and to those who would rather speak.
Against colonialism, imperialism and racism.
So I'm bringing it back to the basics and I—
know that those who supported the struggle locally,
I support your struggle globally.
So thank me and thank you, and we stand true.
And if you're not down, then damn you.

Just do it. Just do it. Just do it. Do it, do it.
Just do it. Just do it. Just do it. Do it, do it.

'94, Mandela on top.
'94, Apartheid have fi drop.
'94, P.O.C. nah go pop.
'94, roots and culture nah go stop.
Black people in Brazil them not yet free,
Black people in Australia, they want liberty.
Study Black history you will see, how long it took Azania to get victory.
Africa rejoice, raise your fists, raise your voice.
Africa bring the noise 'cause you made the choice.
'Cause ever since the oppressor came here, he messed up Azania.

Made ya slaves and he even raped ya,
But I made my X on the paper,
so Mr. Oppressor, I guess I'll see your ass later, alligator.
'Cause the struggle was tough in a rat race,
What a feeling to see a smile on a Black face.
Throw your fists in the air. And to the people over here and over there.
And if you're ready to diss your right to being racist, show a gas face, and say "Naaahhh."
Nelson Mandela's speech "We understand it still that there is no easy road to freedom. Let there be justice for all."

Just do it. Just do it. Just do it. Do it, do it.
Just do it. Just do it. Just do it. Do it, do it.
Oh, what a day.
We had a price to pay.
But, anyway.
We got to move on, we got to move strong
because I'm Black to the bone.
We got to build a home being home alone,
without mama and papa means I cannot grow up proper.
So we got to operate and take it to a level then build Azania, the new world, for the sake of our children.
Pump it up, pump it up, hey.
Stand up, stand up, get up, stand up.
Do you see the change? Do you feel the change?
If you see the change, you got to rearrange your mental state.
Books and pens are great, now.
Knowledge awaits the—
Seeker, the believer digging deeper will become the achiever, and the achiever's going to pass it on.
Knowledge of self is gonna make us strong.
You made the choice. You took the vote
Mandela spoke and said "Never again."
Yes, yes, ya'll.
We should help the man and make sure that the future stays secure or—
Revolution.
If there's one thing that we would like to say to everybody that supported South Africa in the struggle and that is—
Thank you, baby. Thank, thank you, baby. Thank—
Thank you.
I want to thank you, baby. Thank, thank you, baby. Thank you.
Thank you.

Do it, do it.
I want to thank you, baby. Thank, thank you, baby. Thank you . . .

So, it's kind of a thank you song to those who supported the South African struggle but also, like I said, we made those connections with global struggles as well. Also, people say "post"-apartheid, but it was a reality of neoliberalism. The apartheid racial framework was and is still, to some degree, very much in place.

HIP HOP AND HEALING

Before I left POC, I became disillusioned with the music industry, so I got more involved with community development, working with youth in community radio. While being there we got involved with sexual health education and a number of different efforts. ALKEMY was a Hip Hop program that we started that was working with young people at the high school level who wanted to go to university and how we could use Hip Hop arts to introduce different concepts. And this was designed with young people. At university, we were also involved in the workers' struggle, solidarity work. And Hip Hop was also key in the way that work was done and our approach to activism and student politics. When I went to Toronto to do my MA, I continued using the kind of ALKEMY model, now working with young people from the Caribbean, from Kenya, from all over the world, Pakistan, using that kind of model through Hip Hop to deal with issues of marginalization, exclusion, etc.

My current focus is on healing, especially through Child and Youth Work. For me, I found that having done all these interesting things with Hip Hop, in different contexts, different parts of the world, and doing this kind of revolutionary shit, that the inner revolution is super important, because we end up reproducing the hierarchies, the exclusions, the oppressions that we sometimes imagine ourselves fighting against. And spiritual, psychological, all kinds of healing is super important. And so, my focus right now is on how Hip Hop fits into that, not only in terms of how the Hip Hop elements could be used to work in, for lack of a better term, therapeutic contexts, but how the framework or logic of Hip Hop could be used where you don't even need to overtly use Hip Hop elements. The important thing is how Knowledges of Self has impacted the types of work I do outside of conventional Hip Hop practices. And I think I'm going to leave it there. And in the true form of a posse cut, it's on you, yo! [*Laughter*]

EMILE YX?: Hi, everybody. He always makes life difficult for me. I should have gone first, I'm older. [*Laughter*] I want to talk about putting Knowledge of Self into action. My family surname is Jansen, J-A-N-S-E-N. So Jan could have been the slave owner's name and thus Jan *synne* is Afrikaans or Dutch for "Slave or property of Jan." And so, when everybody was into changing their surnames and being "X," I added the Y and the question mark, as if to ask, "Why the hell are you going to do that?" Because the thing about Knowledge of Self is that it's easy to speak information, but harder to implement that information into your life.

STARING DOWN THE GUN BARREL OF APARTHEID

I started b-boying in 1982. And so, for me, that first step was a huge step to take, to actually go out into the circle and do what I was passionate about. But at the same time, I had all these kids in my community who would be like, "Hey, Emile, man, last week you showed me some soccer moves, show me how you spin on the back," etc. And so, it was so automatic that I didn't even realize that I was already learning how to teach and pass this information on to other people. This is footage of a mass rally I attended years ago, but I only wrote this song recently. It's called "Butterflies Fly By." [*Emile plays music video*]

> We're toy-toying with our fists held up high.
> We see teargas fill the sky.
> Butterflies fly by
> Butterflies fly by
> These are the memories etched in my mind
> And won't let me rest until my peoples unblind.
> Butterflies fly by
> Butterflies fly by
> They point a gun at me, today I might die

The crowd scatters, I hear children cry
Butterflies fly by
Butterflies fly by

Now there be many, many memories that's etched in my mind,
but there's one in '85 that plays, rewinds and reminds . . . me
Of the struggle for freedom and equality
Apartheid's legacy still carries on relentlessly . . .

[*Emile points to the video*] So I was in that crowd over there. I actually went through the footage over and over to check for a younger version of myself. But this is the reality of what I grew up with. But at the same time, this is 1985, so I attended this rally. And, basically, the whole song explains me going to the rally, and for the first time in my life, a guy pointed his gun at me. And as the gun passed me, it slowed down, and I thought, "Damn, when is this passing me?" Because it's focused on me, right. And in that moment, my self-worth, in my own mind, was tested because all the time I was shouting, "Freedom or death, victory is certain." I'm 17 years old, I don't know what the hell I'm talking about. [*Laughter*] And at the same school rally, the guy who they bring in to speak has obviously been snuck in. So even though they say it's starting at like, say 10 o'clock, and this is not African time [*laughter*], this is because they need to smuggle him in, right. And so, what happens is, they're like, "Yo, Emile and some of the other guys, entertain us." So, in my own mind, I'm in this conflict. "We're fighting a revolution and you want me to dance?" "Oh, okay, just clap your hands, everyone, let's do it!" So constantly, for me, this period of time, when people speak about the struggle, it was a combination of picking up a brick and throwing it at whoever is pointing a gun at you, picking up teargas canisters and throwing them back at them. And, on the weekend, I go play soccer, and practice Kung Fu and go to a club and dance to Aretha Franklin, whatever. [*Laughter*] So it's a weird history, people make it sound like it's Black or white but it's extremely Coloured. [*Laughter*]

MAKING KNOWLEDGE OF SELF *REAL*

This is another track I wrote, and this happened between 1987 and 1989. I was at college, studying to be a teacher, but at that same time, there was the murder of Ashley Kriel, Anton Fransch, Coline Williams, and Robert Waterwitch. And in 1988, we formed Black Noise. So it was sort of right in the middle of a situation where we had to say something. We were like, "Yo, this can't go on, we need to speak out against what's happening in our country." So this song is actually a slogan that the young kids used, you get the audience, the crowd, and you go like, "Roar, young lions." And they say, "Roar!" [*Plays music video of "Roar Young Lions Roar!"*]

> Roar, young lions, roar
> Roar!
> Roar, young lions, roar
> Roar!
> Coline, Ashley, Robbie and Anton, must be remembered or this battle won't be won.
> I am me because of the true sacrifices of those who sacrificed it all.
> Once more, it's time for young lions to roar.
> Roar, young lions, roar.
> Roar...

These young cadres, or members of Umkhonto we Sizwe, they were my age, right. And for me, I did that song because in South Africa, everybody knows Hector Pieterson, and it really bothered me because to a certain extent this was an accidental hero that people are putting on a pedestal. And I'm not saying that to diminish the person's life. But these young people actually, *knowingly*, fought for our liberation and are never mentioned. There's a very racist undertone in their erasure. So, through these clips and stories that I actually wrote, I put it on a cell phone and just bluetoothed it to kids so they could finally have an image of these people that I'm speaking about. So trying to make that a reality.

With this background, I then, like Shaheen said, reached out to the world. [*Laughter*] I wrote to *Word Up!* magazine and I remember going to my letterbox at home, and there were like 500 letters there. I had to go to the post office to get another bag. I was like, "Damn, I'm never going to be able to read all these letters!" And some of the weirdest things that happened to me were because of these letters, right. I'll give you a quick example. Someone calls, I don't know how the hell they got my number, but in the middle of the night they call up. It's like maybe four o'clock in the morning, right, because I don't think like some people in the US understand time difference. [*Laughter*] So my mom tries to wake me up and, "Hey, Emile, come on there's someone on the phone for you and it sounds like they're not from South Africa." So I get to the phone, and the first thing they say is, "Hey, is your village far from the phone?" "My village?" I said, "No, I took the elephant to get to the phone." [*Laughter*]

But one of those letters was this guy in Dayton, Ohio, of all places. He sent me these photocopies of this book, *Blacked Out through Whitewash*. And as I was growing up I was always wondering where's the information about Black people? I open up a book and there's White folk, sheesh. Switch on the TV, White folks. Constantly, everywhere I go. Superman's White, damn. [*Laughter*] And so, I open up this book, right, and in the book, is all this information about Blackness, about where we come from, and how proud we should be of who we are, our kinky hair, what that all means. I'm completely blown away. And even though I was teaching, I hated reading because I constantly was confronted with information that was not enlightening me. It was all information that was benefiting the status quo.

And so I'm reading this book in the class while the kids are busy on their exercises, and I'm suddenly struck by the thought, "Am I going to be able to change the way young people think?" And it dawns on me that maybe I should ask them a question. And there are 40 young kids, and I say, "You know what? If you were given this option to follow your heart and your passion, and you weren't quite sure how you're going to get paid, but you really love what you do, would you do that? Or would you do a job, crappy or not, but you're getting a salary? Okay, let's vote, who's going to choose the passion over the salary?" And this is a grade five class, right. Everybody put up their hand that they want the salary. I went like, "Oh, my God." Out of the 40 kids, 35 said they would take the salary. And that really broke my heart. And at the same time, I was like, "If I stay in this teaching job, I would not be an example to what I just said." So how do I make all of that information I just read, real? How do I become an example of the outcome of Knowledge of Self? And that, for me, is like what I think everything that we created was because of actually making the knowledge of self *real*.

[*Emile points to an old photo on the screen*] Okay, that's me with the strange, blow-dried hair, over there. [*Laughter*] Blow-drying was big back in the day. I've been involved in Hip Hop for 32 years. We put out this album from scratch—the design, the photo, the layout, everything. I had no idea that we'd be able to do that. And it's all manifestation of Knowledge of Self. You don't want to sign a deal because the status quo will manipulate it for their benefit. So it's constantly asking, no matter what I'm faced with, how do I make real what I'm learning and what I'm reading? A lot of the information was about Do for Self. How do you make ends meet? So I decide I'm leaving teaching and the first thing my mom says is, "Hey, if you leave, you're still going to pay rent, and you're basically surviving on your own." And I couldn't thank her enough for that because what I figured out from that was *the mathematics of survival*. What do I do? How many shows do I need to do to pay the rent? How many shows do I need to do to buy a car, cash? How many shows do I need to do to buy a house, cash? So, in terms of Knowledge of Self, it's about the implementation of what you speak, instead of just speaking.

WRITING OUR OWN STORIES

As the group Black Noise, one of our projects was to go to schools, similar to what POC did. And I'm in the school, and I'm telling the kids, "How many of you read?" And they're like, "Ah, what do you mean?" And then I say, "Okay, if you go to your library, do me a favor and ask the librarian to please give you a book from here, from this area." And then someone shouts, "We don't have anyone from our community who has a book in the library." And everyone, even the teachers at the school, were like, "Woah, that's so true." Are we not writing our own stories? We need to change that. And so, I'm on stage, and I'm like, "Yeah, you need to write your own stories." And the kids are like, "Did you write your own story?" Damn! I love working with young people because they keep you honest. They constantly remind you that your words are not just empty. You are not just saying things for the sake of saying things and sounding like you know something. So I go home, and I'm like, "Oh, hey, a book is just a lot of paper put together with words. You write rhymes. Put some rhymes together and make a book."

What I realized from the process is that sometimes we forget something that's extremely fundamental. And that is that everyone over here

Figure 2.6 Emile YX? teaching the next generation, Mpumalanga (Northern Province), South Africa. Photo by Tanswell Jansen.

has something to give. All of us. You were put here on this earth to contribute *you*. You weren't put here to regurgitate some other guy's information so that you could get a degree. That's not why you're here, right? Sorry to the establishment. [*Laughter*] [*Applause*] Anyway, so for me, it's like an awakening that your God self is being set aside. And I do this with kids at schools. I say, "Name one thing in this room that you see that an artist created." You may join in. Anyone? Name something that you see in this room that an artist created. [*Long silence*] This silence happens in the schools, too. And then suddenly somebody says, "Oh, damn, an architect set this place up." And then people say, "The chair, the light, the design of this machine, the design of the table, the clothing that you have on, the earrings you're wearing, everything that is in the room had an artist's hand on it." And so, cleverly, someone made you believe that being an artist is worthless and being someone that sells the product is the one that should have the work, the money, right? So for me, what it also says is that it's taking away your God self—your creative, God self to create something that only you could think of. Steve Jobs wasn't so spectacular. All of these people that created things, they're not that amazing. Most of them actually stole the idea from someone else. But that's another story. The truth of the matter is, right in this room is a possibility for everyone of us to contribute to this planet, realistically. But we just don't see that. We're like, "Ah, I'd rather work within the confines of what the status quo sets up." Alright.

We have to constantly supply opportunities for young kids. A lot of them are just looking for a chance, an opportunity to showcase their skills. And so, yeah, if you're going to speak about it, then do it. And, for me, Knowledge of Self is about being open enough as a teacher to both give and also realize that you're learning from the process, at the same time. We're all trying to figure out different ways to find solutions to a given problem.

CREATING OUR OWN SCHOOLS: HEAL THE HOOD AND MIXED MENSE

I'll end with this. We decided to just create our own school, the Heal the Hood Project. And the first school we put together there were two young ladies from the community I live in, and two young guys, and it gave them a chance to travel to different parts of the world. They've been to Ireland, Norway, Sweden, Italy, alright. And they got paid a salary every month, and for the first time it was a reality. So young people often ask, "You know, I really want to be an emcee, can you show me how to do this?" Or, "I really want to be a dancer, can you show me?" And then when you give them the opportunity they're like, "Oh, my God, this is really much more difficult than I thought it was going to be." So, for me, I called it a practical school because that's how I learned, from practice and being out, physically there, all the time. And then, I was approached by a project in South Africa, by the government. When they saw me do the school, the Kemoja Project, they asked us to teach 20 young people and I was very worried about doing this. But I taught 20 kids, and it ran for a year. As soon as the World Cup came around in 2010, the government took their money and they left. And when they left, another sneaky character in the corner, a different political figure, I won't mention their names, the DA [*laughter*],

Figure 2.7 Stefan "B-boy Mouse" Benting and Leroy Phillips representing Mixed Mense. Photo by Ference Isaacs.

they came in and what they did was they took the 20 kids that I taught and they asked them to teach in schools, and paid them a salary, but they were not allowed to teach Knowledge of Self. Only the dance skills. So sometimes it's important to understand that things that we do in Hip Hop will not work within the status quo. The status quo's intention with people coming to educational places is to prepare you to work for the status quo.

So for me, learning that made me decide, "Wait a minute, let me use my own example and set up my own school." And I set up a project called Mixed Mense. Mense is Afrikaans for "people." And the kids I selected to be part of the project were from a place called Lavender Hill on the Cape Flats, which has a huge gang and drug problem. The first year I took them to go and see the First People of South Africa. I took them to the Kalahari, and I put them through a process of actually learning rhymes that were dealing with land, all in Afrikaans, obviously, because this was their first language, and the occupation of land, and how the theft of the land gave everyone this might. Stealing this land from our ancestors is what gave them power. Because, although they make it sound like it's just land, everything comes from the land. So, I thought that was important. We did a project about Princess Vlei, an area, a lake where I grew up. They wanted to build a mall and a parking lot on the edge of this lake. And I took the kids there and we sat down and we wrote the rhyme about why this mall should not be built. We put out the CD together, in the same way that I did it before—no record label, nothing, just putting out the CD, putting together the show, touring the kids, taking them to travel to the Kalahari. This year is putting them through all of the process of learning. They are, at the moment, in Washington, DC. They just performed at the Kennedy Center; they performed at the Trinity International Hip Hop Festival, and people are blown away by what they came up with. So, for me, putting your thoughts and your words into action is what Knowledge of Self is about. [*Applause*]

H. SAMY ALIM: That was the 5th element, right there, in action, live and direct from Cape Town, Hip Hop knowledge. I'm sure we have a lot of questions in the room.

QUESTION 1: Has the work that you have done with the kids, has it been helpful in actually reclaiming some of the land?

EMILE: Yo, I think within our minds at this point, only because I work with a lot of the First Peoples way of thinking, I understand that their belief was that they were owned by the land and not the reverse. So, for me, it's very important that when I teach it's about supplying information that is truthful. There's a lot of Khoi-San movement groups in Cape Town at the moment that focus on the occupation of the land. And if the understanding is that land is just for your tribe, then it is not beneficial to, not only Africa, but humanity as a whole. I don't subscribe to race, I don't subscribe to tribe, and I'm trying to get that message across that all of us on this planet come from one people, this First People. You can check it out, anthropologists, and you can find out that the Khoi and the San are our oldest relatives. And that all of this other race stuff is just one hell of a big lie to keep us divided. And so, the thing, for me, the land issue is connected to that, all of the wealth is based on the theft of the land. And so, I try and teach them that information, as well. And, also, for me, teaching them is also about their own sense of self-worth, right, within the context of who we are and where we're from. And I think only once we have Knowledge of Self and a clear understanding can we then work the land, and again, be part of the land. Not oppress and occupy the land, and other earthlings that frequent the land, the misuse of it. So I'm very careful about how I speak to them about ownership. I speak more about this in my forthcoming book, *Reconnect the String: The African Origins of Hip Hop Culture and Its Ancestral Healing Power.*

QUESTION 2: You spoke, Shaheen, specifically about how some of the apartheid censorship was going on as far as the imperialism and capitalists from the US, and how Hip Hop was being censored and not shown there. My question is, how were the images that were shown being filtered mentally? We are shown a lot of "bling bling" here, but we know that's not the reality on the streets, for example.

SHAHEEN: I think that because we were born at a period before this thing called Hip Hop, that some of the very early lyrics weren't so much about those type of images. Earlier on I quoted Grandmaster Flash and the Furious Five, there were a number of songs like that. You had someone who just had a boom box, LL Cool J's "My Radio," and that was the thing, never mind all kinds of ice and bling like that. And so, I think, for me, two things happened. The first thing, this voice. "I am somebody." "Oh, my God, this is music that has an attitude, that has an energy, that has words that speak to me in a particular way," right? And that for me, although the Public Enemys, that phase of Hip Hop, is generally considered as the conscious phase, I think, that there was some kind of political statement, or at least the impact that it had was political to me, in South Africa. That you had young people's voices, young-people-who-were-not-White voices, young people who were talking about just regular shit, those kinds of voices, that was profoundly political, in terms of what was allowed. So the "bling bling" was not so much an issue. In fact, the opposite happened. Hip Hop was the first time that I heard images of the US that contradicted what I saw in Hollywood, and the Disney stuff, and all the happy "land of the free, home of the brave" type of thing. It was the first time that I could make that connection and go, "Wow, this is like Elsies and Mitchells Plain," local areas where we came from.

The interesting thing is in "post"-apartheid South Africa, the thing that I'm concerned about is, very often it's spoken about that young people are the ones that consume particular kinds of images and take it on, and it happens to adults as well. It happens to adults more so, I'd say, in particular cases. And, I think, that the work that we've tried to do through Bush Radio, through the workshops, the workshops that Emile's doing, and a number of other people, Rozzano X and others from the first generation, is to provide some kind of context for South African Hip Hop and context for what it means to push the material over the human spirit. And so we're very fortunate that many of us don't make much money from Hip Hop in South Africa, that this is a "conscious," for lack of a better term, kind of Hip Hop, and especially in Cape Town. And not just in terms of the messages, but also in terms of how the industry has impacted this culture called Hip Hop. The emcee became the thing that was the easiest to add a barcode to and package it. And so, dancers, and DJs, and graff writers, they weren't seen as worth investing in. And so, they became invisible. In South Africa, we didn't really go through that period—since Black Noise and POC were established, there were always b-boys as part of the crew. And the DJ, and the graff artist, and sometimes performing in places where dude's spray painting in a room like this and you're trying to rhyme and breathe, but just to show that what is happening in the States and what industry has done to culture, we are not allowing that to happen here.

QUESTION 3: In terms of both of you speaking of rejecting race, or Coloured identity, etc., I was just wondering what your relationship to Blackness as a political construct was, and its relationship to the concept of nationalism, in your personal politics, but also, within the establishment of Hip Hop in Cape Town in South Africa.

SHAHEEN: In terms of Knowledge of Self, that's actually played out really interestingly because Blackness as a political identity totally rejected apartheid racial classifications and even post-apartheid racial classifications. However, in post-apartheid South Africa, we've seen some really interesting kinds of cases. So you have a de-territorialized Blackness that's connected to Hip Hop that challenges state-sanctioned racial identities, but then you also get responses from folks who identify with state-sponsored notions of Blackness. That's like, "Yo, that's not authentically Black." So you have this kind of reified notion of Blackness competing with this thinking of, "Oh, this is bullshit, this is a political identity." And not in all spheres does it exist, but it's interesting to see how that played out. And even more complicated is that to redress, or address, some of the ills of apartheid, you have this thing called BEES, the Black Economic Empowerment Strategy. And the way that was implemented was very selective. And so, what you had was folks who were classified as Coloured were often excluded from benefiting from those programs and even participating in those programs. In fact, the majority of what you had was White businesses engaged in fraud—and this was actually exposed—where they listed the person who makes the tea as the CEO of the company. That was what happened, mostly. But, what happened was, as a backlash, people who were/are classified as Coloured viewed the selective implementation of Black economic policies as further discrimination. So, under apartheid, Coloured people were not "White enough," and under neo-apartheid, not "Black enough." It's a lot more complicated than that, because if you look at townships, "Black" townships, it's still as impoverished as "Coloured" townships, and so these divide-and-rule policies are still benefiting historical old money and new Black money. That, essentially, is what is happening in terms of those benefiting.

And what's happening that's even more insidious is that you have this national culture of "proudly South African," this branding campaign that wants us to identify with the South African elite more than our brothers and sisters on that side of the Limpopo River, and the Orange River, from Botswana and whatever. And so when they have strife in their country and they rush to South Africa—and they used to house South Africans at some point under apartheid when we had to flee for safety—they have to now be on the receiving end of xenophobic violence. When, if you're from the US, and especially if you're White, from Europe, if you come to South Africa and you take a job, nothing will happen to you. So there's a lot to your question, in terms of how race is implicated in matters that are really the negative impact of capitalism. And so it becomes really tricky in terms of how folks are navigating all of this. So it's not unusual to find someone who has Knowledge of Self, in identifying, to going from Coloured to, "I've seen the light, I'm Black." Then to, "Holy shit, they're discriminating against me,

Figure 2.8 Emile YX? and Shaheen Ariefdien with the Freedom Moves crew. Photo by Abdul Alim.

what now? I'm Khoi-San!" [*Laughter*] And choosing aspects of history and particular parts of our identities in order to survive. In order to survive spiritually, in order to survive psychologically, and materially, right.

And with neoliberalism globally, people are feeling more and more under pressure, feeling more and more under siege. The conditions that we saw that gave birth to the South Bronx, and the Cape Flats, are being spread globally. And in those places, the South Bronx and the Cape Flats, it's even more intensified. And so, for me, it's the question of the negative impact of capitalism and how race is implicated in that, but also how race becomes a red herring, and a way for people to focus on particular kinds of identities and build solidarities around particular kinds of identities that I feel might not always produce the most healthy outcome.

EMILE: A solution, I suppose, is to mix it up as much as you possibly can. And so, I might ask a kid, "You know that click sound you just made, where'd that come from?" And he's like, "What do you mean?" And the word Xhosa means "angry looking man." And it came from their movement, as they moved south towards the San, the first people, and they were given that name, and all the clicks that they use in their language, you understand? So the idea that each of these groups were like ordained by God, that Zulu is people of the heavens, Zulu is no different than Shaka grouping different peoples together. That's all it is. It's a group of tribes that Shaka conquered and forced together and named them Zulu. But when you listen to people speak and say, "I'm Zulu," they make it sound that, somehow, they miraculously appeared. And if you research, you find that within language and within history there is so much fluidity between the so-called tribes and races, and even the Khoi and the San in South Africa, these First Peoples, they are not classified as African. They're not seen as African. How the hell do you not classify the first people of all people as even Black for that matter? Do you understand? So it's very divisive. When I work with communities, I try and get to the middle ground and get people to interact based on the fluidity and the similarity, because we spend a lot of time thinking about the difference. We need to think about the similarity.

3 "Al-shaab yurid isqat al-nitham! (الشعب يريد اسقاطالنظام)"

SUSTAINING REVOLUTION IN PALESTINE AND SYRIA THROUGH HIP HOP

DAM (Tamer Nafar, Suhell Nafar, and Mahmoud Jreri), Omar Offendum, and Ramzi Salti

RAMZI SALTI: Assalamu alaykum. So nice to see everybody here. I'm Ramzi Salti. I teach Arabic at Stanford and I also have a radio show called Arabology on KZSU. It was one of the first shows to actually highlight something called "Arabic Hip Hop." A lot of people who come from the Arab world don't know there is such a thing as Arab Hip Hop. They see Hip Hop as a purely "Westernized" culture, or just the result of globalization and modernity, when it's so much more. Hip Hop can reach anybody, from any background, at any time. This is poetry. This is exactly what poetry used to do to people. Poets are supposed to move people when you listen to them.

Our "poets" this evening include Syrian American rapper Omar Offendum and the groundbreaking Palestinian group DAM. Omar Offendum is a Hip Hop artist, architect (a verbal architect and an *actual* trained architect!), poet, and peace activist who was born in Saudi Arabia, raised in Washington, DC, and now lives in Los Angeles, California. His solo career broke through in 2011 with "#Jan25," which also featured Freeway, Amir Sulaiman, Narcy, and Ayah, a song that both inspired, and was inspired by, the Arab Spring uprisings.[1] His first solo album, *SyrianamericanA*, was released in 2011 to much critical acclaim and, since then, he has had a string of successes, including musical collaborations with Yassin Alsalman, also known as Narcy, or the Narcicyst, an Iraqi Canadian emcee, and British Palestinian emcee Shadia Mansour, "the first lady of Arabic Hip Hop," as well as the classic performance poetry lecture *From Brooklyn Beats 2 Beirut Streets* with Mexican American poet Mark Gonzales (see chapter 9) and Palestinian American Hip Hop artists and filmmaker Nizar Wattad, who were collectively known as the Human Writes Project. Omar is equally known for his art, including his intricate, bilingual Arabic-English lyricism, as well as his activism, which is in part why he was selected as a Kennedy Center Citizen Artist Fellow in 2018–19, one of only five in the country.

The group DAM was founded in the late 1990s by the three members who are here tonight—Brothers Tamer[2] and Suhell Nafar and Mahmoud Jreri[3]—who like to identify as Palestinian citizens of Israel. Their music is known for fusing musical styles while creating a distinct new genre of Arabic rap that combines Middle Eastern beats with a deep urban Hip Hop sound. DAM raps in Arabic, English, and Hebrew and has released more than 100 singles and three albums—*Dedication, Dabke on the Moon,* and *Ben Haana Wa Maana*—in addition to starring in dozens of TV shows and films such as *Slingshot Hip Hop* in 2008, a groundbreaking, critically acclaimed documentary that was directed by Jackie Salloum, arguably one of the most important Hip Hop documentaries ever produced. DAM broke through with their single, "Meen Erhabi?—Who Is the Terrorist?" (over 1 million downloads), and became well known for their raps against the Israeli occupation, though as we will see, they cover a range of issues from racism, women's rights, the experience and the struggle of everyday life in poverty. These artists have long been on the leading edge of global Hip Hop and we're happy to have them with us.

So please let's welcome our brilliant guests tonight, DAM and Omar Offendum. [*Applause*] Let me start with a question that everybody asked me to ask you—Tamer, Suhell, and Mahmoud—about the name, DAM. There's a lot of debate. Does it mean "blood" in Arabic, or does it stand for something else? How did you come up with the name?

SUHELL NAFAR: First of all, I'd like to say thank you for having us. And before we answer this question, I just want to say something. It's really emotional for me to be here, at a table with Omar and Ramzi at the same time. Because unfortunately, we can't have this thing in Palestine. We can't have this in Syria. Omar can't come to Palestine and we can't go to Syria. It's really kind of confusing, and brings up a lot of emotions for me. And now I get to the question. DAM stands for *al-shay' al-ladhi yadum* (الشيء الذي يدوم), something that is immortal. Eternity. In Hebrew, it means blood, if it's without the A. And in English, it's Da Arabian MCs. And we mixed it all together. So we say, "Even if we see blood, Da Arabian MCs will stay eternal, Da Arabian MCs will be immortal."

TAMER NAFAR: Our name, at the beginning, was "*dam*" from *damn*. And it blew up, and it sounded cool when we were teenagers. [*Laughter*] But during that time, we started doing shows at universities and it sounded stupid. [*Laughter*] So we had to find a good meaning, but at the beginning, it was just *dam*—

SUHELL NAFAR: Da Arabian MCs.

TAMER NAFAR: But DAM from eternity, it has a lot of depth.

SUHELL NAFAR: Yeah, *yaani* like when a girl in Cleveland says, "We don't want Arabs here, they're the devil." We're like, *dam (damn)*, we will stay here forever. If somebody says that Hip Hop is something that will pass, no *dam*, we will stay here artistically forever. So, you know, it's about building a better condition.

SALTI: And, now, let me ask Omar Offen—

OMAR OFFENDUM: —*damn*. [*Laughter*]

SALTI: [*Laughter*] So where do you get that name?

OFFENDUM: I mean, Offendum was like a stroke of genius when I was 17 that I wish had more depth to it at the time. When I first started rapping, I was in college. Me and a Sudanese friend of mine I grew up with, we called ourselves the N.O.M.A.D.S.: Notoriously Offensive Male Arabs

Figure 3.1 Omar Offendum and Thanks Joey performing their collaborative album release *Lost in Translation* for CAP-UCLA's virtual performance season, which aired on January 28, 2021. Photo by Phinn Sriployrung.

Discussing Shhh—. [*Laughter*] You know, when I was growing up, when I would act up around the house or whatever, my mom would call me, "effendi, Omar effendi." And for those that don't know, effendi is like a title of nobility or a ranking within Ottoman culture, or Turkish cultures. So, it's like saying "sir" or "Lord," and effendim is the possessive form. So, often in the Middle East, whether it's Turkey or even Egypt, you know, people will say, "effendim," out of respect to you. And me spelling it with an "O" obviously was with the intention of conjuring up offensive imagery here in the states. Offendum, like you know, "Oh, he's gonna offend us," when in reality, it actually means something very kind of noble and respectful. So, for the name to embody the disconnect that happens there linguistically between, you know, something over there and something here, was really important to me, because it in itself was a conversation starter. And then, just on a personal note, my mother's grandfather was Turkish. His name was Omar. He's the one I was named after and he was actually an Effendi. Omar Effendi, so that's kinda where it came from. I also discovered later on that the ancient Greek root word is in fact "*authentes,*" which made me smile as authenticity is what I've always sought to reflect with my work.

SALTI: So, he lives on through your music, Omar.

OFFENDUM: Yeah, I don't know what he would think about my music. [*Laughter*] I've seen one picture of him. It's an old black and white photo. He had a big long curly mustache. [*Laughter*] Big, scary guy.

SALTI: So, for the group, DAM, you have two officially released albums. You've been involved in many other things. The first one is called *Ihda'* (إهداء), which means "dedication." And the second one is playing on KZSU, like every other hour, and is called *Dabke*[4] *on the Moon*. Can you tell us how the first album came about and how the second album is different from the first one?

MAHMOUD JRERI: Well, the first album, *Dedication*, was out towards the end of 2006, at the beginning of 2007. It was a very, very clear obvious direct message that we wanted to deliver. It was like shooting a documentary film, but musically. And that's what we did. It had social, political, and personal songs. It actually had more social songs than political songs, but because we come from Palestine, everyone is concept writing on the political side. I wouldn't call it a political album. *Dabke on the Moon* is much different. We worked with producers coming from the pop world because we wanted to try and experience new things in our music. And it was more like a feature film. It was telling stories. We told stories of prisoners. We told stories of women. Women that are killed in the name of honor, honor killings. And that was *Dabke on the Moon*. I don't know if I would call it mainstream music, but it was definitely different than the *Dedication* album. We tried to experience new things musically and lyrically.

SALTI: Right, which brings me to this question about this song, "*law arjaa bil-zaman*" (لو أرجع بالزمن) "If I Could Go Back in Time," which Amal Murkus participated in. It's a really powerful video about honor killings, which is something that takes place in some of the Arab world, and in my opinion, is a very shameful practice. It was a very gutsy move on your part to do this song, and I'm going to be frank with you, not everybody supported that video.[5] You were kind of criticized for maybe further demonizing Arabs and Islam, at a time where the West seems to be doing that so systematically. But at the same time, when you watch the video, you're moved by the fact that so many women have been silenced. Women have been killed for something as simple as, you know, the very rumor that they have lost their "honor" even in this day and age. How have you received all this high praise and high criticism for that song?

TAMER NAFAR: The reactions we had, there's people who didn't like it. I'll get to that later. But most of the girls, in Lod,[6] where I live—I remember the first preview that we did in Ramallah, the women in the crowd started crying, and we did this song for them. It's not about people who are living in the West, it's about them. And that's how it started. I view honor killings as my problem, for me as an Arab man. I must face it and say, "It's my fault. I want to fix it now." And I think that it reflects the new generation *yaani* the Arab Spring, they got out to change the way they live. So, I think it's a shame. Another thing, when I wrote that song, I was thinking about living in Lod. In Lod, we have had at least 15, 16 murders that are honor killings. And it's girls we know, over sex, and I don't think that's ever a reason for murder. And there's a saying, I feel like most of the men would be dead today if we judged them by the same standards of women. And it's women we know, it's girls we know. If we don't know the women, we knew the guy who killed them. So, we lived that, and I think it's about time that we talked about it, so when we wrote that song, we wrote it for Arab women. And recently I had a call with an Israeli radio station and the host was like, "We have this new single. It's about honor killings, and just to remind you people, only this week, two women were killed," and she mentioned two Israeli women with Jewish names. So, it's not just about the Arab world, it's about violence against women in general.

OFFENDUM: You mentioned before two women here in the States.

TAMER NAFAR: Yeah, lot of Western people see us as bad people. Evil people. And a lot of Arabs only see Palestinians a certain way. And if they see us only in this way, that makes us unhuman. And yeah, these two women, they want us to just be these beautiful, handsome Palestinians, who call out and fight the Israelis, but that's not it, we can't just do that.

Each society has its problems and if I'm brave enough to face it—and I'm talking about a new generation who's brave enough—I think that if you have a problem with us bringing up these issues, you should buy a mirror and put it up in your house, because we have to face these things.

SUHELL NAFAR: Look, there's misogynistic violence everywhere, and it's political, and we have to give knowledge where we can. Us, as kids who started rapping political stuff and then suddenly, you go to protests in Palestine or protests in my city, about the demolishing of a house, and you see people in the protests, walking with you, in the protest that you organized, telling you that they came to this protest because of your songs, it lets you know the importance of Hip Hop. They got knowledge from us for a political reason. We have to do that. If we have influence, we got to use it. And politics means we're not just singing about Palestine. If we're not singing about social stuff, and doing Hip Hop to have fun, we're not being human, we're being fake. Because we're human, and we're all of that. A lot of times we're rapping about Palestine and the dead people who died from fighting. But I don't want to be that person who's just doing Hip Hop about that, because we're more than that.

SALTI: Yeah, I'm going to include Omar in this, because we're talking maybe about resistance being sort of what's expected within all the resistance literature, resistance lyrics. Do you feel that Hip Hop, in terms of its globalization and in terms of your own music, has grown to encompass more topics and broach more subjects than what initially used to happen?

OFFENDUM: I mean, for a long time, while I was doing what I was doing, nobody really knew where I was from. I mean, I was born in Saudi Arabia. I have Palestinian family members, Egyptian family members, and so on. I associated myself with being Arab, more than anything specific. Even though, if you'd ask me, I'd always tell you I was Syrian. But the songs and the way people started to take them in, for a long time, people thought I was Palestinian. You know like, "There's that Palestinian rapper, because he's rapping about Palestine." And then I did a song about the Egyptian revolution. I was on Al Jazeera, and it said "Egyptian" below my name, because they never bothered to ask or inquire. And then the Syrian revolution started and I created a song about the revolution in Syria and then it's like, "Oh, there's the Syria guy. Now we know who he is. He's the Syrian guy," you know? And I mean, to be perfectly honest with you, I'm not shocked by any of that, because I think I've done it myself in the past. Watching music videos, you kind of just start to project onto the person the things that you assume. You think you know about them, about their life. You think you know everything about them, because you've seen a two-minute video clip about somebody. So once I started seeing people do it to me, I was like, "Okay, I see how this works." And, you know, I took a step back and realized that, for me, at the end of the day, I'm a human being who's making art with a particular purpose. I desire to do art as truthfully and honestly as possible, with my experience. I have also written narratives and stories about other experiences I can relate to. As long as I was coming from that place, and made sure it was coming from an honest place, I felt that I didn't need to worry about what people were saying, or how they were internalizing the things that I was saying. That's on them, you know? But it took a long time to get to that point, you know? It's hard, because as an artist, you also have access to people's comments every single day on YouTube, Facebook, and Twitter. I'm like, "Oh my God, I can't believe they just said that about my mother, it's like, 'You never even met her before.'" [*Laughter*]

SALTI: We spoke before the show and I was trying to tell all four of these amazing young men here, how their music has a profound impact on people, despite the generations and language barriers. And we spoke of a young man who unfortunately passed away, who was a huge fan of DAM and who always listened to their albums, like nonstop, and I just remember him always saying, "It makes you feel better. They understand. The music speaks to me." And unfortunately, he was in Jordan and he didn't have much access to much rap music in Arabic. How do you guys feel when you know that you're moving people so deeply and that you're speaking to the experience of people, not just in Palestine, but all over the Arab world, who are marginalized, who are oppressed, who can relate through your music to what you're going through?

JRERI: First of all, *Allah yirhamo, may he rest in peace*. We come from a place that is very hard. There's a big poverty problem, big drug problem, and of course, a huge political problem, as you know. When I speak about my neighborhood, when I speak about my poverty, when I speak about police on Arab crime, or soldiers on Palestinian crime, Arabs against Arabs, when I speak about the right of return for Palestinian refugees, then of course, I will affect many people that feel or live the same thing that I live, because they feel connected to my message. They feel connected to my lyrics, and they can put themselves in that song, in different ways. And the funny thing, I also was affected in the beginning by Tupac and I was affected by him and from his images, 'cause I only saw the images. I didn't understand English back then, but I saw the neighborhood. I saw the poverty. I saw that he talked about political problems. I felt connected to that music, because he talked to me. So, I guess it is the same thing, when you are talking about issues, that they are real and they are happening, then people will feel connected to you and connected to your message and to what you are trying to do.

SALTI: Do you think you're more accepted in the Arab world, in the West, or in say Lod, where you have a population that you can speak to directly?

TAMER NAFAR: I wouldn't know how to measure that, but if I measured it by concerts, this is my third time at Stanford and I've had only one show in Lod. I did 20 shows in Paris and I only had one show in Lod. I had 30 in New York, but I've only had one show in Lod.

SALTI: Why do you think that is?

TAMER NAFAR: I think it's the Israeli passport. I have an Israeli passport and I don't get invited to Israeli festivals, because I'm a Palestinian.[7] I don't get invited to Arab festivals, because I'm an Israeli.[8] So, it's some kind of schizophrenia. I would call it discrimination, *yaani*, it's this new revolutionary music, plus an Israeli passport. And in a place like Syria or a place like Algeria, we cannot go, 'cause there are no embassies basically. I mean, Egypt, before the revolution, they had an embassy. But when an Egyptian singer decides to do something with a guy from Palestine, everybody starts saying, "Betrayer," and the hypocrisy can take over the whole room.

SALTI: Absolutely, because you said that you felt that there's a double hypocrisy going on, because you're seen as Palestinian and Israeli, so you're the Other and you're different, and then, you go to the Arab world, and suddenly, instead of being embraced for the bravery you're showing through your lyrics, you're actually—

TAMER NAFAR: And just to be clear, I'm talking about institutions basically. I'm talking about the people who are creating the festivals. Because when it comes to people, they understand. I think that's the beautiful thing about Hip Hop. I mean, Palestinian Arabic music exists from a long time ago, but have you ever heard of duets between Palestinians and Egyptians? I can count on my hand maybe five duets that I remember in the Arab world. But Hip Hop, how many songs do you have with Egyptian emcees, Omar? How many songs do you have with the Iraqis? How many songs do you have with Palestinians? That's the beautiful thing about Hip Hop. And I don't wanna make it just political and deep and about the Middle East. Check a Lil Wayne album and Drake and you see all this featuring. Hip Hop is a different music, a collaborative form. I recently had the chance to work with a Lebanese artist. I've worked with people who are the enemy according to my passport, but with Hip Hop it's different. That's part of why I love the music. It's so uniting. The word "featuring," it's a revolutionary word and it's been brought in by the Hip Hop world.

SALTI: If it's any comfort, I was in Beirut and I was in Amman last year, and I interviewed so many groups, and the people were always talking about how DAM cannot perform there, in Beirut and these other places, but how the people want it. I mean, the audiences are there and thanks to the internet, are able to tune in. So we're talking about maybe a sad reality that the demand is there, the thirst for you guys is there, but it's these colonial bureaucratic issues, which stop you from actually performing live to people who need you.

SUHELL NAFAR: That's true. We had an invitation to go to Lebanon. That would have been nice for us to go, and to perform there, and the Lebanese will accept us, even if it's the Lebanese government, they'll let us get in.

But then, when we go back home, we won't go back home. We'll go to the Israeli jails. We will be arrested.

TAMER NAFAR: And it's more complicated than that, right? Like I don't know if you remember Ala Hlehel? He's a famous writer, and he has a website "qadita.net." He's a Palestinian carrying the Israeli passport and he had this invitation, because he released a book, *My Secret Affair with Carla Bruni*, it's a funny book. He describes how Carla Bruni comes to Palestine, and wears a *hijab*, so no one would recognize her while she's having sex with him [*laughter*] and it's a funny book. Anyway, he was invited to do this festival, *Mu'tamar Al-Udaba'* (مؤتمر الادباء) in Lebanon (a conference that focuses on Arab literary figures). Yeah and dude thought of something smart, he applied to the *Begatz*. You know the *Begatz?* It's the highest court in Israel. He applied there, and he said, "It's not weapons, it's nothing political, it's just art," and it went on, like, a month or two and they agreed that he will go there and the Lebanese people agreed to accept him. And he didn't go. He was just like, "I just did it for the point." [*Laughter*] "I have a kid, I don't really want to go." It's complicated, you know?

OFFENDUM: I could actually never go to Palestine growing up. It's something I always wanted to do, but the way the laws were set up, if they ever found out, I would never be allowed back in Syria. I couldn't go see my family, and so that's just not a possibility. So I can somewhat relate, you know, to what you guys are talking about. But what's interesting though, is with the Syrian revolution, I'm not allowed to go back into Syria because of what I said on a song. That's the whole irony in and of itself because I was born in Saudi Arabia, and I'm not allowed to go back to this country that I never lived in anyway. But when I go to places like the Gulf, like in Dubai for example, to go do a show there, I get very clear orders not to perform, not even political content, but specifically this one song, because in the hook of the song, I say, "*al-shaab yurid isqat al-nitham*" (الشعب يريد اسقاط النظام) (the people want to topple the regime).[9] And even though it's entirely about the Syrian situation, and it has nothing to do with the Gulf, they don't even want people just thinking that they can even say that out loud, you know? There were Guy Fawkes T-shirts that were made, with the Syrian flag on them, and those were strictly banned. You're not even allowed, nobody's allowed, to wear any Guy Fawkes memorabilia or you'll be apprehended. So I mean it's real.

And, then, I got invited to go perform in Qatar, and I assumed because of Qatar's presumed stance on what's happening in Syria, and support for the revolution, that I would have free rein to say whatever I wanted. Halfway through performing this one song, I noticed that there were some local Qatari guys who were wearing traditional Qatari dress, who enjoyed it, and were chanting along. And there was only like 500 people there, and there was maybe three or four Qataris in their local dress chanting the song, and enjoying it. But as I was doing it, I looked at them, and I was like, "That's going to be a problem." [*Laughter*] And sure enough, right afterwards, I got a warning saying you're not allowed to do that.

SALTI: What song was that?

OFFENDUM: #Syria, *al-shaab yurid isqat al-nitham.* [*Laughter*] And just so people who know, like this particular phrase, *al-shaab yurid isqat al-nitham,* "the people want to topple the regime," started in Tunisia, and then moved to Egypt, and to Libya, and it was spray-painted on a wall in Syria, and that's what ended up sparking the revolution. So it's a very heated kind of thing in the Gulf, especially, you know. So it even shows you how in the Middle East, we hear in the West, especially in the media, they kind of paint it as this one big blob of "the Middle East," but it's so different from one country to another. Life is so different and the things people experience are so different. You can be thousands (hundreds?) of miles away from one of the most horrific, bloodiest disasters that has ever taken place on planet Earth, and have no idea. You'd be in a bubble, and just living life, eating hamburgers and thinking it's all good.

SALTI: Who would've known that two years later, the Syrian Revolution would still be going on. And it's bloodier than ever, more tragic than ever. How do you feel now about that situation and are you going to translate that into your music in the future?

OFFENDUM: You know, it's tough with Syria. My emotions fluctuate every single day. I have family there, and for a long time, my mother and sister were still there, so I couldn't even say the things I wanted to say out of fear for them, and what might happen. Families of activists have been targeted. And not just activists, even musicians and artists. I mean, there's a Syrian American piano player, Malek Jandali,[10] who played at a rally in D. C. and a few days later, his elderly parents got beaten up by thugs sent from the regime. So it was a very real fear when I wrote that song, "#Syria," in August of 2011, and I didn't release it until March of 2012. And the situation changes every day. That's the thing with the Syrian Revolution, it's like they call it the Orphan Revolution because everybody forgot about it, you know.

And we were just talking about this earlier, everybody was so gung ho about Tunisia and Egypt. Then the way Libya ended was kind of weird, and then with Bahrain everyone was like, "Let's just put that one away." [*Laughter*] And what the hell happened in Yemen? And then Syria, like we don't even understand. It's like the toxic revolution. Everybody forgot about it, nobody wants to touch it. It's too complicated politically. It's too much of a mess for people to be able to comprehend. The ramifications are just so huge that it's like daunting to even talk about it, or even to broach the subject. So I mean, it's heavy, but for me, what I've said consistently is that beneath all the political posturing, all the proxy wars, and all the conspiracy theories, there's very real human suffering taking place. It's half a million refugees outside of Syria, millions internally displaced, 70,000 killed, hundreds of thousands imprisoned, and so, it's just a dire humanitarian issue. And for me, as a Syrian, and more importantly as a humanitarian, that's kind of what I feel like I want to focus on, because if you get sucked into the political argument, you'll end up losing sight of the fact that at the end of the day, there will be no Syria to come back to, you know? If nobody's taking care of these kids, who've been out of school for 2-3 years, who are now in these camps, then you know, what are we really fighting for? So the things going on in Syria definitely influence everything I do.

It's also created a huge writer's block. Like, what the hell do you want me to say after this many people have died? What do you want a song to do for you? But what I have done, I think relatively successfully in the capacity that I can, is to use my music and these songs as a rallying point to get people to come together, to raise awareness, and to raise funds for the cause. I've tried my best at least to do that.

But the community gets tapped out after a while, too. One fundraiser after the other. It's like, we have no more to give, and people keep dying, and you just feel helpless, you know? But what gives me hope is hearing the stories of people there. Every once in a while, like in the darkest moment, I'll hear something from, you know, a cousin, or my brother-in-law who does relief work between Turkey and Syria. It really just gives you hope that there will be something to look forward to, or at least feel like these efforts might be worth it in the long run.

One small story to just give a little bit of context, and I guess positivity, there was a man at a farmer's market in Reyhanli, which is a border town between Syria and Turkey, that my brother-in-law had come to. There was a man waving at him like he recognized him, but my brother-in-law didn't quite remember him. He assumed he was one of the people who he had helped give aid to, but he just didn't know in particular who this man was. Anyway, my brother-in-law walked over to the man's stall, and they started talking. The man said his name was so and so, you probably don't remember me. At that point, a customer had come, and the man turned to the customer and started talking about these olives that he had for sale. And they started talking about how difficult it was to get olives now. How olives are more expensive than olive oil, and that's never happened before. This is all because you can't harvest in northern Syria anymore because of all the violence. And the guy said, "Lucky for you I happen to have this batch from my house that I just brought before I came," and so he sold the customer some olives. The guy turned to my brother-in-law and said, "Do you know what I did? I took the winter care package that I got from you and the relief agency," which basically contained, like blankets, coats, shoes and heating oil, he said, "I took that, and I sold them. I used that money to get me a ride to the border. I passed the border, and then in order to pay for my stall here today, I brought olives from my house. I made five times as much money as those olives originally cost." And so yeah, there might be a question of like ethics when someone gives you a donation. [*Laughter*] But this guy actually turned that donation into so much more with the entrepreneurial spirit that all Syrians have, I believe, and turned it into something even more. And that just made me realize, people don't want to just take handouts. It's like the saying, you teach a man to fish and he'll eat fish for a lifetime. So that's the kind of the thing that keeps me hopeful.

SALTI: I think we should leave it to our wonderful audience here.

QUESTION 1: This is a question for DAM. What was it like growing up in Lod, and how did you form as a group?

TAMER NAFAR: Personally, I had a happy childhood. [*Laughter*] It was beautiful, it was charming, until I discovered the world, and I knew that I live in a shithole. [*Laughter*] Like, what the fuck, do you mean to tell me that you're not sitting 60 people in one classroom? I grew up in a bad school, I would say. According to the laws, we're supposed to be 30 students in one classroom, we were like 45. We had the shittiest teachers. When I say shittiest teachers, I mean that I got a broken nose from my teacher. He just grabbed my head, and he smashed it twice. And I love my father, but the first thing he asked me is, "What did you do?"

SUHELL NAFAR: I was in the same bad school until sixth grade, and then I moved to a Jewish and Arab school, kind of mixed. Everyone studied everyone's language, which was kind of cool, and then after that I got introduced to a camera. I wanted to study cinema, but there is no school to do that. I had to fight everyone around to go and study at a Jewish school because that was the only place that I found that they would teach cinema. And that's what I did. I went there naïve and optimistic. But when I got into the school, I started to see reality. I was shocked by how racist the people were. I mean, I was going back to class, and finding on my table, written in huge letters, "Death to Arabs." Or opening the textbook and seeing written on every picture with an Arab, "Death to Arabs." And when the teachers came in, and started teaching, they would give you the worst lessons and propaganda. Like they would teach that our fathers were nothing, and that they came to this empty land, and took it. So I had a lot of really, really hard traumatizing experiences in those few years studying in these types of schools.

TAMER NAFAR: I witnessed these things, and of course it's not black and white. I mean, there's a lot of layers. It's also meeting Jewish people who are like, "Yeah, I listened to your music while I was in prison. Why? I was sentenced to prison for three months because I refused to go into the

Army." And then you go and do shows on the other side of the separation wall, and suddenly you're invited to a village. You go and stay in an Arab village, you go on the stage, and you see how they separate the women and men. I think I'm a part of a new generation who are against these forms of separation. So it's not black or white, it's mixed.

JRERI: And how we formed as a group, it was back in 1999 with Tamer's six-track album, a very bad, bad, bad, bad album. [*Laughter*] It was called "Stop Selling Drugs." [*Laughter*]

TAMER NAFAR: When I recorded it, I remember now. I had a Scarface T-shirt on. [*Laughter*]

JRERI: I was listening to Hip Hop, and I loved that music. And, suddenly, my sister brought me that album, "Stop Selling Drugs," and I was amazed that there is someone in Lod, considered a small city, that had some of that club Hip Hop. So I called him. Tamer invited me to his release party. It had what, 10 friends? [*Laughter*]

TAMER NAFAR: You were the 10th! [*Laughter*]

JRERI: And together we created DAM in the beginning of 2000.

QUESTION 2: So, for DAM, you have that song, "Mama, I Fell in Love with a Jew." I was wondering if you guys could speak on the meaning of that song?

TAMER NAFAR: It's a funny story. It's a sarcastic way to look at the situation with the Arabs and Jews, the Palestinians, and Israelis. It's a love story about me getting stuck in the elevator with this beautiful girl, and she's Jewish. That's the situation. We are stuck in the same place, and you know, we eventually have to talk and negotiate. And we just made it into a cheesy song. [*Laughter*] Yes, we're stuck in the same elevator, and darling you're pressing up, I'm pressing down. That's the difference. It's a sarcastic way to look at the situation. And, also, it's okay to fall in love with a Jew. [*Laughter*] We always say that our problem is not with the Jewish people, but with

Zionism, and with the occupation. We had a problem with the British, we had a problem with the Turks, and now with the Israelis and Zionism.

QUESTION 3: Omar, I was wondering when you're going to make your next song about Syria?

OFFENDUM: I totally understand why people want to hear more music about Syria, about the conflict, and want to get energized and inspired. But that's never how it kind of works with me. I mean, even when I wrote about the Egyptian Revolution, it was one of the first times I wrote about a conflict as it was happening. I typically like to let things kind of settle, and simmer before I speak on them. And to be honest, those songs about Syria, I would say, took 30 years to write, you know? It's not like I just wrote it out of what was happening. It was the combination of the years of dictatorship and seeing how it affected my family, and seeing how it affected the people in the community. And there's a whole lot of words that still ring true and resonate in what's happening now. But the situation is very complicated, and you know, for me to sit here and just write like a chronicle of it? I don't know if it's necessary when you have citizen journalists who are on the ground every day trying to get the story out, and nobody's listening. You know. You can get the real story right there. Like I released a song, "We Have to Change" (لازم نتغير), with Shadia Mansour. It was directed by Global Faction, who's a really phenomenal artist, activist, and filmmaker from London who did most of Lowkey's videos. It's entirely in Arabic. It's inspired by Palestine, but it's much bigger than that. It's more so a dedication to the memory of her cousin, a longtime activist and an important figure, Juliano Mer-Khamis.

QUESTION 4: Omar, how do you determine what your next track is gonna be in terms of language, and who you're targeting, right? Like, in terms of reaching out to the people in the West, but touching people in the East. You have songs in Arabic, English, and lot of your songs you combine them. How do you determine that, you know, without, like, turning off in the case of Arabic, those who don't understand Arabic?

OFFENDUM: I mean, I don't really worry about what's going to turn off or on people. But I do think it's important for people who don't speak Arabic to hear the language, especially here in the United States, in order to demystify this beautiful language. Especially for those people who only get to hear it from an angry dude yelling on their TV. Arabic is a beautiful language, a very deep, a profound one. And I like performing it. It also liberates me lyrically, when I can switch back and forth, and just kind of pull from an entirely different vocabulary and cadence, you know? I've been writing more stuff in Arabic recently. I've been making kind of a conscious effort because I do want to reach out to more Arabic-speaking audiences. But, like I said, in general, I think it's important to do both, because when I go back, and perform in the Arab world, there's also deconstructing the monolithic concept of what America is, and what American culture is, as well. You go back there and you have kids growing up in the Arab world who go to international schools, who watch American TV, satellite TV, and are on the internet all day, and they never study Arabic. They represent a generation that is increasingly feeling "Lost in Translation," something I know all too well growing up as a Syrian immigrant in the United States. Down the line I hope to work on a project that can unearth the stories of the first Arabic-speaking immigrants to America—who mainly came from Greater Syria to settle in places like New York City in the late 1800s. The community included some notable writers like Khalil Gibran, Amin Rihani, Mikhail Naimy, and Elia Abu Madi, who formed the first Arab American artistic collective called *Al-Rabita Al-Qalamiya* ("The Pen League") and became household names in the Arab world, but apart from Gibran didn't gain widespread fame here in the US. My being in a unique position to translate and make art out of their work that is accessible to an American audience a century later will be an important step towards a more nuanced understanding of our shared histories and helping me reconcile my own identity as a Syrian-American in the twenty-first century.

QUESTION 5: With the way that you discussed the issues within your communities, I was wondering how you choose and prioritize issues across these very different spaces?

TAMER NAFAR: It depends, I mean, if we do a show in Lod, we might focus on drugs, house demolitions, and women's rights, for example. If we do a show in Haifa, we might talk about the importance of using the tools that you have to create and make change, because Haifa's the cultural city of Palestine. You have the cinema, we have everything going on out of there. If it's in front of the Israelis, I will talk against the occupation, of course. If it's in the West Bank, then, maybe I would talk about the importance of opening labels, radios, and everything. So it depends, as much as we're united as Palestinians, and even as humans, there's so many ways that we're each different.

QUESTION 6: You're all always dropping a lot of knowledge. What does the 5th element of Hip Hop mean to you?

OFFENDUM: I can't help but find a powerful correlation between the 5th element of Hip Hop and the important status that the pursuit of knowledge holds in Islam. We are taught that the Prophet Muhammad ﷺ said, "When a person dies, his deeds are cut off except for three: Continuing charity, knowledge that others benefited from, and a righteous son who supplicates for him . . ." This important reminder puts so much in perspective for me in terms of how fame and material success are not at all the end goal when it comes to this sort of cultural production. I started rapping as a teenager and always felt the need to honor the great emcees who came before me by doing my best to not only entertain but educate and inspire the way artists like Rakim and Nas did for me. Now that I'm a father I understand just how crucial this approach has been in terms of helping to shape the cultural spaces that my children will inherit in the not too distant future, insha'Allah.

NOTES

1. The "Arab Spring" describes the uprisings and revolutions that took place across the Arab world in the 2010s, which are widely attributed to a series of interconnected events: Cairo's Tahrir Square Revolution on January 25, 2011, the Tunisian Jasmine Revolution on December 17, 2010, and a Hip Hop song by El Général released in early December 2010 (i.e., "Rais Lebled"). For more, see Awad Ibrahim, "Arab Spring, Favelas, Borders, and the Artistic Transnational Migration: Toward a Curriculum for a Global Hip-Hop Nation," *Curriculum Inquiry* 47, no. 1 (2017): 103-11.

2. Tamer Nafar also starred in the film *Junction 48* (2016), in which he played the part of Kareem, a Palestinian rapper who struggles to make music in his crime-ridden ghetto.

3. Palestinian female rapper / singer Maysa Daw joined the group in 2015; see the following link: https://www.papermag.com/maysa-daw-interview-2640045864.html?rebelltitem=43#rebelltitem43.

4. Dabke is a circle dance, usually taking place at weddings and on celebratory occasions, which is deeply tied to Palestinian culture; for more, see Jennifer L. Ladkani, *Dabke Music and Dance and the Palestinian Refugee Experience: On the Outside Looking In* (UMI Dissertation Services, 2002).

5. See Lina Abu Lughod and Maya Mikdashi, "Tradition and the Anti-Politics Machine: DAM Seduced by the 'Honor Crimes,'" *Jadaliyya*, November 23, 2012, Jadaliyya.com/Details/27467.

6. Lod is a city in Israel whose Arab inhabitants were expelled in 1948. The city was resettled by Jewish immigrants, most of them from Arab countries, alongside 1,056 Arabs who remained. Today, the Arab population is 30 percent of the city.

7. In November 2018, Tamer Nafar was disinvited by Tel-Hai Academic College in Israel after having been scheduled to perform a concert there. Tamer responded by saying that was an attempt to silence his voice as "part of the overall war against the Palestinian narrative." For more, see https://www.haaretz.com/israel-news/.premium-israeli-student-union-cancels-israeli-arab-rapper-s-show-over-friction-1.6679742.

8. In August 2019, a concert featuring Tamer Nafar, which was scheduled to take place in Umm al-Fahm (a city located 12 miles northwest of Jenin in the Haifa District of Israel), was called off even though the Haifa District Court overturned an earlier decision by the town's mayor to cancel it.

9. This song by Omar Offendum is titled "#Syria" and the music video (produced by Sami Matar) is at https://youtu.be/TXjEWrhkb6g.

10. Jandali's albums *Syrian Symphony*, *SoHo*, *Hiraeth*, and *The Jasmine Tree* were released at Carnegie Hall's Weil Recital Hall in 2015, 2016, 2017, and 2018, respectively.

4 "The Revolution Will Be Indigenous"

COLLECTIVE LIBERATION, HEALING, AND RESISTANCE TO SETTLER COLONIALISM THROUGH HIP HOP

Jessa Calderon, Gunner Jules, Lyla June, Tall Paul, and Tanaya Winder, with Casey Philip Wong

CASEY PHILIP WONG: Today I feel incredibly grateful to be in conversation with one of the most prominent collectives of Indigenous Hip Hop artists in North America, the Dream Warriors. The Dream Warriors were founded in 2015 by Tanaya Winder with the intention of "heal[ing] hearts by teaching how to unfold into radical, revolutionary love." The Dream Warriors regularly conduct workshops, and each artist in their own respective ways is deeply engaged in Hip Hop pedagogical work. Could each of you introduce yourself and how you got involved with Hip Hop?

GROWING UP HIP HOP AND INDIGENOUS

GUNNER JULES: I'm Sicangu Lakota from the Rosebud Sioux Tribe, south central, South Dakota. For me, I think about how my aunties and uncles were listening to rock and metal, our older cousins were bumpin Hip Hop and RnB, while my mom and sister were pop and rock. My brother and cousins were listening to West Coast music like Bone Thugs-n-Harmony and Nate Dogg. I liked the more melodic music. I sang along to them and learned every word. But at that time, there wasn't a lot of Indigenous people creating music. So when I started, that's what I naturally wanted to do was Hip Hop & RnB 'cause that's all we listened too. It made even more sense after learning more about Hip Hop, and how it burst out of the struggle. We have similar stories to share from the rez.

So eventually, in high school I got a computer that I was able to make music on and that's how it began. I was a sophomore in high school. I was 15 years old. That's really how I began creating, making beats, and there were others who were getting into it. I started writing songs and I was terrible until I made the connection that it was like writing poetry. Plus, I could flow and write bars a little bit, thanks to my older brother, who's still the best rapper I know. He influenced me heavily.

I made my first song as a sophomore in high school, it was called "Come Over Tonight." It was like this kind of vibe-y song. The second song I ever made, ended up being for one of my best friends who was supposed to be on the track with me. But he ended up committing suicide before we could record and it ended up being about him. I was in shock and felt like I couldn't cry about it . . . but I was able to write about it. I just really didn't know how to express the emotion of losing somebody close to me. So then I put it in song. A lot of people heard the song, titled "Lonely Nights and Days," and people would tell me that it really helped them.

And even though I didn't really consider myself an artist at that point, I was just experimenting and soon there was a group of us getting into it, mostly my family. I was excited to write and make music that my friends could listen to. I'd show them on my iPod at school. It's really changed my life. When I first started I geeked out so hard with no YouTube or anyone telling me how to do it. I couldn't have even dreamt of, you know, making it to this point where I am today. So that's how I got started with Hip Hop.

TALL PAUL: For me, kind of how Gunner was talking about not necessarily knowing the historical roots of Hip Hop at the time, I just knew Hip Hop was just so widespread, such a strong, powerful, and far-reaching culture that has reached people all over the world, you know? I was born and raised as Anishinaabe and Oneida in Minneapolis, and it reached me there. It was played a lot in my house. My older brothers and my older cousins were always listening to it. And it was really all I was exposed to from a very young age. So, that is naturally what I gravitated towards when I was a kid, you know. At the time, it was a lot of the East Coast, West Coast thing, and also some of the Midwest stuff like Bone Thugs and Twista. So I had just a variety of influences, and then as I got a little bit older, I got more into Southern Hip Hop too. And the South has been representin for a long time as well, like with Outkast and so on.

What really got me initially interested was just listening to Snoop Dogg, Biggie Smalls, 2Pac, The Luniz, The Fugees, and so on. And when I got a little bit older, I started thinking about maybe I could do Hip Hop for a career. 'Cause my one and two choices for a career, like in many communities of color and reservations and so on, was sports and Hip Hop. I thought about being a football player, but I also thought about being a Hip Hop artist. I thought I would be more of a producer than an emcee, but then as I got older, and actually started to dip my hands into it, I tried producing and it was too technical for me at the time so I just fell back on rapping. And I started when I was about 14 years old, just sat down one day, got bored and started writing raps for the first time. And it was fun and it became a hobby for the next five, six years. And it turned into something that I would show off to my friends or be at house parties and freestyle and stuff like that.

And then when I was about 20 years old, I got into trouble. You know, the lifestyle I was living, partying and getting intoxicated, getting into trouble. I was definitely living a life of addiction and alcoholism. And when I got sober, I needed to find something to fill that void. So I fell back on Hip Hop. I was like, well, maybe I can pursue this more religiously now and actually get into the scene, reach out to some local Hip Hop artists. So, that's what I did. I started sending out, I think, some Myspace messages to different artists back in like 2008. And I ended up getting in touch with some people, got some beats real fast, started going to these Hip Hop workshops that were being held by this group called Big Quarters, learning the process of recording and engineering and performing techniques and so on. And yeah, pretty quickly I was able to write and record my first few songs.

And then from there, somebody told me, well, you want to do this for real? You got to get on stage. And that wasn't something I really had thought about, especially as a kid who had attended different schools, kindergarten through twelfth grade—I became very introverted. When that became a thought process, I was like, alright, well, if I want to do this for real, I'm going to need to get over this stage fright. So I just signed my name up at an open mic called "Voices Merging" at the University of Minnesota. And I walked into the auditorium and there were like 200 people in there. I was a nervous wreck, and I didn't really want to stay, to be honest, but I just forced myself to stay in my seat and wait until my name was called. And then I got on stage, and I messed up quite a bit at first. But then after that I was like, "Alright, well, it can only go up from here, I already messed up." So I started moving around a little bit more loosely, managed my breath a little better, and got through the rest of the song. And after that I was like, alright, I can do this.

From there I just kept signing up for more and more open mics and getting better on stage, getting better with my writing process. I mean, I was spending hours and hours a day just writing and practicing my rhymes. And from there people slowly took notice and it went from being a local thing to suddenly I was performing in California within like three years of starting my career as an artist. Now I've been blessed to travel around the country, and a little bit outside of it as well.

LYLA JUNE: So I want to introduce myself in Navajo . . . Yá'át'ééh shik'ei adóó shidiné'e. Shi éí naaneesht'ezhi táchii'nii nishłiacute-ogon, Cheyenne baashishch'íín, 'Áshįįhi da shicheii, adóó biligaana éí da shinali. Lyla June da shijiní. Taos, New Mexico, dee' nasha. Ákót'éego diné asdzáán nishłiacute-ogon. Diné people, we always introduce our four clans before we speak to establish our identity. I said, "My name is Lyla June and I am of the Black Charcoal Streak Division of the Red-Running-Into-Water Clan of the Diné nation, and I'm from Taos, New Mexico." That's really important for me to share to honor my ancestors.

So I came into Hip Hop through the spoken word world when I was 14, which was quite a long time ago, and I was really deep in the spoken word scene. I was performing and winning national championships when I was 16 and going to Brave New Voices. That whole scene seems to have gotten smaller as I've grown older, but it used to be a really big part of youth culture in the 2000s and early 2010s; I had a fascination with words. My friend, Coral Bernal from Taos, New Mexico, brought me to my first poetry slam and she really helped me see how beautiful these words could be and how powerful they are, and naturally, that turned into Hip Hop. It's spoken word with a beat and it just makes it so much more fun. I mean, if you think of Lauryn Hill, she was like a prophet and she's a woman who was sharing with us how to live in this world, but you could dance to it and it felt good to dance to it. So it was merging both wisdom and joy together. To me, that's what Hip Hop is, sharing wisdom, sharing our way of living, and helping people just exist on this earth while at the same time giving them joy and beauty and connection to their heart and their heartbeat, and so that's how I got into Hip Hop.

I learned how to beatbox when I was 14 and I just loved it and I had a lot of breakdancing influence. I learned breakdancing a little bit and really liked to connect to the various elements of Hip Hop. I used to tag a lot. I wasn't very good at it, but I used to tag up different things and just really connected to that culture. And I always say thank you to the African American roots of that culture because Indigenous peoples are so indebted to the Black community for giving us this gift that has helped us and our people heal so much.

JESSA CALDERON: I was born and raised in Los Angeles County, right, I'm Tongva. So Los Angeles is my ancestral territory. Of course, in LA, we had the Pachuco days in the twenties and that was the mix of the Mexicans and the Natives from this side, right? In the Pachuco days, what they were doing was rhyming, and so smooth. So, that trickled down into all of our generations. And then of course I grew up with Power 106, and my older brothers were bustin out NWA and Death Row Records, and eventually Nate Dogg when he came about. And I would definitely say 2Pac was my favorite artist because he was poetic. I could connect with 2Pac because I was a poet first. I got to learn from all of these wonderful artists, and then when I was about 12 years old, my brother was standing around in a cipher circle where him and all his homies were busting their flows. As I was listening to some of them, I'm thinking that's easy, I could do that. 'Cause I had already been doing poetry. So I just kind of snuck my way into the circle and when it came that I'd be next in line, I just started bustin a flow and I blew everyone away because I was always so quiet. I never really talked, but everybody came up and shook my hand and gave me those props. It was like, "Damn, I didn't know you were a rapper," and that's kind of how that just happened for me.

And then my first introduction to a studio was in my garage. My brother, who was a rapper, he took a fiberglass showerhead and he flipped it upside down and he ran some wires through what was the drain. So now you've got a microphone coming down through the drain and it's just sitting kind of midair. And that's where we would record, bust our flows. And he had a real old, I don't know, maybe like an early '90s computer. We were using FL Studio and that was my first taste of how I was able to hear myself back then, aside from the recordings we would do on those little cassette recorders.

My brother Steven, rest in peace, we called him Custom Rhymes, he definitely was the one who pulled me into rapping and was probably like my only competition. I remember standing around in circles right outside, in the front yard, there was a bunch of people and we would just go at it. Me and my brother, we were the best. I will admit that when he passed away in 2001, I really thought I was completely done with music. My fire just went out. I had no passion anymore. Then my son was born in 2010, and two years after that, he was the one who told me I needed to get back into the studio.

I explained to him that that was a time in my past and I didn't need to do it anymore. And he was very insistent that I needed to get back to the studio. So I told him, you know what, just for fun, let's just go check out a studio. And of course, I posted it on Facebook and it just kind of went crazy. I had some magazine editors and old friends that just really pushed it on me, and it just spiraled. And here I am doing music. I'm a Hip Hop artist. I write all my own songs, and I sing my own songs. This time around, I owe it to my child who at the time was two who pushed me back into music.

TANAYA WINDER: I was raised on the Southern Ute reservation in Southern Colorado, as a member of the Duckwater Shoshone Tribe. I am also Pyramid Lake Paiute and Southern Ute. I really looked up to my sister and all of her friends growing up. They listened to a lot of Hip Hop and so I wanted to be a part of it, too. I was that little sibling trying to hang around with them to be cool. They listened to artists like 2Pac, Nasty Boy Klick, Kid Frost, Salt-N-Pepa, and Bone Thugs-n-Harmony. I have this memory when I was little, I had this really cool yellow Walkman that played cassette tapes. I remember riding in the front seat listening to it, rapping along to Salt-N-Pepa, having a good time, and then seeing my cousin point at me, asking my aunt, "What's she doing?" And my aunt's like, "She's rapping." I've never identified as a rapper, but I remember that moment. I feel like my memories with music stick out. For instance, when I was in middle school, my aunt would take us to the library and we'd check out tapes. My aunt checked out *The Miseducation of Lauryn Hill* and that album changed me. It still changes me. Now I'm a writer and an artist who interrogates love, where we learn how to love, and how we love. Music has always been healing, especially when we think about those moments where we're harmed, or when we aren't loved. Whether it's singing or listening, music has been a lifeline throughout my life.

So I guess it makes sense, looking back on it all, why I founded this Hip Hop artists collective that we're all a part of—the Dream Warriors—because Hip Hop has been so important to me, and to building family, and it's been great to make the space for this chosen music family. As a part of this family, I think about how Hip Hop has helped me find my voice, especially in the sisterhood of Hip Hop. I love my brothers, and that's how Dream Warriors started, with just me and the guys. But I feel like my sisters have really helped me to be less afraid. I never even thought of rapping myself 'cause I just love singing, but I remember Lyla June was like, let's work on a song for murdered and missing Indigenous women. And we were just writing raps in her hotel room, on a gig, and I reached out to Jessa Calderon, I was like, "I want to do a song. I want to try rapping." Some people might be like, "Practice a little bit first, then I'll let you," but Jessa was just like, "Yeah, let's find a beat and do it." Jessa was just really a good sister and encouraged me, it almost feels like we put out that song yesterday, but it's called "Rise and Shine":

> Hook: You are resilient. I respect and appreciate you, my beautiful Indigenous sisters. Rise and shine.
>
> Calderon: My grandmother, an Indigenous woman surviving
> Her land, invaded for corporate drilling and mining
> I stand before you an Indigenous woman thriving
> My generation, an abundance of Indigenous women rising
> We rise like the sun but we shall not set
> Until you've heard every word our sisters have said

No longer do we sit quietly only to accept your disrespect
We speak for our missing and murdered
Our abused and raped whose names weren't even a murmur
It was once understood our women were sacred
European ruling came in and changed it
Made us hate our own faces, left our communities tainted
We have awakened we're taking our places
Restoring culture our children embrace it
Our ancestors stand beside us magnifying our strength
Our same ancestors who didn't back down when war was waged

Hook: It's a good morning to wake, it's a good morning to wake
Rise, riiiise, riiiiiiiiiiiise

Winder: My mother wakes every morning to bless us
Lights sage and sings prayers to the four directions
Asking for protection she lifts her hands up,
Let my daughters know they are always more than enough
Creator made us strong from our spirit to our bones
Put us on this earth to learn, heal, and grow
But the healing doesn't help us when we do it alone
Many hearts one people rising stronger together
A dark night's bright because stars don't get jealous
Shining in a sky that holds everyone's shine
We're sisters, not competition but uplifting,
We're healing these hurts, these historical wounds
Using our power, this connection to the moon
Strong enough to pull tides, the backbone of each tribe
We're creating new paths, tryna do what's right
Rise up with me sisters, it's a good day to shine

[Hook]

Winder: For our aunties and our sisters, all our mothers
Grandmothers, daughters, all survivors too
There's no rising or survival without every one of you
With the light of our fire combined we are unstoppable
Unbreakable, phenomenal, nothing is impossible
Rise, thrive & shine, now's our time

Calderon: Before the conquering we were matriarchal tribes
Sister, take my hand it's the only way we rise
When we reach the top we shall embrace
Enjoy our view and give thanks

Give a toast and a war cry
Native, we grow we don't die
We never give up we struggle through their demise
Still we survive

PUSHING THE BOUNDARIES OF HIP HOP AND INDIGENOUS MUSIC TRADITIONS

WONG: Gunner, I was checking the other day, the track and music video you have for "Patience," with other Indigenous Hip Hop artists. It made me think about how White settlers imagine Indigenous peoples as inescapably locked in the past, as if Indigenous people are already eliminated, do not exist, and have not continued to live, resist, and thrive. Because if Indigenous folks have a present and future, then it questions the legitimacy of the US, its permanence, its history and future. Indigenous presence and futurity exposes the immoral foundations of the US. In "Patience," I see you engaging Hip Hop and Indigenous aesthetics, making something powerful that speaks to the ongoing presence and future of Indigenous people.

JULES: "Patience" was a collaborative track for Antoine Edward's album, *Dimensions*, featuring me, Miracle Spotted Bear, and Spur Pourier. He brought us out to Phoenix to record at one of the nicest studios I've been to. There's a lot of Indigenous artists that are supporting each other and I think that's very important. So I think it was just very powerful and between us a lot of talent, but we didn't know what was going to be created. We were just open to each other's ideas and trusted the process. Antoine led the project and we've already been creating music, blending traditional with modern music.

Spur Pourier and Miracle Spotted Bear are traditional singers originally, so was Antoine actually. Myself, I grew up singing and learning hand game songs and prayer songs for the most part, and we wanted to create something that was kind of transcending those boundaries and we wanted it to be a good representation of the future of Hip Hop in a tasteful way. So it was intentional and came naturally. Miracle and Spur have such powerful voices and Antoine structured the song. He left an open verse at the end for me. We only had limited studio time and I went in the booth and laid my verse and everybody was like, "I didn't know you were going to sound like that," and I was really happy about the way it came out.

It's been really good to work with them. They've been spending a lot of time in Pine Ridge lately, which is a tribe right next to mine, about an hour and a half drive. So I've been spending a lot of time in Thunder Valley and Pine Ridge. Spur and Miracle have their own albums of traditional songs, round dance songs. And then we all come together with Hip Hop. And we were able to come up with this really unique sound. So it's cool we're all connected and collaborating with each other to vibe out and motivate each other not to give up on it.

WONG: I saw your music video for "Another Way," and there's a little boy that's pictured throughout it.

JULES: I composed that one last-minute the night before Mother's Day. I wanted to make a song for mothers, for my kids' mom and for my mom. It's my take on a round dance song. It was my first attempt ever. I came up with the melody, then I came up with words that sounded like the melody. So I'm singing the Lakota vocal inflections. People are like, "Heya, heya," but there's more to it than that. So I just came up with that "Wheyo, wheyah," and then the words, "With you, I found." Like that and it just came out to be really powerful lyrics. I wasn't even expecting for it to be that good but just acknowledging that with these women in my life, I found another way to live my life.

The video that I made with it came a couple of days later. The boy in the video, it's my son, we just got done with Little League practice, that's why he still has the baseball pants on and stuff. And I was just like, "Hey, it's golden hour outside. Son, should we go outside, should we shoot a video to that song?" And he was down, which sometimes ain't the case if he was on his games or something. We went to the backyard and I just filmed it, no stabilizer, nothing. I followed him as he was walking through the trees. So that video, I wanted it to be like forming a prayer. He's standing there with tobacco first and he goes and he walks and then he comes through and he gets to the middle of that space with all the prayer ties and the chair that was already there. My son is with the sage, sitting in prayer, then

Figure 4.1 Left to right, Frank Waln, Tall Paul, Tanaya Winder, and Mic Jordan of the Dream Warriors performing for the youth. Photo courtesy of Jeremy Shockley and *The Southern Ute Drum*.

he comes out. For anybody who watches it, that's how it happened and it ended up just exactly how I wanted it to be.

HIP HOP AND REVITALIZATION OF INDIGENOUS LANGUAGE AND CULTURE

WONG: Alright, Paul, I think I told you that there's been so many times when I do a Hip Hop workshop, I always play that joint, "Prayers in a Song." The way you speak on language revitalization in that track just resonates with so many kids. I'd love to get on record the story of that track. And I know you've been working lately on some music about Jim Thorpe, which is speaking to revitalization on another level.

PAUL: "Prayers in a Song" came about while I was in college. There was a two-year language requirement at the University of Minnesota. And by no means am I a linguist, but it was an opportunity for me to study my language because the Ojibwe tribe is prominent in Minnesota. Ojibwe was taught by my language teacher, Dennis Jones. I took that opportunity to learn the language because I've always had a desire to learn, not really having any exposure to my culture and language. You could say, my family was essentially fully colonized and assimilated into this American society. When I was a kid, there was nobody around me really speaking the language, or practicing the culture. That was something my mom introduced to me later in life when I was about 10 or 11 years old. That was my situation and it created this gap that needed to be bridged within my spirit because I knew I was Native, I knew I was Ojibwe. But I didn't really know what the essence of that meant. I wanted to pursue my culture and language and I picked up on bits and pieces of it throughout my childhood and teen years. But really when I got to college, I was able to get a lot more. I was able to dive a lot deeper, thanks to my language teacher, Dennis Jones.

He would invite us to his house to learn, sweat lodge prayer songs, do different ceremonies. We would see items of ours, whether it might be a feather or other people's spiritual items. And he really taught me a lot of the culture and the language and it empowered me. And something he always said was what you do for the language, the language will do for you. So even though I was struggling to learn it, it's one of the most complex languages in the world. You can conjugate a verb a thousand different ways. But even though I was struggling to learn the language, I wanted to do something for it, to help the revitalization process.

So I had the idea to make a bilingual track in Ojibwe and English. I had a classmate help me translate the chorus, and it just naturally rhymed, and not only that, it naturally fit. The eight-bar section of the beat where the hook is, it was just a natural fit. I had to do almost no touching up of it. I think I had to change one word, but that was more a grammatical correction that an elder told us we needed to make. It wasn't because it didn't fit or nothing.

That gave me full faith in myself to go through with being an emcee, because something that I think is very prominent in the Native community, is a lot of people are close-minded to Hip Hop, especially the older generations. They'll say, why you acting Black? Or why are you rapping?

You should be practicing your traditional ways and this and that. And it's just close-minded, because encouraging the youth to pursue the things that fulfill their spirit is a part of our traditional ways, you know what I mean? It's very close-minded and counterproductive, but my language teacher, he just encouraged me. He's like, if this is your calling and if your spirit calls you to do this, you should do it. And I would say his words rang true as far as, what you do for the language, the language will do for you. After I did that song my career skyrocketed from where it was. I had a video done for it shortly after and that thing shot up to almost 400,000 views overnight, because it went to the front page of reddit.com for that day and just blew up. And I woke up the next day and seen the views skyrocket. I just started getting gigs and bookings, really based off of that song alone, and I still do to this day. And I made that song 10 years ago if not more, so that speaks to the power of that song. And now, with my song "Jim Thorpe," I also had to share this info for Native kids who don't know.

HEALING FROM SOUL WOUNDS AND RESISTING SETTLER COLONIALISM

CALDERON: I often think about how important it is to make use of the platform that Hip Hop gives us to expose the truth that so often gets missed about Indigenous communities and struggles. That's really something that I was thinking about on my track "Injustice." A lot of people don't realize that there's Indigenous people from LA, it's their ancestral territory and there's big reasons for that. When Mexico invaded after the Spanish era, it was still dangerous to be Indian, to be Indigenous from this area, because you're talking about land grabbing, right? And with land grabbing comes massive death, and then America comes, and it's the same thing. In fact, the first governor of California stated, "We are at war with the Indians until they're all dead." We were meant to be exterminated, we were on the run. It was much easier for our relatives to just turn around and say, "I'm Mexican," in order to receive a job and to not die. And so, they were just dealing with a lot at the time and they were thinking protective mechanisms. So fast forward and now the rest of the world thinks that California is just Mexicans, right? And there's so much more to that.

You've got people who are Yoeme, you've got people who are Apache, you've got the traditional people of the land, Tongva, Chumash to Tataviam. There's a mix of us people that are here, in particular California natives.

And in my music, I had to bring that to the forefront, to say, you know that this has been the narrative for these many years, but it's a new day and age and it's time for the truth to be heard. I wanted to talk about the deaths that have occurred here, because for some reason, when other nations outside the US have people murdered at a fast rate, there's media attention. But for some reason, when our sisters and our relatives are being murdered at a high rate, it goes unnoticed. In the 1970s, Native Americans were still at war with the US government. And then we've got our political prisoners and I've talked about John Trudell's family. I've got to talk about Leonard Peltier, he was put in jail as a message, to tell us to stand down, to stop fighting and know our place. And we've seen it again in our generation with Standing Rock and Red Fawn, right?

I make it a point to bring these messages to the forefront. Let people know about what was happening in places like Canada, where there were officers that were taking young boys and dropping them off in the middle of nowhere during winter seasons. And then they were forced to walk back home and majority of them didn't make it. Nobody could figure out what was happening until somebody actually made it home. And it was only when they made it home and talked about it that we found out it was the cops who put them out there.

And then with my song "Home of the Brave," it was 2016 at that point, I really was thinking about Indigenous unity against colonialism. I had to talk about big oil and all of that, because that's something that just never seems to die away and really is prominent in our global struggles to stop the destruction of the earth. I thought it was really important to bring that, but when it came to the music video, what I wanted to do was add really significant places for the Tongva people in that video. And there's a lot of places that people think about as Mexican places, like Placita Olvera Street. The reality is Placita Olvera Street was a prominent place where our people, Indigenous people, were being sold as slaves, right there where that big plaque stands. And right across the street is a place where our people were buried.

And then at the same time, back on "Injustice," I actually had Mashika dancers, who are Mexican-rooted Indigenous people. I mixed them with us, with the bird singers in the California Indigenous style, with my style to just show that, you know what, but we're still here in unity, right? Because I want people to understand that they're Native people too, because I think about the coloniality of these borders. As Native people, we've even put that colonial border in our minds, where we go, "Those people are Mexican, they're not Native," and everywhere below the border, they're not considered Native, because of this colonial border. And in reality, that border didn't exist. There was trading routes that connected us for thousands of years. We held ceremonies with each other prior to the invasions. We need to remember that. We need to bring that understanding back. And I like to remind people from Mexico who even have that mindset themselves. When they tell me, "You're Native," and I'm like, okay, you look just like me. Your ancestors are from Mexico, but they've been there for thousands of years. You're Native too. And it's about bringing that pride back to our people because for so long, especially here in California, it's been disgusting to be Native. They would rather tell people, "I'm Spanish," when they're dark like this, because being Native is looked down upon. So with those types of songs that I'm doing, it's about bringing the pride back for being here for generations. It's about bringing that knowledge forth. We've been fighting so hard just to keep swimming, in these forced colonial ways, that it's hard to acknowledge who we really are and be proud of it, because folks see America first. It's a new time for us. It's a time to be proud and that's what I'm trying to put across in those songs.

WINDER: That idea about unity and solidarity, that makes me think about how lots of people say love is the real revolution, right? I think just, it's not. Not in that way people imagine love, that love that gives people passes without holding them accountable for their colonial mindsets. But the empath in me knows, different people have different soul wounds and those wounds manifest in different ways. Especially if you don't find healing, or depending on what environment you have, it supports or hinders your growth and your healing. I try to think about things in that frame. What do things look like through this framework of a deeper and bigger love, in all its contexts? Whether that's social, emotional, familial, or environmental love, I try to approach things like that, but also how you can hold people accountable with love, in that good way. Love doesn't give people a pass, just because they've been hurt. It gives us an understanding of why people might act the way that they act, but they still need to be held accountable. To me, holding someone accountable with love is restorative justice. And we're still learning what that looks like.

And that's why I think youth work is so important: How can I take what I've learned to help youth, and other people, have the tools that I didn't necessarily have growing up? Everybody needs to be in a position where they can liberate themselves, because we can't save each other. We have to save ourselves. And how do you create a world that can do that? And I think of it, almost if you had a bucket with a bunch of different holes in it, and the water's falling out everywhere. I think that's why I try to do so much poetry. Poetry tries to fill one of those holes. Music tries to fill one of those holes. So that way, that bucket can hold all that we need it to.

WONG: That's so beautiful. You have a lot of poetry that's out, Tanaya, and in those different pieces, I see multiple different themes. But one of the themes is in conversation with love, a love that encounters and heals from violence.

WINDER: Yeah, we have all these inlets coming into us, and you have to think, what's the outlet for it? I think about how with physical things, if you break your ankle or get in a car accident, then you'll have physical therapy, or you need to do a massage. But I don't think enough people think about: What do you do when you experience those emotional traumas? So for instance, I first learned about Murdered and Missing Indigenous Women (MMIW) up in Canada, because my sister lives up there. She did her PhD up there and was doing research and finding out more about it. And in processing this as an educator, as a youth worker, I work with young girls. This is an invisible epidemic, or at the time it was less visible, and how do I help prepare them. Again, in a loving way, in an accountable way, and not a naïve way. And so for me, I feel it's easier to get at these things through art. So that's why I try to write a lot about it, because sometimes I think people can get inundated. As humans, we're not designed to just be bombarded with news and trauma and all of these different things. But that's the reality, that's the world we live in. I try to write songs about it, and do art about that to try to come up with ways that can maybe help us process these experiences, while also helping to educate at the same time.

I don't even want to say it's tied to working with kids, or tied to being Indigenous; it's about being a human being navigating trauma. You need to take time to feel and heal in an ongoing process, so you don't get compassion fatigue, or secondary trauma. Feeling is one of the most beautiful things. When you're depressed, you're numb to things. When I used to drink, I was numb to things. And so *feeling* is so important to me. How do I keep myself well enough that I'm able to still feel *and* be a steward of trauma rather than paralyzed or stunted by trauma? That's why writing about these things really is important to me, because as Indigenous people, we talk about land stewardship, how we are stewards of the land, taking care of it, protecting it, etc. But we also participate in trauma stewardship; we need to take care of and protect ourselves while we take care of others and their traumas, too.

CALDERON: And I would just like to add, I think some of the best songs that any of us in the Hip Hop world has ever written are usually derived from pain. But I think it's really important to acknowledge that we're in a time of space where we need to begin our healing processes. You know, it's been said over and again, this is one of my favorite sayings: I always say that hurt people hurt people. And if we want to see a better future, it really comes down to healing ourselves and healing our communities and understanding that love isn't something that you seek from an outside source.

Love is something that you find from within, healing is something that you find from within and it all starts with us. And if we're going to continue to be broken people, we're going to continue to put that out on people, and it's not cool. And I acknowledge that the majority of this pain and brokenness stems from colonial civilization. It's time for us to really get back into ourselves, to speak to ourselves. You know, it's the perfect time right now that we're all stuck in our houses, to find a small little patch of dirt, and sit with it, and internalize, you know? And I think we are at a time of healing and it's really important to honor that and honor ourselves. I would love to share that with the general masses.

WONG: As Jessa and Tanaya were speaking about solidarities and healing, it made me think about a song and video you have, Lyla, "All Nations Rise."

JUNE: My intention with "All Nations Rise" was to push myself and our people higher. When I wrote the hook, I was like, no, you can do better than that. Try again, and I wrote a different melody and I said, no, push it higher, and so I pushed it higher and I just wanted to give the best gift I could to my people in the spirit of service and inspiration. And so my goal was to help Native people see their own beauty and to wake them up. The inspiration for that song actually came when I was driving in Aztec, New Mexico, which not too many people know about that town, but a lot of Diné people live there. I saw a young man walking on the sidewalk with a black hoodie on, and his hood was up, and he was just looking down and listening to music. And obviously, I shouldn't judge what he was thinking or saying, but he just looked like he had given up. He looked defeated. I actually wrote that song for him to say, "Stand up, boy. It's not over. You got to get up." And that's really what that song was for, was to get our people to stand up again and say, hey, the battle has only just begun, because we walk around like we lost the war, right? "Oh, we lost to the Americans. we lost the war, right? "Oh, we lost to the Americans. We lost. Game over." And I was like, "Nope, no, no, no, no. Game has only just begun. Get up. We got shit to do and we need you, and you have the power, you have the beauty, you have the ancestors within you and behind you to make your wildest dreams come true. So stand up!"

And of course, the second half is in Spanish, which is very similar to what Jessa was doing in saying, "Hey, I see you as Indigenous. I honor your indigeneity, even if you speak Spanish and I speak English." If the border was a few hundred miles North, I would be Latina, but because I'm on this side of this imaginary border, I'm Navajo. So I was bringing those nations together, too, and I wish I could have brought Portuguese into it to honor the Brazilian Indigenous folks. And all these are all colonial languages, of course, but that's what a lot of Indigenous peoples in these different parts speak.

WONG: There's an Afro-Indigenous Hip Hop scholar, Kyle Mays,[1] and one of the things he argues is that Indigenous Hip Hop is one of the largest arts and political movements, cultural movements, in Indigenous North America since the Ghost Dance movement in the late nineteenth century. What do y'all think about that?

CALDERON: Sure, when the Ghost Dance went about to all of the nations, it was to instill pride and to make sure that people didn't lose themselves to this White world, and when you think about the Hip Hop that many of us are attributing to our communities, it holds true in that same sense. Many of us were shamed for being who we were, but still internally wanting to have that pride, at least for myself. I always knew who I was. I never backed down to my teachers who were trying to tell me my history, and were calling me out, and lying in front of everybody, including that fourth-grade mission project that so many students had and often still have to do in California schools. I was that one kid that always stood up and spoke out where many of my friends just shut up and shut down. So it's a struggle in that aspect of growing up Native in such a colonial world, because you feel so much shame. You feel like you don't even belong in your ancestral territory, and so often we revert to drugs, alcoholism, and suicide because of the lack of feeling like we belong. And that shouldn't be, because little brother, little sister, you are in your ancestral territory. Everyone else is an invader, so if anybody else doesn't belong, it's them, and I think doing this music is about that.

I'll give a perfect example for you right now. My son at three and four years old, he had a long braid. Every single day of his life he had to deal with being called a little girl and being shamed for having long hair. And he didn't ever want to cut it, but he always had to have his little Dodgers cap on, always. One day, he's four now, he can't find his Dodger cap and we got to go and he's panicking, straight panicking to the point where he starts crying. He cannot leave without his hat. I'm like, what are you talking about? So on the drive, I found his hat. I'm trying to pull it out and I ask him what's going on? And he's like, "Well, if I have my hat, then maybe less people will think I'm a girl," and I'm like, "Dude, you've been wearing that hat and people are still being ignorant. That's not you, that's them." So I pulled up Frank Waln, and I said, I want you to hear the song, and I wasn't even a Dream Warrior at that point. And I play where Frank Waln's talking about being proud and never again tucking his hair, and so on. And then there was a song called "My Stone," which really related to my son because I'm a single mother and his father has never been around. And at that point, my son's like, "Play it again, play it again, play it again," and after that, he stood so strong in his power when people came at him sideways and ignorant, and I helped instill his pride by playing Frank Waln, and that's what we're doing as Native people, is helping our peoples to want to learn their language by incorporating it in our music and to want to get back into knowing their traditions because we're speaking on being proud about it.

And so now that we're giving them a platform to say, "Hey, those people relate to me in a way that nobody else has." Yeah, I loved Hip Hop because there were struggles that were somewhat relatable, but man, there's struggles that are right here in my yard, and Indigenous Hip Hop has moved to address those struggles. In that way, we're instilling pride back to the people to want to connect to their roots. We're connecting to the community and bringing power back to us and allowing us to stand in our power.

JULES: My first thought brings me back to the Religious Freedom Act of 1978, which allowed us to practice our religion. And whenever I think of the Ghost Dance, I'm thinking of the nighttime dances. I'm not really well studied, but just from what I was told is we had to practice the Ghost Dances at night because it was against the law to practice it. Bureau of Indian Affairs (BIA) cops or the police were actively trying to catch and stop them, and basically, a lot of our people historically were pathologized as mentally ill or something. If our spiritual leaders were medicine people, they were being taken away whenever they were coming after us for practicing our own religion, trying to do the erasure that Jessa was talking about.

I think my other connection between the people in the Ghost Dance movement and us as Indigenous Hip Hop artists would be just the resilience. We're still finding ways to practice and to use our power that we have, our connection that we have to our culture, to those spiritual practices, to the connection and using that as a power to share, the power to bring people together, just like the Ghost Dance. I don't know anything about other nations practicing that, but maybe just with Hip Hop music, with that, being able to use that same power, those same connections, that same energy to still press on and to still share our narrative, and we're still being silenced in a way. I think it's difficult to really get into mainstream media with our narrative because it's the truth from our perspective. And so I think in a similar fashion, it's just that resilience to continue doing it, even though they're still trying to suppress us.

Relatedly, right now I'm working on this "LANDBACK campaign." It came to life following the Mount Rushmore protest in 2020 and they proposed that we do a soundtrack for the campaign. We had the conversation, what would that look like? We were like, that'd be cool to be a part of it. And it's basically going to be the soundtrack behind the movement. And they gave us the freedom to create the creative direction for it. We recorded three songs yesterday and they're all definitely going on the album. We're so hype about it.

JUNE: Hip Hop is a groundswell in Indigenous culture and in the Indigenous world. I would say that this influx of Indigenous Hip Hop and just Indigenous music in general that's coming out is doing powerful political and cultural work. It's being spearheaded by people like Frank Waln, people like Supaman, and before that, of course, you have Keith Secola and different rock musicians in the sixties and seventies. Music spearheaded by the American Indian Movement itself in the sixties, which paved the way for us to be who we are and just the contemporary Indigenous music scene.

I think it's definitely incredibly important for Native people in the sense that, when Jessa's having a hard day with her son, she can put on a YouTube video, and there it is. That couldn't have happened even 10 years ago, sadly. Very recently where we couldn't go on YouTube and find ourselves there and find not just ourselves, but our beautiful selves, who we are, how we shine, what we talk about, what we hold close to our hearts. And there's still that honor there—and her son, Jessa's son's name is Honor—that honor that our ancestors walked with in the face of genocide and robbery, we still hold that today and it shines through our music. It shines through our Hip Hop, and it's just one more way that we, as Indigenous youth today, in the twenty-first century can carry on that legacy of dignity and honor of what our ancestors stood for and the ways in which we want to be leaders, not just for our own people, but for the whole world. People look to us for how to exist on this planet and we're carrying that on today through Hip Hop.

COLLECTIVE LIBERATION AND ENVISIONING INDIGENOUS FUTURES

WONG: Y'all have me thinking about the role of education, like this fifth element of Hip Hop, and more broadly about what type of education we need for liberation. What does that look like? How does Hip Hop inform that for y'all? What is the education we need for organizing together and getting past our environmental circumstances, getting past these colonial mind states, and from this place where some folks feel like we can't change?

JULES: I can only speak like for what changed me, I guess, because it's always different for individuals. But like, Tanaya, the way you were talking about identity definitely has always been important, and what does it mean to have that lack of identity. And I think all art forms are part of that, including Hip Hop. And I mean, there's just some things, like art, there's no Lakota word for art. It's very much just a part of our lives, you know?

I grew up in an Episcopal family and eventually parted from it after my grandmother passed. After that, I found spirituality. My uncle used to practice our ceremonies. I think gaining that knowledge of self, it's so simple and so powerful at the same time, the teachings and the language that is used and even the interpretation of language. Language is so powerful. Especially as you're learning and being educated about the basics, the ways of life and how we're all connected in this world, and gaining those understandings. And then along that journey, I started to learn about our history.

I went to a tribal college, Oglala Lakota College. If I didn't attend a tribal college I may have never learned about treaties. I would never learn about local history, none of that. Once I did, it was just like, okay, now I know the truth. It's just impossible for me to go back to just being uneducated ignorant, and accepting that. And like Lyla said, now we're just thinking every day about these things, and it's nonstop. And sometimes I even have thoughts, like, man, I kind of wish that I could not think that way sometimes, right? But I think it's just, once you learn the truth about history and how we were affected, it's like, What can we do for the youth? How can we offer paths to that truth and regain identity and power? How do we support them to be able to stick up for themselves, and all Indigenous people moving forward?

I think it's so important to have that foundation, the education and ancestral knowledge and stories. And us, keeping in mind that we are influencers, whenever we're working with the youth, we need to lead in a good way and use those teachings of the Lakota, having those morals and those virtues to live by and to guide us.

WONG: And that makes me think about another scholar, Nick Estes, and his book, *Our History Is Our Future: Standing Rock Versus the Dakota Access Pipeline, and the Long Tradition of Indigenous Resistance*. He's talking particularly about the context of the Oceti Sakowin, but I see that idea of relating the history to a post-settler colonial future in a lot of your works.

JUNE: Yeah, we work with the NDN Collective[2] and they talk about radical imagination. Like what does it look like when we've won? And I started crying when he talked about that because as Indigenous peoples, we don't often get to even think that way. We're too busy fighting off today's onslaught, everything from our kids need food, to our water's getting poisoned, to our women are going missing, to our language is going extinct, and on and on. I mean, every day we're fighting dozens of battles at once, and it's fucking hard to just wake up and be Indigenous, generally speaking. I think that for him to ask us that question of what does it look like after we've won, there's an aching in my heart, a good kind of aching that says, wow, no one's ever asked me that. I grieve for that fact that I've never been able to think about that. And then after that grieving, immediately there's celebration because now I'm thinking about that for the first time. And what I think what we see as Dream Warriors, among many other things, one of the things we see is our youth are safe. Our youth love themselves. Our youth feel empowered and our youth have the older sisters and brothers they need to not just survive, but truly thrive and be the people they were born to be, whatever that is, whatever they choose that to be, and so that's what I see.

JULES: I think Lyla is spot on, especially with the NDN Collective. We're here working on a project for them. Someone was talking about a future where our people thrive, and we actually wrote a song about that. It's like, what does that even look like, and what is it afterwards, and it just feels so good to imagine. Lyla articulated that so well and definitely, it's all about the youth and it's really exciting. I'm just excited to have that thought of what the future could look like because we grew up thinking by 2020, we're going to have spaceships flying around, and flying around in cars. That colonial ideology had us not even thinking of what type of energy we'll be using and nowadays we're thinking that we need to live more simple and leave places better than when we entered them, including this earth.

We're always talking about the Seventh Generation prophecy[3] and it coming to life. I think with this movement, with the movement of Hip Hop, and the influence that is happening on a broader scale, and the education that's happening, it's definitely a larger movement and the change must be radical enough to change the systems that are in place that oppress us.

CALDERON: For me, it's about reaching further than just Indigenous people because we all know how sacred the land is. Now we need to reach out to the colonial mindset and get them to understand how sacred it is. I do see that slowly happening, but it needs to happen at a faster pace. For instance, we've got people that are non-Indigenous now who go to turn on their faucet and there's contaminated water coming out. They can't drink their water and so now it's slowly happening that they want to begin to listen to us, but it's almost to the point of no return. So these things need to happen now, and you know, we are in California, in LA, and we're dealing with these fires out here in California. There's Indigenous ways that were held in place pre-contact and there were safe burns, controlled burns. And we would come in and we would trim things down and then we would burn them. Then we'd move to our other location and then come back to this location when everything was abundant and ready for eating and using once again. We would go back and forth to our two areas in that way to take care of the land. When the Spaniards actually came the second time around—because the first time there was a controlled burn happening with all the smoke—the second time around they came, and they're like, wow, it's like a paradise. It's beautiful. And what they failed to understand was it was manicured by the Indigenous people who practiced their sciences to take care of the land and keep things safe, healthy, and beautiful.

And until we get back to that, we're going to continue to struggle in these ways and the scary thing is it's believed that a lot of these fires are actually happening for money purposes. That a lot of, for instance, the water being contaminated is happening for money purposes. Somebody's benefiting on one end of it, and what it comes down to, as I say in one of my songs, I mention how the Cree have this saying about how you cannot drink, you cannot eat money, so what's going to happen when everything is used up? When there's no more fish? What are you going to eat because you can't eat money, and we need to understand that now. We cannot live without water because we're 80 percent water. Try going without water and see how well you do, and we can't go without our foods because that's what keeps us sane and moving. That's what gives us our electricity.

So it comes to the point where we have to all understand Indigeneity and that mindset of what it is to honor the Earth and understand that she has life, she's breathing life into us, through these trees that we keep destroying and causing fire to and giving us life through the fruits that come from these trees and so on and so on. Her bloodstream, if you will, is that water that feeds us, that bathes us, that cares for us, and the way that the ocean and the fresh water, they all play a part in our lifestyle. Me personally, as part of an ocean people, we honor that ocean.

I remember in 2016, as a paddler, we usually paddle from the Ventura coast out to Limu, which is now forcibly known as Santa Cruz Island. With the big oil spill, we couldn't even touch the water. By the time they deemed it safe, we started paddling again out in the ocean and I could see spots of oil, fat spots of oil just floating on by and I'm thinking, this water is touching my face right now. What's going to happen to my body? And it comes a time where we have to understand that the Earth is more sacred than money and really put that action into place to better the future for the next generations, instead of just thinking for ourselves here and now.

WONG: You got me thinking about how we understand each other, and how we're in communication with the world, our relations. And for instance right now we have this new acronym, "BIPOC." You know, Black,

Indigenous and People of Color. So what does Blackness mean next to Indigeneity, how do frames dictate relations? I know in the past 20 years there's been a lot of academic folks taking up Black and Indigenous ideas, which are not mutually exclusive, and how Indigenous scholars are pointing out how that process is putting these important ideas through a White gaze and destroying a lot of what they represent. How do you all as artists envision having the type of conversations that could switch mind states to address these things that we're talking about?

WINDER: Yeah, I think it's really tough. You brought up BIPOC and I was just hearing that with some of my friends who work in public health and different things, too. It's such an interesting term. Like one of my friends was like, "Do you think that it's performative? If people actually mean it to include Indigenous people?" I feel like the questions you're asking have been like my life. I feel like it's been navigating these circles. Like how do I talk to my own people? How do I talk to people from my community? How do I talk to other Indigenous people? And that messaging, even though some of it is the same, like some of it changes. Like it's almost like you're entering a different river, and you have to get your grounding first before you can try to walk across.

JUNE: I think it's really important to consider the connection between Black and Brown peoples in this conversation. Some say there's no Native people in football generally, but a lot of those Black guys, they're part Native. Because, here's the thing: When we met each other in the South, we had both been tribal people. We were both being oppressed. We both held unity and compassion as the highest value. We understood each other very deeply. And there was a lot of intermarriage. Ninety-eight percent of our people were obliterated in the Native American Holocaust. So that creates a genetic bottleneck where you cannot go on as a people. So we intermarried with a lot of Black folks and White folks too. A lot of the Scots-Irish people, same thing. They had been obliterated by the British crown. They had their languages prohibited. Welsh was prohibited in schools as late as the 1930s.

And so in this discussion of Indigenous Hip Hop, I think it's really important to acknowledge that there's a lot of as they call it, Black Indians, right? There are a lot of people who are Afro-Indigenous, and they are just as Indigenous as me and any of us here. And I want to make a space for them to claim that and to witness them as Indigenous relatives, even though they might not "look like it," whatever that's supposed to mean. And that also relates to just the origins and the elements of Hip Hop, to breakdance, right? There's a breakdance move called the "Indian Step." And if you look at our grass dancers, they're top rocking, totally top rocking. I mean, I actually used to grass dance when I was young. I was like that weird girl who wanted to grass dance, because it's a male dance, but I loved grass dancing. And when I learned to breakdance, it was like so easy.

And we have to honor the connections, even Kool Herc in the New York area, that's Indigenous land. But a lot of Lenape people, the Indigenous peoples of New York—Lenapehoking as they call it, they look Black. You know, you go hang out with the Ramapough Lenape, many of them look Black. And so I just wanted to honor that connection, as we discussed, and pay homage to Black folks for giving us this art form and also pay homage to the fact that we are very, very interconnected on this continent and most Black folks are also Indigenous, maybe Chatah, maybe Chickasaw, maybe Mvskoke, maybe Seminole. There was a lot of intermarriage.

WINDER: I'm so glad you said that, Lyla. 'Cause that just makes me think, like growing up in ceremony, that's one of the first things like we hear, "all my relations," like we're all related. Like that everything has a spirit, like rocks have a spirit, plants have a spirit. So, they deserve the same level of respect that we do as human beings and that we're all connected. And I think that's part of our charge in this role as Indigenous people, is how do we get people to understand that, understand that life is precious, to understand everything has a spirit. And to understand that because we are all related, like how can we make living easier? You know, how can we make living bearable to make sure everybody is taken care of? And each day is a ceremony, each day a song, each act that we do is a ceremony. And I think all of us try our best to bring that same level of intention and honor and spirit to everything here.

JULES: The revolution will be Indigenous. I heard that somewhere on multiple occasions. And I think it's the truth and we're all a part of it, witnessing it and it's beautiful. It's led by love and being a part of the Dream Warriors collective, I know the love and care is genuine. And sometimes it's almost overwhelming because we get into our emotions but it's okay. The hard work that Tanaya does and the others, it's just such an honor to be a part of this collective. And I just want to thank Tanaya for reaching out for me to be a part of it. And you know, it's so good for my spirit to be able to be surrounded by people who are just so driven by love and make music and that are Indigenous. We have this space, and I appreciate that.

NOTES

1. Kyle T. Mays, *Hip Hop Beats, Indigenous Rhymes: Modernity and Hip Hop in Indigenous North America* (SUNY Press, 2018).

2. The NDN Collective is an Indigenous-led organization dedicated to building Indigenous power by decolonizing and transforming systems, and providing tools and strategies for Indigenous self-determination and movement-building (see more at ndncollective.org).

3. Among the Oceti Sakowin, the prophecy of the Seventh Generation foretells that after seven generations of living under White settler colonialism, Indigenous descendants will rise up and bring back their cultures and languages. See also Nick Estes, *Our History Is the Future: Standing Rock versus the Dakota Access Pipeline, and the Long Tradition of Indigenous Resistance* (Verso, 2019).

5 "Luchando Derechos" in Neoliberal Spain

HIP HOP VISIONS BEYOND RACISM, XENOPHOBIA, ISLAMOPHOBIA, AND THE GENTRIFICATION OF EL RAVAL, BARCELONA

La Llama Rap Colectivo with H. Samy Alim

H. SAMY ALIM: La Llama Rap Colectivo, as a Hip Hop group, formed here in Barcelona, in the racially, ethnically, and culturally diverse neighborhood of El Raval, a home to many immigrants and first, second, and third generations of Communities of Color from all over North Africa, the Middle East, South Asia, and Latin America. El Raval is a community of about 50,000 people, almost half of whom are born abroad, many of them Muslims from Morocco, Turkey, Pakistan, and Indonesia. Most tourists to Barcelona have never heard of this neighborhood—or if they have, it's only recently—but it's a relatively hidden, oppressed, working-class district in a city that now rivals London and Paris as one of the most popular tourist destinations in Europe. As developers continue to gentrify El Raval, community members are forming politically active coalitions to resist further displacement and loss of important cultural nodes. The community has a long history of art and activism, and you can now see the proliferation of anti-gentrification campaigns. Local residents of El Raval are protesting on a regular basis, occupying buildings and plazas set for destruction and hotel development. It's within this context that La Llama Rap Colectivo was born.

Hip Hop has taken root here in Barcelona and across Spain, but here we focus more specifically on Hip Hop as local knowledge. We delve into

Figure 5.1 Sitting, left to right, Susi Álvarez Mariño and Andy Robinson; *Standing, left to right*, Waqar, Mr. Michael, and Casey Philip Wong. In the studio, Barcelona, Spain. Photo by Abdul Alim.

art, activism, and the challenges faced by folks here in El Raval—and importantly what Hip Hop is doing to continue the struggle for human rights, and how La Llama Rap Colectivo, in particular, breathes life into the phrase "Luchando Derechos"[1] by continuing a legacy of community art and activism in the area.

We know La Llama has previously worked on educational projects at the Associació Joves TEB[2] (a youth association), which was founded 30 years ago in 1992. Youth all work *tirelessly* on Hip Hop workshops, media and digital storytelling projects, and various educational projects that address a wide range of social issues facing youth by drawing upon local knowledges to resist the oppressive systems that make life difficult for working-class Communities of Color in Spain. La Llama is one of many groups emerging now to give hope to a new generation working to transform the circumstances, to paraphrase Tupac, that they were "given."

So let's get right into it. You're now both giving workshops at TEB, but you started here as kids? How did you get involved with TEB?

COMING OF AGE THROUGH HIP HOP: RESISTING ANTI-BLACKNESS IN BARCELONA

WAQAR: Well, I was 11 years old when I discovered Hip Hop. When I first started to write, I did it to vent, like rap was a way you could put your concerns down on paper. And I found out about TEB through my uncle, who's also a rapper. I remember being in the schoolyard, writing raps, and my uncle told me, "There's this place where you can go record for free and they have a radio station," and I came here. I found out that my uncle used to come to TEB, too, and he knew our director, Susi. And when I first met Susi, I was a quiet kid. I've always been very shy, and rap opened me up. I learned how to talk with people, to communicate, to learn how to express my emotions. Shortly after coming to TEB, I formed a group with my uncle and a friend called Huellas Negras, and we talked about social issues.

ALIM: "Huellas Negras"? Wow! Why did you choose that name?

WAQAR: Blackness was looked down upon, and we felt like we were looked down upon. I'm the Blackest in the group, and we wanted to leave a mark, a black mark, like footprints, saying no to racism, it was political, you know? We talked about politics, but we focused more on social issues, on building a critical consciousness, so it was the right name for us. And I was like 13 or 14, just a kid. And after we formed the group, I learned that there used to be a "Rhyme Workshop," but it had been suspended. Susi restarted the Rhyme Workshop for us, and facilitators came from all over. They taught us how to rap, and how to write, and that's how I started out here. I remember Susi gave a lot of the workshops. I remember she taught me, because I was a kid—Susi has been here for many years.

MICHAEL: When I started coming here around seven years ago, I was 14 and already making rap and into Hip Hop. I used to rap around the neighborhood and in other places. I put on a concert, recorded some things, and then I found out that here, apart from there being a studio, I knew that Susi had been working with young people who were into Hip Hop, especially on rapping. I also knew the group Waqar had from the neighborhood. I knew that they came from here, and so, one day I came with the intention of making music, because there was this Maqueta Workshop (Demo Workshop). You could come here, make songs and record little demos. Since I started coming, my brother came, other people came.

ALIM: You all started very young, to make your own music and write rhymes. Why Hip Hop? You could have chosen whatever you wanted, but why was Hip Hop attractive?

MICHAEL: I think we young people liked it because it came out of the Bronx, from that type of working-class neighborhood, and we came from a working-class neighborhood. And I joined because I liked writing poetry and I listened to Nach and those artists that made a more poetic type of rap. It was like, one day I listened to my first Nach song "Efectos Vocales,"[3] and I said to myself, "I want to do that, man!" Man, it's the best song! He played with the A, with the O, and with the E. It was the first rap song I ever listened to, and I said, "Fuck, man, I could have started lower and gone up!" And I already had some things written, you know, so I started grabbing internet instrumentals and playing around.

WAQAR: For me, Hip Hop was important because you could relate. I felt that I could relate to so many songs, when I had personal or family problems or any type of problem that you have in the neighborhood, you know, especially in our neighborhood, because it used to be like a ghetto and you lived through many kinds of things. For example, I began listening to Tupac and I liked his songs. He was my hero! The message pulled me in, because I read his subtitles and said, "Hey, I can talk about crime and so on," but the message he was giving was very important, you know, that you can be anyone, and if you want to, you can be whatever you set your mind to. It doesn't matter where you grow up. He really inspired me, because I could see inside myself that I had a lot of things to say.

"PEOPLE HERE ARE WORKING PEOPLE": THE MISREPRESENTATION OF EL RAVAL

ALIM: For people that are not from El Raval, can you explain how your neighborhood has changed?

WAQAR: Well, there used to be a lot of drug trafficking, the streets were narrow, there was a lot of crime and it was very unsafe, right? And now the streets are wider, but the problem is that now, there is gentrification going on in the neighborhood, you know? Our neighborhood has been treated with a lot of prejudice in the media. They constantly say bad things about our neighborhood. They say there are prostitutes, there are drugs. Well, there are those things everywhere. Look, our neighborhood has bad things, but if you only focus on the bad things and you don't see the positive ones, then it can only be normal that people are afraid. I believe our neighborhood has as many bad things as positive things but I value more the positive ones.

MICHAEL: And then, something might happen here, and something outside on the outskirts of the city, the suburbs. And whatever happens here is given much more attention and they talk a lot more about what happens here than about what happens elsewhere. So people that live more in other types of neighborhoods, more high class, then it's like, come on, man . . . But of course, it's not the same when you say, "Look, there's drugs in this neighborhood" than "There are drugs in El Raval," right? What sells more? You know, people have a morbid curiosity, and if you can talk about El Raval, well . . . Look, some time ago, someone was stabbed here and so there's a lot of talk and everything, there's a lot more, social media and the media, you know? "El Raval again . . . " And so they take advantage when something bad happens, "So many bad things are happening because there is so much immigration . . ." But don't give me that shit, it can happen any place, right? The thing is there are a lot of different cultures and the media manipulates this all the time. People from here are working people. Our parents are families that have never been well off economically, you know? So then, we are these typical families that work so they can feed their children, you know? And that work a lot of hours to feed their children. And so you grow up with these values that your parents instill in you, that, hell, my mother works a lot of hours so we can have an education, so we can have food, so we may have a house. The housing issue, it's very expensive, and . . .

WAQAR: I can relate in another way, too. It's like the same thing that happens with Muslims, you know? When a Muslim does something, it's because of their religion, but when a White person does something, then he is mentally ill, things like that, you know? We are working class, humble people, that earn a living to pay for rent, pay for food. I don't think that money defines who we are. We are people from different parts of the world, but we're united. In fact, my grandfather is the one who came here and brought the family, and we are one of the first Pakistani families in the neighborhood, maybe the first one. We've been here for more than three decades, at least. In fact, look, I had the same teacher in elementary school that my father had. My family comes from Pakistan, specifically from Kashmir. Azad Kashmir. "Azad" means free, and it's called free Kashmir since there is no conflict. If you go to the other part of the border, there's conflict. You can't live in peace there.

MICHAEL: My mother, well, my family is from Madrid. They all came to live here. My father is from Morocco. But what is cool about this neighborhood is that you can find people, even from Lithuania, and from everywhere, yeah, or people who have very rare family histories like Greek and Hindu. The blend of cultures that you find here, the multiculturality is enriching. And you learn a lot. I have friends from all over and I have been brought up in school with people from Ecuador, Colombia, and from all over, Venezuela, Bolivia.

"BRUTALITAT PROU IMPUNITAT": RESPONDING TO THE POLICE MURDER OF JUAN ANDRÉS

ALIM: So, during the years that we have been working together, it seems like there have been some very disturbing incidents that have happened, and I said, "I can't believe that you have the same problems we have." Because, in the US, we have a lot of problems with police violence . . .

Figure 5.2 Street art in El Raval, Barcelona, Spain. Photo by Abdul Alim.

MICHAEL: Yeah, in this neighborhood there has always been a serious problem, right? Because there has always been this sort of struggle between police and the young people in the neighborhood, because we have always been looked at in a bad manner. The police are prejudiced. They have always been prejudiced, everywhere. And when you are Moroccan or from some other "foreign" place, or according to them, you look a little suspicious, then you are somebody that I can stop, I can ask for your documentation and I can take you with me or I can beat you. In fact, in 2013, and we created the group because of that, in 2013, the police killed a man here in the neighborhood, and we just exploded. We created the first song because we were fed up, man, always, but that was like the last straw. It had never happened that the police killed a neighbor from here, from this neighborhood. We created the group right then and there.

WAQAR: The song we made is called "Luchando Derechos"[4] and it's against police abuse. And the Mossos afterwards, when they murdered

Juan Andrés (our neighbor),[5] that was the boom, right? It shocked us all so much!

MICHAEL: I saw it on TV, but . . . I know there was a problem between two neighbors from that street. It seems like they were arguing, so the police came. Then Juan Andrés, the person that was killed, they stopped him. But the thing is that around eight policemen came to stop one person, which is not necessary, you know? It always happens like that, right? They are going to stop you because you are at the public square sitting down, you know, eating seeds and here come 10 of them, makes you feel like a criminal. So many officers fell on him and he didn't understand. They started talking, a little annoyed, arguing, and he rebelled, because it's normal. You're not going to let them abuse you. So they started to beat him, right there. And they said that no, that it was him, and that since he was on drugs, his heart had stopped. And, so next day, the police were going by people's houses who had recorded this and forcing them to erase the videos they had recorded. In fact, they did not convict those policemen, I think they only left them without their jobs for two years and made them take some classes on Human Rights, or something, so they can learn about rights, but they have even gone back to work again just a couple of months ago. If you kill somebody, man, and you are a policeman, and you can keep on working? I don't understand, man! All the neighborhood united against the police. There are some groups, there are some strong collectives here, in favor of Human Rights and against injustice. And later they created a square called Ágora Juan Andrés, in memory of our neighbor. That was a place that was abandoned. The neighbors cleaned it, fixed it, painted some murals and graffiti, and have kept it as a public space for the whole neighborhood, with gardens. It is a space for everybody. Whoever wants to go in, can go, stay there, do whatever they want. And then, people hold meetings when something happens in the neighborhood, about some injustice, the neighbors hold their meetings there to see how they can face the conflict, that problem, demonstrations, many things . . .

WAQAR: Yes, in fact when this Juan Andrés thing happened, there was a campaign started named "Justicia Juan Andrés" (Justice for Juan Andrés). After that, there was another campaign called "Ojo Con Tu Ojo" (Keep an

Figure 5.3 (Top) Street art in El Raval, Barcelona, Spain. Photo by Abdul Alim.

Figure 5.4 (Bottom) Street art in El Raval, Barcelona, Spain. Photo by Abdul Alim.

Figure 5.5 (Top) Street art in El Raval, Barcelona, Spain. Photo by Abdul Alim.

Figure 5.6 (Bottom) Street art in El Raval, Barcelona, Spain. Photo by Abdul Alim.

Eye on Your Eye), which was for people who get their eyes taken out with these rubber bullets that they shoot during demonstrations. And all those campaigns got together to file a complaint against the police.

MICHAEL: Now they want to force the people out from the square. We were in a demonstration there last month. So it seems that they got a letter, like an eviction notice, that they had to clear the place because the company that used to have land there is now claiming the land. And that doesn't make much sense because the neighbors found the place abandoned. It was all full of trash, all dirty, and what they did was clean it up, take the stuff away, leave it pretty, fix it up, and now that it's all clean, now you want to throw them all out, right? They want to fine the people like twenty thousand euros or something. It doesn't make sense! I'm sure they want to build a hotel there or something, right? And since it's occupied by the people from the neighborhood, they don't want to have them get in their way. The people are still there and, in fact, we don't know when they are going to go there to clear them out. But the day it happens, there's a night stay planned, so everybody will go there with tents to sleep and occupy the square. And fast.

WAQAR: That's why in the song "Luchando Derechos" I wanted to send the message of that the police mistreats us because of how we look and also, more in general, for the system, it seems like they complain about us, but the system does nothing for us either. When you are a kid and you want to find a place to play, there are none. So you start to learn that you have to be on the street. But then you are on the street and the police come, so ... In the video, "Brutalitat prou impunitat" means "Stop the impunity and the brutality," it's in Catalan. We also say "Justicia Alik" because Alik Manukyan is an Armenian that was in the CIEs, the immigrant centers, and he was also killed there and then they said he had committed suicide.[6] But for us it's the same. Somebody who drives you to a point where you want to commit suicide, for us that is murder, because it's psychological, right? You have to stay there for two months minimum, six maximum, and then they deport you to your country. For me these immigration detention centers are worse than jails. At least in jails, you are in there because of a crime you committed and there's not that much abuse in jails either, from the police, because there are public officers. And here there is certainly no dignity, right? Because when you go to one of these places you gotta have hygiene and food and there are places with no nurses, that when you are sick, they don't take care of you, you know? And in the video, we tell the truth about how the family is coping with it, how we are, or the people who live these situations.

"VERDADES OCULTAS": EXPOSING RACISM, XENOPHOBIA, AND ISLAMOPHOBIA IN SPAIN

ALIM: And so you recorded the video for "Verdades Ocultas"[7] in front of the Foreigner Detention Center. Where is it located?

WAQAR: In the free trade zone. Isolated.

MICHAEL: Sure, in places not easy to get to, because if this was inside of Barcelona, people would be there, demonstrating at the door all the time. Instead of that, to get to this place, you have to take a bus. There was a demonstration to shut down CIE that day and we took a bus and seized the moment to record the video. In fact, the latest news from Barcelona was that they were going to close it, but then they said they were going to reform it, and that's where they are.

WAQAR: We were there to record, because, since we were talking about racism and all. Once we got there, the people asked us to perform.

ALIM: You weren't you afraid of being there?

WAQAR: No.

MICHAEL: No, because in the end, you have to consider that there were hundreds of people. Imagine, in any case, if they had done something to us, it was hundreds of people against five policemen and it's impossible. In fact, in the part where I rap, I am the last one to rap, but I was the first one to record. And you can see that in my part that there are some Mossos d'Esquadra, the police force in Catalonia, that go here [*Michael points to the screen at the officers*] and talk with some other officers to ask them to stop us, because they were listening. But no, they didn't say anything to us, and I didn't feel unsafe or anything. This filled me up on the inside, you know? Because I really felt it, people that are undergoing all this mistreatment and all . . . You felt supported, because everybody was looking, backing up what you were doing.

WAQAR: Yeah, even Ada Colau, the current mayor of Barcelona, was there in fact. In the song we say that we have the most powerful weapon, right? We use this music to sort of defend ourselves. "To shatter these racial walls!" right? Because, according to us, this is racism, because you're taken in only for not having papers. Whoever tells you there isn't racism here or in Europe, it's a lie. There's racism in Pakistan, in Germany. I went to Germany with a company that I used to work with, on a company trip, and they stopped me only because I looked like a Syrian, only because of this, and I was traveling with my bosses. I mean they told me that . . . I asked them, "Why did you stop me and not them?" Because they were White and I wasn't. It hasn't happened to me in a long time, but here if you look like "the wrong kind of person," just because of prejudice, they can stop you.

MICHAEL: For example, if you see an immigrant here say "I feel Catalan," there will be many people who are going to say "No, you're not Catalan, you're from over there, from your country." From this neighborhood, you can hear typical comments, like "Go back to your country!" you know? The typical, always, right?

WAQAR: Yeah, it happens a lot. Like there used to be many Nazis here, but there was a fight between immigrants and Nazis, and they threw them out of the neighborhood, the Nazis. I think racism is growing *and* people are becoming more conscious also, at the same time. Because there are a lot of ignorant people that say, "There's no racism in my country," but sure, there is no racism because you haven't experienced it. And not everybody is racist obviously. Because there are Catalans that will tell you, "Sure, you can be Catalan." But what I mean is that there are some people who, just as there can be some Spanish people who if you tell them that you are

Spanish, they will tell you that you are not Spanish, because of the color of your skin, right? You have to be White for example, right? And since we've had so many generations of immigrants here in Catalonia and in Spain, it's normal that a person that has been born here will want to identify himself as Spanish or as Catalan or how he pleases, right? I am telling you this because it happened to me once that a Catalan lady asked me: "Where are you from?" And I told her that I felt Catalan, right? And she told me: "You are not Catalan." There are many cases like that one. And also, for example, you go to the Social Security office and just because they see you with a different skin color, or from another country, they think that you don't know how to speak Catalan or that you don't know how to speak Spanish, and these things happen. *Or* when you speak well, they tell you: "Oh, you speak Catalan very well" or "You speak Spanish very well." Of course, since he is White, if he speaks well they are not going to tell him that. If you were born here, if you didn't speak well, then it wouldn't make sense. Because, for example, if I had been born in Morocco and I didn't speak Arabic well, it would be strange, right? The strange thing would be that I didn't know how to speak it, not that I knew how to speak it.

MICHAEL: Yeah, and I also think that the media, television, news and all of this, encourage this racism, right, with the news they show. "Two Moroccan kids have a fight in El Raval and stab such and such." And so, they keep making comments, saying things that promote hate against Moroccans. Like what happened with the terrorist attack in Barcelona about a year ago, right? It seemed like all the Muslims were bad, man, and it's like, no, man! And then, a year goes by, and the king and the president come here to supposedly assume their stance, like "I'm interested in what happened here." And then for the rest of the year they are with this conflict that Catalonia is not Spain, and that if you leave Spain, we are going to throw you out, and now we are interested in you. That is what bothers me too, right? The two faces the system has. And sometimes you're scared because of what is going to happen after one of these attacks, right? Because, you know, when something happens with Muslims, it becomes widespread and the next day we have attacks on mosques or against women who walk alone with a veil. They don't bother men, but when they see a woman with a veil alone, that's when they attack. They take the veil off. Or police security increases, and then, any Muslim person or that looks like one, is suspicious, right? It's like, "I am going to look at you, thoroughly, even if you are not doing anything, just to see," right? So you are walking along and, "What's in your backpack?" It doesn't make sense!

WAQAR: In the song when I say "dunya," dunya means "world" in Arabic. And what I meant was that this world is everybody's and that it's nobody's. It's for everybody, right? But nobody owns the world. I'm also talking about Guantánamo, that this place is worse than Guantánamo. Because in Guantánamo, it's an unfortunate place, right? But people that go there have committed terrorist acts or broken the law, right? In this case, they are in there because of their face. Supposedly, of course, the ones the government wants. Here, of course, if you have money, it doesn't matter where you come from, they will welcome you with open arms. But if you don't have money and you don't have papers . . . And in our song "Protesto,"[8] we made it with Juli, who is an artist from Barcelona. It's against the "Ley Mordaza," which was a law approved in Spain.[9] It's against freedom of expression, so for example, there are artists here that are in jail just for insulting the king, for example. In the video, we are in Plaza de Cataluña for 15M. There was a demonstration here, 15M (May 15), where all the struggles got together. It's the biggest demonstration there has been in Barcelona and in Madrid, and people got united that day to protest.

"LA LEY MORDAZA": STATE REPRESSION AGAINST RAP
AND FREEDOM OF EXPRESSION

MICHAEL: "Mordaza" is this bandage that they put on your mouth, you know? In the movies sometimes, haven't you seen that they put a bandage over your mouth and they tie you up, that is a "mordaza." "Ley mordaza," it's a law to keep us quiet. The video shows that we live in a Francoist era, because when Franco was alive, people didn't have many rights, because he was a dictator. And I'm saying that it's as if we are still living in those times, because there's still an enslaved society and a racist society. Yeah, we are working here, but we are slaves to this system and the system is prejudice. Then it says, "Being an Immigrant Is Not a Crime," and it's about the CIEs. It's the "Tanquem on CIEs" campaign. Tanquem means "Let's shut them down." It's with them that we made the "Verdades Ocultas" song, and they came to TEB and explained to us what was going on there. When we go to these places, we sing the songs that talk about what people are fighting for, so people are always there, involved, backing each other up. The problem is that they sell you the idea that there's freedom of expression, that you can say whatever you want, but when you do it, then they arrest you. So you say, "What can I talk about?" They aren't putting him in jail for killing somebody or something. It's for his songs, because he sang things against the king.

WAQAR: Well, there are a few rappers that have experienced that. There is Pablo Hasél, Valtónyc, Ajax and Prok. And by the way, the last thing I know about was Ajax and Prok. This city council from I don't know where, in Madrid I think it was, invited them, knowing what type of music they play, they invited them, they sang, and the next day or something, they had to pay a fine for singing what they sang.

MICHAEL: Yeah, because there's a song they have about the police, where they talk like they're messing around, right? "The police comes, they take away your joints, then they smoke 'em." And so they talk a little about the police, right? And then, because of that song, because according to them, police cars and policemen appear on the video, they received a fine and they had to pay twenty thousand euros, or if not, three years in jail. And they were like, "What? Is this serious? It's not like we are saying anything bad about anybody." If I want to hire him and I know he sings against injustice and I am a right-wing person, well I don't hire him, man! But on top of that, don't protest and file a complaint!

ALIM: Well, what did they say against the king?

MICHAEL: No, just things in general, because they talk about the things that are in the media, man! That the king goes hunting with public money. The king and all his family and all his grandchildren have a lifelong salary without working!

WAQAR: In fact there is a song by Pablo Hasél[10] called "Death to the Borbones."[11] The Borbones are the kings and he explains there that the king doesn't contribute anything to the country, and that there is a lot of hypocrisy, right?

ALIM: That's strong critique!

MICHAEL: Yeah, yeah, but it's because they have caused that rage, right? When they come to the demonstrations and beat us up, when they throw us out of our homes and they throw mothers with their children out of their houses. You have caused this, so don't complain if you have caused this, you know?

WAQAR: And the hypocrisy, right? Because he just made up a song, he just said "Death to the Borbones," but the Mossos d'Esquadra killed, murdered Juan Andrés, and look at them. There they are, they have their jobs, their houses. It's like they're coming after us, after the people that fight for equality, for rights.

MICHAEL: The king, here in Spain, his role is like a figurehead. Because the president, yeah—even if later on he doesn't do much, but the president does work. But the king, his role is irrelevant, right? So then it's like, you are getting rich, man, with our taxes, and when I sing this in a song, on top of that, you arrest me, man! The television talks about that, too, and you don't censor the television and I sing what the television tells me about you. So you censor me, but you don't censor the television.

WAQAR: Yeah, they're scared of the people, and of rap artists, because they're putting rappers in jail and not another type of musician. They want to scare us, if you want to know the truth. Because I think Hip Hop in Spain has grown a lot, and it's been here for many years and it's growing and every time there are more of us that contribute to Hip Hop, and Hip Hop contributes to us, too. There's like a united struggle also, in Hip Hop, in favor of freedom of expression. And I think that scares them, because we are young, there are people who have studied.

ALIM: I thought maybe it's because they are talking about the struggle between Catalonia and Madrid. So, it has nothing to do with this?

WAQAR: No, not at all. The protest signs you see are for the prisoners, for the politicians that wanted independence. They are incarcerated.

MICHAEL: Because they wanted Catalonian independence. And since the government is against that, they have put those politicians in jail so they don't have to grant independence. And so, now, the part of the Catalan people that want independence, demonstrate, right? They took out those politicians that only wanted independence. That is what I was telling you, right? That there is this independence conflict of "we won't grant you independence," but then, there is a terrorist attack in Barcelona and you come to clean up your image, "and I worry about the Catalonians" and "I worry about the people in Barcelona." And now on top of that, you are not president anymore and your salary is for the rest of your life. You, your four-year term has ended as president and you are not president anymore, because they voted for someone else, but you still get paid! It's like, fuck, man! I want to be president too! [*Laughter*] And here you are at home, getting paid, relaxed.

ALIM: And you are not afraid to talk about this issue in particular?

MICHAEL: They've told us many times, but no, because I think that for me, if they put me in jail because of my songs it's because they are more afraid of what I can think of than of what I can do. So if they are putting us in jail and censoring us it's because they are afraid.

ALIM: Have you rapped about the subject of Catalonian independence?

WAQAR: No, we haven't. It's not that we are afraid to speak about independence, it's only that I, personally, prefer less borders, but I also respect people who want independence. We have never talked about "Let's make a song for Catalonia," because I don't feel Spanish or Catalonian, I feel from the world. Sometimes, when they ask me, I answer, "I'm Pakistani, Kashmiri, Spanish, Catalan," I couldn't care less, you know? I am, I feel from the world and I feel more from El Raval than from any other place, and I don't think it's an important issue for me. I think there are more important issues. I am not in favor of the politicians being in jail, for example, I support that, but independence, no . . .

MICHAEL: Everything that has to do with change, I think can be positive. If we become independent, and if independence goes cool—if they don't want us independent it's for some reason. So I believe that if we do it, I think it's going to go better because much of Spain's income comes from Catalonia. And not only that, it's a selfish way of thinking but, not only will jobs be better, but people might live better, and I believe that, if there is a change and it goes well, cool. And if it goes wrong, well, I think we should try out all that has to do with change. When they were voting on the referendum here, the police went to where people were voting, grabbed the ballot boxes and beat up the people, so they couldn't vote! They grabbed the ballot boxes and took them away. But it wasn't the local police; it was the national police.

WAQAR: It's a dictatorship. For me, it's a dictatorship because if the people are not free to vote . . . Police from Madrid came all the way here. I was shocked, too. I saw the videos and . . . [they beat] women, old people!

THE GENTRIFICATION OF EL RAVAL AND THE STRUGGLE AGAINST NEOLIBERALISM

ALIM: You guys are on fire! Who came up with the name "La Llama"?

MICHAEL: We were tossing around names and "La Llama" came up because it has two meanings, right? It means the flame, of fire, right? Because we are trying to send a message too, right? We are trying to give a message of hope, and bring light, lighten up the neighborhood with our rhymes. And then there is also the animal called llama that *spits*, so we play with that meaning too—to spit truths. And we also play with the meaning of this animal's name to spit truths and to spit on reality. But the fire is the flame, so you can say "the flame is alive," in some circles, right? Where maybe they're talking about a revolution. You can also use it as in the flame in the fire, but, you know in that demonstration, the flame is alive, you know? The people are coming and going and the atmosphere is hot . . .

WAQAR: What I see is that people who don't have economic means, who can't afford an apartment, are being thrown out, right? Or the houses that they are living in, they are raising the rent or throwing them out of their properties, to build hotels. And I think that they are using poverty to throw people out and make something "cooler" out of this neighborhood, right? More for tourists . . .

MICHAEL: Yeah, in fact, many years ago in Las Ramblas Raval, here in La Rambla, El Paseo, where "The Cat" is and all of this,[12] where today you can find stores and hotels, it used to be all houses and apartments, and they kicked the people out to make Las Ramblas Raval. In the end, it's all for tourism, for economics, so that it's pretty. And they threw the people out of there, and they sent them to other neighborhoods, to other places.

ALIM: So, this is why you were talking before about gentrification. Right where the Barceló Hotel is, and all, those were houses?

WAQAR: Yeah, in fact, a short time ago, they made another hotel in front, and it was a place that was in use—they were making art there. And then right there in Drassanes there is another one. There is a sort of "solar"—a public space where there's nothing—and they want to make another hotel.

MICHAEL: It's like an empty place, and they don't worry about it at all until people start using it and start engaging in cultural activities there. And sure, we care because it was a place that was occupied, open to the people, they could do cultural things, beautiful things. It had been abandoned for a long time and when people begin to organize cultural activities for the neighborhood, then they want to make a hotel there, "Oh no, no, now we are going to make a hotel."

WAQAR: The same thing is happening with the Ágora Juan Andrés, which was a place full of cockroaches, rats, syringes, everything. I think that they are afraid that people will unite. I think that in the poor neighborhoods, in the ghettos, people are more united, right? Because there's so much suffering, so much poverty, so much hunger, scarcity and all, and I think that brings people together. Suffering makes people get together and I think people in the upper classes are afraid that we will unite and make a revolution and so they want to divide us. Because I think everybody has to make a living, because we are—they got us imprisoned. The system has us going from one problem to the other, and of course when you're earning a living, you're working, you don't have time to engage in cultural activities or to be in the neighborhood making a life for yourself, right? And what used to happen, when there wasn't so much gentrification in the neighborhood—for example, you walked down the neighborhood and you knew the people who were in the neighborhood. Now you walk down the neighborhood and you don't know most of the people, because they are outsiders, from nice neighborhoods, that have money, right? But before, they certainly were the same ones that had always been here, the ones who had lived here all their life. Now that doesn't happen anymore. Now there are apartments that are only for tourists, for example, right? There are people that are only renting to tourists with a lot of money, right? Look, what I see when I'm walking on the streets—usually, in the restaurants here, there is a person outside that invites you in to eat, right? And what I've noticed is that these people only go towards the tourists, right? They don't go towards the people that live in the neighborhood: "Hey, would you like to eat?" They just straightaway [*he makes a gesture with his hand as if shoving somebody*], "Not this one . . . This one is an outsider."

MICHAEL: Different people are arriving. In the past, there weren't many hipsters—this movement, where they all wear their horn-rimmed glasses, a beard, and very vintage clothes. Now there are a lot of hipsters, because a lot of people from here have had to go. And then, people who can definitely pay for the apartments come to live. In the end it's because they can pay. I mentioned hipsters because it's the largest collective there is, but outsiders come, and these are people who would have never come to live here a few years ago. And now they come and pay for an apartment, because it's downtown, after all, this is downtown now. Now El Raval is "cool." It's not "dangerous" anymore. There are a whole lot of Airbnbs here. The owners who own blocks throw the people out of there and rent their apartments to tourists and they make more money, because I can charge a tourist twice as much as I can charge you. And they throw you out of your house, and go get a life! Because they rarely help you. There are many empty apartments but they don't usually help you and give you another house. It may be a mother and her four children and they won't help you, man. So, it's like, how . . . ? In the end, for us, people that live in Barcelona, there are no advantages, no supports, right? You are like locked up and that's it, and now and again, depending on where you're from, you have the police there, right? And then, people from the outside certainly have more freedom, right? And it's like, in your own city, you can't have freedom!

THE RELATIONSHIPS BETWEEN HIP HOP ART, ACTIVISM, AND EDUCATION

WAQAR: That's why we focus on Human Rights. In fact, every year we participate or they call us for "Ciudad Defensores por los Derechos Humanos" (Cities Defending Human Rights) and different collectives come from different parts of the world. For example, last year a person from Palestine came, or from Syria, who is an activist, a doctor who is there helping the refugees, and it shocks us, right? Because we are with such important people, who are making a huge impact on the world.

MICHAEL: Activists from all over the world that work for Human Rights in their countries or that are in some internal struggle, and we go there with students, we make a presentation, or a talk. The good part of that is that we rap about Human Rights, and when we rap about Human Rights, well, many people got interested, not only in our rapping there but in us going and talking about Human Rights.

ALIM: That's right. This is another form of education, that, well, doesn't always have to happen at school. How would you describe the relationship between Hip Hop and education?

MICHAEL: Beyond our workshops in schools where we teach kids how to rhyme and life skills, etc., I would say there is a relationship in that Hip Hop is a cultural movement that encourages unity, from my point of view, and there is a very big collective that makes up Hip Hop culture, breakers, graffiti artists, DJ's, MC's, everybody, right? There is like a unity and it encourages this, right, that we, the people come together more. You can take all of this over to education in the sense that rap is a genre that speaks about anything, right? We can talk about education. We can speak about Human Rights. We can talk about the street. And so, it is a tool that you can use, right? If you want to raise awareness, if you want to educate, if you want to, not to change an idea, because I don't want to change your idea, but I certainly want you to see that there are different options of that idea and not only one, you know? For example, why does prostitution exist? It's not because girls like it, but there are cases, where some *have* to do it, because there is no other option, to feed their children, right? And I think that other genres of music like pop can't do that as well, because they always speak of love, things like that. And yet since Hip Hop addresses many issues, you can use it as a tool to educate young people and raise awareness in them, mostly about what is happening.

WAQAR: Well, the message we normally send is about what's happening, right, the truth about what is going on in the world or the things that we live through. I think it's important also for society to know what young people think about society and the system in general. We use Hip Hop as a tool for change, because we believe that we can change the way people think, right? For example, let's say somebody sees that I am Black, and so, they might think "this guy is a sexist," or things like that. In "Voces Mudas,"[13] for example, we make it clear that we believe that women and men are equal, that we are not above them. And not only men and women, but among all the different people that exist around the world, that we are all equal. I think creativity has a lot to do with it also, right? Because when you make music, you create, and I think that creativity in education is very important, because education has always, mostly in my era, everything was boring, right? "This is like this." And no, I think that music is freedom, right? Because you can create and say, "I want this to be like this," and you can educate yourself in another way. You are more free in the mind, right?

Figure 5.7 Right to left, H. Samy Alim with La Llama Rap Colectivo and his students, Barcelona, Spain. Photo by Abdul Alim.

You are not there, with so much information in your mind that in the end you are not going to use. I think that in music there are values that can help you in life, because Hip Hop has given me many values which I think they didn't teach me at school. I think what Hip Hop can offer to education is this genuine contact with the student, right, this something intimate, which I think you can't get in traditional education. Hip Hop provides an opportunity for a more intimate relationship with that student, that makes you know how that young person is doing.

ALIM: Yeah, and what I've also seen is that with Susi, you and everybody, it feels like a family, that is the word that fits better.

WAQAR: Yeah, I feel like in a family, not only with Susi, but with all the people that come here, with Eva, with all the educators that come here. We all feel like a family, and one likes that, right? Because maybe one day you are sad and at home, and so, well, you come here and they ask you what's up. That's what a family is about, right? Being there in the good times and in the bad times. And the important thing is that the new, young people that come here can also feel like family, you know? That's what's important. Let's see, for example, when we say "we are a family," well, it's like a smile. They don't need to talk, because you can see it. And the respect they have for us too, right? Because I am not related to them. And they respect you. Me, for example, they call me brother, right? The Pakistanis that come here, well, I am like an older brother, and that shocks me, right? Because they don't have to. It makes me feel happy, and it makes me respect them more, be more fond of them.

NOTES

1. This directly translates as "Fighting Rights," which loosely can be understood to mean "Fighting for Our Rights."
2. Since 2021, La Llama Rap Colectivo operates out of Xamfrà: Música /Escena/Inclusión Social en el Raval: https://xamfra.net/. Their music and videos are produced by Drako & Antiqua Deorum: @antiquadeorum: https://www.instagram.com/antiquadeorum/?hl=es. Their official YouTube channel is: https://www.youtube.com/watch?v=2ATtqDm7TXA&list=PLqiLaALuJGInTC_R33_QJzsdRGHcEJyRE.
3. Nach is considered by many to be one of the most influential Hip Hop artists in Spain. Known for his poetic lyricism and creativity, he has produced numerous critically acclaimed albums over the last 25 years. See his music video for "Efectos Vocales" at https://www.youtube.com/watch?v=eOTbm-NvLII.
4. See the music video for "Luchando Derechos" at https://youtu.be/2ATtqDm7TXA.
5. Read more about the tragic and violent police murder of Juan Andrés Benítez at the hands of the Catalan police: https://english.elpais.com/elpais/2013/10/23/inenglish/1382538293_863505.html.
6. See more on Alik Manukyan at https://www.equaltimes.org/inside-spain-s-immigration?lang=en#.YDRnDS-ZPxg.
7. See the music video for "Verdades Ocultas" at https://youtu.be/ZNh_wiKeuHs
8. See the music video for "Protesto" at https://youtu.be/mH6ZrzHV_Nw
9. Many believe that La Ley Mordaza was passed "to help the ruling party maintain its hold on power by discouraging the anti-austerity protests that have

snowballed into widespread support for the populist Podemos party." Read more about La Ley Mordaza, "Spain's Ominous Gag Law," at https://www.nytimes.com/2015/04/23/opinion/spains-ominous-gag-law.html.

10. For more on the jailing of Pablo Hasél, see https://time.com/5941707/pablo-hasel/.

11. See Pablo Hasél's song "Death to the Borbones" at https://www.youtube.com/watch?v=Dxj90JiVMFY&feature=emb_logo.

12. Colombian artist Fernando Botero created a cat sculpture that was installed in the Raval Quarter in 2004, contributing to the ongoing racialized gentrification of El Raval. For more, see the following interview with Barcelona-based collective Etcétera: http://insurgentnotes.com/2018/01/gentrification-and-class-struggles-in-barcelona-spain-interview-with-etctera-collective/

13. See the music video for "Voces Mudas" at https://www.youtube.com/watch?v=RDirlPRVoaE.

PART II Hip Hop Organizing for Abolition, Reparations, Healing, and Growth

6 1Hood

HIP HOP ART, ACTIVISM, AND MEDIA CREATION IN PITTSBURGH

Jasiri X

So what's the state of the Black world, when the hood raised Black boys and Black girls?
Before you pass judgment on us, Jasiri X gon give you somethin to discuss
See, these streets will come talk to you if you understand the language
Corners become famous the more blood they stained with,
the more murals painted when shells hit the pavement
We need three Jesuses to come and save this
We need Moses Abraham and David, all 12 Disciples
to wash away the blood on that hand that held the rifle
'Cause life so hard, he like whoever showed they face tonight is getting robbed
When your home is a grave, the streets is a maze,
and so many cats blaze it's hard to see through the haze,
and crime pays way more than minimum wage,
and plus the lead from the gauge will take a swim in your waves,
Loosen your braids, leave bald spots in your fade,

> like you got your hair cut with some raggedy blades
> The truth is, we no better off than when we were slaves
> Malcolm X and Dr. King probably spinnin in their graves
> It's gotta be the last days, 'cause I can't take no more
> And these kids, they don't Harlem shake no more
> They in the kitchen, cookin up cakes galore,
> kickin down doors and "everybody face the floor,"
> and they got guns that will make you shake and contort,
> and they don't shoot ball, they shoot 38s for sport,
> Getting tried as adults when they case hit the court
> Getting sent to state prison getting raped, Oh Lord
> What did we do to deserve this condition?
> But we can't even function without herb in our system
> And every hit we take from the spliff blurs our vision
> And the next day just means another murder victim in the summer
> Just means we born to get dumber
> Coroners putting bodies under covers,
> and in between sheets like the Isley Brothers
> He told his mother that he loved the hood, but the hood will never love ya
> What's the state of the Black world, when the hood raised Black boys and Black girls?
> Before you pass judgment on us, Jasiri X gonna give us somethin to discuss

I wrote that piece—"The State of the Black World"—because I was going to a lot of these forums, and the adults from our community, I felt like, were looking down and passing judgment on my generation in a particular way, kind of like, "We did all this fighting during the Civil Rights movement to get you these opportunities. What's wrong with your generation? Why don't you pull your pants up? Why don't you just go get a good job?" And I felt like, man, when you come into our communities, you know, some of us are in situations where we're really raising ourselves at a very young age, where not only mom's gone, but dad is gone too, grandma is holdin it down, you know what I'm saying? And the responsibilities and the things that we have to do, a lot of times we're making adult decisions at a very young age. And we're forced to do things a lot of times that we don't wanna do. And these people who are judging us, don't come into the communities that we live in. So I always say to adults, "If the young people don't know, whose responsibility is it?" Is it our responsibility that we don't know? Or is it the responsibility of those that know to come to us and give us the knowledge and the understanding that we need? That was the message for them.

My name is Jasiri X. I'm honored to be here, and thankful to have all y'all attention for these couple minutes, know what I'm saying?[1] I'm originally from a place called Chicago, Illinois. I'm from the Southside of Chicago. I don't know if anybody is familiar with Chicago, Illinois, or the Southside of Chicago. In Chicago, it's funny because right now there's a lot of conversation around the violence in Chicago, about Chicago being called Chiraq. Chicago has been a gangster-hit city since the '20s, since Al Capone. Chicago has always been a place where there's just been gangsters, know what I'm saying? My father was in a gang in Chicago called the Black P. Stone Nation. That goes back. If you're familiar with that history, want to study that history, look up a guy named Jeff Fort, who was a gang leader out of Chicago.

I lived in a neighborhood in Chicago called Roseland, that they called the Wild Hundreds, if you're familiar with that terminology. Because of that history, I got to an age where—the neighborhood I was in—there wasn't really a question what you were going to be down for. You was going to represent your hood. It just was, what it was. So my mother, not wanting me to follow in the footsteps of my father—I have an older sister, but it was more so the things that I began to get involved in. You know, she was like, "You ain't gonna get my son." So she moved us from the Southside of Chicago to a city outside of Pittsburgh, a suburb, called Monroeville, Pennsylvania. So I went from a school that was 100% Black and a neighborhood that was 100% Black, to one that was 95% White. It was a wake-up call for me. My given name is Jasiri Oronde. I was raised socially conscious. My mother raised me to know my history. I have Indigenous blood, or Native blood. My grandmother is Cherokee, my mother raised us as we're Black, love Black, be proud to be Black, but I really didn't understand it until I arrived into this environment. And I'm getting called n*gger. And I'm punching people in they mouth, you know what I'm saying? And I'm getting suspended, you know what I'm saying? All of these things are happening, and it caused me to really kind of decide how I'm going to handle these situations. I'm thankful for my Mom for instilling that history in me because it gave me the skills and the ability to not—unfortunately, I might want to beat everybody up, but I'm not going to be able to do that, you know what I'm saying?

So, I became an activist when I got to Gateway High School. We organized the Black students to form a club. We did activism to get our high school to teach a Black history course at the school. That was the beginning of my activism, and my introduction into Hip Hop. My best friend at the time, he got some turntables for Christmas, and he was like, "Write a rap. I'ma be the DJ, you gonna be the rapper." And I wrote a rap, and it was terrible! It would be like somebody tossed me a trumpet, and said, "Play the trumpet!" I'm trying to play it, and it's going to sound terrible. But I just kept doing it. I was nurtured along the way. When I was bad, people encouraged me. People wouldn't be like, "Man, you terrible, you should never rap!" For some reason, people encouraged me, and as I got better, I started to find my style and find my voice. But I hit some roadblocks.

I graduated high school at 17. I went to the University of Maryland, College Park, which is right outside of Washington, DC. And I wasn't really mature enough to go into that situation where I had complete independence, and I was in this city. I began to make some decisions. I'm smoking, I'm drinking, I'm partying. I ended up leaving Maryland, transferring back to the University of Pittsburgh. But when I came back to Pittsburgh, none of my friends were in college. My friends were participating in another type of lifestyle. Me and my friends, we had our own apartment, our place became the hangout. In my mind, I'm like, "Well, I don't need college. I'm going to be a big rapper anyway. I'm just gonna smoke and drink and get my party on, 'cause I'ma be a rapper." But I had no concept of the music business. I thought one day Russell Simmons was just going to come knocking on my door, Diddy was gonna come knocking on my door, like, "Hey man! I heard there's this dope rapper here in Pittsburgh!" I had no concept of how I was going to take my music to another level. I began to participate in things that I shouldn't have. I'm going to be honest. I just happened to be the lucky one, that when things went down, I just didn't get caught. There was times when I should have been caught. There were times where I got pulled over with stuff in the car. But by the grace of God. That's the only thing that separated me from the individual that's mass incarcerated right now. Or, when the shots went over, thank God they missed me. That's the only thing, the grace of God.

I basically reached a point, when you're 20 and you're still in that same room that you grew up in, and you're looking at the little Michael Jordan poster that you had in your pad when you was in eighth grade, there's a point when that's not cool anymore, know what I'm saying? I had to begin to find out what I wanted to do. For me, one of the things that school did for me, and I'm not trying to disrespect school, school made me not like to read. This is personal, because school made me read stuff that I had no interest in. "I don't care about these people, or these subjects." What I had to do was go find books and subjects and things that I cared about. I would go to the house, we had some older dudes, who were mentoring us, mostly negative things, but they had a lot of books! They always had books about our history, and I would always ask to borrow they books, and they'd always tell me, "No, you ain't borrowing my books." It made me think, "Man, you know, I'm gonna get me some books." Reading about myself, my culture, my history, it revolutionized my life. It caused me to really begin to say, like, "Okay." One, it caused me to put the weed down, for me. Because if you smoke all day, you won't have any production, like, "What am I gon do?" It forced me to really begin to take steps in order to secure my life, to secure my future. It made me concerned about the world outside of me and my environment.

FREE THE JENA 6

For example, and I'm gonna backtrack a bit. Myspace is what launched my whole career. This is how far back I go. I did a song, have you ever heard of the Jena 6? In 2006 there was a situation. Have you ever heard the term, "the wrong side of the tracks," like, "You're from the wrong side of the tracks"? This is how they divide communities. In the South, the way they divided White and Black communities was by the train tracks. So Jena, Louisiana, was a place in 2006 that was still like in 1950. The community was divided. So the train track was here, on one side was the rich White community, on the other side was the poor Black community. At their high school they had a tree. The rule was, only the White students could sit under this tree. This was 2006. So a Black student sat under the tree, and the next day White students hung nooses from the tree. It caused all this racial tension in the town and in the school. Because of the racial tension, they had a meeting at this school. At this meeting, they gathered all the Black students, and they had the district attorney for that town come in and tell the Black students, "If you all don't chill out, I can end your life with a stroke of a pen." Just the Black students. The White students have a party off campus, a Black student goes to the party and he gets jumped and beaten up. The next day in school, him and his boys see one of the dudes that jumped him, and what they do? Jump him! Instead of getting suspended, they get charged with attempted murder. Even though the guy didn't spend one night in jail, and one of the guys got 10 years in prison for a fight. Just imagine, you fight in high school and instead of getting suspended, or in-school or whatever you get, you get 10 years. He was one of the best football players in Louisiana, had a college scholarship to LSU. His life was over. We found out about this through Myspace. This was when YouTube first started poppin. We find out about YouTube. So I was like, "I'm going to make a song about this."

I put it on my Myspace page, and I sent it to a website called Allhiphop.com. At that time, Allhiphop was like the biggest site. I'm at work, my man called me like, "Yo, your song is on the cover of Allhiphop.com." I left my job, because they block them websites at schools, I couldn't get on the website. I was like, man I'm happy. Somebody sent it to a radio host named Michael Basin. At the time, Michael Basin had a syndicated radio show that aired on all the major Black cities all across the country. I didn't know who he was when he called me. They called me, they was like, "We gon put your song on the radio." They said my name, Jasiri X, and I started getting calls from people all over the country. People were like, "Michael Basin, he's like Oprah on the radio." Then I got scared, like damn. Then he played my song, and it started getting played all across the country, and I was *gone*. I didn't even have a video at this time. All I knew was I wanted to make more songs like this. This next one is closer to home, called "America's Most Livable City."

"CLIPSBURGH, PISTOLVANIA": AMERICA'S MOST LIVABLE CITY

Pittsburgh, Pennsylvania—Steelers and Wiz Khalifa—and that's pretty much all it is right now. Pittsburgh is America's "most livable city." According to *Forbes* magazine, this is the place, of all cities in the United States, this is the most livable place. This is the place where you'll be the most happy, which has the best living you can find, Pittsburgh. When you come to Pittsburgh, if you ever come, when you get off in the airport it says, "America's most livable city." The same year Pittsburgh was named the most livable city, according to the United States Census, we were told we had the poorest Black community in the country. Poorer than Detroit, poorer than Cleveland, poorer than Chicago. The poorest inner-city Black people live in Pittsburgh. "Most livable" for who? That's the glaring contradiction of being Black in America.

> Welcome to America's Most Livable City
> Please ignore the invisibles with me
> See Pittsburgh rebuilt its economy
> but we still lead the Nation in Black poverty
>
> Welcome to America's Most Livable City
> Just ignore the invisibles with me
> And state ya business,
> 'cause here the place ya living
> depends on ya race and privilege
>
> They call it Clipsburgh, Pistolvania
> Where block dictators will launch missiles to bang ya
> Where hot metal come whistling out the chamber
> To maim ya twisting you like Wrestlemania
> And what's crazier the bishop won't pray for ya
> Ya families so poor they can't even afford a crate for ya
> And in them skyscrapers bruh they can't wait for us
> to move out the hood so they can take it lace it up
> Transit cuts a brother can't even take the bus
> This is the ugly truth no need to make it up
> Then some magazine comes along and places us
> As most livable in the USA, what?
> Say what? Guess they didn't survey us
> 'Cause life is cut shorter than razors where they raise us

Judges are racists and quick to hang us
And police taze us until we never wake up

Welcome to America's Most Livable City
Please ignore the invisibles with me
See Pittsburgh rebuilt its economy
But we still lead the Nation in Black poverty

Welcome to America's Most Livable City
Just ignore the invisibles with me
And state ya business
'cause here the place ya living
depends on ya race and privilege

And downtown it's a bunch of new buildings
Glass and steel cathedrals the cost a few million
They make billions to treat a dude's illness
With medicine and pharmaceuticals so who's dealing
But the schools are failing screw children
Just make sure the office has a see-through ceiling
Pitt University and CMU killin
Classes cost thousands I don't see you fill 'em
How we gonna get a job in biotechnology
if all we ever learn is survival psychology
And why we so poor if y'all revived the economy
but we don't get nothing besides an apology
Tear down the projects and put up a Target
then build new homes so they can stimulate the market
But move us out the neighborhood so we can never harvest
The only thing we guaranteed in Pittsburgh is charges

Welcome to America's Most Livable City
Please ignore the invisibles with me
See Pittsburgh rebuilt its economy
but we still lead the Nation in Black poverty

Welcome to America's Most Livable City
Just ignore the invisibles with me
And state ya business, 'cause here the place ya living
depends on ya race and privilege

The neighborhood in the music video for "America's Most Livable City" is called Formosa Way. In the music video you see row houses, and they're all abandoned. When people don't have a place to live, they go and still live in these abandoned buildings. Formosa Way is in an area of Pittsburgh called Homewood. A lot of people in Pittsburgh consider Homewood as the worst, the most dangerous, area in Pittsburgh. In my lyrics I say, "Tear down the projects and put up a Target," that's actually my neighborhood. My neighborhood was called East Liberty. East Liberty had housing projects. They tore down the housing projects, they put up a Target, put up a Whole Foods, they put up a Trader Joe's, and the whole neighborhood began to change economically. We got pushed out, and then they made all these great changes to the neighborhood to make the neighborhood better. Now when we come in there, we get racially profiled and harassed. That's gentrification. All of that was and is still going on in Pittsburgh.

1HOOD: OUR POWER IS IN OUR UNITY

So, we started an activist organization in Pittsburgh called 1Hood. Our program came out of a study they did in Pittsburgh about how the media covers Black men. They studied all the local media in Pittsburgh, newspaper and television. They said 90% of the time when they talk about Black men in Pittsburgh in the media, what do y'all think the subject is? Students respond: "Gangs, murder, crime." Basically crime, drugs, murder, right? The other percentage is what you think? Sports. We either commit crimes or we catch a football in Pittsburgh, right? When it comes to quality of life stories of Black men in Pittsburgh, it was less than 3%. So we basically said, look, our generation we really ain't lookin at the news. You all look at the newspaper? Do you all watch the local news? Unless you're on it, or know someone on it, you don't watch the local news. Where do I get the news? I wake up, I turn on my computer, or I pick up my phone, "What's happening on Facebook? What's happening on Twitter? What's happening on the ground?" That's how I find out what's going on, not necessarily the TV. So we said, look, we want to teach Black youth in Pittsburgh how to analyze media, create their own media, and tell their own story. Because the telling of your story is powerful. Oftentimes if you don't tell your story, somebody else will come in and tell your story and they'll do a terrible job of it. Oftentimes if it's someone White they'll center themselves in your story. You'll find your story be about them and not you, about how they came into the hood and saved you.

At the time we started 1Hood, Pennsylvania led the nation in what they call "Black on Black crime," us killing one another. Our thing was that, our power is in our unity. Why are we fighting one another, and killing one another, when we're not the cause of the problem, you know what I'm saying? You hustlin on the other corner isn't the reason why I can't find affordable housing. Whatever neighborhood we live in, we all suffer from poverty. We all suffer from schools that are not as good as other communities. We all suffer from lack of affordable housing. We all suffer from police brutality. We're all dealing with these same issues, but we take our frustrations out on one another. We felt like the real solution was for us to come together in unity, and deal with the root causes of our problems. And then, in our unity, we can have more power to really get the things that we want to get done, you know what I'm saying?

Before I became a full-time artist, I was in the high schools. I worked as what they called the teen parent advocate. I basically dealt with teen fathers. I had to wear a suit when I worked in the high school. Because if I didn't, they would think I was a student. I would be in the bathroom, and teachers would come in like, "What are you doing in here? You 'poseta be in class!" And I'd be like, "I work here, what are you talkin bout?" And teachers would see me and be like, "Man, can you take some of these bad students and kind of talk to them?" And they would mostly be young Black men, and so, because I rap, I was like, "Yo, like we're gonna do a Hip Hop club!" So I started Hip Hop clubs in the schools, and I had a student in one of my Hip Hop clubs at a school—Taylor Allderdice—and that student's name was . . . Wiz Khalifa.

WIZ KHALIFA: CONNECTING ARTISTS TO COMMUNITIES

I met Wiz when he was 16 years old. And what was different about him as a student was—this was before he smoked weed, so at this time, he wasn't smoking or drinking. He had no tattoos. No Amber Rose. Wiz was a straight A student. That's the reason he got the Wiz part of his name. He was more mature. When I met him it was like I was talking to somebody my age, I wasn't talking to someone young. He had a level of maturity and intellect that was very different. Like I said, he got straight As. You know,

Figure 6.1 Jasiri X with youth of East Palo Alto, California. Photo by Abdul Alim.

you see him laughing now [*imitates Wiz's laugh*], dude is smart, you know I'm saying? He knew at 16 that he wanted to be a professional rap artist. Like he was very clear, like this is what I want to do. Not as a hobby, like, "Ah we chillin and I'm smokin on somethin, I'ma kick a little freestyle, I'ma snap this freestyle real quick," not like that. Like he was, "I'm studying the craft, this is what I'm gonna do."

So the way he got discovered in Pittsburgh was that, he had a job, and he was using his money to go to a studio in Pittsburgh called ID Labs. The guy who ran the studio was a dude named E. Dan. If you ever see ID Lab's Production, it's these dudes from Pittsburgh. Basically, E. Dan called his man, and he was like, "I got a guy in the studio named Wiz Khalifa." The dude he called was named Benjy Grinberg. Benjy at the time was working with Def Jam and L. A. Reid. He came to Pittsburgh, saw Wiz, and they started Rostrum Records around Wiz Khalifa, know I'm saying? I literally watched this dude go from a high school student to an international superstar, to where like he's performing at the Grammy's. I watched how they do it. I saw when Wiz got signed to Warner Brothers Records, and then dropped from Warner Brothers Records. And then people was clownin him, "You got dropped and dah-da-dah." And then I saw him put out an independent album, *Deal or No Deal*, which launched Taylor Gang Entertainment. Then I watched him do *Kush and Orange Juice* and the rest was history.

I know his whole family. The Khalifa part of his name comes from the fact that Wiz's grandfather was in the Nation of Islam. Wiz's grandfather is a well-respected community activist in Pittsburgh. His Mom is really involved in the community in a strong way. That's another part of Wiz—even though he don't really rap about it—that he has in him. He was just back in Pittsburgh, went to all the high schools, came and gave away five thousand backpacks to the students and stuff. My students were there. I've had some opportunities to kick it with him, but you know I just haven't taken him up on it. But anything we've ever asked Wiz or Rostrum to do for 1Hood, they've done. And this is part of the reason we started 1Hood, because I seen it was possible. And what I wanted to do was help other artists. I felt like if we could connect the artist into the community like Wiz is, then we can have these artists who will want to come back to Pittsburgh and begin to really help other artists. I saw Mac Miller do it too, but it was kind of a different way, 'cause Mac Miller went to that same school.

JORDAN MILES: TELLING OUR OWN STORIES

I feel everybody is an artist. You might not feel like you are, but everyone is an artist. I say that because you all have a unique story. You all have a story of where you came from that is unique to you. To me one of the most powerful things that you can do is to tell your story, particularly if you are one of the "Others" or the minority because people will look at you and assume they know who you are or what you're about, know I'm saying? In the "America's Most Livable City" video, did you all see the dude who had a neck brace on, and he looked all crazy? That was a guy in Pittsburgh named Jordan Miles. So, we told the story of Jordan Miles—it ended up being a national story.

> Now here's a little story I got to tell
> about 3 officers you don't know so well
> It started way back last January

with officers Ewing, Sisak, and Saldutte
They ran into a boy named Jordan Miles,
a real good kid who for sure was mild
But he was found guilty before a trial
'cause he's a young Black man in the wrong part of town
Jordan is a kid that gets good grades,
not a thug braggin that he's hood-raised
He takes care of his grandmother cause she's older,
went to performance arts school and plays the viola
He never did a crime one day in his life
His favorite TV show is *CSI*
When he graduated he wanted to learn
how to catch a criminal like Lawrence Fishburne
Then one night like he always did
He made the short walk to his grandmother's crib
'cause grandma didn't like to be alone
by herself at night so Jordan stayed in her home
Now these 3 cops were undercover
so they could sneak up and snatch a brother
catch you in the act pull the gat and bust ya
throw you on the ground pat you down and cuff ya
rollin through the hood looking for they next victim
like every other night so they know how to pick 'em
They saw Jordan walking they lips they start lickin
"There's a young Black male hell yeah let's get him"
They jumped out the car as the tires spun,
yelling "Where's the drugs, where's the money and guns?"
Jordan stops walking, his face was stunned
He thinks he's being robbed so he starts to run
He didn't get far before the cops catch 'em
Now they got 'em they gotta teach him a lesson
Because he ran that means they gotta wreck him
They slam him on his neck and start to chin check him
Blow after blow till his face was swollen
He thinks their gonna stop but they just keep going
He calls on God whispering the Lord's prayer
They grab him by his locks just to rip out his hair
Beaten and bloody they finally handcuff him
but then when they search they don't find nothing
Their minds was boggled then lies start to follow
Let's say inside his coat he had a Mountain Dew bottle
and we thought that it was a weapon

we had to hit him cause he resisted arrest and
Let's take him to jail and get him drug tested
because if he's high we won't look so reckless
Now Jordan's Mom is really scared
'cause she called his grandma's and he isn't there
What, he's in jail? She headed there on the double
It must be a mistake Jordan's never been in trouble
Outside the jail and she saw this man
who was beat so bad it made her think "Damn"
It looked like he was hit by a bomb
then he walked right up to her and said "Mom"
She was shocked she couldn't believe
that disfigured face was her son indeed
She fell to her knees she couldn't even breathe
Her son has been a victim of police brutality
She rushed Jordan to emergency
And every time she looks at him it hurt to see
her son in a hospital bed in pain
Police took no blame and claim it's how they trained
Jordan got charged but when it went to court
We found out the police falsified their report
They said a neighbor called the cops crying
She got up on the stand and said "Stop lying"
Now the whole community wants justice for Jordan
And the cops charged for the crimes they reported
Call the DA and tell him to press charges
we demand justice and we just gettin started

So we actually told this story. This is one of the first videos that we actually had an action at the end of the video. Jordan was basically going to his grandmother's house like he did every night. He's from a community, Homewood, that I was talking about. They have what they call the "jumpout boys." The jumpout boys are undercover cops. They jump out and they want to catch you dirty. They want to catch you with drugs and guns. In this neighborhood, Homewood, if I'm walking through Homewood dressed like this they'll pull up to you and be like, "Lift your shirt up." So I then have to show that I do not have a gun on my waist, know I'm saying? Or they might pull up and jump out and tell you to get up against the wall, frisk you, make sure you don't have anything. Jordan was an honor roll student, he played the viola, he not in the street. So when they jump out on him, and they're like, "Where's the drugs and guns?", he actually thought he was being robbed, because they were undercover. They didn't have police uniforms on, didn't identify themselves as officers. So he starts to run, and slipped on the ice. And the unwritten rule with cops is if you run and they catch you, they gon give you somethin to run from. So they beat the dude, like that, you know what I'm saying?

They beat him to the point that his mother went to pick him up, she didn't know who he was. She was like, "This dude look like the elephant man, who's this?" When he said, "Mom," and she looked, "Oh my God that's my son." And that's when she took those pictures, and then the story came out. The police said he had a Mountain Dew bottle in his coat, and they thought that Mountain Dew bottle was a gun, and that when they jumped out to grab him, that he resisted arrest, which is crazy. The dude is 5 feet 6 inches, 125 pounds. One of the officers that beat him actually trains other officers in martial arts tactics—he's like a black belt martial artist. So they have to try to justify themselves. So then they said a neighbor called the cops and said she saw someone suspicious in her yard. They pulled that neighbor, called her to the stand, and she was like, "I didn't call y'all! I know him, I see him at his grandmother's house all the time."

Even though that happened, the cops were not found guilty. In fact, the cops got awards from the city after they beat Jordan Miles. We were trying to pressure the district attorney who had the power to charge the cops. We put this video out. We had people calling all the way from Japan. We shut the number down, people were calling, "We want these officers charged." It didn't lead to them being charged, but it led to a civil suit. He actually ended up getting money from the city. Of course, when he went to the civil trial, the city of Pittsburgh said the arrest was illegal, but that there was no police brutality, yeah. So this is why I do the activism I do, because I don't want to wait until it's me, or someone in my family. I want to try to intervene and stop the stuff before it gets to me.

BLACK LIBERATION THEOLOGY

My most recent album is *Black Liberation Theology*. I put it out for free. I use a lot of samples, I can't clear them, it's a whole conversation about selling music online. If you want to get into the business side of it, we could get into that side of it. Black Liberation Theology is an idea of the Black Liberation Movement combined with Christianity. I wanted the album cover to look like a Bible, but then I wanted the words Black Liberation Theology to look like a gun. I was going to do something different, but a friend of mine was like, you should create a cover that when you see it, you want to listen to it. The album is a response to what's happening right now around police violence with Black and Brown folks. When do we have a right to fight back? My album is dealing with questions like that.

One of the things that also helped me is I'll jack another artist's beat who's more well known. I use a lot of Drake beats now. You see I don't look like Drake—all light-skinned people don't look alike!—my eyebrows are regular size. [*Laughter*] I'm a fan of Drake! I used Drake's "Worst Behavior" because there was a group called the Dream Defenders that were using that "Never Loved Us" part. They were saying America never loved us, and they were using it around the question of police violence. So I did a remix of Drake's "Worst Behavior" and used that "Never Loved Us" part. In this song, "#NeverLovedUs," I talk about another incident of police brutality in Pittsburgh where a young man named Leon Ford was shot five times by the police and paralyzed.

> Every time I ride around hearing siren sounds
> Some crooked-ass cop might fire rounds
> And the shot might lie me down
> Somebody got to tell my mom they paralyzed her child
> We need Malcolm with the M-1 and then some
> Booby Seale with the shotty filled get some
> Man we need Farrakhan security
> For every Black child that made it outta puberty
> Black leather jacket black shotgun Huey P
> Bet you'll see them bullets fly nigga duty free
> Before I'm crucified like a cross on ya jewelry
> By crooked police in the hood on a shooting spree
> Ask Leon almost had to read his eulogy
> Shot five times by the cops so brutally
> In a wheelchair and still gettin all the scrutiny
> Even though America truly be actin on her worse behavior
>
> Did we pay more attention to Michael's new Jordans
> than the outcome of Michael shooting Jordan?

For protection do I need a rifle when performing?
If we start turnin up will they try to murder us?
Dangerous Black kids we ain't welcome in suburbia
All we want is justice and equality the nerve of us
Still deny services criminalized by journalists
Turn the other cheek and get killed by Christian conservatives
Mass incarcerated in prison is where they herding us
Callin us thugs you see 'em try and Richard Sherman us
They act like ain't nothing worse than us
But be the first to bust last to get searched and cuffed
We ain't forget you used to purchase us
Left us swinging from the trees or you burn us up
Now we organized and ready to stick the merchants up
So give them purses up
For you see us on our worst behavior

Andy Lopez was only 13
7 shots from a sheriff left him in the dirt leaned
To his mother and his father had to be the worst scene
Do you know what hurt means?
When you see your child dead and his shirt seems
liquid from the thickness of the blood still squirting
Dear God can you answer me 1st thing?
Can you wipe the earth clean
of all the hatred in this world and let the church sing?
Amen turn to today's hymn whose gonna save them?
'Cause in North Carolina Jesus they slayed him
In the back of a cop car cuffed they sprayed him
Then told us that he killed his self like Satan
So when you see me on MSNBC
Or on Huff Post Live and I bust 45s
Until I see America shut both eyes
Call the hearse to claim her on my worst behavior

DO WE NEED TO START A RIOT?

The last video I want to show y'all is, "Do We Need to Start a Riot?" A lot of times they'll call me "conscious" because they don't want the hood to listen to what I have to say. So I have to try to break through that label. The first song I was able to do that with was this song in 2012, "Do We

Need to Start a Riot?" It's just funny I do that song in 2012, when all the stuff start jumpin off in Ferguson, and Anonymous and all these people start tweeting out the video. So I use—remember 2Chainz had that song "Riot"?—I use that song. The first part of the video we filmed at this big rally we did in New York City. The second part we went to LA because it was the 20th anniversary of the LA riots, so we went to LA where the riots started and we filmed the second part of the video. LA is really like Little Mexico. I was with my man Javier Gonzalez, so I be in LA blending in, trying to blend in, you know what I'm saying?

There was a famous video that came out of the riots where a White dude was driving a truck through an area where the riots happened, and they ran on the truck. The man in this video is the one who pulled the guy out of the truck, and they ended up beating him up. So he ended up doing time, and what was interesting about him—his name was Henry Lewis Watson—he didn't apologize. Like they were trying to get him to apologize, but he was like, "No," and he went and did his time. When we were shooting the video where it happened, it's maybe about 10 of us, he rolled up on us. He's still the OG of that neighborhood and was like, "What y'all doin in my hood?" And Javier knew him, and he told me to tell him what the video is about, and I'm like, "It's a video about the 20th Anniversary of the LA rebellion." And the guy is like, "The LA riots happened because of a dude who got beat up by the police called Rodney King." Rodney King's funeral was that day, and I was like, "This is a video we're doing, it's called 'Do We Need to Start a Riot?'" Here's the video:

> Ramarly Graham, they shot him
> Alan Blueford, they shot him
> Ken Chamberlain, they shot him
> Kendric McDade, they shot him
>
> Darius Simmons, they shot him
> Bo Morrison, they shot him
> Wendell Allen, they shot him
> Justin Sipp, they shot him
>
> Scared rappers be quiet
> Scared preachers be quiet
> Scared leaders be quiet
> You're in the presence of warriors

Scared rappers be quiet
Scared preachers be quiet
Scared leaders be quiet
You're in a warrior's face boy
You can't call this a race war
'Cause we the only ones they got hate for
That get shot down when the gauge roar
But we always willin to take more
From Emmett Till on that lake floor
To Trayvon, Rekia Boyd
Mumia, Troy it's we destroyed
Since I'm public enemy I bring the noise

Marissa Alexander, they locked her
Jasmine Thar, they shot her
They keep trying to kill us
But they never get indicted
Our people crying loud
But them scared rappers stay quiet
And if we don't get justice do we need to start a riot?

In 92 those riots grew
Peace treaty, red unites with blue
In LA the Crips and the Pirus
Put aside the feud and started riding true
Said the NOI was behind it too
Then police came in to divide the crews
Steal a homie's car then drive it through
Another gang's hood then fire the tool
Our unity is our biggest weapon
When I ask this question you feeling threatened
But imagine your child being killed for less and
It's 45 days for the killer arrested
Mad at me 'cause I'm givin a message
But if we can be killed by Zimmermans
And they can get off 'cause of privilege
Then are we really citizens
Get beaten to death if you a immigrant
Go back to your country is the sentiment
They call us monkeys say we ignorant
So we get killed they don't give a shit
Now what would you do if you were living this?
To protect your kids from this?

If ya child got killed would you live with it?
Would you slit you wrists would you get the fifth?
Would you care about ya job or ya benefits?
If they said they murderer was innocent
No trial no jury no sentencing
And you saw how foul this system is
but they keep tellin us to be patient
They keep tell us to keep waitin
They keep tellin us that we hatin
And when we're killed 'cause we Black that we racist

Howard Morgan, they shot 'em
Then for 40 years they locked him
They keep trying to kill us
but they never get indicted
Our people crying loud
But them scared rappers stay quiet
And if we don't get justice, do we need to start a riot?

EXPANDING 1HOOD

At one point in time 1Hood was just guys, just brothers. But then this young lady, she came to 1Hood, and was like, "I'm gonna be a part of 1Hood." And we're not gonna kick you out, know what I'm saying? So we went to the people that support us, and was like, "Can we have young women as well?" They was like, "Cool." So now we have singers, we have music producers, we have spoken word artists, we have Hip Hop artists. We have a studio that our artists can use, that's free to use. We have video equipment that they can use to make their music videos if they want to. The idea is also to show them how to use social media to get their stuff out, because I got out on Myspace, Facebook, Twitter, Instagram—that's how I got my music out. For me, the most helpful in my career of all social media has by far been Twitter. Like for me, I've met the most people on Twitter. That's how I met Lupe, that's how I met Talib. All of these people I met first on Twitter. For me, Twitter has been the most productive, but I'm gonna get a Snapchat.

One of the other things we do for our students is we help them put their projects out. We also help them get physical CDs if they want to perform and sell their CDs. One of the most recent students is a sista named Black Raw Medusa. She released a project called *Still Waters Run Deep*. Another student just graduated this year, from a high school in Pittsburgh, his name is Apollo, his project was called *Ill Lucidity*, which was interesting. His project, he starts off asleep, and then the last song was "Lucidity," and he wakes up. So he was on some real ethereal type of things. Tyhir Frost graduated as well this year, he did a project called *IDL (I Depend on Life)*. We are really proud of all of them and will continue to support their art, activism, and media creation. We need to tell our stories.

NOTE

1. I'd like to acknowledge Andy Robinson's "Advanced Drama" class at the East Palo Alto Academy High School in East Palo Alto, California, where I delivered the first version of this talk on November 20, 2015. I am grateful to Casey Wong for the invitation. I spent hours with the students that afternoon, building with them, and making connections between what's happening in Pittsburgh, East Palo Alto, and hoods across America. One Love. 1Hood.

7 "Protection from Police Who Hinder Respiratory Airways"

HIP HOP THEATRE AND ACTIVISM WITH KUUMBA LYNX IN CHICAGO

Jacinda Bullie, Jaquanda Saulter-Villegas, and Leyda "Lady Sol" Garcia

CASEY PHILIP WONG: What's good, how's everyone doing? I have the honor of introducing three legendary women, Jacinda Bullie, Jaquanda Villegas, and Lady Sol! They're the founders of a truly community-rooted Hip Hop organization out of Chicago, Kuumba Lynx.[1] Kuumba Lynx utilizes Hip Hop arts and culture as a vehicle for creative expression, cross-cultural dialogue, community building, and preserving what they describe as "the essence of what Hip Hop means to marginalized communities."[2] Kuumba Lynx offers us a rare perspective on Hip Hop knowledges, pedagogies, and futures as they've been thriving and engaging in "liberation through artistic expression" for over 20 years.

Kuumba Lynx primarily facilitates programming in Uptown, Englewood, Little Village, and Austin, but program participants represent over 27 Chicago communities. From Auburn Gresham to Humboldt Park, and from South Shore to Rogers Park, Kuumba Lynx serves youth with experiences and perspectives from across the world. As of 2020, Kuumba Lynx's program participants are 55% Black or African American, 30% Latinx, 1% Native, 5% White, and 9% identifying as "Other." Kuumba Lynx serves youth ranging in age from 8 to 18 years old (70%), but also serves transitional age youth from 19 to 25 years old (30%).

Let's give them a big welcome! [*Applause*] They're going to have us begin with a cipher outside, do some breathing exercises, and then have us return to introduce the groundbreaking work they've been accomplishing. Let me pass the mic!

LEYDA "LADY SOL" GARCIA: Thanks, Casey! Even though we're going to be presenting a lot today on our education and organizing work from the perspective of spoken word, we also believe in the educational and liberatory power of movement and dance. I've been a street dancer since I was a young person myself, and eventually became a professional street dance educator, creative director. When I'm going into spaces, I believe it's important to share movement. I like for our participants to articulate differently. Why? Because when they get out into this world, everything is not "Yah!!" [*Laughter*] The energy doesn't look that way, doesn't feel that way. We need to learn how to shift, and contract, and release. We need to learn how to breathe to deal with that trauma. We're creating pieces to rewrite the narrative of our traumas, and so when you see some of our performance pieces, you'll be like, "Oh, I wasn't expecting that from them." They're supposed to be spoken word, right? [*Laughter*] That's all I have to say, let's move! (Kuumba Lynx leads the group in a dance cipher and then breathing exercises).[3]

JACINDA BULLIE: We feel good? We feel rejuvenated? Alright, now a little about us, we started as a performance ensemble, with the three of us—me, Jaquanda, and Lady Sol—so Hip Hop theater is, and continues to be, central to the work that we do. But our work doesn't live on this traditional stage. Our work really lives in the places that we inhabit, beyond just the theater, the stage, and moves toward enacting and thinking about how you reclaim space. We kind of root our work in the Mississippi Freedom Schools[4] and the idea of, "Who better to teach and empower and liberate folks in terms of literacy than those who look like us and come from where we're from?" For us, the whole peer exchange and peer support piece is huge, this is truly a community-based organization.

JAQUANDA SAULTER-VILLEGAS: When you enter this space, the community that we have here is very supportive of who you are and where

Figure 7.1 (Top) Jaquanda teaching at the 5th Element Symposium. Photo by John Liau.

Figure 7.2 (Bottom) Lady Sol speaking to the audience at the 5th Element Symposium. Photo by John Liau.

you're from. It's like family. We let our young people know that our conscience has to be open to the idea that life extends from people who have been here before you, to people who will come after you. That it's not just a single or individual journey, it's a community journey.

ACTIVISM AND THE CITYWIDE MOVEMENT IN CHICAGO

BULLIE: Our youth don't just come in every Monday, Wednesday, Friday, and clock in hours, you know? They don't just come in to put in "learning time." As you get further into it, our youth start to realize that we're about creating a lifestyle change for everybody, and it's a way of changing yourself and the world. Our youth-on-youth component to this work gives young people the opportunity to feel valued. They get a chance to talk about injustices that are happening in our communities, discuss how we have the ability to change those things, and that's what "connected learning" is about. It's really for young people to walk out of these spaces feeling confident in who they are in the world, and feeling confident that they can and do make valuable contributions.

We see Kuumba Lynx as part of a citywide movement in Chicago, and it still is. In fact, right now, today, our mayor wants to spend 95 million dollars on a new police academy. When we talk about investing in shit like that, like that's the disruptive work we're interested in doing, and we're real vocal about that. We're really pushing for divestment, defunding the police, and thinking about what it means to reinvest in other things.

One of the ways that we're doing that is something we call a train takeover. A train takeover is a big piece of how we get that word out. It's not a traditional way of organizing folks, but it's mad powerful when 30 young folks get on a train for two hours, go car, by car, by car with a very clear message. And it's honing this artistic excellence that none of us are short on. We're not short on emcees and creativity, right? We have an abundance of that, so that's just one example of how we use that creativity, that wealth of what we have, that capital that we have to really impact, critically think about, and take action with our bodies and artistic works that we have created. And as one of our strategies, train takeovers been mad popular in Chicago in the last like year and a half. It's a really dope tactic that we're proud to be a part of.

And before we take part in these actions, we facilitate space with young folks where we engage in real-time dialogue about issues that are impacting them. And when young folks have this space, magical things happen, right? As the adults, we do not ever trick ourselves in thinking that as facilitators of the space, we know it all. We also partner and organize with folks that do work more deeply in areas we're working, or have a different lens, a lens that sees partners in allyship with us. So we don't focus on balancing out or compromising our perspectives or lens. Like we're real clear about what our lens is, and we just try to galvanize folks that support that lens and build with them.

MANDATING CURRICULUM ON POLICE TORTURE IN CHICAGO PUBLIC SCHOOLS

One of our partners is a group of folks called Project NIA (i.e., "nia" meaning "with purpose" in Swahili), who we've been working alongside for a decade in different capacities. But one of the things they were working on was an ordinance in Chicago to condemn and collectively heal from the violence committed by a police superintendent, a man named Jon Burge, who was charged with the torture of innocent folks.[5] Innocent folks who had been spending decades in prison. So we partnered with them on this ordinance, and Chicago became the first city to propose an ordinance like this—what came to be called "the reparations ordinance." And it was specifically for folks who had been survivors of Jon Burge's torture, and we really invested in this work. Our young folks had an opportunity to work side by side with folks in the community to get this ordinance passed. And it passed. Like straight up, survivors of police torture and abuse got to hold the city accountable. And I just want to name like a few of the things that folks received. The children of survivors will have free college, and the families will have free therapy and mental health services, right? They also got some compensation, which don't mean shit, like 5.5 million dollars: divided up amongst the survivors. That's like a new TV for each person, right? Like let's be real.

But the formal apology and mandated curriculum for public schools in Chicago, you know, we talk about reparations and we talk a lot about reimagining a more just world, right? A lot of us have that rhetoric in some way or another, but what does that really mean? Because we often talk about this pain narrative, but we don't talk about the joy narrative, about what we accomplish through our coming together, through community. We don't talk about defining what our joy looks like in this work or what our reimagined world will be composed of. And this is that, in real time, young people witnessing what a reimagined world looks like, and can look like as we organize. How we heal. How we move forward. How it's important to be honest with the shit that we've done, so that we can move forward. And the one piece that I want to elaborate on real quick is that education piece, the curriculum on police torture in Chicago public schools, you know there's always challenges with this shit, right?

So this fall, that curriculum was ready to go for public schools in Chicago. And it was about to roll out. Within our communities there are the children of police, and their parents went wild. They're fighting it right now. They're saying it's wrong. They don't want the curriculum in public schools, even though we have an ordinance that's like, yo, this *has* to happen in every Chicago public school. These people are challenging it and shutting it down and teachers are crumbling and saying, "Well, I will just take a section of it out. Do I have to teach the entire piece?" Like, you know, you know how this happens. We fragment shit and then before long, we miss the point of it. Our children miss that crucial education that we fought for. And so as a liberator, as an educator, as someone who is facilitating a learning space, what do you do? Like, folks fought hard to have your back and now they're backing out.

But with that said, because of these pushbacks, we have to celebrate our wins. Our young folks were a part of that journey towards getting that ordinance passed. They met with the survivors when they got out. It shifted their lens, and I mean they are like true abolitionists now from this experience. And that is powerful. And this is an example of the Hip Hop spoken word piece that four of our young people created and performed:

> False confessions
> Felony arrest
> Arts repressed
> Ain't no rest in a race for voice
> They bring chain cuffs over here bigger than a monster

On our block, block, block, block
Trauma
Impact
Heavy
Interrogations from birds bursting of false confessions
$9,968,191 tax dollars spent on defending Jon Burge
Against claims
Of police torture
It's coming
First time I saw man burst into little boy
Was between wetback and PHD
My father rolls down his window like he is supposed to
The officer asked him to get out the car
Assuming his brown couldn't be without traffic
Drugs couldn't be without his Brown
Michael's
Melanin
Poster child for police pension
After hours of questioning and searching
My father reminded me of institutional genocide
The deliberate death
torture of a people
Bomb blast
Release of energy breaking our sanity whatever Black blood be
Bullying by boys in blue is bound to bruise
Every 28 hours they suspect, fire, seize, fire, search, fire, and criminalize
Reparations are owed to the 110 Black men
Badges are nothing but shooting stars
Fights with oxygen masks
Protection from police who hinder respiratory airways
Resist propelling nuclear poison
Resist learning division through obsidian balls before third grade
Resist 'cause we are punished for it anyway
We need this land to acknowledge us
And make amends
Ready, aim, fire, bomb, blast, hit
If you don't watch for civilians,
ISIS, Taliban, Al Qaeda, back at you

(*Singing together*)
They shot down a boy
They said he was a thief

Strange things have happened here
And stranger would it be
If we met at midnight
Murdered in the streets
Don't preach about terrorism when you keep it breathing . . .

SAULTER-VILLEGAS: As we support young people to write pieces like this, we challenge and push them to engage our literary communities, to embrace both written and oral traditions. In Chicago, there is a huge literary community, and in particular, we've been a part of the Louder Than a Bomb community since its inception. We believe in the work. And it's obvious that the work has a huge impact on our city.

SUSTAINABILITY AND LONGITUDINAL EXCELLENCE

BULLIE: So, related to impact, we've also got to talk about how we show up, and about the way we enter, exist, and exit community. When you have partners in this work, in this life and the next, you gon show up, right? I was talking to Lady Sol, we were talking about sustainability, and what we call longitudinal excellence. Because we are in this work, but what helps your work sustain itself?

For us, longitudinal excellence is really about encouraging ourselves in healthy ways, unpacking our own experiences. It's about better understanding what brings us to this Hip Hop pedagogy work, and knowing why it is important to sustain that work. And it's about what we've worked to do, you know, create an institution. We're building an institution as a collective of artists and activists and human beings that listen to our hearts, and that are invested in our life purpose in this physical existence.

We are developing an institution in the margins, that we're pushing to the center and out of the margins. So this work is happening in the margins, but by creating this institution, if you will, we aren't censoring ourselves, and remaining outside of the margins now. Like we aren't about censoring ourselves, or letting others censor us. We're about saying, "This is how we do it," unapologetically, accessing spaces that traditionally we have not been able to access. I mean, honestly Lady Sol mentioned to some of y'all before we got started today, like, we don't do this. We do not facilitate sessions on university campuses about what we do, about our practice. We read a lot of theory about what we do, but we've never been asked to share what we do, so you know we, we're thankful that you are here and open to listening. Hopefully this has given you a brief insight into our work. People tell us all the time, get out the factory and see what you do. Because people are writing about you constantly, in so many ways. But this is the application of that writing.

SAULTER-VILLEGAS: Speaking in real time on institutions, the margins, and that longitudinal excellence, we have to speak on that from our experience. What does it look like for an organization or institution to have longitudinal excellence that came about from, you know, three sistas? Three 19-year-olds, right? Yeah! [*Applause*] So, 21 years later it looks like us creating transitional leadership, developing what is needed to sustain this institution, our community, and this work.

Currently, Jacinda and I are moving out of operations and into another role in the organization and youth that came through our organization are taking over. So yeah give it up. [*Applause*] It looks like us debating with that new youth leadership about how we are going to organize our institution. We just had a very deep debate the other day about titles. Because now that they've received this title, they are loving it, which they should in their own right. Because you know they worked really hard, and earned this, right? But for us to have the opportunity to call ourself a director, like what does that mean? Like, what kind of power are you holding now, and how are you going to spread that power with new generations of youth, and not get in your ego, as a director? And there was a lot of pushback, misunderstandings, but we're generatively working through that, unpacking that. Like, the new leadership is asking us like, "Why do you think we have to structure our institution like this? Like isn't this holding us back? Like, why?" And we don't have to structure it in these ways, that's the beautiful thing. We can change all the rules, right?

And so that's what longitudinal excellence looks like. It looks like health and wellness, and how important that is to the people who work in our organization. So guess what that means for us? Every other Friday, you go be you. You go learn and love on you. You go heal. We're not going to come on Fridays. You're going to get paid for that. You are going to go and take care of yourself. It looks like, you know what, there are some dynamic artists in the world and we want them to come in and work with you as a staff. Not for students, we are not bringing them in for the students, we are bringing them in for you. Because you had art in your heart when you started this work. Why does it have to go, because you are working in an office? Continue to grow, for each other. That's a part of our practice, right?

How do we exist in these institutions? Do we have to re-create these institutions in the ways they have always existed? And I say, why not change to our new social conditions? Isn't that the work? Re-create that. Reimagine that and make it so it works for a new community. So it works within a new, not-for-profit industrial complex bullshit situation, right? [*Laughter*] We're gonna change it. So that's what we've been doing and why we're throwin up this pic of us [*picture of Jacinda, Jaquanda, and Lady Sol*], right now, because it really also does come back to our 19-year-old selves, and what was that fire in our hearts, right? What was that fire, what was that motivation, that intention, behind the work, and all that is really filling in these so-called gaps, y'all? Addressing how society fails us. And the fact that we have the power to do that, has always been there, and is amazing, and we need to hold onto that, and when needed, reignite all that. [*Applause*]

BULLIE: So thank you for being here with us. We'll open it up to a little Q&A if we have any questions. I will come around and give you the mic. Pass the mic.

QUESTION 1: Wow, you all are moving so much of the community! Do you guys get any assistance or support from governments, or like anybody within the system that supports you, or backs you up?

BULLIE: We know the game, so we apply for grants. It took us about 12 to 14 years to get funding, but it never dictated the work. And the reason I think we can sleep at night is because we have had mad conversations about who we take money from. Specifically, government money, we negotiate that all the time. And very recently we decided not to replicate the shit that's been failing us, but to dream it differently and finesse funds to do so. If that makes sense without me saying too much. So we can go to sleep at night. So we can have five people that can eat off of this work. Full-time people, they don't got health insurance yet, but they got that weekday off. They got a space and place that still honors their creative self. And they get a little money to eat, write, and to live. Because at the end of the day, survival is real, right?

QUESTION 2: Hey, so this is so inspiring. The young people we saw earlier in Kuumba Lynx videos seem to be totally bought into making art about like systems of oppression and social change. Do you run into a situation where some young people are like, "I am not trying to talk about that, I just want to do this other thing"? And I ask because our organization has that issue.

LADY SOL: I always think about what it means to be inclusive, what it means to allow your participants to engage, and to be heard. It was important to begin by asking y'all, like, "What are you listening to? What's your favorite song right now?" And you know, we integrate that and have that inform the approach to the work we're doing. How can our personal lives and how we're living help us think about the work differently? It really is about that ongoing dialogue, ongoing questioning. But also, to be real, you have to make it fun. They ain't gonna show up if the shit ain't fun, right? [*Laughter*] You have to find some fun, center the joy. You know, we celebrate each other. All the time.

BULLIE: It's that piece, like you know, acknowledging that we turn up, right? [*Laughter*] That we all have fun. It's important to have that brave space[6] to like go through that piece of you. But then to analyze and think about why that's a piece of you is also important. So, like carving that space, like we all have that 10 minutes of ratchetness in us, right? [*Laughter*] Or 10 seconds, maybe not 10 minutes, I don't know. [*Laughter*] But that's just the point, like it's in us all in some way or another, y'all know what I'm saying? It's in us, let's just acknowledge that we like to have fun, we like to know all of the pieces of us. But yes, we have to constantly question what moves us, all the time. Why is it moving us and what is it rooted in?

QUESTION 3: This is more like a thank you. So, I didn't get to partake in the outside festivities you facilitated before this session, but it looked really amazing. You came inside and I was a part of the whole breathing exercise, which was phenomenal, and I am going to try to say this without getting super emotional. But, as a Black woman, having that moment today gave me time to really reflect on something that was in me, in my whole entire core, that I was struggling with, that I actually got to let manifest today. That fear of allowing my daughter to grow up in a world that I've lived in, where I've been taught that six figures and corporate is the way to go. And I look around here at this elite institution that we're in right now, and this is what you strive for, for your children, and you lose sight of passion. As a young mother to her, I was never able to do anything that I was passionate about. So yes, I work this six-figure job, the way you're supposed to go, but you're not passionate about your job. You hate going there.

And then I look at women who have, for 21 years, done something that their heart has brought them to do for a community. And I think about how holding myself back from doing what I love to do is impacting my daughter, my beautiful daughter I have sitting right next to me. I want to let her know that the sky is the limit, and there's no boundaries set, and let her know that she can pursue being a singer. She wants to be a singer. I know we're taught to say, "No, that is not a job," and I am like, "Oh honey, that is beautiful, do what you want to do." I know so often that children do what we do, not as we say, and I am going to take the very same advice for myself. So I thank you ladies, because you had a PowerPoint slide up there that said, "Be bold," and I will take that with me when I decide if I am going back to my corporate job or not. I will be bold, and I will do what my heart leads me to do and also take care of my family. But I realize that I definitely need to be bold along the way, for me, my daughter, and the Black girls who look at us and see what is possible, and I thank you ladies for, for everything.

LADY SOL: Thank you so much! Aw, big up yourself.

BULLIE: Big up to everybody in the room.

SAULTER-VILLEGAS: Yes, big up. So, that's a good place for us to end. Let's close out with a call and response, repeat after me, everybody say: Peace.

Love. Respect. For everybody. We respect. We appreciate. We nurture. We give back. To mother earth. We give back. To our souls. We give back. To our community. So we may grow. [*Audience repeats after Saulter-Villegas*]

LADY SOL: Thanks y'all!

NOTES

1. *Kuumba* means creativity in Swahili. *Lynx*, in this case, has a dual meaning. First, to have youth find the courage of the lynx, who are small but known for their courageous roar—hence youth voice! And second, *lynx* meaning unity and connectedness to youth communities around the world, creating real community.

2. Shout out to Thomas Plank, a Stanford undergraduate researcher who played a crucial role in connecting, building, and learning with Jacinda Bullie, Jaquanda Saulter-Villegas, and Leyda "Lady Sol" Garcia about the incredible work of Kuumba Lynx.

3. We believe moving, breathing, and setting the vibe is necessary for effective Hip Hop pedagogy, and aimed to model this in our workshop. With this intention, we created and made use of the following playlist: (1) "Step Into A World" (KRS-One); (2) "Planet Rock" (Afrika Bambaataa); (3) "Skelewu" (Davido); (4) "Sauce It Up" (Lil Uzi Vert); (5) "Fight the Power" (Public Enemy); (6) "Bodak Yellow" (Cardi B); (7) "HUMBLE." (Kendrick Lamar); (8) "Give It Up Or Turn It Loose" (James Brown); and (9) "Lighters Up" (Lil' Kim).

4. This is a reference to Paulo Freire's notion of a "problem-posing" education. See Paulo Freire, *Pedagogy of the Oppressed, Fiftieth Anniversary Edition* (Bloomsbury, 2018).

5. From 1972 to 1991, Jon Burge is known to have sanctioned, and participated in, the torture and coercion of confessions from more than 120 people, predominantly Black, in Chicago. For more, see Laurence Ralph, *The Torture Letters: Reckoning with Police Violence* (University of Chicago Press, 2020).

6. Reflecting growing understandings among activists, educators, and intellectuals about the possibilities of "safe space," acknowledging limitations of the framing of "safety" in regard to how we learn, dialogue, and reach toward social justice amidst ongoing complicities with systems of oppression that we are often not able to find autonomy from, Kuumba Lynx invokes "brave space." Brave spaces center the courage to say what needs to be said in the interest of justice, while being mindful of our relations, and how we exist together. See more in Brian Arao and Kristi Clemens, "From Safe Spaces to Brave Spaces: A New Way to Frame Dialogue around Diversity and Social Justice," in *The Art of Effective Facilitation: Reflections from Social Justice Educators*, ed. Lisa M. Landreman, 135–50 (Stylus, 2013).

8 Ripples of Hope and Healing

SUSTAINING COMMUNITY BY CREATING A SOCIAL JUSTICE ARTS ECOSYSTEM

Sonya Clark-Herrera, with Measha Ferguson Smith, hodari blue fka Adorie Howard, Reagan Ross, and Casey Philip Wong

JEFF CHANG: We have our friends from the Mural Music & Arts Project (MMAP) in East Palo Alto with us. One of the themes of the 5th Element has been about recognizing and respecting multiple literacies and multiple knowledges. And this basic idea has led us in the direction of thinking about pedagogies that are critical, culturally relevant, and culturally sustaining.

Tonight we're focusing on Hip Hop as local knowledge. We want to start from the idea that, rather than the traditional role of authority, expert, and the agent of transmission, the teacher's role in these kinds of pedagogies is decentered to a certain extent. As in Maisha Fisher's (Winn's; see chapter 17) wonderful ethnography of the Power Writer program in the Bronx led by Joseph and his students in an after-school program, there is a complex dance that's happening in the classroom between the teachers and the students in that different people are taking the lead. So it's about a process where oftentimes the teachers completely disappear. They become the students. And among the student themselves, whoever's leading "the dance" changes quite a bit. So, it's a different understanding of teaching and learning. It's more like a potluck. Everybody is coming to the table with their own food and everybody is going to eat together and

Figure 8.1 Isaiah Phillips AKA Fat Boy AKA Randy McFly performing for an excited audience. Photo by Mural Music & Arts Project.

have fun together. And Joseph is the host, the guide. He is the authority in the room, but he wields his authority like he is sort of passing the mic around. So he moves from being an agent of *transmission* to an agent of *transformation*.

By centering students' stories, we are actually centering local knowledge. And what do we mean by local knowledge and why is it important? Well, local knowledge is our caches of experiences, of languages, of ideas, of cultures, that students are bringing into the learning setting with them. In this sense, learning becomes a really important site to produce and reproduce community. These are living knowledges—growing and evolving. Embedded in these local knowledges are ways of doing, thinking, and being that allow the community to continue to survive and thrive. Earlier, we talked about Hip Hop as a lived, local culture with knowledges embedded in it. The slang, the dance, the graffiti, the raps, the poems, all these different sets of knowledges were peculiar to these neighborhoods, even as new knowledges continue to be produced and evolve.

In this era of Common Core and national standards, it could be argued that local knowledges are even more important than they've ever been. And why is that? Well, the argument in part for national standards is that in order for us as a nation to be competitive in the twenty-first century globally, we have to raise our educational game because we want to develop individuals who will continue to maintain our supremacy in the economic and social order. The argument for Hip Hop pedagogies, on the other hand, is that they allow us to *sound* democracy—and I'm using "sound" here as a verb—to bring about a process of learning that strengthens and sustains the cipher, the community. So the larger social question becomes: Can a place of learning become one that not only builds individuals who are ready for the world but also grows and sustains the communities around it? And do these goals even have to uphold each other? As we see the incredible teaching and learning practices, the creative and expressive practices, of our friends here from MMAP, we further ask how arts pedagogies are helping us to reach those goals and moving us toward a transformation of individuals, of communities, of the nation, and of the world.

Just to situate MMAP, and get a brief glimpse of East Palo Alto, it is a small, 2.5-square-mile working-class community of color with

Figure 8.2 Girls writing rhymes at the Mural Music & Arts Project. Photo by Mural Music & Arts Project.

approximately 29,000 residents. While the median household income of nearby San Mateo was $70,819 in 2010, and $74,335 in Santa Clara County, the median income of East Palo Alto was $45,006. The city is also facing rapid gentrification and resegregation, with median home prices in EPA rising from $279,000 in 2012 to $704,500 in 2020—in just eight years. Eighty-nine percent of children in the Ravenswood School District are eligible for free and reduced-price meals.

MMAP began in 2001, employing local teams to design and create murals in East Palo Alto. Since then they've served 12,591 youth, created 235 murals, produced 162 original songs, and so much more. They've created an environment to grow and transform youth, they've created a culturally relevant and sustaining space. There are six main programs in their youth leadership academy: Health Education through Art, the Teen Mural Program, In-School Electives, Public Arts Consulting, the Graffiti Arts Project, and the flagship History through Hip Hop program.

I'm now going to go ahead and turn it over to Sonya, the co-founder of MMAP, and our research team at the Institute for Diversity in the Arts— Casey, Adorie, Measha, and Reagan—who have been working closely together to understand how MMAP engages in processes of transformation with youth and communities.

A LABOR OF LOVE: FORMING A SOCIAL JUSTICE ARTS ECOSYSTEM IN EAST PALO ALTO

CASEY PHILIP WONG: We're honored to have you here, Sonya, and the MMAP family in the house! [*Applause*] Sonya, let's walk through your journey with Hip Hop and activism, and your experiences with Hip Hop pedagogies and starting MMAP in East Palo Alto. How has Hip Hop been a part of your life?

SONYA CLARK-HERRERA: First time I think I can remember reciting lyrics to Hip Hop was in seventh grade, so '83. If you play any song from that era, of course I can recite the lyrics. At that time my family was living in Whittier, even though we would go out all over Los Angeles, but we were listening to East Coast rap because that's what there was. I loved EPMD and Big Daddy Kane. All those guys. Kool Herc, for sure. In high school I really got big into Public Enemy because it was so political. Hip Hop was a little angrier, but really exciting too. I love that era. Then I went straight into LA hardcore because that's where I was and they were really accessible and they performed everywhere, at the gym, at the quinceañera. So it was a very different time. I got a chance to meet everybody in NWA, but obviously I didn't sit down and hang out, like, "Hey, how are you doing?" [*Laughter*] Because I was a little girl.

After high school I moved around a bit, and ended up in New York. Being in New York was awesome and where I met The Roots. That was a big transition point. *Illadelph Halflife* was being recorded at Battery Studios in New York, and we spent a week in the studio with them. We hung out, got to know every lyric on that album. That album was great to me. Everybody had a DJ in their apartment, in their house at all times. Everybody always had records, we all had systems. Biggie was around, we'd see Big Pun at the club all the time. Everybody was always out. It felt like everybody knew each other, it was a very small arts community in New York. That's what it was like in the '90s. De La Soul was always everywhere. I got to know those guys too because their manager actually was Kweli's manager. They're all UVA guys. In New York it started to be fun to be pedantic. Instead of just being angry over there, it was cerebral and we'd talk shit about what they didn't know and it was all subversive. You kind of felt powerful.

In the '90s I was doing visual art. When I was younger I danced so I did a lot of that really embarrassing stuff with big, puffy pants. I did spoken word. I've done some rap, but doing visual art was a lot easier for me. And because we were doing visual art with a lot of Mexican flavor, there was nothing like that in New York at the time. I was working with a lot of artists, we had 20–30 visual artists. I loved doing that. Also, the people that sold art like we did back then were still using slide projectors and wearing suits and talking about museums and doing Europeans prints. We just laughed at that and called it such bullshit!

WONG: Your engagement with Hip Hop became political in high school with Public Enemy, but what was your relationship to activism growing up?

CLARK-HERRERA: We were always politically active. My parents were. My father and uncles worked in academia, and my uncle did all sorts of work on minority populations and health disparities. My dad was building free clinics when we were little. He was getting in trouble for calling out mayors for stealing money and one time there was a firebomb at the clinic. All sorts of crazy shit that happened when my parents were very active. My dad was in the paper for getting in trouble for protesting, then we'd go paint. When I got arrested for protesting my parents were so proud. They were like, "Aww." They had us marching, riding, walking. Every Sunday we'd have to write all these letters to whatever senator was doing something wrong. They would drag us there because the youth voice is always the best. They'd be like, "Now tell them, Sonya."

There's not a time I don't remember doing that. They were always fighting the power. I hope that I've raised my kids the same. My son's first time we went to a basketball game the cheerleaders were cheering, "Go Greyhounds," or something and he goes, "Power to the people! Black power! Power to the people! Black power!" He did not understand. My son had never been to a basketball game. He had only been to political rallies. He was like six and he'd never, ever learned to cheer, he'd only learned to chant. So we were like, "Oh shit, we've got to teach him how to do that." That's how my parents brought us up too. My brother and I always knew that we would be in some sort of service to the community and that community would be first and that we were nothing without it. We've always been active.

WONG: Wow, so you're doing Hip Hop, visual arts, and involved in activism, and you end up in East Palo Alto and start MMAP. How did all these things come together for you?

CLARK-HERRERA: We were brought to the South Bay because Eugene got into law school here, and we lived in East Palo Alto because he was Black and I was Latina, and we didn't feel comfortable anywhere else. I knew I wanted to continue my New York lifestyle with arts, and move more toward effecting change. You can only effect change in the way that you know how. You can only do something well if you're passionate about it. So I think Eugene, my husband, wanted to use our experiences to develop knowledge. I wanted to work with teenagers. We always knew we wanted to work with teenagers. We were both terrible, terrible teenagers and I can understand the angst of a teen. What is the most important thing to a teenager? Honesty and respect. Those are the only two things that they really need, and so we get along really well. Then I knew the arts is the only way I felt I could communicate all of my anger. Whether it's listening to music, making music, writing about how I felt while we were dancing to that music, it's always about the arts. Everything fun in the world is. It's the way you look at everything. And no one can tell you you're wrong with art. It doesn't matter what anybody else thinks. It's art. It's the best weapon and mechanism for social change.

And thinking about East Palo Alto, at the time, there was no sidewalks, no trash cans, no streetlights, no IKEA, no Home Depot, I mean, there was not a lot. I was thinking about how we could wrap around a community that already had this beautiful history and multiple layers of exciting, difficult, and hopeful stuff. You can only do that with art. So using art was the way that we felt we could best give back. I couldn't do what my parents did. They built clinics. They made free clinics wherever we lived, even though my dad was a professor and he always worked in another clinic, he spent all his days doing stuff. So did my mom. That was their volunteerism. They had degrees in that area. We didn't have that opportunity, me and my brother. My husband was in law school, and I had just finished with grad school, studying genetics. I had two bachelors. One was in biology and the other in social science. Nobody wanted a part-time master's geneticist. I didn't really have a whole lot, and I'm going to give back somehow?

When we decided to get started doing youth and arts work, we knew there was a lot to do, so we tried to partner with all these entities and organizations. We formulated what would become the Teen Mural Program (TMP), the founding program of MMAP. Every time we went to talk to an organization, they wouldn't know that we were the artists. They would say stuff like, "No kid's going to understand how to do that shit." And, "No poor kid really knows how to do that and that's not going to work." They're like, "We don't want your murals on the outside because those kids won't be able to do a good mural. If you do it personally, you can. But not if they do it." They just gave us a ton of shit and they didn't really think it would work. And so we said, "Fine. We'll do a mural on the inside." But we also believed that you couldn't expect kids to do anything without giving them a training seminar.

So we had a training seminar where we recruited kids from all over. And then we had this one mural that we did for the Boys and Girls Club that was part of just get your feet wet, dabble, see if you like it. We knew we only needed 15 kids, so we had like 30 kids for that first thing. The kids thought we were crazy because we insisted on paying them. Because I was like, how else do you get poor kids to shake their families? My mom would've been all "Mm-mm," shaking her head no, "go babysit and bring some money home!" We realized the challenges when 100% of our kids that year had parents who were incarcerated. 100%. No one had documents. 2001. No one had any documentation. So we had to go to grandmas and churches to try to find some way to pay them.

And then at the end of the summer we had this big unveiling. We had 300 people, we cooked for it. We brought a Grammy award-winning band, Quetzal. We had this beautiful event, and in the middle of it the head of the Boys and Girls Club and the then-mayor, Ruben Abrica, said, "Why would you stop here? Why don't you do a mural for every school in the district. That's 13 murals. Will you commit to that?" In front of all these people. I'm stoked, I'm like, "Yeah, totally." And the next day was 9/11. Literally we all partied that night really hard because we were so stoked. All these people from LA were staying at our house; luckily they drove instead of flying or they'd have never gotten out of there. And then the next morning we lost my largest installations of art that I'd ever made, because I did a lot of my art in the World Trade Center. Because that's where the banks were. So that's where we sold art. So we lost a lot of art, we lost a lot of friends. That was our beginning.

But that year, we learned a lot. We decided to do four programs a year. Just try to get these murals done. The community was so behind us and it was so great. And the kids, we never did a recruitment. We still have never really done recruitment. The kids find you. Like they know if you're doing something or you're paying them or it's fun. And I remember we were out painting one day and these other kids came up and started giving shit to this kid, Alan, like, "Oh, oh, you like to color?" And he was like, "At least I get paid for working," you know, like, "Fuck you." The fact that we paid them kind of justified it. It was a job. And they didn't have to admit that they needed to be with us, that they needed this kind of support. So we had all sorts of kids. We realized we couldn't get the Latinos to come if the Black kids were there, especially for the girls. And so we'd have to go house to house and knock on the doors and say, "No, we're there as well. They'll be okay. They're going to be fine." But there was so much racism. It was very much the beginning of the transition of this community. So there was a lot of that. But it's not the kids that are bigots; it's the parents. And if you let the kids understand each other, they're all fine.

So we used to call ourselves a consortium. A consortium of artists and activists who cared about the community of East Palo Alto, working to make a difference. And that was really what it was. The board, the group of people that were serving them, the artists, the staff, interns from Stanford. We were just a bunch of people who actually gave a shit, but had no real money to do anything. But we could do this, together. And now we get a lot of kids to college, but it's not a straightforward path. We had some really great kids, but it was tough. We had kids that would get in one fight and be kicked out of their school. Like we had every type of kid. You realize how many kids deal with trauma and poverty and different parenting strategies. In our first two years, we had three people have someone in their family have a baby without *anybody* knowing they were pregnant. How is that possible? What's happening in their lives? There's not a lot of honesty and there's a lot of fear. We started getting our girls to have more interaction with other girls, bringing in more mentors, and having more events that would bring in volunteers. So we invented this advisory board, people that could talk to them about, "You got to be careful, man. Don't be drinking like that, don't be smoking like that." You know?

We learned a very ugly lesson, early on, about transitional age youth. There was this one kid—I was working with a community leader who had this kid, Mike. And Mike starts the program as a *senior* in high school. We didn't recruit, so we couldn't say, "We don't want you," so we took him. Very challenging kid. Great kid, but on the precipice of disaster, right? And we take him and we love him, but we only have funding till 18-years-old, because that's the only thing we've ever done, and that's all we have. And so he's with us for those six months, does some great work, and then we spit him out. That never was good for us. We tasted it, we hated it, we knew something was wrong. We just didn't have it structured for the transitional age youth.

Within a year, he and a couple other guys who were also not alumni from the program but kids that we'd known, well they're still all locked up. One was involved in this very high-profile murder. I still don't believe he did it and I still visit him in jail. But somebody killed somebody and these were all East Palo Alto kids, retaliating against each other, because they had nothing to do except to argue with each other. If we would've kept one or two of those kids that wanted to be of age and in our program, none of that would've happened. Because all they were was bored and stupid. And for sure Mike wouldn't have been entangled in this and now he's been incarcerated for years. It was at that point that we were like we got to figure out a way. So we started hiring transitional youth as part of our model, staff members, junior staff members, interns. We've been so proud of keeping these kids, or a few of them at least. And so we just started doing this and we started doing it in a way where we thought we were making some progress.

A few years after we got started one of the kids was like, "We're tired of muraling. Can we just rap? Can we make beats? Can we do that?" And we're like, "Hmm. Okay." They felt like we did all this research to do the mural, most of us would paint, and then half the time some of the kids were not as interested in painting. They'd be washing brushes or making jokes and started writing rhymes and started rapping. We began to pilot early versions of what would become the Hip Hop program beginning in 2004, but it wasn't until 2007 that the program really took off.

Around that time, East Palo Alto was having a lot of gunrunning. They stopped selling drugs as much and started trafficking weapons. When they started trafficking weapons, there were a lot of busts, raids, and shootings. And so our kids couldn't walk home from schools and we couldn't keep them out at night. So our Teen Mural Program used to run four times a year, and you would do it after school. So one time we're at Costaño Elementary School painting a mural and there's a bust. Streets are closed, kids can't get home, we're stuck. So we stopped doing the Teen Mural Program except for during the summer because it wasn't safe. During the summer we can work during the day, but during the school year it's basically an after-school program for kids who don't have any affiliations with their school and get dumped back in the community. We would keep them there till 7:30 p.m., feed them, and then boom. It wasn't safe. So we had to stop doing that during the year. And that was a really hard thing to swallow. At that time we supported those kids interested in making a Hip Hop program because all you need is a studio. That's how the History through Hip Hop (HHH) program formed.

HISTORY THROUGH HIP HOP (HHH) PROGRAM

The HHH program was different. It was a very challenging program to transition to, but the kids loved it. They were prolific and they did well. Then they had a lot of concerts. I mean, they've played at The Fillmore and The Warfield with big artists, you know what I mean? We've given

Figure 8.3 Student DJing at the Mural Music & Arts Project. Photo by Mural Music & Arts Project.

them a million opportunities and they've had some fun. And then in the middle of things we'll have like a shooting, or human trafficking, or whatever. The whole thing has to shut down and you have to focus on that, and that's just what life's like. So every single season we've had some major thing happen. Everybody being pushed out because of gentrification, the small drug war. And that just changes the landscape and the kids can't focus on getting whatever they want recorded and things just have to extend. And that's what we have to do, and that's okay.

Compared to our other programs, I think kids knew they had more ownership over it and they knew that they were driving it. This was about expression and creativity and it was way cooler to them. Even the art that came out of it or the videos that came out of it were all really them. That's why it's also slower, because it's legitimately youth driven. They always give it their all. And that was the excitement, and that's why I think it was so successful. It was also the people that were running it. You're talking about like Jidenna, who's now a Grammy-nominated Hip Hop artist, Chitty, Teff, Sean, Bronson, Tunde, Demetric, Remi, and all the guys from Stanford. Remi was in the second Teen Mural Program that we had, at 14. Then he went to Stanford, was a Gates Scholar. I still remember when Eugene flew up to Portland to help him with his essay. I mean like that's how important he was. Now he's a man and he's married and he's a restorative justice coordinator at East Palo Alto Academy and it's so awesome. I have so much hope for that school knowing that Remi's there, because I've known him since he was a child.

Another exciting part was how HHH brought everyone together. TMP did that, but not like HHH. In East Palo Alto the churches are all segregated by race. The different clubs were always like that too. Like the Tongan kids played rugby, Black kids played football, and the Latinos played soccer. Like everything was super segregated, except for our program back then. Now a lot more stuff, thank goodness, is desegregated. But we had them together. One time there was a Latin kid hit by a Black kid in the street, with a car, and the police had to come out. There was retaliation. They would come to us and talk to our teenagers because they knew they were the ones that were going to be able to do something. So we had this really incredible group of kids that I think made some huge strides in East Palo Alto race relations. And that had to do with just giving them a place to talk about things and be respectful to each other. And we'd take in boys and girls. If something would happen, we would sit there and figure it out till it was done. I mean, it was like a family.

WONG: So what does HHH programming look like? If I'm in the room during the school year, what's going on?

CLARK-HERRERA: HHH begins with research for five weeks, which we all do together, and then the last seven weeks we put together the project, so it's a 12-week program. After the first five weeks we'd have the kids separate into visual arts and then performing arts, there'd be dancers, rappers, DJs, and beatmakers. Essentially there's different cohorts by the four major elements of Hip Hop. And then you'd have the last week when we'd all get together and do this community unveiling, because part of it is bringing this to the community. And we'd have the kids explain why they did what they did and to invite them into the process, let them see the youth. I'm sure you've seen our logic models. Youth are supposed to be recognized in their community and the community's supposed to understand them as active participants and the youth are supposed to feel like they're being listened to. So that whole piece is why unveiling is so important, for the kids to be proud of something. And because at that time, which still really is the case, they were all bused out of their community for school. This was the only time they get to highlight what they did to their parents. Their parents wouldn't go all the way out to their schools, but they would come to the unveilings.

But like right now, with what Teff has lined up for this cohort, we're studying Michelle Alexander's *New Jim Crow*, so that's like really compelling. But even more compelling is the people that he's bringing to meet with them and interact with them, and also the music people that he's bringing. Like Gavin, who did all this stuff for YG, like merchandise and all of his music. So YG's coming. We have a lot of people that Teff knows and cares about that are willing to come work with our kids. So our kids have a chance to meet with Dom Kennedy when he comes, we all get to go. Our kids have a lot of opportunities to interact on a higher level.

MMAP'S IMPACT ON YOUTH AND COMMUNITIES

WONG: Thank you so much for sharing about your journey, Sonya, and the incredible work of MMAP. We're so grateful for you. With the help of hodari blue, Measha Ferguson Smith, and Reagan Ross, we're now going to turn to some findings from our research. It should come as no surprise that we found that MMAP moved beyond just sustaining languages and cultures, to sustaining the youth and communities speaking and enacting those languages and cultures: what Samy and Django Paris would call *culturally sustaining pedagogy* (see chapter 10). MMAP gave power to youth themselves, allowing young people to grapple with the racialized,

Figure 8.4 Student completing a mural. Photo by Mural Music & Arts Project.

classed, and gendered forces acting upon their lives. MMAP engages Hip Hop and the arts not just in the interest of honoring, fostering, and perpetuating the power of Hip Hop, but with a direct focus on sustaining young people *themselves* as they confront racial capitalist-contrived poverty and exploitation, hyperpolicing and mass incarceration, gentrification and resegregation, toxic masculinities and gendered violence, and other forms of systemic violence and injustice.

We also found that MMAP's work with youth directly contributed to giving power to families, neighborhoods, and the community of East Palo Alto through what we're referring to as "ripples of hope and healing." MMAP has helped create a social justice and arts ecosystem, with Hip Hop in particular, functioning as a leading creative instrument for positive social transformation. We're thinking about Hip Hop pedagogy as more than just educators directly teaching and learning with young people, but also how educational practices with young people create the possibility for broader social change by linking together families, neighborhoods, and the larger community of East Palo Alto.

CHAPTER 8

MEASHA FERGUSON SMITH: Hodari and I would like to now offer an example of these "ripples of hope and healing" by sharing our experiences working with young people in MMAP on the creation of the song "Street Religion," and an interview with Tanisha, one of the young people who produced it.

HODARI BLUE: Tanisha was one of the first people I connected with at MMAP. I was sitting at a table doing my own thing where Tanisha was working on a song with Yolanda, another student in the program. On this day, Tanisha was super interested in chatting with me. When I think of her now, I think of her wearing a headband, her hair in a bun, a blue sweater, and some clean Air Force 1's. She was a sophomore at Woodside High School then, and we often carpooled together to San Francisco for HHH summer programming at Spotify. With that brief background, I would like to share the song "Street Religion":

Street Religion

[*Chorus*] Be careful with them boys in blue, boys in blue
Watch yo back 'cause they might shoot at you, shoot at you
Better be wary of your neighbors too, neighbors too
Tenth commandment said they flip on you, flip on you,
Hold up, hold up, hold up,
Live by, die by, street religion
The mission to live by, die by, street religion
To hate to live by, die by, street religion
Don't think I'll live by, die by, street religion

You ever heard bullets and sirens, and sat there in silence?
So sick of the violence, tensions is risin,
Every time it got hot, more bodies they drop,
Commandments forgot, this new jack city go crazy,
Purple times rock-a-by babies, these boys can't help but wreak havoc,
'Cause the game is the deadliest habit, we just dealin with the drugs we was handed,
You know about rock and how it landed, crack rock ain't no different from Plymouth,
In the gang you gotta get it how you live it, in the hood more dyin than livin,
Bow down to the streets that we live in, be careful of the street religion,

[*Chorus*]

Heisman for the one time, click clack before I lose mine,
If my brother fight, then we fight,
Cousin fight then I'm right wit him,
On the block posted wit night vision,
If you had to try me, get right wit him,
You ain't from where I'm from, you ain't seen what I've seen,
I done seen homies bleed til they can't breathe,
Nah this ain't no movie, nah we not actin,
But we bout that action, Janet Jackson,
And as, I lay, me down, to sleep,
I pray, the Lord, my soul, to keep,
Should they, get me, fore I, wake,
I pray, he keep, my family straight

[*Chorus*]

They don't know, they killin my people,
They just want green, like their first name Cee-Lo,
They wanna do evil, oh he used to stack C-notes,
In that peacoat, til his PO got pissed off, peeled off,
Cops shootin pistols, and they stay shootin, me those,
Judge don't lay me down like the Beatles,
'Cause the system get foul like a free throw,
They don't know, the way they be perceiving us,
In the back of car, CNN and CBS,
Switching up stories, so devious,
And all of this bullshit, they feedin us,
They feedin us, They so childish,
It gets tedious, when you're tryin to save the world,
Drownin in greediness

BLUE: And now an interview clip with Tanisha.

It's really like what we've been through or seen, or ... We know somebody who been through it, like ... like there was this one time, there was a part in "Street Religion." You ever heard bullets and sirens and sat there in silence? Like, I hear bullets and sirens, almost every, not almost, every night, and I just sit there like dang like, there's nothin you really can do, besides sit in silence, like, that's all. When we did that, we did "Street Religion," it helped me get over when my uncle got shot, 'cause when that happened, I was like, my grandma could be outside and somethin happen, my little cousins could be outside and somethin happen. It still had a heavy impact on me, like, when she did that I was like, dang, was she there? All the stuff she rapped about, I was like, that's like the whole night, like what happened that time from beginning to end. It definitely helps me tell the truth about EPA, about anything, it could be about your day, it just helped me like release everything.

BLUE: Young people are often very much aware of the fact that what is happening around them is unjust. Hip Hop, in this case, provides the space for self-expression and deepened connections in that process.

FERGUSON-SMITH: Relationships are the threads between each individual in a Hip Hop space. These relationships and the love and care that exist between youth is what allows for them to make critical reflections on their own lives and critical connections with the people around them. It allows them to feel safe enough to share. In doing so, it's something that lightens the individual weight each person carries and allows for them to see themselves in others. When you can see yourself in someone else, you feel a sense of connectedness that reminds you that you are not alone and that the things you are going through are bigger than you. Reflections validate the experiences you might feel afraid to share because of the ways they have hurt you. But releasing them almost acts as surrendering experiences to the collective, to the community, to be held by beats and harmonies, footwork, sacred ciphers—instead of in your body.

Also for folks of color, queer folks, low-income folks, and people marginalized in any way, this release becomes an avenue for connecting about the things that mainstream media and education distorts, pathologizes, and criminalizes about you and your community. It becomes a personal duty to do so, to get the truth out. But you gotta feel loved and cared for by somebody first. The young artists at MMAP are coming into the sacred knowledge of how they can help themselves to do more than just survive, but to return to wholeness.

CARE, AFFECTIVE LABOR, AND SUSTAINING COMMUNITY ORGANIZATIONS

REAGAN ROSS: MMAP is also an effective Hip Hop organization because of all the affective labor that occurs in MMAP spaces. Affect means "relating to, arising from, or influencing feelings or emotions." Affective labor then is labor that relates to and impacts feelings. It's labor that shows care, and it is often associated with people on the feminine spectrum, and is thus marginalized in terms of its importance. In an interview with former MMAP staff member Aria, I asked her whether there were any students that she felt particularly connected to. Aria immediately named two girls, Donna and Esme. I then asked how she went about building her relationships with Donna and Esme:

> I don't know. I just love those kids, like I was always checking in on them, asking how they were doing, asking how things were going. They could call me or text me any time during the day or night. I used to get so frustrated, it was kind of like always something—a request for a letter of recommendation in like two days, but I always did it. I was totally in it in terms of supporting them in any way that I could. I also wasn't afraid to ask them hard questions too about what was going on in school or at home or whatever. Like Donna, I taught Donna how to drive. She and I will always be like sisters.

When we interviewed Donna, she spoke about Aria too. She spoke about how she and Aria would meet up when Aria was back in town and how Aria helped her apply for colleges and taught her how to drive. She described Aria as her mentor, and then went on to talk about how that inspired her to be a mentor for others. So, we can definitely see the ripple effects of that care.

The affective labor—the care work—that MMAP does is crucial to MMAP as a community-based Hip Hop organization. Care work allows young people to feel safe and comfortable enough in the MMAP environment to speak on personal, intimate situations. Affective labor is a foundation for exemplary Hip Hop pedagogy. However, this affective labor can sometimes come at a cost. Aria offered a critical caveat: "We bit off so much more than we could chew in terms of our staff bandwidth, and so it felt like we were just always working day and night to do as much as we could." She went on to talk about how she felt like in MMAP you never got the opportunity to step back and make sure the work was sustainable. Not just from a financial perspective, but from a *people* perspective, that is, making sure staff members weren't getting burnt out.

We have been talking about sustaining community by creating a social justice arts ecosystem, one where ripple effects of hope and healing are felt

Figure 8.5 Mural Music & Arts Project showcase in East Palo Alto, California. Photo by Abdul Alim.

both within and beyond the organization. But as we conclude, we need to consider the question: How can we honor, foster, and sustain the affective labor of educators within organizations like MMAP? We know this is a struggle confronted by many organizations that are full of love but are often also cash-strapped. We are hoping we can hold onto this question as we theorize how to build, move forward with, and sustain organizations doing social justice, Hip Hop, arts, and activism work with youth.

9 Beyond Trauma

STORYTELLING AS CULTURAL SHIFT AND
COLLECTIVE HEALING

Bryonn Bain, Mark Gonzales, A-lan Holt, and Michelle Lee

JEFF CHANG: So we've got four people here who have been pioneers in the realm of developing and telling stories, and teaching through poetry and spoken word pedagogies. Bryonn Bain, who is best known for his groundbreaking piece *Lyrics from Lockdown,* is with us. Bryonn is an Associate Professor in the UCLA Department of African American Studies and Department of World Arts and Cultures / Dance, and has been doing important work around the prison industrial complex for years. He brings together Hip Hop pedagogy with work with incarcerated folks as well as work in the community.

Then we have two local legends. Michelle "Mush" Lee is the Executive Director of Youth Speaks, and now serving as their Senior Advisor of Pedagogy. Youth Speaks is one of the organizations that pioneered Hip Hop pedagogies back in the late '90s and is now the leading purveyor of youth poetry around the world. Thousands and thousands of kids will be here again this summer to participate in the Brave New Voices program that you may have seen on HBO. She's recently launched the Whole Story Group, where she is helping leaders build powerful stories.

We have our very own A-lan Holt. A-lan is the Director of the Institute for Diversity in the Arts, a Sundance Fellow and SF Film Screenwriting

Fellow, and a frequent contributor on-air at KQED Arts. But most important to tonight, A-lan is a groundbreaking poet, playwright, and filmmaker, best known for her short film *Inamorata*, and her collection of poems, *Moonwork*.

Last but not least, we have Mark Gonzales. Anybody who's been around me and Samy for the last three years knows he's one of our favorite people in the world, and an amazing thinker around the question of healing. Mark's been busy the past few years, and notably released a beautiful book, *In Times of Terror, Wage Beauty*, and is in the process of launching a center for art, hope, and innovation in Tunisia, The New Medina. I'll hand it over to Mark. [*Applause*]

WHAT IS A STORY?

MARK GONZALES: I work specifically on what it means to be human, and how human beings learn ideas and identity. A large part of my work has to do with trauma and how human beings harm others, or harm themselves. And where do we learn that? And where do we learn that that's okay, to the point where we have this reality with so many of us dying at such early ages? The methodology I developed is called *wage beauty*.[1] It's a four-part methodology for healing trauma: name, frame, speak, grow. And what I want to talk about today is actually around this concept of stories. But first, there is a need to not only just use language but to define the language we use. What do I mean by stories?

I grew up not loving stories. Stories to me were things like this, where my father and my grandfather and his brothers and sisters would be like, "Oh, let me tell you a story," and it'd be like, "Oh God, let me get the hell out of here, please no!" 'Cause to me stories were just things that parents did and things that parents did weren't cool and so I wanted to be cool. So it's like if you are doing stories, I'm out. Until I realized that stories are a medium. They are more than phonemes; they are more than curated sounds and words. And we can even get into different levels of stories and ceremonies and what they hold for different cultures on the planet. But the reality is a story is a medium. It's the medium through which we learn to read the world and ourselves and a story is very different than a narra-

Figure 9.1 Mark Gonzales sharing a story. Photo by Shara Lili.

tive. Most people use them interchangeably but they are very different things. A story is an account. It has a beginning, an end, it can be past, it can be future, it can be fictional, it can be prophecy, but a story is an account of an event. A narrative is when you tie stories together in order to advance an idea across thousands or tens of thousands of people to the point where it becomes what we call normalized.

Like I said, I'm interested in the question: How do human beings learn how to be human? And it's interesting because if we look at the role stories play in human existence, *stories are the ancient tool of identity*. Telling stories is literally how human beings learn to be their specific type of human. Every culture, every society, every tribe, every group of people on this planet have set up a system of stories that teach them about themselves, what came before, what will come after, and their belief in the sacred, the divine, etc. It's what drives us. It's how we learn behavior, what is acceptable and what is not.

Something interesting in this time that we live in is that most of us I see in this room as I look around are situated within an ecosystem of stories. And there's two types of stories most of us would probably relate to. One is the narrative of invisibility, meaning if stories are the engine of identity and we're looking at larger narratives across our society, across this planet, wherever we look, we are not there. You're invisible. People who look like you, people who pray like you, people who speak like you, people who live like you, they do not exist in the stories that you are situated within. And if they do exist, then they're demonized. They're always on the negative side. And because stories are the engine of identities, we learn to be invisible. We learn to play small. We learn to shut up. We learn to live in the shadows. We learn to hide. We learn to suppress and oppress ourselves in terms of cycles, or we learn to be hyper-demonized and hyper-vigilant in terms of we always have to be on our game, always have to be on our toes because we are ready for something to be done against us at any time.

And this is to me what really gets interesting in terms of stories, wounds, and healing is that people have been in fights over a word. You can see entire families break up over an argument, people who are blood relatives. And so if we know that these words can harm a person to the point where people who came out of the same womb are no longer talking to one another over a few words, then what is the effect of a harmful social narrative on the physiological and psychological health of entire groups of people? How does that affect us inside our body and inside our brain? In the US currently, if we look at anxiety and depression, there are 180 million adults in the US. There are 200 million prescriptions for anxiety and depression alone. We have more prescriptions for depression and anxiety than we do adults. If we look at suicide, self-harm, in the US it's at the rate of one million per year that people attempt to take their own life. Meaning people will choose the grave over another breath, feeling that the grave is a better place for them. And that's not an isolated event. It's a cumulative statistic, meaning each year it's one million, plus one million, plus one million. Meaning by the time you left high school, on average 18 years old, 18 million people had attempted to exit this earth from this nation alone. What is the effect again of a harmful social discourse on the physiological and psychological health of entire groups of people? Why are we so sick inside our brain, inside our body? And where did we learn this from? Or in the words of Malcolm, "Who taught you to hate what God made you?"

TRAUMA AS COLLECTIVE AND CUMULATIVE

And this is where it really gets into the fields of historical trauma, which asks: What are the ways that dominant groups affect secondary groups through segregation, displacement, acute and chronic violence, economic destruction, cultural dispossession. Trauma is an individual experience, not one million people being hurt, but one person being hurt who has a family, a daughter, a son, a grandmother, a grandchild, one million times over. That's what it means when you bomb a country, when you displace a people, when you reshape the cultural gene pool of an entire society and what they believe is normal. And it doesn't just affect them in terms of statistics or in terms of whether they lived or died, but there are three primary responses: psychological, social, and physiological, meaning how it affects our bodies, our minds, our spirits.

Even though we're taught about trauma as an individual experience, it's actually more a collective and cumulative experience. An interesting study out of Emory University was recently done in terms of genetic memory and how genes carry not only physical traits, but parents who go through extreme duress, their children are more prone to fear biologically than their parents were.[2] So genes carry emotional DNA as well. So, we really have to understand what's going on to harm ourselves so much. And if we think about, we all had creation stories that are beautiful. So, why is it that so many of us when we begin the story of our people we began with the story of invasion or wounds? We've completely ignored our origins, and when we do that, we no longer tell the stories of beautiful creation, we begin and make pain the beginning point of our existence. And if the beginning point of your existence is pain then the mind starts to believe that pain is infinite because there's not a time before it. And if there's not a time before something, there's not a time after something. And what you've done with your storytelling abilities is you've normalized that reality. You've normalized your wounds. You've normalized the pain.

And that's what we have to get back to in these conversations. Most of the things we're addressing within our communities, our homes, our schools, our societies, are not problems. They are symptoms. And as long as we see suicide, self-harm, street violence, interpersonal violence, intimate partner violence as a problem versus a symptom, we will never be able to address the root causes. And if you don't address the root causes, you are going to continually play catch-up.

It was interesting, in his recent dialogue with H. Samy Alim, Harry Belafonte asked, "Where are the radicals?" (April 30, 2014, the St. Clair Drake Memorial Lecture, Stanford University). And I thought about this actually for several weeks because I know people who would be classified as radicals across this globe. Whether or not you believe in armed struggle, whether or not you believe in direct action, whether or not you believe in economic shifting, I know people across the globe who are willing to do whatever it takes to love their people. People are not checked out and they are not numb. They are shellshocked. And if we look at epigenetics—that it's not just a generational reality but also an intergenerational reality— then we have to understand that maybe what most of our communities are facing in these times is intergenerational shellshock.

BEYOND HEALING AND TOWARD GROWTH

And how do the people begin to heal from this shellshock, and move beyond healing to growth? If we are only talking about healing, then literally we are saying the best that we can do as humans is to restore ourselves to the baseline that we came out of the womb. We are not here to heal; we are here to grow. How do we center a discourse around growth, a discourse around not just surviving but living and not just living but thriving. What does it mean to thrive? How many of us are engaging with one another on *that* story? And not doing it in ways that throw our elders under the bus, but literally, remember that whoever raised us for better or worse had a childhood, and had experiences that would shape the way they would forever raise us. Our parents were children once. There is no intergenerational healing without intergenerational forgiveness. And if we are not doing that, we are setting ourselves up to be cast out when we are elders.

So I humbly encourage us to think about the ways in which we might see story as a medium, as an engine for new possibilities and realities. Are we only doing this within performance spaces? And that's beautiful, but we had a conversation at the World Islamic Economic Forum, which was the gathering of over about 5 billion dollars in capital from across the globe, literally asking, "How do we define value? Where did we learn the story of success? What is the story of wealth?" Wealth is literally an accumulation of capital. Capital is that which has value. So what do I value? I value family, so how is wealth related to family? Perhaps this is how we start new economies, with new language, frameworks, and mental models. [*Applause*]

AN ETHIC AND PRACTICE OF RADICAL LOVE

MICHELLE LEE: I represent Youth Speaks.[3] We started in 1996 in San Francisco: James Kass, Marc Bamuthi Joseph, Paul Flores. It was really the idea of some young, really enthusiastic visionaries who were at San Francisco State in the MFA program and were like, "Dude, why are we studying all these White writers and why are all the classes filled with

Figure 9.2 Michelle Mush Lee teaching the 5th Element class. Photo by John Liau.

these White students who don't have a critical analytic lens on race, class, gender, sexuality, etc.?" We were teenagers then. Now I've worked with young people for 12 years in Oakland, and San Francisco, all over the Bay Area. In this field that I've dedicated my life to—Hip Hop education, knowledge, spoken word, pedagogy, youth-centered arts education, and youth development work—we don't always have the answers. Tonight, I hope that I can move you, and we can connect through a spirit and through my intentions and thoughtful words.

At Youth Speaks, we talk about three things being at the heart of our practice: safe space, radical love, and ethics of a participatory audience. I'll go into those in a second. I want to start with love. Who here has been in love? Okay, good to know. Cuties, you two up front, okay. I see you. I'll say my entry into writing was not through poetry. I had a really, really, awful, messed-up breakup when I was 19. It was my first love, and it was devastating. It was like the worst thing that had ever happened because that's just what it is, man. So I had nothing to do. I started painting. I was alone. I had no idea what I was doing, but I was messing around with acrylic, and oil, and linseed, and turpentine. And I just drew. And what ended up happening after nine hours of straight painting—I didn't sleep that night—was this piece. It was the first time that I had felt that free in a long time. There were no rules for me. And what I ended up painting that night was a picture of a naked man hunched over with no head. [*Laughter*] Sorry, is that too much? I'm trying to be honest.

And I ended up leaving the country, and I went to the West Indies, and I lived there for about six months, and that's where I started writing poetry. And at the time I thought that I had been painting my first love. He broke my heart. And I thought it was him. Twelve, thirteen years later, I realize that I was actually, with every stroke, painting a little bit of him and a lot of every moment that I've ever felt abandoned. Every moment that I had walked into a room and somebody looked at me as if, maybe she doesn't speak English. Maybe she's too hood. Mark was talking about invisibility, and my entire life, if you don't already know, I've never been White or Black. I've never been incredibly rich nor incredibly poor the way my parents grew up. I was always somewhere in between. I was always the hyphen or the pause between Asian and American. And for me, that just meant that I didn't really matter or exist.

I say that because I want to start with love. If today is all about healing, I don't think that I can begin to talk about any type of pedagogy, any type of theoretical framework, without talking about love first because that's what drives my work. And I think that's kind of simple, but real talk, I think it should be simple. I don't think it needs to be more complicated than that. And when I hear otherwise, I'm always ready to challenge that idea. At Youth Speaks, we believe in love. We are compelled by the radical notion of community over self, sacrifice before greed, love over hate, peace over war, hope over hopelessness, to speak, act, believe, and risk it all before becoming mere spectators of history. So as a representative of the organization, but also as a woman and most recently a mother, my work is concerned with helping young people find, develop, publicly present, and apply their voices as agents of change. Our method, our motivation, or in other words the how behind the why, is pretty simple. It's to embody what I chose to call tonight *an ethic of radical love*. And it's not something I invented. I will be honest. Before going into that, I have been reluctant to talk about love because I'm a woman and I'm an artist, and anytime you put those two things together everybody's like, "She's going to talk about love. She's going to talk about her third eye." [*Laughter*] And plus, I was like, "Yo, I gotta bust stereotypes, you know what I mean? I'm busy, people. I can't talk about love."

But to love, by nature, is a radical act. It's dangerous because there are so many risks involved with loving young people who do not come from your body, including stepchildren. I have discovered that at the heart of every worthwhile, challenging, fulfilled learning experience I've ever had, was a fertile environment for learning to happen, a place where active love leans in and finds home. This home we call safe space, and this is what Mark was kind of referring to earlier about the narrative of invisibility. As People of Color, we survive by creating and retelling our mythologies. We have to because Margaret Cho on *All-American Girl*, that fucking wasn't enough for me. Because half of the cast wasn't Korean and when they spoke Korean, I saw through that bullshit. And I was so disappointed because I had waited months to watch that. I was like, "Finally, somebody who looks like me." I was juiced. [*Laughter*] But I watched it and then I was so disappointed because it wasn't the language of home. It wasn't the language that my mother tucked me into bed whispering.

As People of Color we survive by creating and retelling our own mythologies. The heroes and heroines of our cultures are castrated by mainstream avenues of knowledge sharing. One half of our birthright is the right to do simple basic things like eat, work, and live in peace. But the other, for real, is to see and be seen. It is the right to exist culturally because the pain of invisibility is almost too much to bear. And I would say that is one of our greatest obstacles as educators in the twenty-first century, is to give people spaces in which they can investigate, interrogate, tell, and reimagine their own story. And this is where I end, with ethics of a participatory audience. What does that really mean? It means, yo, you got invited to my party. Come straight. Show love. Don't hate. Applaud and listen. That's what it means. It doesn't mean you come and you are passive. I'm not here to entertain. I'm not even here to knowledge drop, really. I need you just as I need the young people in all the learning spaces where I am invited. It's a reciprocal relationship.

If my students have taught me nothing else, they've taught me this: that every new learning experience requires two things, wonder and love.

The love that I'm talking about is not passive or permissive. It is not superficial love. It is not an obsession of power disguised as love, but an experience based on reciprocity, brave and honest conversation, rigorous curriculum, high expectations all the way around, with personal, intellectual, academic, and spiritual impacts and outcomes that are carried by a young person throughout his, her, or their journey in this life. King once said, "I'm foolish enough to believe that through the power of love somewhere men of the most recalcitrant bend will be transformed because we had the power to love even our enemies."

Can I ask you guys to do one thing with me before we move on? Please think of five people who have loved you powerfully. I want to share a prompt, "blessed be." We are thinking along the lines of meditation, prayer, ritual, words of forgiveness or celebration. Start your poem with "blessed be" and the names of five people who have loved you strongly. Next, staying on that same line of prayer and meditation, I want to know if anybody here has been dissed recently? Okay. Think about five people that you would consider your enemy. Could be personal, it could be big, institutional, systemic. I want to challenge you to say a prayer for those folks. "Blessed be the girl in fourth grade who kicked me in my face for packing rice and kimchi for lunch. Blessed be the child who has memorized their abusers' hands before ever learning to say, 'What happened to me was not my fault.'" Bless those who have trespassed against you, those who have used you. Why? Because intentional forgiveness is the first step towards radical love. Before we write, before we talk about changing the world and our impact in it, we start with love. Thank you. [*Applause*]

FINDING HEAT AT DAWN: ENVISIONING SAFE,
SUSTAINABLE FUTURES

A-LAN HOLT: As an artist and playwright, I resonate with so much that you shared, Mush. In the past few years I've really been focusing on learning the daily intricacies of a practice that yields art; that kind of art, like commitment, has to love despite it all. And love, I am finding, continues to be it all: continues to align, most prominently, the infrastructure of this work for social change. These days, I am learning how best to love; how

Figure 9.3 A-lan Holt speaking at the 5th Element Symposium. Photo by Shara Lili.

best to create the healthiest space to work and continue writing plays with a rigor and kindness that comes from having a strong, patient practice in these chaotic and rapid times. I am learning what it really means to live sustainably. And for me, these days, sustainability comes from finding heat at dawn. Comes from making the decision to sleep the night before, and eat better, and take in less toxins. To break fast with poetry, and water, and all these gentle things we sometimes forget. These gentle things the poem reminds us are ours. These small rituals of health that make the struggle for justice more sustainable overtime. I think about the words of one of my favorite poets, Solmaz Sharif, "I have always valued that within these moments of crisis and urgency and urgent action we need those patient moments too," Sharif says. "So maybe the poem is that space for patience, for deliberation, for a kind of concentrated slowness within an otherwise chaotic and rapid world."

These mornings I wake up at dawn. A ritual I began in January that has become the root of my healing and artistic practice. I find the dawn to be a healthy space to wake. The new air is cold and sharp. Some mornings the heat in our apartment works and the chilled hardwood is warmed and gracious to bare feet. Most days it is still dark and wet outside: too cold for these California bones to shake themselves awake, and so I lay and dream myself a patient poem. A poem that begins with finding my heat. There is a psychological component to heat. As mammals it provides a sense of warmth and safety. It reminds us of home. It is how we connect with ourselves and our sense of security.

In the context of my creative practice, one that is very much rooted in work toward social justice, I consider heat and the role it plays in creating strong emotional foundations for artists and activists. Twyla Tharp, in *The Creative Habit*, gives one example which I love. She says:

> A warm, secure dancer can work without fear.
> In that state of physical and psychic warmth, dancers
> touch their moments of greatest physical potential.
> They're not afraid to try new movements.
> They can trust their bodies, and that's when magic happens.[4]

I argue the same of artists and all people working toward social change. A warm, secure artist can work without fear. They are not afraid to try new ideas, they are flexible, they trust and connect with their bodies, they trust and connect with their creative work. As a writer, I didn't always understand the importance of incorporating movement into my practice until I understood the nature of heat. Here is what I've learned about heat.

We search for heat everywhere. In clothing, water, exercise, food, bodies, cigarettes, alcohol, wayward lovers. We search for heat everywhere. Some of our heat sources support us long term, and some of our heat sources do not. We know we feel supported when we know we feel at home. Home is rooted in consistent safety and security.

At the root of our art making is an attempt to create a work of art that envisions safe and sustainable futures. In this way, I believe that we create in order to re-create our conditions.

Our heat sources are always connected to our bodies. As artists our bodies must be supported if the magic is to happen, and if we are to create the kind of work that transforms our current world, if we are to create things that move us toward just futures. So every morning I wake up at dawn and I slow down enough to find my heat.

WRITING IMPOSSIBLE WORLDS INTO EXISTENCE

Mornings are that place where I am finding peace: those quiet pockets of time when most of the inhabitants of my world sleep. These small spaces span a couple of hours all my own. They become a space to write (or dance) or be alone, by myself, alone as I need to be, alone to create these small universes, these intricate new worlds, these plays. Indeed, these days I am learning the mechanics of what it means to carve out space for this type of mending work. And oh, what a gift the morning has been.

As an artist I am learning every day what true commitment feels like. What it means to inspire yourself in a tangible way to write. Write despite the rent, or the lover sleeping beautifully beside you, or the heartbreak, or the days when the work does not slip into poetry as easily as it should. Write. Write. And be in love with that thing—writing. Be an active lover in a practice that requires you to bend, and respond, and nourish, and live with, and sustain, and protect these glimpses of scenes, these visions of possibility, until they suddenly break into play. Then guide that play back until it again breaks into something bigger than itself: a work for many audiences, an opportunity to come together as a people, a vision for something new. Art practice for me has always been a system of care, rooted in intimate community and in service to social change. It allows space to practice transforming generational curses into cures; like my play *8ball* about a family during the 1980s crack cocaine pandemic, or my film *Inamorata* about infidelity and reconciliation among two women in love with the same man. Finding connections across difference and mending relationships troubled by trauma are the intentions behind my work no matter the medium. I work on an intimate scale creatively because it feels like a more manageable arena to consider such seemingly impossible terms like safety and stability in my body, on my block, within my city and community as an artist, mother, and Black woman. I write impossible worlds into existence because visioning is a collective act, one that invites new ways of being in relationship, one that acts as a useful tool toward collective liberation.

HIP HOP, SPOKEN WORD, AND PERFORMANCE THEATRE IN PRISONS

BRYONN BAIN: Peace, peace. How y'all doing?

> Mephistopheles
>
> The world is so upside down I dial 999
> And say: "Operator, put the Devil on the line!"
> Too many people on this planet are poor and dying
> Not player hatin'—I'm giving Satan piece of my mind
>
> The Devil has me on hold 400 years
> But my eye is on the prize I keep the phone to my ear
> When he clicks over he says, "Can I call you back, my Man?
> I'm on the other line with my Uncle Sam."
>
> Sam needed a hand with a business plan
> And was mad that one went bad in Afghanistan
> So I say, "Yo, just call me back in a couple of years!"
> Wanted to tell him go to hell, but he was already there
> Most people miss the Devil when he walks right by
> They be looking for his tail or two horns in the sky
> The Devil doesn't look demonic, doesn't act deranged
> Drives a solar-powered car and rocks Armani exchange
>
> Met him on a sunny, summer afternoon
> I was hanging at my house about to barbecue
> Brothers was getting mad cause all I had was tofu
> When Lu came through and grabbed a couple of brews
>
> The Devil got drunk about half past two
> Seen him slip some bacon in the vegetarian stew
> Stole some old lady's dentures so she couldn't chew
> Then kicked down a little kid wearing corrective shoes
>
> But what I really can't stand didn't go down there
> I don't care that he be tripping after too many beers
> What I hate is all the suffering that seems to surround me
> Cause he got cash ruling everything around me
>
> Got my moms at three jobs just to make ends meet
> Brother stabbed up in the street last week
> Older cousin overdosing on cocaine
> Homey took a bullet to the back of the brain

So I wasn't bout to stop when my phone call failed
I get out my PC to send the devil email
Copy his address off an old CD-ROM
It's WickedMutherfuckerAngry@God.com

I write: Devil, I'm directing this letter to you!
Time your wicked ways 'round the world was through!
But before I get another word out on the keys I hear: Beep beep!
Beep beep!! Beep beep!!! Now who the hell is this paging me?

Take my celly off my hip
So I can see what it says
"Lucifer left you a message."
Is all that it read

So I open my phone
So I can retrieve the voicemail
Mephistopheles left for me
He said . . .

"Sorry that I haven't gotten back to you
But that ain't the only thing I ain't been able to do
See, I been chillin like a villain on vacation with my crew
On a beach in a black hole far from you!"

I look up at the letter I just completed
Double-click on an icon so it was deleted
The Devil hadn't been to earth in six centuries
The world is how it is cause that's how people want it to be

Got my moms at three jobs just to make ends meet
The government don't give a damn if poor folk eat
Brother stabbed up in the street last week
Another brother needed Nikes on his feet

My older cousin overdosed on cocaine
Since CointelPro the ghetto ain't the same
My homey took a bullet to the back of the brain
NYPD wanted somebody to blame

We are living in a material world
Living and dying in a material world
Living working dying in a material world
Like spiritually anorexic boys and girls. [*Applause*]

Figure 9.4 Bryonn Bain performing *Lyrics from Lockdown*. Photo by Lee Wexler.

It's an honor to be here with my brethren and sistren to rock with y'all today. When I was 15 years old, I was invited to perform in a prison in upstate New York. It was almost like a dare. My brother K was like, "It's a captive audience. They can only boo us so much." [*Laughter*] So I was like, "Let's go do it." So we did it, right? We went, we rocked, we banged on the table, we freestyled, we spit, we sang holiday songs, and the OGs took us afterwards, broke bread, and we were just hooked. We were like, "We're going back every holiday season." We did that till I was in my mid-20s. And when I was in my mid-20s, I had an experience where I was put into a correctional facility that wasn't on a voluntary basis. [*Laughter*]

And so that experience changed my life and led me into going into prisons in a more political way. And as an artist, my father sang Calypso music on his way from Trinidad to the Apollo theater in Harlem. And I grew up hearing all these songs, everything from Mighty Sparrow and Harry Belafonte to Led Zeppelin, you know what I'm saying? That was the gumbo in my house, and it really forced me to think about being incarcerated and incarceration, that problem, in a much bigger way. So for the next 10 years after that we're going in prisons and began organizing to do work in prison. I began courses at Columbia, at NYU, at the New School, going into Rikers Island. At LIU in Brooklyn going to Boys Town Detention Center. But a lot of my thinking was shaped by the experiences of over a decade of doing work at Rikers. We had toured prisons in half the states in the country, doing Hip Hop, spoken word, and theater as a tool for healing. The wardens, COs, wouldn't let us go in if we said, "Listen, we have a revolutionary agenda to reappropriate resources for the liberation struggle, so we here to actually begin that process." [*Laughter*] So we said, instead, "This is about spiritual growth and healing, right?" And honestly, at first, it was just game. And in the process, we realized, actually, the word became flesh. That was actually the real core of what we were doing.

RIKERS ISLAND: BUILDING CURRICULUM IN REVERSE

So the first time we went into Rikers Island we were like, "Okay, we're going to revolutionize these young brothers." Rikers Island has about 13,000 incarcerated men and women. It's the largest penal colony in the world. During any given year, there's four to five thousand teenagers, 16–19 years old, incarcerated at Rikers. They spend $167,000 per year per person at Rikers Island because there's so much movement between the 10 jails that are there. And the New York state public schools spend less than $15,000 per student per year. They spend over 10 times the resources to actually incarcerate young folks in New York City as they do to actually fuel their education. So when I hear folks talk about, "The system is broken, we gotta fix it," I'm like, "No, actually, the system is working exactly as it was designed to work." Right? To make Black and Brown folks slaves and hard workers for White folks, and to make White folks—unless you come from the upper echelons of the socioeconomic ladder—a cog in the wheel. To not inspire you, to not cultivate your imagination.

So, in Rikers, our plan was to go in and to teach them their first lesson. "We're going to teach Assata Shakur." We were like, "Yeah, the Black Panther Party. Here's the history of the Panthers." They were like, "Uh, what is this?" They were bored out their minds. Until one of the young brothers said, "Wait a second, isn't that like Tupac's auntie?" And then another brother said, "Yeah, wasn't Tupac's mom locked up when she was pregnant with him and everything?" And because Tupac Shakur, at Rikers Island, is like Jesus Christ [*laughter*], all of the sudden, we had their attention. So we reverse engineered the curriculum and I went the next summer. I interviewed 50 young brothers, one at a time, to find out what was on their playlist. If you were stranded on an island, what would you listen to? What are the songs you know all the words to? And so we built the curriculum in reverse to link the literacies that they have to the literacies we know they need to have access to institutions of power and privilege that we already had access to. And so those courses have been going on for about 10 years at Columbia, at NYU, at the New School. And it's been transformative.

I only learned later on that these were some of the ideas of another lawyer turned educator by the name of Paulo Freire, alright, who went to law school and said, "Wait a second. I would use these skills in a different way." He challenged the whole banking concept of education. People are not ATMs. You don't deposit ideas into people to get them to regurgitate them at the end, alright. Education should be about liberation. I learned later on that, actually, Paulo Freire influenced Augusto Boal. We began to use theater in prisons and I was introduced to this in law school by the warrior-lawyer Lani Guinier, who brought in folks doing theater in prisons in Cornell. I said, "Wait a second. I'm supposed to be doing that."[5] And it blew my mind to learn this other way to look at theater.

At the same time, if anybody here has been to a theater in a Black community, you know what that experience is like. How is the experience of theater different in a Black neighborhood? Besides the fact that we bring our own food, what else happens? [*Laughter*] What else goes on? The audience talks back! "Girl, you better run! What's wrong with you? Get up off the ground. Oh, my God! I can't believe it. What? Oh! A brother gotta die in the first few minutes every time!" You know what I'm saying? So, Boal said that yeah, that's the way it's always been. Historically, theater hasn't been the Aristotelian form of theater where we passively just absorb. We interact. Can I get an amen? "Amen!" Can I get a hallelujah? "Hallelujah!" Somebody say holla. "Holla!" It's all the same spirit. This is the ancient ritual that we are participating in, right, from the ancient drum circle to the haiku masters traveling around with their 17 syllables to the poetry cipher, the slam, the Hip Hop emcee battle. That same spirit.

So Boal said, "Listen, we need to take it back to that space." So we began using theater in an interactive way, in a participatory way, in prisons, and linking Hip Hop and spoken word with that.[6]

DECOLONIZING THE MIND

I want to share one other quick story which kind of captures, I think, the ideas, the theory and practice that most of our work has been motivated by. Che said if you want to engage in protracted struggle, you have to engage both the theory and the practice of change, right, theory and practice of revolutionary struggle. So one of the master teachers I had the privilege of studying with was Ngũgĩ wa Thiong'o. Ngũgĩ wa Thiong'o is from Kenya and in his area in Kenya, the people spoke Gĩkũyũ. So Ngũgĩ grew up speaking Gĩkũyũ, but in his school, the British were there with their colonial occupation. They forced the kids to speak English. That's half the story. The other part of it is that they would beat the children when they spoke in their native language, Gĩkũyũ. But they didn't beat them right away. What they would do is they would actually take each student one at a time. Class is going on and then all of the sudden, somebody would speak out in Gĩkũyũ. They'd give that student a little black stone and go on with the lesson. A little while later, somebody else speaks out in Gĩkũyũ. The first student would then pass the black stone to the second one and they'd go on with the lesson. And then somebody else speaks out in Gĩkũyũ, and the black stone gets passed on to them. And so at the end of the day what happens is the teacher would go to the last person who had the black stone, and would say, "Okay, now it's time for you to get your lashes. Go pick a little branch from the back behind the school and before we beat you, we're not going to beat you quite as badly if you tell us who gave you the black rock. Okay?" So he gets 10 lashes instead of 20, and it goes on and on to the end of the day.

So the lesson in this was very powerful. It was twofold. The students were learning, one, to devalue all things African, and overvalue all things European, all things White, all right, European culture. Because we know that language is not just a communicator of ideas. It doesn't just carry ideas. It's also a carrier of culture, right? If we talk a certain way, it says something about where we're from, you know what I'm saying? Or if we talk like that we come from a different part of the planet, then that culture is carried in the language we speaking, right? All of your culture, if you're from New York, you know what I'm saying, your neighborhood might tell you where you from, "son," you know what I'm saying? So all of the language that they were actually censoring was communicating so much more than just, "Don't speak your language." It was teaching them, "You are less than this. You are inferior to this. So participate in your own oppression. Give into it. Let it go."

The second powerful idea which ties into the idea of spoken word and Hip Hop pedagogies is they were also learning the power of divide and conquer. They were learning that you can actually better yourself by separating yourself from your brothers and sisters. You, by distancing from those who your interests are in alignment with, you actually can further yourself. And I think that is a lesson that too many of us have embraced in so many of these elite institutions. Adam Clayton Powell Jr. said one time, "Harvard has ruined more Negroes than bad whiskey." [*Laughter*] Alright? So, for me, bringing together these university spaces with folks who are incarcerated is a part of what I see as a much more radical project, which is about much more than just critical literacy and life skills. Those are important parts of it, but it's also about rethinking and reimagining where resources and where power is located in this society. And I end with that so we can get into our conversation. Thank you very much. [*Applause*]

JEFF CHANG: There were a lot of themes that resonated, I think, between the four of you. The power of love and the power of counteracting generational transmission of trauma, and how it gets remade and reproduced every generation, and the power of looking at the word and being able to undo that, I think came out pretty thoroughly in all of those.

QUESTION 1: For all of you, what has been the most fulfilling thing you've researched or participated in?

LEE: I gave birth at home without drugs. [*Applause*] I would have to say for many reasons, that's been really incredible for me. The way that I love young people has a motherly touch to it. And that has taught me an expansive type of love. The way that I love my son must be the way that I love my students. And that's why I'm still in public schools because that's the goal. I'm not going to give up on the system, even though, as Bryonn said, it's a setup and it's working beautifully. But there's still hope wherever there is real love.

BAIN: Well, actually, my son came a month early, and basically, I was in the bedroom with two phones in my hand—a phone in each hand, in my underwear—and he just appeared. The ambulance came five minutes later, you know what I'm saying? So it was not expected, it was not planned. I try to eat natural and organic, but for childbirth I want to be in the hospital with the army of doctors and nurses who do this every day, with the latest technology. But definitely that's one of the most fulfilling moments.

I think in terms of the context of spoken word pedagogies, I had one amazing moment that just was very different for me. The first time I actually got to perform and lead workshops in a correction facility that was mostly White was years ago in Springfield, Ohio, the Clark County detention center. I went the first day, performed and did workshops, and I said, "I'm coming back in a couple days. We're going to do a slam. So y'all get ready." We gave them some tools to work with and there was a young boy, 15 year old, James, who was sentenced to 98 days. He requested to stay a 99th day to be in the slam. And then he won. [*Laughter*] So he left the next day with the wind at his back and a whole new relationship to language and words. Like, "Yeah, I won that. Yeah, I took first prize." So to be a participant in that process, to me, was an unforgettable experience.

CHANG: One of the things that you all raised was this sense of responsibility that you have as teachers, right, as parents, and as teachers. You're sort of talking about them being the same thing in some ways. Your parental skills are your teaching skills, and your teaching skills are your parental skills. We're trying to empower the students to be able to tell their stories, right, their traumatic stories, often. And then the class ends, and we leave the prison, we leave the school, the quarter ends, we're off to our next thing. But the stories that are being released bring with them all these emotions, and people then have to deal with the aftermath of telling these stories, sometimes publicly, sometimes for applause, and points, and rewards, that accrue to everybody around them but themselves. So what are the ethics and responsibilities that we have as teachers to these students in these pedagogies that are meant to be liberating, but at the end of the day we're not there anymore?

BAIN: We began touring prisons every summer. It was a very grassroots tour. Every summer we would go for several weeks and just try to really link local communities to folks who are incarcerated. And I think what happened is we decided, ultimately after five years of that, that we would focus at Rikers to sort of be able to maintain relationships in an ongoing way after the applause dies down. So I think that was part of rethinking our work to actually think about the whole continuum of the experience of incarceration. In New Haven, for about a year, I did a series at Whalley Avenue Prison which is like the Rikers of Connecticut, right next to Yale, right? It's like all the universities are next to prisons and oftentimes there's no dialogue. So we had this poetry group there and I remember—because it was like folks from 16, 17 to 60 years old who were there—poetry was the only space where they could actually be vulnerable because in the facility you have to wear your mask the whole time wherever you go, you know what I'm saying? It's just a rare thing to have somebody shed a tear or anything like that at all. So the safe space that Michelle touched on before was an important part of that. I mean, I was literally ripping up my love poems because these cats were going so deep with theirs. But I think, really, creating a way for the thing to continue without you being a necessary part of it, right, making yourself somehow irrelevant by really developing miles of rotating leadership. So first day of class, I always create our community contract. So we decide what are the rules that we need to be in this space to feel safe, supported, encouraged, respected, and then I will lead that. But then by the second, third class, somebody else is sort of leading the recitation of the community contract so that the spirit of that thing is preserved without my participation. I've gotten all these other local artists to be part of the process, so it's not dependent on me for it to continue to survive and thrive.

LEE: The kind of principled ethical and moral responsibility we have is to create safe space that's consistent and dependable because sometimes— and I don't mean to be dramatic—straight up, that is the only consistent, dependable thing in a young person's life. And I really mean that. It's just not hyperbole. So for me it's like you open up a young person and they're talking about being raped by their uncle. And this is over a course of three years though. A young person that began with us, and not with myself, but with another mentor at Youth Speaks, started writing about banana pancakes in their first after-school workshop. At the end of three years before leaving for college out of state, they shared a beautiful, self-possessed poem about sexual abuse and incest. And I think that that can only happen when there's a consistent place for them to go week after week. It's both presence and love. And I feel like at some point, it almost is like parenting. And I think some people might really hate this answer, and I'm okay with that. But it's like you raise your children the best way you know how, up until a certain point, and then they gotta go.

CHANG: I'm going to cry, Michelle. You're going to make me cry. My son's going off to college in three weeks, so I'm like, "You're doing this on purpose, I know you are, Mush!" [*Laughter*]

LEE: And to an amazing program, full scholarship. The idea is we work with someone like Jeff's son, Johnny, who has been with us for three, four years. And the point is not to have him necessarily open up to continue processing the same trauma with no container for that trauma to be held, but it's like now you have the tools, whether it's writing, whether it's knowing how to ask the right questions, I want you to be equipped to create your own safe space in the ways that makes the most sense for you. It doesn't have to be Youth Speaks style, but here are the tenets of our pedagogy. Here's what we mean when we say "safe space." It means be prepared. It means asking questions that lead to questions. It means wearing the hat of a learner as well as a teacher. And then loving. And when he goes to the University of Wisconsin, Madison, the hope is that he will go and model healing and voice for other young folks who may not have had that type of interaction with mentors, with positive adults in their lives.

GONZALES: I'd say in about 15 years of work and over several hundred organizations, I can think of less than 10 that have a mandatory introduction to trauma and growth foundations for the facilitators in the space.

And I'd say it's something that, structurally, creative and youth development spaces are failing miserably in. And it's only been in the last two years, partially due to the funding structure shifts and what they've been mandating for non-profit-based organizations, have they been looking at what goes on through the process of writing. And we have to remember that through the process of writing, the body remembers. And so when you're asking people to write, time is not a constant as much as a concept. You write and time bends. Language is a time machine. And so you ask someone to write on something and you're sending them out of the room. And so we use a very just simple process, an axiom, you could say, which is do not open wounds you're not trained to heal. And that's just across the board. Do not use your lack of knowledge as an excuse to not open conversations, though. Because the reality is that one student who wrote about sexual trauma, if she's a young woman, represents the one in four young women in the US who've had a childhood sexual violation or trauma. If he's a young boy, it's the one in six young boys who've had a childhood sexual violation. So it's a lived experience for far too many people within this country, but we don't speak about it.

I am also thinking about the role of the teacher. And I think we have to really go back and ask: What is the educational system we're in? Because historically, if you even look at sacred education or if you look at most non–1800 to 2000 Western education, is that there's not just a centralized space of random people with the credential who are separate from the community who are being paid to grow children. They're rooted within it. So the people who see the children are the people who see them when they go home. And I think we have to really ask as education structures are completely shifting in these days and ages, how do we return to those relationship-based engagements? So even if we don't have all the answers, we're engaging whole person wellness versus structural liabilities. Because I think that's where the conversation of trauma currently is within most institutions. It's not, "This person is wounded, and we're all wounded, so what is our own accountability in healing collectively?" It's, "We have to report it because Child Protection Services says we have to report it," which then begins a legal procedure, which then introduces courts, and prisons, and foster systems, and the taking away of children, which opens up an entire conversation. And that's not the way I really want to engage creativity and healing. I really want to engage, what does it mean to be a whole person, and what does whole person wellness look like?

LEE: I want to just say that our work is not a substitution for mental health services. And not to say that mental health services are the perfect model. But I feel that as educators we have to own that, and we have to own that culturally as well. That's not who we are, and if I feel like a young person is tinkering on the edge of some real serious self-hate behaviors, I have to step aside and let the right community of folks tend to that. Healing is also the responsibility of audience members. It's not to just take in. It's your responsibility to find a way to speak to that poem or that poet in some way. It is not a free show.

QUESTION 2: What type of advice would you guys give us high schoolers about getting through life, the struggles that we go through during our daily lives with the police or misrepresentation at our school? We're misrepresented at our schools because we're Brown. People look down at us, thinking that we're only capable of doing wrong things and we're just bad because that's just how we're viewed in our hood or in our area. What type of advice would y'all give us on how to get through life?

LEE: It's a sister to sister question, fellas. [*Laughter*] I'm going to go ahead and step up. I'll just say—wow, this is a very Zen kind of mom moment—which is, don't allow the misperceptions of you to shape your actions and thoughts because then we become the stereotypes. We become the misperception that we're attempting to shatter through language. Spoken word and writing isn't about becoming published, not for me, at least, and I don't think for our brothers here. It's about how do you become literate in this world. How can you sit in a class like this five years from now and feel like you deserve that seat? That you don't constantly have to prove yourself to your peers. Like you can go, like Jeff was saying, toe-to-toe with anybody, whoever that other is in your mind, the imaginary other. Because sometimes we build it up. Don't let it turn you into a monster because it can really break you. It can really turn you cold and angry, and all your poems are just going to be like all of my poems when I was 19.

"Fuck you!" [*Laughter*] "I'm Asian!" And maybe sometimes it's going to one extreme so that you can come back and find a balance.

GONZALES: I think the one thing that's kept me alive is constantly just remembering this: "You're never as alone as you think and we may just be in the majority." And when I remember that, things get a little bit better. I used to look for, I think, answers, and then I realized I needed to look for questions. And I think that that was one of the setups that I was caught in, like, "No, no, no, you've got the wrong answer." And I was like, "I don't even like this question. What questions do I want to center?" And I really think about that word, centering, these days. I don't like this language of what they call resistance and fighting back. I've been rooted and lived a lot of my life in that language, and I realize it just always put me up like, "Okay, I gotta be ready to go." [*Hands up in a defensive fighting posture*] And I realize even the best we were thinking about was like, "What's an alternative look like?" And I'm like, "No, I want to center what's important to me." I want to create my own universe and my own galaxy. What's in there? And who's in there? What are my values, and what are my dreams, and what are my hopes, and how do I just stay alive long enough to figure it out? When I look in my family, that's the thing, literally. My cousins and all their dramas, and their prisons, and the addictions, and all the different realities they've lived through and we've lived through, and I just think about those who lived past 25, which, ironically, is when the brain finally solidifies itself. Those who lived past 25, they eventually figured it out, and that was it. There was no like, "Here's the magic answer," etc. It was just keep alive. Keep alive and things get into place eventually, and we figure it out.

And the other thing—I don't really like the concept of advice. I think, for me, it's more along the lines of just knowing that if you need anything, ask us. I mean, that's to me really the kind of stage I see my life at, which is just trying to be a resource for people who need anything. Not advice, but literally a phone call. Like people need bail money, food money, an ear, a ride, a laugh, a place to kick it, a breath, a word. Word. But I don't assume. I just say, "Just let me know." That's what I offer up. If you need anything, just let us know. And if we can give it, we can give it.

BAIN: My grandfather passed just a couple years ago. He was 103 years old. We thought he was 101. Six months later we found out he was lying about his age. [*Laughter*] But when he turned 100, I went to go see him and I remember saying, "Grandpa, what do you eat to live to be 100 years old?" And he looked at me, he said, "Boy, I ate everything but people." [*Laughter*] So he just crushed my whole vegan, macrobiotic theory, to the chagrin of many folks in the Bay Area. But he also never left Trinidad, you know what I'm saying? He didn't come, eat all this food here, plugged up with hormones. But I think it was more than just the good country vittles that kept him alive as old as he was. It was also that he was surrounded by people that loved him, you know what I'm saying? He was surrounded by all his community. People traveled from all over the island to come and meet the oldest man in Princes Town. He was surrounded by all that. And then when I looked at trends of folks who live to be 100 years plus, that actually is a common trend. Folks are rooted in a community. So I would say, surround yourself by folks who love you, who are going through what you're going through, who can help you get through it, who know your heart, who know your spirit, who know where you're headed, who believe in you.

For folks who are at the college and graduate level, this may resonate with you a little bit more. I was told by an elder, "You should have a personal board of directors." I was like, that's such a corporate image. [*Laughter*] But I think it's the same thing. Five, six, seven people, a small cadre, a cell of people—some your age, some older—who know your heart, who know where you're headed, who can be there for you as a sounding board for those moments of crisis, of transition, where you're trying to figure out which way you're going. My younger brother was told when he was in high school he was going to be dead or in prison by the time he was 25 years old by the principal of the school, Mr. Sam Black. I'll never forget that. So, yeah, but my brother works at City Hall now. He wears a suit. He was on the path for a while. When I got into law school and had my Harvard Law School acceptance on the fridge, he had half a ki in the fridge behind it, you know what I'm saying? But he found a way to actually turn things around and is doing great things, and I think that capacity is in all of us. That capacity to actually defy the odds is in all of us. And your greatness doesn't come on the heels of your gift. Your greatness comes on the heels of your great adversity, the challenges you face, and how you overcome them and show the world and those around you what you're really made of.

GONZALES: I think one of the things that our kind of current secular way of being has normalized is this idea that this life is all there is, but there's many different relationships with time. I come from a community and a tradition that believes we walk with angels and we walk with ancestors. Wherever you go. People ask me, "Don't you get stage fright?" It's like, "Nah, can't you see? We got homies up here. We roll deep wherever we go." And so when you talk about an ancestral advisory board, to play off of the idea of the personal advisory board, it's not just some abstract, poetic idea. We've been trained to believe we're alone, but you are never as alone as you think. Who walks with you? Who are you walking with? And the world just gets a little bit lighter when you walk like that. [*Applause*]

NOTES

1. Mark Gonzales, *In Times of Terror, Wage Beauty* (Wage Beauty x Think Disrupt, 2014).
2. Brian G. Dias and Kerry J. Ressler, "Parental Olfactory Experience Influences Behavior and Neural Structure in Subsequent Generations," *Nature Neuroscience* 17, no. 1 (2014): 89–96.
3. See more at https://youthspeaks.org/.
4. Twyla Tharp, *The Creative Habit: Learn It and Use It for Life* (Simon and Schuster, 2009).
5. See more in Bryonn Bain, *The Ugly Side of Beautiful: Rethinking Race and Prison in America* (Third World Press, 2013).
6. See more at http://www.lyricsfromlockdown.com/bio/.

PART III Hip Hop as Critical, Culturally Relevant, and Culturally Sustaining Pedagogy

10 "Where the Beat Drops"

CULTURALLY RELEVANT AND CULTURALLY
SUSTAINING HIP HOP PEDAGOGIES

Gloria Ladson-Billings, Django Paris, and H. Samy Alim

H. SAMY ALIM: What are *culturally relevant*[1] and *culturally sustaining pedagogies*,[2] and how do they relate to our conversations about Hip Hop knowledges, pedagogies, and futures? And how do they address the rapidly changing demographics of the United States, particularly when it comes to the shifting demographics of race? We know that very soon the majority of elementary school children in this country will be students of color.[3] So this, in my estimation and many others' estimation, requires a necessary and radical shift in mainstream educational research and practice. Educational scholarship must contend with these shifts or risk becoming irrelevant, not just to People of Color—although some people will nod that it already is irrelevant to us—but scholarship risks becoming intellectually irrelevant as well. In other words, this is not a plea for inclusion that you're going to hear tonight. It's not a cry for a seat at the table. But what you're witnessing here tonight has the potential to radically shift the terms of the educational debate. This is the current moment.

These pedagogies, while spanning the last two decades, are really pedagogies of the future. I speak for all of us when I say, I can't tell you how hyped I am to be joined by these two brilliant guests tonight. Gloria Ladson-Billings is one of the most influential and beloved educational and

Figure 10.1 Left to right, H. Samy Alim and Django Paris listen to Gloria Ladson-Billings drop knowledge. Photo by John Liau.

race scholars of our times. As the Kellner Family Endowed Professor in Urban Education at the University of Wisconsin, Madison, she is a critical race theorist and a Hip Hop pedagogue. Django Paris is the James A. and Cheryl A. Banks Professor of Education at Washington University in Seattle, where he directs the Banks Center for Educational Justice. The more Django and I engaged Gloria's work, the more we thought critically about its implementation in White mainstream institutions. And I know this is something Gloria's been dealing with as well—the ideological incorporation of her pedagogical theory, or more directly, the whitewashing that's been happening in relation to this work. And we keep seeing over and over again in whatever media you watch or listen to, the reemergence of deficit theories to describe Communities of Color, whether they're neo-"culture of poverty" arguments or the new "language gap" arguments that you're hearing so much about. These are hotly contested areas. This is what we'll be talking about tonight and this is the relevance of the 5th Element to broader discussions of race, culture, and education.

The last thing I will say is that, even in a short time with Gloria, as you will see tonight, she manages to mentor you. She is in a constant state of teaching, giving of herself, committed to the present and the future, and for that I'm ever grateful. And without further ado, Gloria Ladson-Billings. [*Applause*]

HIP HOP(E): REINVENTING CULTURALLY RELEVANT PEDAGOGY

GLORIA LADSON-BILLINGS: I've called my remarks Hip Hop(e): Reinventing Culturally Relevant Pedagogy. Most of you know me from something called *culturally relevant pedagogy* (CRP), probably because of this book, *Dreamkeepers: Successful Teachers of African American Children*,[4] which is in its second edition now, or if you know me as an academic, you know me from an article that was in the *American Educational Research Journal*.[5] Or you might know me from the work that everybody hates in the mainstream, Critical Race Theory.[6] In fact, Wisconsin is such an open records state that I got to read my tenure dossier and all the letters that was in it. And someone who was very, very prominent said, they loved the culturally relevant pedagogy work, but they were "less sanguine" [*laughter*] about this Critical Race Theory piece—that's mainstream for "I hated this" [*laughter*]. "Less sanguine." But that is a part of the work I do and people know me from both of those places.

When we talk about CRP, we've been talking about this notion of a focus on (1) student learning or academic achievement, (2) cultural competence, and (3) sociopolitical consciousness. The student learning goes without saying. That's a part of what you're supposed to be doing. Kids are supposed to learn something as a result of being in a classroom with teachers. We always have an argument of depth versus coverage: how much do you get done. And we have this notion where people think that, "Well, if you have a high failure rate, then you're rigorous." It's very prevalent on college campuses and literally college professors will brag about how many people didn't pass their course. And all of that came from a tradition in which we thought of education as if it were not a net but a sieve. In other words, you would get everybody in and then you pushed through those you thought were smart enough. You pushed through those who could take honors. You pushed through those who would go to Advanced Placement. You pushed those through those who could go to Stanford. But part of the demand today in K–12 education is another metaphor, not a sieve but a net. It's not that some should get through but *all should be successful.* That's always been the focus of culturally relevant pedagogy. How do we ensure that everybody is learning?

The cultural competence piece is this ability to be firmly grounded in one's own culture of origin and fluent in at least one other culture. In my dream world, our students leave school multiculturally competent, speaking many languages, being comfortable moving in and out of various cultural settings. At minimum though, they ought to be bicultural. So that means even White mainstream students have a responsibility to be able to have cultural competence beyond the culture that they start with. It is not what we often see in various helping professions like nursing or social work or counseling, where people say, "I'm doing culturally competent nursing or counseling," which they basically mean is, "I have a list of dos and don'ts for operating with those people." That's not what I mean by cultural competence.

And then the third piece that almost never makes it above the line is this notion of sociopolitical consciousness. And that is what, in short words, I would call "the so-what factor." When students say, "Well, why do we have to learn this? So what?" Sociopolitical consciousness is helping students understand the application of their work to solving real problems. This is not a new idea. This is an idea that comes to us from Thomas Jefferson. The whole point of education, "Above all things, I hope the education of the common people will be attended to; convinced that on their good sense, we may rely with the most security for the preservation of a due degree of liberty." So it doesn't say anything about getting a job. It doesn't say anything about getting into elite colleges. That says, if we're going to preserve democracy, the people have to know something. So the idea of sociopolitical consciousness is a critical piece to those three. So that's what it has been from its inception and my early research. But we're now in a place that I would call evolution.

I ask this question all the time. How many of you are on Twitter? Right. So I get more hands in a college audience. If I do professional development with teachers, I don't get anybody, right? [*Laughter*] Because when I go into schools I see signs like this, right? "No cellphones." And I try to remind people that what the kids are working with are not cellphones. They have computers in their hands on which they could make a call. Now, not the old school flip-phone you got with the factory ring [*laughter*], okay, that's a phone. But that's not what the kids have. The kids have smartphones. And so if you are going to be working with young people and you're not out in the social networks that they're in, Twitter, Instagram, Tumblr, not so much Facebook for them. If you're not there then you don't even know what the conversation is that they're engaging in.

NEW CENTURY STUDENTS: MOVEMENT, VERVE, COMMUNALISM

So, there are some tendencies of what I call new century students. One is that they think multitasking is an efficient work style. And I know this because I have one of these folks living in my house, right? [*Laughter*] So the computer is up, she got her smartphone, she's insta-messaging, she's trolling YouTube, she's watching TV. I mean, she's literally doing all these things at the same time. So even though the cognitive psychologists tell us this not an efficient work style, it's the preferred work style of what I call new century students. They've come to think of themselves as consumers rather than students. So they are shopping, and one of the things they are shopping for are courses that they like. And they often are not willing to pay for anything less than a B, because if you're going to be buying, why would you buy a D, right? [*Laughter*] But that's a mentality that has come about among new century students. They receive their news via push notices, internet sites, blogs, even the *Daily Show*. They're not going to get their news from the 11 o'clock news report.

They're interested in social justice but not so much social welfare. So that's one of the things that reflects the tension between things like healthcare. I hear young people saying, "Well, I don't want to pay for a bunch of old people's healthcare. I'm not sick." Okay, who been paying for your healthcare up to this point? A bunch of old people, right? [*Laughter*] You did not pay the bill when you left the hospital after you were born, but somebody had to pay the bill. Or the debate about Social Security, right? "I don't want to pay into Social Security. Let me just invest my money where I want to." So they do care about social justice but not as concerned about social welfare.

And for all of the faculty in here, I'm telling you, email is an old technology. Stop sending these people emails. They not reading them, okay? And for them, library research is something that they do on a computer desktop, which means they're not as likely to be opening up a journal and flipping through it. They go to the article they're looking for, whereas when you and I used to go to the library, we'd get the book, and then we'd be like, "Here, I got another good article. Oh, here. Got another good article." [*Laughter*] But our students don't do that. They go to the one article you assigned or they'll text you and say, "Is this in a PDF?" I mean like, "Can you just like get it to me instantly?" So we need to think about these tendencies. And they value staying connected. So places that tell them, "You can't use your cellphone," really are antithetical to the way in which they're used to operating. And they have very different conceptions of copyright, intellectual property, and plagiarism rules, right? Because they live in a culture which is sampling. They live in a culture which is about mash-ups and pulling things together.

Now, what I'm arguing when I tell you these things is not that we have to adapt to their standards, but we have to understand them. So that means as teachers, we have to help them understand, "Here's what constitutes copyright. Here's what I mean by plagiarism." So that they understand that they can't just grab stuff and call it their own. I would say 20 years ago, when we said "digital divide," we were talking about differences of race, class, certainly the socioeconomic levels. But I would say that the new digital divide is a generational one, right? That even in some of the most remote places I've been like rural South Africa, the students have what they call mobile devices. Even when their teachers don't have it, they have it. I was in a class in a township and the teacher was explaining to me, "Well, we can't be doing all this kind of stuff because we don't have these technologies." I turned to the students, I said, "How many of you have mobile devices?" 100%. "How many of you are on Twitter?" 100%. So me and the kids is going back with the tweets and the teacher is not even in the picture. That's where the digital divide is; it's a generational one.

And because it's this generational divide, what we're now seeing is, I would say that Hip Hop becomes common culture. Not Black culture, Latinx culture. It becomes common culture for young people in terms of their affect, their dance, their music, their dress. I'll often have teachers who will say to me things like, "Well, what if the kids are not into Hip Hop?" And my response is, "Then you ask that same question about Shakespeare." Because what if they're not into Shakespeare? We will teach what we value whether the kids are into it or not.

Returning to *Dreamkeepers,* in work from 1989, it focused on cultural history, revealing those kinds of things that textbooks omitted. These teachers that I worked with were very deliberate in inserting the kids' cultural history into their teaching. It also had a focus on community issues. Things like urban renewal, or concerns of veterans, or homelessness. But it had a limited focus on student culture. Only one teacher in my study used rap to teach poetry. For the most part, what was youth culture was not a part of that 1989–1991 study. But today's dreamkeepers need to include popular culture to the understanding of what we mean by culture; they need to recognize Hip Hop's longevity and its power. We keep talking about this as if this is a new thing. Hip Hop is over 40 years old.

In talking about our students as being new century students, in some ways I think of them as shape-shifters. They're much more difficult to pin down into neat categories of race, ethnicity, language, and culture. And examples of that have to do with their taste. Their sports heroes include Kobe Bryant and Jeremy Lin. They will follow Gabby Douglas and Lolo Jones. They listen to Justin Bieber. Well, maybe nobody listening to Justin now [*laughter*], because he's a criminal. But they were listening to Justin and Bruno Mars and Nicki Minaj. It's just not these neat narrow categories. They go across all kinds of genres. So part of what I think I have to do in my work is figure out how to connect the old and the new. So I have some work from Wade Boykin from 1983,[7] where he talks about these nine dimensions of African culture: spirituality, harmony, movement expressiveness, verve, affect, communalism, expressive individualism, morality, and social time perspective. And way back in '83 said, "I'm seeing these dimensions in African people around the world."

Well, I've been looking at ways in which these dimensions are showing up among new century students versus what I would call American values of: rugged individualism, competition and free enterprise, rationalism, control over things like the environment, or controlling time, change, equality/egalitarianism, privacy, future orientation, and self-help. Neither set of values is wrong. They just are. And so when you have these value clashes, if people subscribe to one versus the other or aren't able to code-switch in their value orientations, it's times like that that you have cultural conflict.

So if you go back to movement, *movement* is the emphasis of interweaving of movement, rhythm, percussion, music, dance that is central to psychological health. The old school movement would reflect something like maybe Alvin Ailey, but this would be a new school movement. It's still movement. *Verve* is the propensity for high levels of stimulation, energetic and lively action. Of course, schools call this ADHD [*laughter*], okay? But instead of medicating people, if you were in New Orleans, you're going to see verve and it's old school verve. Been there for centuries. But this is also verve on the ones and the twos, right? *Communalism*, this commitment to social connectedness and social bonds, and responsibility that transcends individual privileges. So being in that choir, right, "We're singing together" is about having a crew, right? I love the Wu-Tang Clan. And I love them because they worked together as well as individuals. And so that is that expressive individualism—a cultivation of distinctive personality and a proclivity for spontaneous, genuine, personal expression. Best example of that is if you ever go to a Black church. Oh, she gon wear that hat. I don't care if everybody else got that. She gon wear it the way she wear it. The next person gon have it cocked totally different, right? [*Laughter*] But there is also expressive individualism in my new century students and the way in which they both got on jeans, they both got on T-shirts, but there's a way in which each is carrying himself to express himself. Orality being that preference for oral and aural modes for speaking and communication. And speaking and listening treated as performances, so not just what's written but what's said, and what you hear.

As an example, I want to share a piece from Native Americans. I showed this when we were at the American Educational Research Association a couple of years ago, because I think once again, we get caught in thinking, "Oh this is a Black thing." This is an artist called Tall Paul (see chapter 4) of the Menominee Nation and he's out of Minnesota. [*Plays music video*]

> I feel the light and effects of assimilation
> In a city night erased by bright lights, skyscrapers . . .
> Imagine what it'd be to live nomadic off the land and free
> Instead, I was full of heat like a furnace,
> 'Cause I wasn't furnished with the language and traditional ways of my peeps
> Yeah, I used to feel like I wasn't truly indigenous . . .
> Definitely native, take responsibility for being educated
> My people and customs originating from early phases of history
> It's deeper than fried bread and contest powwows

I just want you to see the language, because that's a language that's dying. I've had countless students who have done dissertations on language revitalization among the Menominee, and yet it's not until this young man decided to put it in a form that young people could connect to that it had an impact.

Lastly, I just want you to know what we do at UW Madison and it really would kill me if me I didn't give a shout out to our First Wave scholars. The First Wave program at the University of Wisconsin, Madison is unique in this country, probably in the world, because you're not really going to find a program at a university—at a major university—that embraces Hip Hop culture, that embraces spoken word, that embraces Hip Hop theater, and really acknowledges the power that all these art forms are having. So our First Wave students are students that get scholarships because of their Hip Hop artistry. They have to study a major that we have. We recognize their skill and what that brings to the university. And that is a four-year scholarship because you have this artistry. [*Applause*]

KNOWLEDGE, HIP HOP, AND CULTURALLY SUSTAINING PEDAGOGIES

DJANGO PARIS: So following Gloria on the podium is basically like following your favorite emcee to the mic. So imagine following Lauryn Hill or Mos Def or Tupac, right? They just killed the set. Everybody goes wild and then they give you the mic and you're basically wondering what to do. But I'm giving big time thanks and praises to be sharing this mic with Gloria Ladson Billings. I've been thinking about the 5th Element and about *knowledge*. Whose counts where, for what purposes? It's clear for instance that the knowledges and the practices and bodies of Black and Brown and Native people count quite a bit in the domestic and global marketplace. Think Hip Hop and Black music more generally. Think college and professional athletics. Think the prison industrial complex. But once we get into pre-K–12 through university classrooms they often count quite less, if they count at all. And the knowledges and practices of people of color only do count if they can be assimilated into certain American stories of progress, of opportunity, of meritocracy, of dominant norms of cultural practice. And so we continue the battle to make spaces for fully realized and complex engagements with the knowledges and practices of many of our communities.

At heart, this battle is what culturally relevant and culturally sustaining pedagogy (CSP) is all about. What Jeff Chang and H. Samy Alim have done with this class then is part of a long tradition of making spaces and places for the knowledges and people and Communities of Color. Of course, here we are in the Bay Area, a place so crucial to making a space for ethnic studies. So my deep thanks to Alim and Jeff, two of my intellectual and cultural justice heroes, for continuing that tradition in ways that join the 5th Element, our knowledges, with the larger project of learning and cultural justice. So tonight, I'd like to talk just a little bit about CSP, which is an emerging concept that owes its deepest depth to Gloria's work on culturally relevant pedagogy. And also many other scholars who have worked to forge strength-centered frameworks for teaching students of color.

Let me say up front, and this will not be a surprise to many people in the room, but as a Black student born to a White settler mother and a Black Jamaican father up the road on these Ohlone homelands in San Francisco, I did not experience culturally sustaining pedagogy in California's public schools. [*Laughter*] It was clear early on that schools did not often value or attend to the practices of Communities of Color. And yet living within and across racial and ethnic communities showed me that multiple and valuable languages, literacies, literatures, and cultural practices did exist in the world. [*Displaying a family photograph*] And here I am, for example, in 1982 in Kingston, Jamaica, with my grandparents, a seminal moment in my journey toward consciousness about multiple Englishes and multiple ways of Blackness in the world. I also show this photo because of that dope Adidas outfit. [*Laughter*] I also show this photograph to pay homage to Jamaica, birthplace of my father, birthplace of the father of Hip Hop, DJ Kool Herc, and to remind us of Jeff Chang's prescient sentence in, *Can't Stop Won't Stop: A History of the Hip-Hop Generation*: "The blues had Mississippi, jazz has New Orleans, Hip Hop has Jamaica."[8] And the truth is I am a reggae head first. I actually brought these three mixtapes with some good, fresh reggae that I got from my younger brother Marley. That's his real name. [*Laughter*] I mean, if my name is Django . . . [*Laughter*]

My experience in public school, a Black young person with a Black immigrant father and a White mother, growing up very poor with a complicated class history that included college for three generations in Jamaica, these are some of the anchors of my own work, and why I commit my life to understanding and seeking to perpetuate and foster the practices of young People of Color, while also seeking to engage and extend them, in the project of cultural justice. So take just a few seconds to think of the following: Why this course for you? Why the 5th Element? Why and how are Hip Hop knowledges and youth cultures and, specifically, the youth cultures of Communities of Color crucial to the work you do in the world or want to do in the world? So kind of hold that. I mean, what are your commitments? And if you could just write down one word that captures that commitment. Maybe that word is "love" or "power" or "Blackness" or "revolution." It can be in any language. But just if you could, just hold one word for me that captures that commitment of why the knowledges of youth matter to you? I mean, one of the things that these anchors and commitments help us through is the difficult times, and they also make us cherish the joyful ones. They also give us concrete experiences, the things that you were thinking about, the reasons those words mattered to you.

Recently, I've come to see this pedagogical and curricular silencing through the concept of Toni Morrison's "White gaze."[9] One of the things that Alim and I ask in our 2014 article is: What would our pedagogies look like if this gaze and the kindred, patriarchal cisheteronormative, settler colonial, English monolingual, xenophobic, ableist gazes weren't the dominant ones in teaching and learning? What would liberating ourselves from these gazes and the educational expectations it forwards mean for envisioning new forms of teaching and learning? What if indeed the goal of teaching and learning with Black, Native, Latinx, Asian, and Pacific Islander young people was not ultimately to see how closely students could perform White middle-class norms of language, literacy, and cultural being, but rather was to explore, honor, and extend, and at times problematize, their heritage and community practices? It is from this place, somewhere beyond the dominant gazes and with our hearts and minds centered on our youth and communities, that we begin thinking about CSP, which as Gloria so perfectly put in her recent article, "uses culturally relevant pedagogy as the place where the beat drops," as a remix that does "not imply that the original was deficient but rather speaks to the changing and evolving needs of dynamic systems." Or put another way, a kindred way in building with Jamaican reggae, the Hip Hop tradition, CSP is a sort of dub side, what we call a version, building new possibilities using the same culturally relevant riddim to focus the work on the current moment.

CSP seeks to perpetuate and foster—to sustain—linguistic, literate, and cultural pluralism as part of education for positive social transformation and revitalization. We believe this term, stance, and practice is increasingly necessary given explicit assimilationist, monolingual, monocultural educational policies and the continued pervasive domination of narrow visions of achievement based largely on White middle-class norms. HB 2281, the K–12 ethnic studies ban in Arizona, is a particularly egregious example of such policies. And let me say Arizona, where I taught high school in the early 2000s, is a place that I love, with many extraordinary people and communities that have been on that land forever, and others who are newcomers to that land. I would hold up the former Mexican American Studies program in Tucson, Arizona, as an exemplar of the real CRP, and the real CSP before it was closed by the state board of education that claimed through HB 2281 that teaching Chicana/o and Indigenous histories, literatures, and practices, and even teaching dominant canonical White literatures and practices in critical ways, was essentially "anti-American." And I want to give a shout out to master teacher Curtis Acosta, who has done exemplary work in the program.

One example of the sort of critical cultural wealth fostered through the Mexican American Studies classes is this student Mariah Harvey, testifying before the State Senate as the classes were about to be closed. [*Plays video*]

STATE SENATOR: So whoever has been elected to talk about this program please come forward.

MARIAH HARVEY: My name's Mariah Harvey. I do believe that these classes are necessary to learn. Anyone opposed to the knowledge of youth is just—you're not getting it. You have to be ignorant beyond anything to not want the youth to have knowledge. We invite you to come and see our classes unannounced just so you get a real sense of what we're talking about.

STATE SENATOR: Thank you. You're very articulate and eloquent.

HARVEY: Thank you. You're more eloquent.

So, her thoughts about opposition to youth knowledge, right—"You just aren't getting it." The criticality needed to respond to the wack "articulate and eloquent" comment from the state senator shows school learning *can* join the brilliance of our young people.[10]

THE NEXT AMERICA: EVOLVING CULTURAL SHIFTS

Given current US demographic shifts toward a majority multilingual, multicultural society of color embedded in an ever more globalized world, fostering cultural, linguistic, and literate dexterity as Gloria was talking about is no longer simply about valuing all of our communities. Although I think that's important. It is also about the skills, knowledges, and ways of being needed for access and success in the present and the future.

So this data is from Paul Taylor's new book with the Pew Research Center, *The Next America*.[11] I mean, just look at that for a second, right? So, in 1960, the US was 85% White. Today, that's down nearly 25% to around 62%. Within 25 years or so, when many in this room are in their 40s, which I might say is a very great decade to be a part of [*laughter*], there will be more People of Color in the United States than White folks, with Latinxs being the largest group by far, Asian Americans the fastest-growing group. The percentages of Native peoples growing slightly and Black folks pretty much holding it steady like we always have. [*Laughter*] So like 12%. Now, to take this to schools as Alim was talking about, California schools already serve a majority of color, as do many other states like Arizona, which makes moves like English-only ethnic studies bans and affirmative action bans particularly pernicious and desperate forms of hegemony. Indeed, nationally, White students today, as Alim said, count for just over 50% of the public school students. So, 2000 was the first year there were more so-called "minority babies" born in the United States than White babies. The overall point is that this country is changing and really quickly. And as our society continues to shift, so too does what Lisa Delpit called the "culture of power" way back in 1988.[12] We can no longer assume that the White middle class, linguistic, literate, and cultural skills and ways of being that were considered the sole gatekeepers to the opportunity structure in the past will remain so as our society changes, and of course, check out Alim and Smitherman's book *Articulate While Black*[13] for more on that.

In essence, we need to work on pedagogy that will join all those babies of color who'll be flooding schools in the next five years, and also their White "minority" peers, and will prepare them for access to the plural, multiracial, multilingual, multicultural world of today and tomorrow. And to build on what Justice Sotomayor in her dissenting opinion said to the Michigan affirmative action ban, she said in her dissenting opinion, "You can't wish away racial inequality." And I would add for Justice Roberts and others of like mind, you can't wish away demographic change and all that comes with it. It is also obviously the case that demographic change alone does not guarantee social and cultural change (in the short term, as we see in Arizona, it often guarantees White supremacist backlash), but it does create a moral imperative and ongoing opportunity for an education that sustains our communities.

Connected to these demographic, and social, and cultural shifts are shifts in the ways that young people are living race and ethnicity. And oftentimes in our teaching, in our asset pedagogy teaching, we have really thought more statically in terms of the connection between race and culture, and Gloria was alluding to this before, right? And so in my own work, for instance, Black students were participants in Black Language (BL) and Hip Hop cultures but so were Latinx students, so were Mexican American students. So were Pacific Islander students. And so, one thing that I would like to say though about this is that sharing in BL across race and ethnicity, as I've looked at in some of my work, is not just about sharing in Black-originated words or grammatical constructions, right? As the late great June Jordan said, and I love this, "The syntax of a sentence equals the structure of your consciousness." By sharing language these youth are sharing ways of seeing and naming and being in the world across their racialized and ethnic communities. And coupled with language sharing in my work was participation, which won't surprise you, in Hip Hop culture.

So a young man I call Rahul, a Fijian-Indian-American young man born and raised in South Vista, a friend and also a dope emcee, wrote one song where he flowed:

> 'Cause I'm the one with the most hustle loot
> It doesn't run in my family so I call it a new root
> From the Fiji Islands to this ghetto beautiful place, I rose from the streets, teaching me to kill it on any type of beat
> From rock to country, to Hip Hop to rap
> Yeah, you know me as the first Fijian to ever do that.

As Rahul told me in his sophomore year, "It doesn't matter what race you is. If you can flow, you can rap." When the White gaze is the dominant one in our teaching, we have been so focused—with very good reason—on preserving and valuing the heritage practices of distinct Communities of Color as they contrast with dominant White practices that we have tended to devalue the cultural, linguistic, and literate flows within and across Communities of Color. While it is of course true that racialization and racism continues to be experienced differently (anti-Blackness, anti-Indigeneity, the model minority myth are distinctly experienced, yet related, for example), ignoring the changing ways race and ethnicity and cultural practices are lived is in many ways a divide-and-conquer mentality. Indeed, we should remember that coalitions of distinct experiences and common ones were at the heart of the ethnic studies movement, and I believe are at the heart of much of global Hip Hop cultures. And so in teaching, we need to resist reinforcing static unidirectional notions of cultural difference without attending to shifting and evolving ones.

MIGRATING INWARD FROM A PLACE OF LOVE

I'll end by "migrating inward," which I think is one of the most important movements we can make. And that is that most of the work in the asset pedagogies tradition has been purely positive. "All Hip Hop is conscious." "All youth culture and funds of knowledge are wonderful and need to be perpetuated in the project of cultural justice." We're critiquing that, as many have, and saying, "Of course, that's not the case." As in all cultures, cultures have both things that we want to extend and things that need to be revised in the project of cultural justice. But let me just say one thing on this "inward critique" that is really important: It can really only come from a place of love, right? The critical work of joining youth in challenging and changing problematic beliefs and practices can only happen from the inside and center beyond the White gaze and other dominant gazes from a place of love, understanding, and respect. And too many of us as teachers and people, as researchers, as families, aren't really in that place yet. And I think this is an important thing to think about. Maybe we can take that up a little bit. As Alim and I talk about, we need to stop "half-stepping" asset-based pedagogies.

And so let me just end with this: The struggle for educational justice for students of color continues. We all know that. We ask youth, families, educators, researchers to join us. And we ask those of you here, those who're involved in the cultural work of the arts of education, wherever teaching and learning happens, we ask you to join with us to take the struggle further in the full knowledge that our practices and beliefs, and as Toni Morrison reminded us, our lives, have depth and value in their own right and must be sustained in ever more critical ways as our nation and world changes onto the dub side of theory and practice for educational justice.[14] [*Applause*]

QUESTION 1: What are the implications that culturally relevant and sustaining pedagogies have for teacher education, and teacher learning, and teacher-student involvement?

LADSON-BILLINGS: Let me just raise the question I raise whenever people say, "Well, why should we do this or how?" What are we trying to produce? I think I have a pretty good idea what the neoliberal agenda wants to produce—workers. Workers that don't ask any questions, that don't challenge, and they certainly don't organize. They just come and do a job and they're just glad to have the job. But I think what culturally relevant and culturally sustaining practices are trying to produce are human beings with strong democratic sensibilities. So those are two very different goals, and I think as a teacher, that's the question that anyone who is teaching has to ask themselves, "What is it that I'm trying to produce? What do I want to see at the end?" Not just this moment. Not just what the test scores say. "What kind of people do I want to have a hand in shaping?"

PARIS: Yeah, I mean, it's been pretty clear, as Gloria was alluding to, what kind of people schools have been interested in shaping for centuries, really. And the students that schools have been interested in shaping are, as you said back in 1994, it's really an assimilate or fail model, right? You either assimilate to certain ways of doing and being or you don't succeed, or there's other places waiting for you—the school to prison pipeline. And so these are deep questions that teachers need to ask. I think one of the really exciting things for me is that Gloria asked the question in '94, "What's happening that's good for Black students? Where's that happening, right?" And so one of the questions that we continue to ask is, Where are extraordinary educators doing work around relevant and sustaining pedagogies, right? And there are lots of them doing work inside schools and community organizations. And there are young people doing extraordinary work that teachers need to join. And so looking at it rather than from what Eve Tuck[15] calls a damage-centered perspective or a pain narrative to the sorts of sustaining things that we see going on is one place to start.

QUESTION 2: How can each of us, given our different styles and ways of being, contribute to the larger mission of CRP / CSP? And how can each person contribute to building this society?

LADSON-BILLINGS: We have to begin to look for the commonalities. I mean, people have asked me over and over, "You teachin what? You doin Hip Hop what?" But I see an incredible commonality between your generation and mine. I'm a child of the '60s. Well, we wanted to get some stuff done. I start my class off with the Last Poets, right?[16] And one of the things that I think is interestingly happening to society is that the overall agenda's figured out that the 18–25-year-olds are the most dangerous people in the society. So you either have to neutralize them through narcotics, lock them up, or convince them to go along with your program. And that's been really effective except that Hip Hop has revitalized this whole notion of young people as movers and shakers in the culture. And I would say, you cannot let people do those other three things to you. That you have to continue on with this consciousness that has been raised in you. And each of you has a sphere of influence. You have people who'll listen to you. You have people who'll respond to you. And you can't just do it with just your friends. You have to get out there and be able to spread this word. That's what Hip Hop has done for us. I think it's important that we promote the stuff that's happening that is positive in this culture and medium because it is really what is going to sustain people, especially in institutions like this.

I don't know how many of you have read the history of Stanford University. Actually, *read* it. Because I read it before I came here and when I finished reading I said, "Mm-hmm." And looked at my admittance form, finished reading and said, "I am not who you all are looking for." [*Laughter*] But I came in with that awareness. So I didn't let being here frustrate me because I kept saying, "They ain't build this for me." Ellwood P. Cubberley said, "I don't want nobody like you in this building."[17] So I had to go in spite of that. This is one of the first times I've been on campus and I didn't do through the Terman Building, because I love going through there. But Lewis Terman thought I was an idiot, right? "Black people don't know nothing." And I used to go through there. My classmates would say, "Why do you always walk through this building?" [*Laughter*] I said, "I just want this man to know, guess what? I'm still here. I haven't left. I'm not going nowhere." [*Applause*] And that's really our claim that we are still here after everything that has been done to try to destroy us, to wipe us off the face of the earth. We are still here. And so as you sit in classes that don't speak to you, I mean one of the things that you say over to yourself, "You know what? I'm going to be here next week, too. I don't know if I'm going to make it but I'm going to change it. I'm going to make it speak to me."

QUESTION 3: You talked about approaching things from a place of love, but we can't ignore the fact that there does still exist a dominant culture, a White dominant culture. So we know we don't want to assimilate, but at the same time, what is your vision?

Figure 10.2 Left to right, Django Paris, Gloria Ladson-Billings, and H. Samy Alim at the CSP Retreat, Santa Monica, California. Photo by Django Paris.

PARIS: I would just say one quick thing and that is, things are changing so rapidly, right? That one of the points we try to make in our work is it's really a false position that we put ourselves in and we've been put in. And that is that we either need to assimilate or fail, right? That you have to lose senses of self to gain new senses of self and ways of being in the world. And so cultural linguistic dexterity, literate dexterity, and so forth is now the goal, so that's a false choice. And we need to make sure it becomes even more so going forward. And so I feel like as teachers, as families, it's a crucial opportunity now as things are rapidly accelerating in terms of changes in racial and ethnic demographics, right? And age demographics too. And so it's a crucial moment for us to take advantage of what we've known for a long time as Communities of Color about cultural and linguistic dexterity, about double and multiple consciousnesses, right? Du Bois 1903.[18] It's a crucial moment for us to take advantage in pre-K-university to make multiple ways of knowing central to the discussion as they are in *this* class. In my undergrad classes, in my graduate classes, teachers that I work with are trying to not make the White gaze the dominant one in their teaching, in their curriculum, in the ways they think about the world and the ways they're open to students thinking about the world. And so I think we need to continue to build that up as youth grow and join us, right? And so we can't be trapped by thinking the dominant White gaze is going to be the only one going forward or that it's the only one now.

LADSON-BILLINGS: And I would also say that we have a responsibility to develop in our students a critical consciousness, so that they begin to understand that that which is from *them* is often being reinterpreted and sold back to them. This is them looking at what kids are doing. So one of the things that's been really exciting to me is looking at the internationalization of Hip Hop. I've been on six of the seven continents—I haven't been to Antarctica—but on the six of the seven continents I've been on I have seen a representation of Hip Hop on every last one of them. That's the power of this movement. I took some students to Sweden last February and that's crazy, right? I live in Wisconsin and I'm going to take some people to Sweden in February. [*Laughter*] But we're literally walking down the street and I'm hearing this beat. I said, "I don't know what those people are saying but that beat is fresh and we're going in here to listen to this." And so here they are in Swedish, rapping, flowing, the whole thing. So I'm saying, this is again something we are giving the world. The international song of protest is "We shall overcome," since the Freedom Movement of the '60s. Even in Tiananmen Square, the gentleman is standing in front of the tank with "We Shall Overcome" on his T-shirt. And yet we have children who don't understand that their culture is constantly giving to the world. What they're being told is they don't have anything. "That's street stuff. Don't bring that in here. That's slang, don't do this." They are literally re-cultivating the world and yet they don't understand that what they're being asked to take in is already theirs. And so I think developing that critical consciousness is incumbent upon us. We have to teach our kids what it is they are already contributing to the world.

QUESTION 4: I'm in my teacher education program right now and I just constantly feel frustrated in the schools that I've worked in that the system just isn't set up to teach CSPs. And this speaks to me so much, and that's the kind of educator that I aspire to be. And I'm terrified of my first year and knowing that this is what I want to do in my classroom. And I know that the schools that I'll be working in don't support this. What is one practical piece of advice that you would give pre-service teachers or current teachers?

PARIS: Can I just do two quick ones and then I'll let Gloria give the real answer. [*Laughter*] No, but I mean, so one is maybe it's not so practical, but I think it's essential. And that is to remember that we're part of a long movement for justice, right? And that folks who were working for the abolition of slavery, enslaved people, folks that were working for the women's right to vote, marriage equality, weren't waiting for that to happen before they acted, right? And so it's always been a struggle. And that frustration and that feeling like it wasn't built for the justice work I'm doing is there. And so to know that and to remind ourselves of that daily. I think the other thing on a practical level is to find other teachers who are doing similar work. And to collaborate and to make small professional learning communities within your own school, across schools, and again to have support from veteran teachers and from other new teachers that are trying to do the work. What are you studying to teach? ["Bilingual elementary."] Yeah, I would also just say there's a lot more room in the classroom and within even the most scripted type of situation than we might think. It is going to be hard. But if we push there is room there.

LADSON-BILLINGS: And what I would add to what Django has said is really get to know that community so that you could build those allies beyond the school walls. So that you'll have parents that will be up in arms if they think you're going to get moved out. Because it matters that the parents and the community members see you on their side. One of my former students is one of those examples of a teacher you should get to know. This year in my culturally relevant pedagogy course I Skyped in four teachers to talk about their work, and one of them is out here at Mountain View High School, Steve Kahl. Twenty-five years ago I was Steve Kahl's professor and supervisor at Santa Clara and he's helped change the entire assessment protocol at Mountain View, because he said, "I was tired of what they were doing. And so I kept doing workshops and stuff on it and the teachers invited me. 'Well, don't just tell us about it, come work with us.'" And so he moved out of Independence High School where he was back up here so he could work with these teachers and the entire Mountain View district is now looking at different ways of formative assessment. So yeah, make those connections and collaborations with people.

QUESTION 5: If you had to make your dream institution, or place of learning, what would it look like?

LADSON-BILLINGS: My school already exists. It's called the High School of the Recording Arts.[19] It's in Minneapolis, where kids who have been pushed out and kicked out of other institutions have found their way back in. They create public service announcements, they use their talents in Hip Hop culture to do this work, and they are again reconnecting with school. So for me, that already exists.

PARIS: It is interesting to think about how many of these spaces do exist but how we don't hear about them, right? So that's one thing. I think that to build on what Gloria's saying because that's a fully realized school. Another thing we can think is really expanding what we mean by school and what we think of as school. So I've been just getting to know Detroit as a community and as an extraordinary community. And one of the things that I'm learning from folks that have been doing work in Detroit for a long time, and you could ask dream hampton about this, but is the work that is already going on in Detroit, as dream shared with us a few weeks back in Michigan State. Thinking about the 5 Elements Gallery[20] in Detroit or some of the community gardening and urban gardening that's been going on, and the public art. And thinking of these community organizations that are already doing extraordinary learning work with youth; how to link those with schools or think of them *as* school. And so I think that's one of the things also to think about.

LADSON-BILLINGS: And from an international perspective I'd tell you to check out the United Alliance Community Center that's done by Charlotte

O'Neal and her husband, who was in exile for 42 years as a former Black Panther in Tanzania.[21] They are inviting people from everywhere to come. And check out some of the videos that they've produced. They invite people to come and see what they're doing and to work with them and teach. So I think that, like Django said, there's places all over, and not all of them in a structured school setting.

ALIM: Speaking directly to the international aspect, and where learning happens outside of school, I think Heal the Hood in Cape Town, South Africa (see chapter 2) and La Llama Rap Colectivo in El Raval, Barcelona (see chapter 5) are also doing brilliant, necessary CSP work in often difficult and challenging contexts. Much respect to them. Much respect and thanks to you, Gloria and Django. Peace everybody.

NOTES

1. See Gloria Ladson-Billings, "But That's Just Good Teaching! The Case for Culturally Relevant Pedagogy," *Theory into Practice* 34, no. 3 (1995): 159–65.

2. See Django Paris, "Culturally Sustaining Pedagogy: A Needed Change in Stance, Terminology, and Practice," *Educational Researcher* 41, no. 3 (2012): 93–97.

3. See R. Crouch, S. B. Zakariya, and J. Jiandani, *The United States of Education: The Changing Demographics of the United States and Their Schools* (Center for Public Education, 2012).

4. Gloria Ladson-Billings, *The Dreamkeepers: Successful Teachers of African American Children* (John Wiley & Sons, 2009).

5. Gloria Ladson-Billings, "Toward a Theory of Culturally Relevant Pedagogy," *American Educational Research Journal* 32, no. 3 (1995): 465–91.

6. Gloria Ladson-Billings, "Just What Is Critical Race Theory and What's It Doing in a Nice Field like Education?" *International Journal of Qualitative Studies in Education* 11, no. 1 (1998): 7–24.

7. A. Wade Boykin, "The Academic Performance of Afro-American Children," in *Achievement and Achievement Motives: Psychological and Sociological Approaches*, ed. Janet T. Spence, 321–71 (W. H. Freeman, 1983).

8. Jeff Chang, *Can't Stop Won't Stop: A History of the Hip-Hop Generation* (St. Martin's Press, 2007).

9. Toni Morrison, interview by Charlie Rose, *Charlie Rose*, PBS, November 10, 2008.

10. Seven years after closing the program, the law was finally overturned when a federal judge ruled that HB 2281 had been written and enforced with "racial animus" against Latinx and other students and educators of color.

11. Paul Taylor and the Pew Research Center, *The Next America: Boomers, Millennials, and the Looming Generational Showdown* (Public Affairs, 2016).

12. Lisa D. Delpit, "The Silenced Dialogue: Power and Pedagogy in Educating Other People's Children," *Harvard Educational Review* 58, no. 3 (1988): 280–99.

13. H. Samy Alim and Geneva Smitherman, *Articulate While Black: Barack Obama, Language, and Race in the U.S.* (Oxford University Press, 2012).

14. We delivered this lecture in 2015 and our thinking, our work, and the world has certainly changed since that time. And yet even as we may now see ever more clearly the connections between White supremacist backlash and the growing majority of color in the US nation-state and globally, as well as connections among Indigeneity, Blackness, land, and possible liberation, so much of what we shared in this lecture remains vital as so much about racism and intersecting forms of oppression and our beautiful collective resistance has not changed.

15. Eve Tuck, "Suspending Damage: A Letter to Communities," *Harvard Educational Review* 79, no. 3 (2009): 409–28.

16. See Abiodun Oyewole, Umar Bin Hassan, and Kim Green, *On a Mission: Selected Poems and a History of the Last Poets* (Henry Holt, 1996).

17. The building that houses the Stanford University Graduate School of Education is named after Ellwood P. Cubberley.

18. W. E. B. Du Bois, *The Souls of Black Folk* (Millennium, 2014 [A. C. McClurg, 1903]).

19. See more at http://hsra.org/.

20. See more at https://www.blac.media/news-features/5e-gallery-in-detroits-historic-corktown-district.

21. See Sheila Smith McKoy, "An Interview with Charlotte O'Neal," *Obsidian: Literature in the African Diaspora* 10, no. 1 (2009): 98–109.

11 How Hip Hop Means

RETROSPECT FOR BEATS, RHYMES, AND
CLASSROOM LIFE

Marc Lamont Hill

H. SAMY ALIM: Marc Lamont Hill is one of the leading intellectual voices in the country. He is also author of two Hip Hop texts: the foundational and award-winning *Beats, Rhymes, and Classroom Life: Hip Hop Pedagogy and the Politics of Identity*,[1] as well as his co-edited volume, *Schooling Hip-Hop*.[2] He has also written *The Classroom and the Cell*, with Mumia Abu-Jamal,[3] and the *New York Times* bestseller, *Nobody: Casualties of America's War on the Vulnerable, from Ferguson to Flint and Beyond*.[4] Marc, trained as an anthropologist of education, presents so many themes in his books that we are dealing with directly here in the 5th Element.

There are many reasons why Marc's *Beats, Rhymes, and Classroom Life* is one of the best case studies of Hip Hop pedagogy in the scholarly literature. First and foremost, Marc brings a much-needed analytic rigor to a field that demands it. The text is both celebratory and critical of Hip Hop pedagogies, of Hip Hop itself, and of American educational institutions. Also, as Gloria Ladson-Billings writes in the foreword, this book flips the discourse of the "achievement gap"—that we're always hearing about in the media and sometimes on this campus—which positions students as failures, to a discourse of a "cultural gap," which positions schools as failing, highlighting the *perennial problem of curriculum being disconnected from community and culture*. All of this is happening within the context of what sociologist Prudence Carter refers to as the "opportunity gap," in which schooling occurs within a context of growing economic and social inequalities.

As a teacher-researcher, Marc worked to discover the potential and the pitfalls of Hip Hop pedagogy—not only who we let in by these new methods, but also who we marginalize and exclude by these methods. We don't think of Hip Hop pedagogies as potentially exclusionary, but they can be. As he demonstrates throughout his work, the use of culturally relevant, in this case Hip Hop-based, pedagogies inevitably creates spaces of both voice and silence, centering and marginalization, empowerment and domination. Marc engages the politics of identity and centers culture in educational processes. While others may be willing to push aside issues of identity and culture as if they don't matter to how students learn, Marc tells us that, in fact, we should be foregrounding them. Let's give a big round of applause for Marc Lamont Hill. [*Applause*]

WHO AM I TO DO THIS WORK?

MARC LAMONT HILL: Peace everybody, how y'all doing? Y'all good? So, family, I want to begin as my instructors would have me. Susan Lytle, one of the great literacy theorists of our generation, as well as my former doctoral advisor Kathy Schultz, would always encourage me to situate myself in the work. As anthropologists, we have historically been taught not to do that. Until the "crisis of representation" of the '90s, we were told that it was a grave sin to explicitly locate yourself in your work. We were taught to have "a view from nowhere," a kind of Archimedean point of objectivity from which we should do our research and produce our analyses. Of course, many degenerate into mere navel gazing, where self-indulgence is disguised as reflexivity. But somewhere in the middle of these extremes is the idea that we can situate ourselves in the work and ask the fundamental question—as all of you should be asking as researchers and scholars, as teachers and cultural workers—"Who am I to do this work?"

When I think about who I am to do this work, the first place I land is not the University of Pennsylvania, Temple University, Morehouse College, or Teachers College; it's not all the schools I went to or taught at. It's North

Philly, Hunting Park, 1222 West Luzerne Street. And it was there that this project began. *Beats, Rhymes, and Classroom Life* was prefigured long before I got to graduate school, or even undergraduate school, because I was in the midst of Hip Hop. I grew up in the hood, listening to Hip Hop. I was surrounded by the sounds, sights, and spectacles of Hip Hop. And it was like my womb, it was what protected me. In many ways, Hip Hop raised me. It helped me to understand what was going on inside of a neighborhood that I was often excluded from.

I wasn't allowed outside the house because they was always killing everybody in Hunting Park. Every Saturday, somebody got killed. So my parents were like, "You're going to stay in the house." Kind of like how Nas talks about in "Project Window," Hip Hop was my window into what was going on in my own neighborhood. I was the kid who got on the school bus from all-Black North Philly to the mostly White Northeast Philly, where I could have a decent education—not a great education—but a decent public education. It's that 1954 *Brown v. Board* idea, right? Not that anything magic would happen if White people were in the building. Your IQ doesn't go up when White people are in the classroom. But the number of books and teachers might go up. And so I was on the bus ride up there, leaving North Philly and going to this new and strange place. I was trying to make sense of my own cultural identity at the same time that Hip Hop was trying to do that, too. And so to that extent, before Hip Hop entered the full-fledged gangsta rap moment, there was this cultural nationalist moment going on with the Native Tongues, especially A Tribe Called Quest and De La Soul. So Hip Hop in some ways helped me to understand my own racial identity. It helped me to make sense of new ethnic, racial, and ideological possibilities. Hip Hop in many ways provided an education for me.

There was also this gap between who school thought I was, who my neighborhood thought I was, and who Hip Hop thought I was. There was a gap between who my friends from the neighborhood were in their schools and who they were at home. I had friends who were writing rhymes on the back of napkins and on paper. We would be in the park on the corner and I'd hear people spittin and rhyming. I'd meet people who were able to consume large amounts of information. We were in the midst not just of Hip Hop's expansion but also an expanding Islamic community. People were joining the Five Percenters, learning Supreme Mathematics, and memorizing everything!

But school only focused on what they couldn't do. My peers were writing rhymes, and school said that they were illiterate. On the other side of Hunting Park, Puerto Rican and Dominican youth were working in their parents' stores and counting change without a register. But school said that they couldn't do math; they were not numerate. So, there was this huge gap between who school thought people were, and who I knew them to be. My people were smart, clever, precocious, and resourceful. In school, they were just "illiterate." They were just "behavior problems." They were just "struggling readers." They were just "at risk."

So by the time I got to graduate school, I brought all that with me. I began trying to make sense of who I was, who my friends were, and what these educational institutions that I occupied were. And I wanted to do so for the purpose of fixing them. I come out of the Africana intellectual tradition that says that the word can't just be the word, the word has to be made flesh—we have to actualize this knowledge. Knowledge has to be used in the interest of something, for the purpose of something.

I started to take these Education classes, where I kept hearing words like "deficit." I kept hearing words like "gap." And it was fascinating because I just couldn't understand how there was an achievement gap, and how we were reifying the gap through the language itself. We weren't talking about achievement gaps between Whites and Asians, despite the same difference in performance on high stakes testing. We weren't talking about "White-on-White crime," despite the fact that White people are killed by other White people 95% of the time. My point is that, even in a progressive graduate school, there was still a gap between how I understood my neighborhood and how the literature was talking about it.

And there were only a few places that helped me understand that gap in a different way. There was the culturally relevant and culturally responsive pedagogy literature. We stand on the very sturdy shoulders of people like Gloria Ladson-Billings, Geneva Gay, and Carol Lee for that reason. There was the multicultural education movement, pioneered by giants like James Banks. There were some critical pockets of possibility, but far from enough. So I decided I needed to figure out how to close that gap between who kids were and how school saw them, but also between who they were and who they could be.

Figure 11.1 Marc Lamont Hill teaches the 5th Element class. Photo by Abdul Alim.

I entered graduate school in 2001, and at that time a couple of really interesting articles came out in the *English Journal*. One was by Ernest Morrell and Jeff Duncan-Andrade, which was a very short piece, it was like six pages, and it was about how you teach an English course using Hip Hop texts. I was like, "Yo, now we gettin somewhere!" And then I went back and read Carol Lee's brilliant scholarship using signifying texts, particularly *Their Eyes Were Watching God*, as a way to scaffold literary interpretation to improve inferential and cognitive reading scores.[5] And I was like, "Yo, all right, now we're onto something. I know this stuff works. I know that my tradition has some value and some merit to it. How can I use it?" And so the first thing I did when I had a chance to do a teaching practicum was return to the old high school where I had taught Spanish and English. I wanted to see what would happen if I was using Hip Hop texts to teach literary interpretation.

HOW DOES HIP HOP MEAN?

As someone trained in the discipline of anthropology, which has had a significant impact on the field of education for more than half a century, I was interested in raising particular questions. These were different questions than I would have had if I were exclusively interested in student outcomes. We live in a world obsessed with technocracy, outcomes, numbers. And so, a lot of the questions that were being asked at that time were, "Does this stuff work? If I take Hip Hop and I put it in a classroom, will it work?" I cared about these questions too. I also wanted to know if it worked. But Carol Lee showed us, quantitatively and qualitatively, that it worked. Gloria Ladson-Billings *been* showing us that this stuff works. So, for me, the question became less about, "Does this work?" and more about, "What does 'work' mean? What else is going on while it's working?" Let's assume for a minute that people have great outcomes and are achieving. Cool, y'all are achieving, but it don't mean y'all ain't got issues. Y'all at Stanford, I know y'all achieving, and I know y'all got issues. [*Laughter*]

So, for me, it was a question of what else is going on. I was interested in the cultural dimensions of the class, the identity work that was happening, the power relations that were happening. If you tell me that in the middle of a classroom suddenly the students know more than teachers about this text that we're engaging, that we're suddenly witnessing what Michel Foucault called "the insurrection of subjugated knowledges," then what else is happening simultaneously in this classroom? What's happening coterminously? What's happening concomitantly? That's what Black people do when they get a mic! [*Laughter*] I wanted to know the stuff that was happening at the same damn time! That's my translation for the ratchet. [*Laughter*]

And so, I went into the classroom again, this time for my doctoral research. I decided that I wanted to ask some fundamental questions within a classroom where Hip Hop was *at the center* of this. And I wanted to ask them for several reasons. I'm going to take a step back now and tell you what conversations I was trying to intervene in. And what I saw was a literature in Hip Hop Studies that I thought was really interesting. We were studying Hip Hop in the academy. Tricia Rose's book came out in the early '90s, 1994.[6] There was Russell Potter's book.[7] I mean there wasn't that many, we knew all of them. Dr. P, William Eric Perkins, did the edited volume.[8] So, there were like maybe five books at the time. And by the time I got into graduate school there were a couple more, but not many.

I was trying to make sense of Hip Hop. But the thing about the work was, one, it was all textual. In other words, people were reading Hip Hop texts and interpreting them. "This is what this lyric means," "This is what this idea means," etc. And, for me, meaning is important but I wanted to ask some situated questions as well. In the musicological world Christopher Small has this idea of *musicking*.[9] And it asks the fundamental question: Why are people consuming or listening to this music at this time and in this place? Guthrie Ramsey also asks that question in *Race Music*.[10] Why are these people listening to this music in this time, at this place?

So I understood that Hip Hop was dope and there's all this interesting stuff. I can analyze Lil' Kim lyrics and understand the sexual empowerment dimensions of it and I can look at the use of irony and mood in Biggie and I can unpack some of the really interesting layers of Ras Kass, right? And that's fresh and that's cool. But I also wanted to know: How are people using this text? How are people making sense of this text? What does Hip Hop mean to them? Because there's often a gap between the expectations we have for what people are going to do with the text and what people actually do with the text.

At that time, I was also engaged in the critical pedagogy literature. And in some ways the critical pedagogy literature—which was often labeled "critical sociology of education" at the beginning—was my strongest theoretical apparatus because it was also asking questions about text. In 1968, there was like Philip Jackson, *Life in Classrooms*,[11] looking at the ways in which schools operated to reinforce the "hidden curriculum." By the time we get to Bowles and Gintis in '76—*Schooling in Capitalist America*[12]— and Bourdieu in '77, we were asking really interesting situated sociological questions about schools and how they function and reproduce inequality.

But then there was the turn to cultural studies within critical pedagogy that happened in the '80s and even more so in the '90s. Suddenly, a small group of education scholars were engaged with the Birmingham School, which offered us the cultural studies tradition. I don't want to get too far on a tangent, but cultural studies in a sense was trying to make sense of the everyday. Cultural studies was based on this idea that cultural was ordinary. Culture wasn't just the property of the bourgeois humanists, the Matthew Arnolds or Q. D. and F. R. Leavises of the world. It wasn't just the property of an overly pessimistic Frankfurt School thinker like Theodor Adorno. These folk saw culture as an exclusive and transcendent sphere. The cultural studies tradition taught us that culture was located in the ordinary. Like Emerson, the Stuart Halls of the world reminded us that there is magnificence in the quotidian, joy and beauty in the everyday.

Cultural Studies was showing us the richness and complexity of everyday cultural practices, from music to film to fashion. And it was stuff that we needed to not only consume, but critically engage. As people like Henry Giroux taught us,[13] culture had to be understood as a site of pedagogy. This meant recognizing pedagogy in spaces beyond the classroom. There's pedagogy in a store mannequin. It tells you what you're supposed to look like and what you're not supposed to look like. There's pedagogy in a political ad, as it helps to shape our social and ethical priorities. And there's pedagogy in popular culture, which is a vigorously contested terrain on which we come to understand what we're supposed to value, what we're supposed to consume, which identities we are supposed to perform.

So I wanted to understand the pedagogical relationship between individuals and texts. But, again, many of the critical pedagogy people were trying to do that on *behalf* of young people, on *behalf* of schools. They would look at a film like *Lean on Me* or critically examine a rap song, and tell us what the text signified about young people, schools, and other dimensions of the social world. And that work is necessary. We need to unpack a movie like *Lean on Me* because that's a straight-up Reagan Era narrative: Bad kids, bad school, no resources, bring in one awesome charismatic leader who "got tough" and transformed the school with no new books, no resources. That's almost always the narrative, right? I mean *Dangerous Minds, Dead Poets Society, Summer School, Pride, Freedom Riders*. Bad kids, bad school, no resources. Usually awesome White person comes in, changes the day. The only difference in *Lean on Me* is that he was Black but same narrative. So that stuff is cool, but the way that we interpret the text isn't necessarily how other people take the text up. So, for me, the question was, How can we link a conversation in critical pedagogy that unpacks the structures and latent messages, etc., in these texts to an analysis on the ground of how people are making sense of the text? I wanted not just text but context. And so, for me, as an ethnographer, that was the question to take up. What does Hip Hop look like in everyday practice? The problem was there weren't that many people doing it. Ian Condry did it with *Hip-Hop Japan*.[14] Greg Dimitriadis kind of towed the line in a very brilliant way in 2001 with his book, *Performing Identity / Performing Culture*, which was like a drink of water in a desert to anybody studying this.[15] That was the first book we were like, "Oh, this is fresh and smart." So, I was doing that.

And then there was still the question of cultural relevance. I said, what if we imagine Hip Hop in the tradition of Gloria Ladson-Billings and said this is a form of culturally relevant pedagogy? We know that students learn better when texts are connected to their cultural experience, when texts speak to their linguistic orientations and registers, when the characters in the book look like them, when the narratives and experiences are connected to them, when the pedagogical interactions speak to some of these values and traditions. (And, of course, we cannot essentialize Black culture into a singular set of experiences. At the same time, we can locate commonalities and points of contact.) So I was trying to make sense of all of that. But, in the conversation about cultural relevance, I was trying to say, "What does it mean to be relevant? And what kind of culture are we talking about?" So, if a text is culturally relevant, what does it mean for a text to be culturally relevant in the context of Hip Hop? What does it mean for me to turn on Kendrick Lamar and hear, "Sing for Me, I'm Dying of Thirst"? That might be culturally relevant but that doesn't necessarily mean that I want to take it up within the classroom space. Aretha Franklin used to sing, "Don't play that song for me. It brings back too many memories," right? So there's this way in which the text itself can be problematic and in which it can create contradictions in the classroom.

ENTERING THE FIELD: HIP HOP LIT

I wanted to know when this cultural stuff comes in, again, what else is going on? So I went back to the school that I call Howard High School in South Philadelphia. I went to the principal and said, "Yo, I really want to do this Hip Hop course." He said, "I would love to do it. But we have the PSSA," the high stakes test *du jour* in Pennsylvania. "And we're only teaching to the test. It's all we're going to offer." I said, "Okay, that's unfortunate, but I think this could help." He said, "No, I can't risk it. But I have these other kids in the night school program." He called them the "throwaways." He said, "You can have them." I said, "Okay, cool." It wasn't my favorite idea but I said, "Cool."

So he takes me to the evening school, the Twilight Program, with the "throwaways." These kids are a range of ages, but most are between 15 to 19. I also had one kid who was 23, the same age as me. I said, "Well, I need a teacher. I want to co-teach this with somebody," for lots of reasons. Partly because I actually believe in co-teaching as a form of knowledge production and co-generative dialogue. Also, as a teacher-researcher I thought that having a second teacher would be helpful for me in terms of collecting data and taking notes.

They gave me the perfect teacher. He was smart. He was accomplished. He'd won the state teaching award. Of course, six months before we started, they decided in the great wisdom of public education that, "This guy's such a great teacher. We should make him an administrator." So they took him out of the classroom and I needed a new teacher. And they eventually gave me the person I call Mr. Columbo. He was a little less engaged and wasn't a strong classroom teacher. We didn't complement each other in the same way. He didn't suffer this academic stuff much. He had a MA degree in English from a very nice, local graduate school, but he didn't think much of it. I think he saw our class, in retrospect, as a day off. Like, "You'll come in and teach. I'll do the housekeeping stuff." His exact words were, "You teach the Hip Hop stuff. I'll teach the real English stuff."

So we come into the classroom and we design the course, which we called "Hip-Hop Lit." The idea was, again, that we would teach it like a regular English course. The only difference is instead of Yeats or something we'd have Lauryn Hill. So we divided the units up by theme—roots of Hip Hop, love, family, neighborhood, despair, politics. Inside of each unit, we would have literary themes, literary devices, and literary approaches that we wanted people to learn. So we would take a text like "Manifest" by the Fugees. We would read those lines and we would make sense of tone and mood through Lauryn Hill's verse: "I would spend nights overwhelmed by God's test contemplating death with a Gillette but no man was ever worth the paradise manifest." So then as we get to the "contemplating death with a Gillette" part, we would interpret what that line meant. Some students said, "She's trying to kill him." Others said, "No, it's suicide." I was less interested in determining the dominant reading and more interested in having them nurture their inferential reading skills. That's the foundation of the ideas that got me into the course. They took pre- and post-tests, and did just fine, but that wasn't the point of the study. I wasn't interested in whether their reading scores would go up with a whole bunch of 50 Cent and Eminem. I wasn't interested if engaging Jay-Z would raise their cognitive scores. I was interested in what was going on in this classroom. And from that focus, three big ideas emerged.

MANAGING HIP HOP'S POLITICS OF AUTHENTICITY

The first thing that I found useful, instructive even, was the class's conception of authenticity politics. In chapter three of the book [*Beats, Rhymes, and Classroom Life*] I talk about the idea of "realness," which was an emic concept that emerged out of the data. One of the main classroom conversations was about what constituted "real Hip Hop." Each unit featured Hip Hop that I thought was dope. So I had Biggie, Jay-Z, Common, Nas, Digable Planets, and NWA. So there was a rich and diverse body of texts that I brought to the classroom. And I wanted students to consume these texts because I thought they represented real Hip Hop.

But there were debates in the classroom about what real Hip Hop was. For some of the students, real Hip Hop wasn't what I offered, but rather the stuff they listened to on the radio. And they were like, "Yo, I don't know Digable Planets." They didn't see that kind of text as real. Other people attached themselves to the class because they saw real Hip Hop as the stuff we taught. Other people saw real Hip Hop as the underground, so they were dismissing Jay-Z and Biggie as real Hip Hop. We had "the heads" in the class, the self-identified arbiters of what real Hip Hop was. And they were like, "No. This ain't real Hip Hop. Real Hip Hop is like Pharoahe Monch, Kweli, Mos Def." So there was this internal debate in the classroom about whether the texts themselves were authentic.

Now, this was fascinating because in a normal English class nobody's really questioning the legitimacy of Shakespeare. We have accepted that the canon is just the canon. But in this space we were debating that. And for me, that was cool because one of the points of a class like this is to question canonicity—not just to question what's included in the canon but to question the very idea of a canon. But sometimes students didn't want to engage texts that they didn't think were worth their time because they were not legitimate. And I was like, "You all, it's cool, we don't need a canon. Canons are bad." We need bodies of knowledge that we appeal to but, as Dewey said in *The Child and the Curriculum*,[16] it should be a map of previous experiences and should be constantly alternating and shifting based on human needs, based on the constitution of human knowledge, social convention, etc. There is no trans-historical, realist canon. And they were like, "Yeah. That's cool, Mr. Hill, but *you* got a canon." I was like, "What are you talking about?" They were like, "This class is a canon. Ain't no Lil Jon on there. Ain't no 2 Chainz."

And they were right. Because I had made a decision that certain things didn't fit either. So the takeaway from that piece for me was that oftentimes when we do progressive pedagogy, when we even do Hip Hop–based pedagogy, we have it in our minds that we're destroying the canon when sometimes we're just changing the canon. We're just aiming it in a different direction, you dig what I'm saying? I was making the very same high / low distinctions that other people were making. The same way the Frankfurt School was owning classical European music and dismissing jazz. How do you dismiss Coltrane?! But I was doing the same thing. I had Nas and Biggie because in my mind that was street genius. Nas was a pavement poet. I was like, "Yo, I can justify all this." And the Hip Hop intellectual canons were making such a strong and strident case for this kind of Hip Hop. And that was cool, but I was dismissing the ordinary. I wasn't finding magnificence in the quotidian. At the time, 50 Cent was the hottest thing in the world, and I was dismissing it because it just had no value to me. "This isn't intellectually rich enough." So they forced me to manage my own authenticity politics around the Hip Hop canon.

There was also the question of racial authenticity. Who can be in this space? Now, for me the point of this class was that everybody could be in this space. The best of our tradition isn't about reversing the relations of a person. I didn't want to give a gun to the rabbit, right? I didn't want White people or non–Hip Hop heads to get excluded from the class. I wanted everybody to feel and be able to engage these texts. But it was very interesting the way the politics of realness informed and governed the class. This was marked as a Black class. Real in so many ways was a proxy for race. So when people talked about being in the class, people said the Hip Hop class. They meant the Black class. When they said, "We will be covering Hip Hop topics," they meant Black stuff. They even referred to the students, those are the Hip Hop kids, but they were talking about certain kids. And so there was a very particular way that the class operated with this implicit, tacit, unspoken racial calculus that suddenly Blackness was centered in a way that it never had been before. Now, of course, some of you might say, "Well, yeah, so what? Whiteness is centered in school all the time." But that wasn't the point of the class and I'm not sure that that's the right way to teach. In fact, I'm sure it's not the right way to teach.

So there were these interesting performances of realness in the class because people felt like they needed to be real, i.e., perform a very particular notion of Blackness in order to work. So there was this one girl named Lisa. Lisa would come in with bamboo earrings. She would speak African American Vernacular English, which is cool. I know plenty of people that talk like that. And I know plenty of Black people that don't. But her friends were like, "Yo, Mr. Hill, she only talk like that in here." She's from South Philly. You all watched *Rocky*, right? She had that kind of thing going on until she got into the class. Then all of a sudden, she'd act like she was in a whole different world. The first day of class she came in with a picture. She was like, "This is my daughter. She's Black, you all." Because she wanted everybody to know that her daughter was Black, because her daughter's father was Black. And given American racial politics, obviously, one drop and you're Black. So she was trying to buy into the class vis-à-vis her daughter's Blackness, her own language practices, and also through the stories they were telling in the classroom, the conversations they were having. They had to have real stories, stories that reflected what they thought Hip Hop realness was. And for them Hip Hop realness was constructed as poverty, violence, and also racial oppression. So they had a very narrow notion of what Hip Hop realness was, which speaks to a broader conversation outside of classrooms. How do we imagine authenticity and realness?

Now, on a kind of intuitive intellectual level, we would say realness is just a one-to-one correlation between how you live and how you say you live.

Back in the day we talked about "studio gangstas." There is this whole way in which Hip Hop has governed itself by saying you need to have a one-to-one relationship between what you say and what you do. But it's not that simple because nobody says, "Will Smith keeps it real. He really does go to Miami," you know what I mean? [*Laughter*] He's not lying, but realness has never been as simple as that one-to-one correlation. It's also been undergirded by all sorts of expectations about how race is performed, how poverty and marginality are performed, vis-à-vis our understandings of race.

And so all of that was happening in the classroom in a very interesting and complicated way. So when kids said, "I don't want to talk in class because I don't have a story that's real enough," they never said it was honest enough. They were saying they didn't have a story that they thought matched a particular understanding of what a Hip Hop story or experience is supposed to be. Because Hip Hop has these major grand tropes that are talked about like the outlaw, the trickster, all of these figures that govern a real Hip Hop narrative, as Imani Perry describes in *Prophets of the Hood*.[17] The outlaw, that's what Tupac is, right? "Hit 'Em Up." Or the trickster who gets through by guile and wit, the signifying monkey tradition. The pimp, the player, the boss. So there's all these stories and expectations that were governed by realness.

WOUNDED HEALERS: THE UNDERSIDE OF RELEVANCE

This next chapter is the one that was the toughest for me to write, and it might be my favorite one: the "Wounded Healers" chapter. The Hip Hop–based education classroom created a kind of environment that not just sanctioned but encouraged storytelling. And it makes sense because so much of Hip Hop is about the narrative, the autobiography or the fictive autobiography, creating space to tell who and what you are. Don't get me wrong, the traditional canon has story. Ain't no shortage of stories in American literature, but the investment and the connection that the students had to the stories in Hip Hop Lit were different than the ones they had to other stories. So if I were reading a story about love and it's coming from Lauryn Hill "Manifest" or Eve "Love Is Blind," they connect to that in a different way than they connected to *Romeo and Juliet*, which is interesting in its own ways. Sometimes traditional American literature actually had greater connections to their own experiences and themes than some of the Hip Hop stuff, but nevertheless they felt connected to these Hip Hop stories. So as we began to read and hear these stories, students began to engage, analyze, critique, and draw meaning from the text. But they did it by connecting the text to their own experiences.

We read Beanie Sigel. Now, I'm also from Philly. I'm obsessed with Philly. I tell my daughter all Black people started in Philly and then walked to Africa. [*Laughter*] There was a lot of Beanie Sigel in the class. Freeway. We read "Where Have You Been" by Jay-Z and Beanie Sigel, a very painful, powerful song of them talking to their absentee fathers. Then they make "Still Got Love for You" on the *Dynasty* album, which is part two, where they respond to their fathers' responses, to hearing about their own pain as children. To me, I'm just teaching a unit on metaphor, tone, and inference. But as I'm teaching that, the students aren't just talking about mood and tone. When Jay-Z talks about waiting for his father to come pick him up, they would say, "This is a painful moment and so the mood must be this and the tone must be that because there's no way his father could leave him and he not feel pain. And I know that, because in my own life, my dad left when I was six and I didn't see him again." When you have these kinds of narratives coming up in the midst of a classroom, it becomes overwhelming.

Now the first thing you might say as the teacher is, "Well, why don't we cut that part out? Just tell them about mood and tone. I don't need the other stuff because when I'm teaching Edgar Allen Poe we ain't getting no personal stories about ravens." [*Laughter*] But the problem with that is that we're engaged. Now I'm taking it back to the scholarly literature. I want you to see this connection between the gaps in the scholarly literature and the work that I'm doing in the field. Remember, I started by saying I'm in a conversation about culturally relevant pedagogy and I wanted to know what we meant by "culture," what we meant by "relevant," and we also said we wanted to be in that conversation about what's going on *while* Hip Hop-based education is working. So I'm saying, "Okay, it's working." They know mood and tone now. But I've brought in a story about fatherlessness in a neighborhood where kids are fatherless and I've connected it to artists who students attach to their own identities, who they regard as real. They love

Jay-Z. The school was five blocks from Sigel Street. Literally. When Beans is saying, "You was an abusive pops. Fuck, you left me out to dry, stuck," that connects in a whole different way. Not just to White folk but even to reading Baldwin, Hurston, or even Morrison because, for them, those Black authors were still elites, people in the mainstream literary canon. It was still different than what they saw with these Hip Hop texts. This shit was real and they felt it and so if I'm going to bring in a culturally relevant text I got to be prepared for the consequence. And this was a conversation that the literature on culturally relevant pedagogy had not taken up yet seriously. So part of what I was adding to the conversation was a consideration of not just the benefits of relevance but also the underside of relevance. What's underneath this thing? How do we account for the pain and trauma attached to these texts? What happens when you play that song for me that brings back "too many memories"? What are we going to do now?

I was just beginning to figure this out as I taught the course. And it was hard. Not too much later, we're in our unit on politics and we read "La Femme Fetal" by Digable Planets: "It was 8:49 on a beautiful ninth day of July. There was not a cloud to speak of so the orange sun hung lonely from the sky." It's a whole kind of critique of American abortion, a critique of the Supreme Court's conservative justices like David Souter and Clarence Thomas. It's a critique of the moral contradictions in America around women's reproductive rights. We also read Common, "Retrospect for Life," from his second album, which featured Lauryn Hill. One of his dopest albums, man. The refrain in the song is "316 dollars ain't worth your soul," referring to the price of a regretted abortion. Lauryn singing the hook, "Why didn't you stayyyyy" from Stevie Wonder's song, "I Never Dreamed You'd Leave in Summer." Amazing, beautiful, and painful song. I felt like if I'm going to teach about abortion, I would need a balanced approach. I see things quite differently now. But that's where I was as an educator at the time.

On the day we taught the texts, I was running late. I texted Mr. Columbo asking him to "put the question on the board," as we would do prompts every day to get students writing and thinking. I asked them questions like, "What'd you think about the text? Who do you think made the right decision? What would you do in this situation?" Stuff like that. I got in the classroom and we were starting our normal routine and I had the students go around in a circle. But something strange was happening. Almost nobody was writing in their journals. but the women in the class were definitely not writing. "Why y'all not writing?" I asked. No one was saying anything. "Somebody going to say something?" I pleaded. Nobody's saying anything. Silence.

Eventually, a student named Keneka spoke up and said, "They're not writing because they don't like the topic." Now Keneka and I had a very particular kind of interaction because I had taught her previously as her Spanish teacher. So this was like my third year with Keneka and our relationship was playfully antagonistic. If I asked her to do something, she'd say "I don't want to" and roll her eyes. I'd say "Whatever. Just do it." And then she'd smile and do the work. That was the norm.

But as a teacher some days you have had enough, you know what I mean? It's like, "Alright. Enough of the back and forth. We at that point now where I just need you to do the work." I was like, "Keneka, alright, I'm not asking you to speak for everybody, just . . . " She's like, "We don't like this assignment." I just thought she was being difficult. I thought it was one of those days that was just going to be tough. After all, all kinds of stuff happens in people's lives and you don't always know what's going on. I thought the students were just being obstinate. I was like, "Yo, that's not an acceptable response. In this class we offer . . . ", and I begin a whole explanation of how the class operates and what an appropriate response is and how to offer analytic specificity. And finally, in the midst of my diatribe, a student who never says anything was like, "Mr. Hill, they don't like it because it's about *abortion*." Keneka was like, "Duh."

And then it finally hit me. I'll tell you what I missed because I think it's much more important to tell you about the failure of that moment. One, as a teacher I didn't listen for silence. We often think about silence in education as a form of disrespect or disengagement, as anti-intellectualism or incapacity. We think if you're silent something's wrong. We see it as empty. What we need to do as educators is listen *to* and *for* silence. There's something powerful in silence. Silence can be resistance. Silence can be engagement. Even in music sometimes there's a moment of silence, a moment under a beat, before a beat, after a beat. Sometimes there's a track going dead for a minute. Half a beat, it's stunning. Silence matters. I was listening for a voice, but I couldn't understand how to listen for silence. And in this case, silence was speaking far more loudly. It wasn't disengagement; it was discomfort. I wasn't locating my male privilege or how my question negated a whole range of possible experiences. I was in a class of students aged 15–23 who were in night school oftentimes because they had kids. I knew that. Keneka ain't have no kids but there were all these silences in the class that I didn't consider. There were all these opportunities that I didn't consider because, "We in Hip Hop class. They connected to this text, they know this text, they are free to speak." No.

People will tell you all the time: "This is a safe space." There is no such thing. Places are always replete with power. Power is situated and it's engaged in very particular ways. We cannot have a classroom where there ain't no unequal power relations here. "We all equal. This is democratic because we got Hip Hop." No. There might be new relations of power. There might be new dominant discourses. There might be new subjugated knowledges. But at the core there is a power relationship here that we must analyze and unpack.

But I couldn't see that. Part of that was just old-fashioned patriarchy. Some of that was me having a kind of naïve conception of what Hip Hop–based education classes could do, and more broadly, what Hip Hop could do because I didn't completely understand how Hip Hop can also silence people. Read Gwendolyn Pough's work, *Check It While I Wreck It*.[18] Part of how and why women "catch wreck" in her book is by intervening in spaces that are almost exclusively male because female voices are often silenced. That's why we got street fiction. That's how we end up with Nicki Minaj. And I don't mean that in a disparaging way at all. I think what Nicki does is amazing. I think if anything is problematic it's our critiques of Nicki and how viciously gendered they are.

The next day in class Keneka didn't come back. I wanted to apologize to her but she didn't come to class the next day or the next day. And then the following week came with no sign of her. She wasn't there. She finally came back and I pulled her aside and said, "Yo, I'm really sorry about what happened." She said, "It's okay. I wasn't mad at you or anything. You probably didn't notice but last summer when y'all said I was looking fat, I was actually pregnant and I had an abortion and I didn't know what to do and that song brought back a lot for me." Then, I went back and looked in her journal from the day where she refused to write. Oh, she wrote. She talked about how women have to make choices for themselves and made it very clear that she was struggling with this issue.

The takeaway around this is really about authenticity. But it's also about storytelling and it's also about *wounded healing*. The concept of wounded healing is what frames that whole chapter. The idea of Chiron, the Greek figure who was hit by an arrow soaked with the blood of Hydra, is that he was the great healer. But once he was hit with that arrow he had a wound that could never be closed. So he went through life as this sort of tragic irony, the ignoble paradox of healing everybody else but never being able to heal himself. So, for me, the classroom became a space of wounded healing, where people were healing each other through storytelling. Whether it was reading a rap text or affirming each other, what I call co-signing in the classroom, where you tell your story and I tell my story to make your story feel better because part of what you want to know sometimes is you're just not the only one going through this.

When Lauryn Hill says in "Manifest," "I tried to call the cops. That type of thief you can't arrest. Pain suppressed will lead to cardiac arrest. Diamonds deserve diamonds. He convinced me I was worth less." Woo! Her words created a community of people who could talk about heartbreak and pain, and not just for women and girls. It created a whole space to talk about masculine pain and how we understand and perform gender. We were able to heal each other, not in the kind of pie in the sky way, but in the sense that we were able to affirm each other's narratives, to let people know that they weren't alone, that their stories matter. In critical race theory we talk about *counterstorytelling*. Part of why we engage counterstorytelling is so that we know that there are other people doing this, that there is another narrative that might actually be just as significant as the dominant mainstream narrative but we have to retrieve those narratives from "the bottom of the well," as Dereck Bell would say, and resituate them in the middle of a class. That's what the class enabled us to do.

WAYS FORWARD

The last chapter of the book is where I want the field of Hip Hop–Based Education to go. Sadly, years after I wrote that chapter, I feel like we still need to be moving in those directions. This book wasn't about pedagogy in the kind of procedural way of you walk into a classroom and here's how you teach, but I did want us to think about the pedagogy in three ways. One was the pedagogy of Hip Hop. We need to spend more time making sense of not just *what* Hip Hop means but *how* it means. That means the processes by which Hip Hop comes to take up meaning. That means that we can't just do a textual analysis of a lyric. We could do that all day but I'm interested in the political economy of Hip Hop, the circulation and consumption of Hip Hop, the way in which texts come to arrive in the places that they arrive. I also want to unpack Hip Hop not just for questionable gender politics, hypermasculinity, or violence. I want us to think about what it means to think about Hip Hop through a queer lens, for example. What would it mean to make sense of Nicki Minaj's Roman character, not just as a kind of performance or as a kind of carnivalesque figure but also as a kind of reimaging the boundaries of gender performance. What would it mean to look at this through different lenses, such as political economy, queer theory, or disability studies? What would it mean for us to apply new units of analysis to understand what Hip Hop means and also, again, how it means because that's a whole other level?

Pedagogies about Hip Hop. Forcing us to reconsider what critical media literacy looks like, to have a pedagogy that engages conversations about the culture so that when we come into a classroom, even if it's an English classroom, if I'm going to smuggle in Lil Wayne then we're going to have to have a conversation about geography, the role that geography plays in Hip Hop. Think about the role that the geographically specific, what Murray Forman calls "the extreme local," plays in Hip Hop. There's a level of geographic specificity that enables a kind of ghetto patriotism and a kind of ghetto nationalism that I think we haven't fully unpacked within Hip Hop. There's a kind of conversation that we could have about identity, and when we come into a classroom we need to have it.

Then finally pedagogies with Hip Hop, which is, How do we use Hip Hop in the service of actually teaching traditional subject matter? Because some of you are like, "I hear all this but I just want to teach math. I need my kids to know how to count." That's cool but I would argue that the "pedagogies of" and the "pedagogies about" will actually enable the "pedagogies with." You actually will teach better knowing this stuff. But as Lee Shulman talks about content knowledge, knowing your subject matter and pedagogical knowledge, like knowing how to teach English, or how to teach social studies. I'm saying that this stuff can be woven into that conversation in such a way that as we're teaching English or math we can think about this because for so long this was the exclusive province of English and language arts. Everybody was like, "Hip Hop, you can teach poetry, cool. But I'm a science teacher." And then Chris Emdin (see chapter 12) comes into the picture and says, "Wait a minute. The cultural politics and aesthetics of the battle might be helpful not just for English but for science."

Let me pause there and say thank you and take some questions. [*Applause*] Brother all the way in the back. You, the White guy. I realize "brother" as a racial signifier was probably confusing. [*Laughter*]

QUESTION 1: I'm interested in your concept of wounded healing and your thoughts about how your work with these students would have been different during the schoolday with general education students. How would that have affected your work and in doing your research?

HILL: Let me talk about process, first from a level of practice because that would have been the thing that I'd be studying. One of the things I highlight in the wounded healers discussion is that most of the moments that I analyze happened within the rhythm of teaching. So, to that extent, I don't think it would have been much different because I think it would have still happened within the rhythm of the conversation. I think what's more difficult in a traditional schooling program is two things. One, the curriculum is overdetermined by accountability expectations, by high stakes testing, by top-down measures, by deskilling attempts at teachers such that I can't even get into an actual teaching rhythm. I'm just reading a script. So, to that extent, there's just no space for those conversations. So I'm not sure that test-centered models of traditional school work, not just for what I was doing, but for any kind of effective pedagogy. It's just not effective for anything except making you good at taking tests. And I ain't never seen a job-wanted poster for a good test taker, so I'm not sure if that's even a worthwhile goal.

The other thing is what Arlie Hochschild talks about in *The Managed Heart*.[19] There's a whole body of work in the '70s and '80s in the sociology of emotional labor. Emotional work is the kind of stuff you do within the context of your job or another space to demonstrate proper emotion, such as smiling. A waitress does emotional labor because you have to smile even when you're pissed off. Being a counselor, you have to look interested even when you're dozing off in the back of your mind. And if you're doing wounded healing in a classroom, where you've got five sections and you got five periods of kids who are talking about fatherlessness and pain and drugs, that's emotional labor for the teacher. And you're a person and you're carrying all this stuff and I don't want to ever underestimate how taxing that is on your spirit.

I had one class every day and I would go home. And it was research. But imagine the day-to-day grind of doing that, period after period, semester after semester, carrying all that stuff on you. It would be like a priest that did nothing but confessions all day. It's draining on you, so you also have to find mechanisms for resting the self, for detaching in certain kinds of ways, and for not investing in each narrative in the way you did before without becoming plastic. It's a unique set of skills that doesn't usually get nurtured in teacher education programs. You just start taking on all this stuff and don't know about it. That's why sometimes out-of-school spaces are better for it. The problem is we've divested from out-of-school spaces, the spaces that are most productive for this kind of work. Because of the neoliberal agenda and our obsession with prisons, we've gotten rid of all the programs that stop us from going to prison. Early childhood education, arts, music, sports. As a result, the school becomes the locus for all kinds of stuff, not just reading, writing, and arithmetic, but stuff that just happens there because it can't happen anywhere else. Part of that is just the dysfunction of education and that's what we have to wrestle with, too. So I guess the ultimate answer is, I know what my practice would have looked like but I don't know what my process would have looked like because I might have been overwhelmed and crashed too, you know what I mean? But in terms of what I researched, I think I would have approached it the same way.

QUESTION 2: Harry Belafonte's going to be here in a few weeks and in the vein of what he says, do you think that artists, Black artists and Hip Hop artists, should be held accountable to promote certain things that will help the youth that they're impacting?

HILL: I believe in the relative autonomy of art so I don't ever want to constrain what people do and what they produce. I don't want to infringe on anybody's First Amendment rights to say stuff either, though that becomes a straw man argument that gets invoked when people are held accountable for the impact of their words. People say, "I have a right to say . . .", but that's rarely in dispute. But I'm in a position now in my life and my career where I literally challenge artists to do more and say more, you know what I mean? I haven't met Chief Keef yet but when I do, I want to say something to him. But I'm also like, he's a teenager and so part of me wants to say, "Well, okay. Chief Keef has had a set of experiences that produced this kind of content, life experiences. Chief Keef is dealing with some issues." I don't want to negate that, but I also don't want to let that go unchecked and unchallenged. People rap about killing people all the time. People rap about all kinds of stuff. And some of it I enjoy. Do you know what I mean? To be quite honest, I like 2 Chainz album. I love Pusha T. Pusha T, I almost wanted to go sell crack this summer—Pusha T will have you leaving school and selling crack! [*Laughter*] And to some extent, I can detach who Pusha T is as a character from the music, the same way I can separate Al Pacino from Scarface. But young people have a connection to these characters that they don't have to the Terminator or to Scarface or these people. So when they see Chief Keef, they believe in his narrative in a different way. So these artists have a greater responsibility.

I don't want to nullify their right to do that kind of art, but I want to challenge them to be better and to do better and I find that when people know more and understand how their work is being taken up, many artists make different decisions. The Christians have a saying, "God loves you just the way you are but loves you too much to leave you that way." That's sort of how I think about Hip Hop. I love Hip Hop just the way it is, but I love it too much to leave it that way and so I always want to challenge it.

And the only time I draw lines is—for example, I was one of the people who protested Rick Ross's "You Ain't Even Know It" remix, where he said, "Put molly all in her champagne, she ain't even know it / Took her home and I enjoyed that, she ain't even know it." Because I'm like now you're actually endorsing rape, and for me, that's a line no one should ever cross. People say that's an arbitrary line. It might be subjective, but it ain't arbitrary. I'm drawing a line on rape. It's not arbitrary at all. That's a line I draw and I talked to Ross about this. Even when he came to *Huff Post* we talked about it. I told him, "I didn't like what you did. I didn't like the response." I hit Ross up right after it happened and said this too before I even went on Twitter, so I'm willing to challenge artists and have difficult conversations. I'm also willing to encourage our people, our consumers to turn that stuff off. If we take the profit out of misogyny and out of homophobia then they won't do it. Corporations don't have feelings; they have interests and they're all economic.

QUESTION 3: My question was about the story that you shared about abortion and how you found yourself becoming the manifestation of male privilege as an educator in that situation. Were there other times where you found that topics that you're trying to incorporate in Hip Hop–based education have become alienating to female students, or perhaps silenced their voices in favor of a more masculine narrative? And how have you dealt with that in classrooms where female students are often subdued in the first place?

ALIM: Yeah, well that story really spoke to me because doing this kind of work you do get confronted with a lot of situations that are really real. In fact, when Marc was teaching Eve's "Love Is Blind" in Philly, a couple of years before that I was teaching the same song with 10- or 11-year-olds. Not because I picked it, because I wouldn't have picked that song, but because students picked it. Eve is rapping about her friend who was abused by a guy and at the end of the song, boom! The gun goes off and you're led to believe that Eve actually killed the guy, right. So, this was going on in a situation where I was just using Hip Hop in the classroom to get kids to write and think critically, and they're writing all this beautiful stuff about it, while in the same neighborhood "the Baltimore rapist" is walking around outside the school picking off young women on their way to school. That was something I was not thinking carefully about, as a man, even knowing what was happening. I didn't connect it. I didn't anticipate the young girls' struggle with sexual abuse, or that they might want to discuss murder as a solution to it. I wasn't ready for that.

Another story, which relates to Marc's Nicki Minaj comments earlier, happened when I was teaching this Hip Hop course to high school students and it was going so well. We'd have these gender debates, these race debates. And then there was one moment where we got in a really heated conversation about Foxy Brown and Lil' Kim. So when Marc says that we can't *a priori* tell what youth are doing with texts, that's a crucial point. I couldn't necessarily read what young women were doing with Foxy and Kim and we had this conversation that gives me chills up until this day when I talk about it. I was asking students what they prefer because that was my starting point, what they were engaged with, not what I thought was cool. A student got really quiet, basically shut down, and later told me that the reason why she fought so hard for Foxy and Kim was because in some of their songs, especially Foxy, she talks about rape. And as a student the only place this young woman felt comfortable having a conversation about rape was through her engagement with Hip Hop music. Not at school, not with her parents, not in church, not with any other sanctioned community. So those kinds of issues come into the classroom in a very real way and have you questioning your patriarchy and privilege—and the whole purpose of education and how society has failed young girls. As Marc said, once you start dealing with cultural relevance and the "ugly underbelly" that is revealed, you do also have to deal with these issues.

The other thing that I think Marc might want to speak on maybe is the hypermasculinist tendencies that we see coming out in some forms of Hip Hop culture. Even in the cipher arrangement that some of us laud so much, "Oh, that's where Hip Hop equanimity is at its finest. Male and female, it don't matter, White, Black, it don't matter." We construct it as all about the skills, but it's actually a place that's loaded. And when you create a classroom environment based on that, do you also then bring those dynamics into the classroom with you?

HILL: Absolutely. That's the stuff you have to think about. You have to think about the hypermasculine tone of the text, even representation. How many male authors versus female authors are on the text? Remember I talked about that second piece, pedagogies about Hip Hop, that's where you can unpack some of the gender dynamics of this with the critical media literacy. I think one of the interesting love songs in Hip Hop is "Ms. Fat Booty" and the title kind of belies the narrative I think because it's one of the few texts where men talk about vulnerability and love. "Weeks of dating late night conversation. In the crib, heart racing, trying to be cool and patient." He's talking about falling in love. "Flu-like symptoms when shorty not around. I need more than to knock it down. I'm really trying to lock it down."

It's a song where he's being vulnerable. He's talking about pain but he also says he wants to knock it down. He also says, "I smashed it like a Idaho potato." Now, the imagery is cool on a certain level but that's also an opportunity for us to talk about sexual violence because if in every song, the metaphor for sex is "I hit it," "I tapped that," "I beat it up," "I smashed it," "I pounded it," "I killed it," if every metaphor we use to talk about sexual engagement is one of violence, then we might be normalizing it without even thinking about it. So by the time we get to Rick Ross talking about "molly in her champagne, she didn't even know it," that's only this much past the line because we've never contested the other expressions of violence before. And there's nothing wrong with vigorous sex; I'm not trying to foreclose on erotic possibilities, right. But that has to be something that is done with agency and with consent from all parties involved as opposed to a kind of very masculinist, aggressive understanding of sexual encounters that suggests that the only time men engage in sex is one of violence, one that has nothing to do with female pleasure, female desire, or female interest (see chapter 14). And we just smuggle that into every Hip Hop narrative, even the love songs.

For me, that's the work of pedagogies about Hip Hop. That's the work of decoding those texts. That's the work of engagement. We could have a class on Hip Hop and by the end we have students thinking about sexual violence. How dope is that? To me that would make the whole class worth it.

QUESTION 4: As Hip Hop continues to mature, what do you think is next and how do you think it's going to continue to mature?

HILL: There are now multiple generations within Hip Hop. I think it's a beautiful thing that it's shifted and grown. I'm not comfortable with all the directions that it's grown. I think that Hip Hop has become part of a broader neoliberal bourgeois project to some extent. That's troublesome to me. It's troublesome to me that Hip Hop is voting for Obama instead of challenging the authority of the state. That's just problematic for me and

Figure 11.2 Left to right, H. Samy Alim, Marc Lamont Hill, and Jeff Chang engage the audience.

that's not anti-Obama per se although it kind of is. I would just love a rap song about predator drones in Yemen, like, saying this is not okay. For me, part of it is about wondering if Hip Hop is becoming more and more politically unsophisticated, less and less politically engaged, less radical. That's probably the best way of putting it. I worry that Hip Hop is moving in a less radical direction. That scares me.

I worry that Hip Hop hasn't grown in gender politics at all, but then in all these fresh ways that Hip Hop is moving. And you're going to have dream hampton here next week. I'm sure she'll talk a little bit about *Decoded.* Jay-Z talks about this in *Decoded* as well.[20] Hip Hop made being a deadbeat father not cool. A whole generation of young people didn't have fathers and they rapped about not having fathers. And we rap about killing people, even Rick Ross raps about rape. As disgusting as that is, nobody raps about being a bad father. Nobody raps about, "I don't see my kid." We have the power to unlearn some stuff, too. So I think Hip Hop has done a good job of dealing with that particular issue. I think Hip Hop has done a good job of dealing with the adult process, the maturation process of the human being. I'm not sure what the aims and the ends are of all of that. I think sometimes we've created the wrong aspiration. You know wealth building, all the kind of neoliberal fantasies there. That scares me as well.

There's going to be another form of music, though, and it's going to be different and fresh and new and y'all gon say it's not as good as Hip Hop and y'all gon hate on it. You're going to think your kids are crazy. That's just what's next. At the same time that that's happening, Hip Hop is going to become institutionalized, same way Jazz is. There's a Nasir Jones Fellowship at Harvard, y'all. Nas got a fellowship named after him at Harvard right now. That was unimaginable 20 years ago. Hip Hop is going to become institutionalized. There are going to be debates about it, and there's still going to be b-boys on the corner, and people all around the world using Hip Hop as a soundtrack to their resistance. I think it's going to be a complex thing but I know Hip Hop will live and I know the next great thing will also be a testimony to our genius and our brilliance and our possibility.

Thank you all. [*Applause*]

ALIM: Did we not learn some shit tonight? Dr. Marc Lamont Hill everybody.

NOTES

1. Marc Lamont Hill, *Beats, Rhymes, and Classroom Life: Hip-Hop Pedagogy and the Politics of Identity* (Teachers College Press, 2009).
2. Marc Lamont Hill and Emery Petchauer, eds., *Schooling Hip-Hop: Expanding Hip-Hop Based Education across the Curriculum* (Teachers College Press, 2013).
3. Mumia Abu-Jamal and Marc Lamont Hill, *The Classroom and the Cell: Conversations on Black Life in America* (Third World Press, 2014).
4. Marc Lamont Hill, *Nobody: Casualties of America's War on the Vulnerable, from Ferguson to Flint and Beyond* (Simon and Schuster, 2016).

5. Carol D. Lee, *Signifying as a Scaffold for Literary Interpretation: The Pedagogical Implications of an African American Discourse Genre* (National Council of Teachers of English, 1993).

6. Tricia Rose, *Black Noise: Rap Music and Black Culture in Contemporary America* (Wesleyan University Press, 1994).

7. Russell A. Potter, *Spectacular Vernaculars: Hip-Hop and the Politics of Postmodernism* (Suny Press, 1995).

8. William Eric Perkins, ed., *Droppin' Science: Critical Essays on Rap Music and Hip Hop Culture*, Critical Perspectives on the Past series (Temple University Press, 1996).

9. Christopher Small, *Musicking: The Meanings of Performing and Listening* (Wesleyan University Press, 1998).

10. Guthrie P. Ramsey, *Race Music: Black Cultures from Bebop to Hip-Hop*, Music of the African Diaspora series, vol. 7 (University of California Press, 2003).

11. Philip W. Jackson, *Life in Classrooms* (Holt Rinehart Winston, 1968).

12. Samuel Bowles and Herbert Gintis, *Schooling in Capitalist America: Educational Reform and the Contradictions of Economic Life* (Haymarket Books, 2011 [1976]).

13. Henry A. Giroux and Roger I. Simon, *Popular Culture Schooling and Everyday Life* (OISE Press, 1989).

14. Ian Condry, *Hip-Hop Japan: Rap and the Paths of Cultural Globalization* (Duke University Press, 2006).

15. Greg Dimitriadis, *Performing Identity / Performing Culture: Hip Hop as Text, Pedagogy, and Lived Practice* (Peter Lang, 2009).

16. John Dewey, *The Child and the Curriculum, Including the School and Society* (University of Chicago, 1902).

17. Imani Perry, *Prophets of the Hood: Politics and Poetics in Hip Hop* (Duke University Press, 2004).

18. Gwendolyn D. Pough, *Check It While I Wreck It: Black Womanhood, Hip-Hop Culture, and the Public Sphere* (Northeastern University Press, 2015).

19. Arlie Russell Hochschild, *The Managed Heart: Commercialization of Human Feeling* (University of California Press, 2012).

20. Jay-Z, *Decoded* (Spiegal & Grau, 2010).

12 The Magic behind Science Genius

HOW HIP HOP CAN TRANSFORM SCIENCE EDUCATION

Christopher Emdin and The GZA, with Bryan Brown

CHRISTOPHER EMDIN: The field of science education has not seen a revolutionary approach to teaching and learning ever. And we know that the history of science necessarily positions other students of color in particular as outside of being those who are experts in that domain. And so, the work essentially is to move science education and flip it on its head—to engage with folks who are science educators on the cultural turf of the young people, rather than the cultural turf of the discipline. And then most importantly, let young people see that they have the brilliance, the intellectual acumen to be successful in those disciplines, because the notion that "science is hard," "I can't do math," has been so engrained into their consciousness. So what we're trying to do with Science Genius is this consciousness shifting, and we'll expand more on that tonight.

GZA: Mic check. [*Laughter*] Growing up in the '70s and the '80s, I was not readily exposed to the hard sciences. Science existed in tertiary forms during my youth. It was not until my music career had matured that I was exposed to science as an intellectual pursuit. When I was younger, I had a cousin who had inserted some tweezers in an electrical socket and he got the shock of his life. [*Laughter*] And we took him to the doctor. The doctor

THE MAGIC BEHIND SCIENCE GENIUS   299

Figure 12.1 Left to right, The GZA, Bryan Brown, and Chris Emdin discuss Hip Hop and science education. Photo by John Liau.

said that it was his rubber sneakers that had saved his life. So this information was fascinating to me. Would he have died if he was barefoot? How is rubber or wood not conductors of electricity, but metal is? So this had left an impression on my mind for years. And music has always been a part of my life. When I was younger, I got into Hip Hop around the age of 11. I would go to the block parties and watch the DJs spin back and forth. In between that and going from turntable to turntable, I would also watch the MCs recite their rhymes, these young street poets. So we got into Hip Hop. We found our calling. But being that we were always asking questions about science, we decided to incorporate those things into our music in some of the works we were writing. These two forces in my life formed the background for my involvement with Science Genius, science education.

EMDIN: I think what's powerful about what GZA just described was when he said—this young person had this experience and he saw somebody almost die and he heard a story about saving his life through the sneaker. And that captured his imagination. And for young people who come from those backgrounds, there is no structure within a traditional school that allows that student to be able to interrogate those kind of questions with their teacher. So the traditional structure of science education is, "Here's the information, take it, memorize it, give it back to me." For a young person like GZA who walks into that classroom and says, "This dude stuck the tweezers in there and he's still here and a sneaker saved his life," the traditional science classroom doesn't have the space for that question to even be asked. But we know that experientially is how scientific knowledge is built. And so, part of what we're doing with science education is also creating a space within a traditional classroom where young people have a voice to be able to investigate what they're inquisitive about. And then the teacher takes that information that the young people gives them and then layers that with the science. See, when you have that layering going on, then a young person gets turned onto the discipline. If I start with the content first, I may never ever get to the experiential piece. But the experience first is how you turn them onto science.

BRYAN BROWN: Science is the last discipline in education that I'm aware of to incorporate Hip Hop as a pedagogy. We have somehow avoided it fundamentally. What are you actually doing in classrooms with Hip Hop to teach science?

EMDIN: The basic task is in allowing the teachers to realize that the traditional structure just can't work. The structure of the classroom has to be malleable enough for us to use new practices. Then once that layer happens where the teacher's like, "Okay, well, maybe they can do something different and not just answer questions," it's like, "Well, what are they going to be able to do differently?" And that piece involves, one, playing music. So when the students walk into the classroom and they hear an instrumental that they can hear outside of the classroom, somehow psychologically there's a blurring of the divides between the in-school and out-of-school worlds. So the second thing we're doing practically is bringing the music from the youth communities into the classroom. So you start with changing the space. Then the third thing is understanding the language of science and the language of Hip Hop and making those things come together. So this is based on Dr. Brown's work, of course.[1] It's this idea of if a kid says something and it is a complex word with five syllables, and they learn the definition of that word with another bunch of words that have multiple syllables, do they really understand the construct, just because they can spit it back to you? The answer is no. So what we're doing now is also saying, "Let the kids be able to describe the scientific ideas conceptually, using their own localized language, using their own hood talk." So that's the third thing, and then the next component is the notion that you can use your own words and there's a space for it. How do you craft rhymes utilizing your conceptual understandings and your own language to describe these scientific ideas? And then lastly, of course, is the age-old Hip Hop art of competition, where the kids know that they're in competition with kids in other spaces. So to make sure that their rhymes are rigorous enough to be able to go through a rigorous battle with somebody from another space.

GZA: Well put. [*Laughter*] He's a tough teacher. I go into the classroom as a musician and provide a model for students to explain their scientific concepts through recitation and rhymes. My thing when I'm in a classroom is just showing them how to structure a rhyme, how to put it together, what words to use, where to put them, and how to make the story compelling and descriptive and visual.

BROWN: You're one of the best emcees in the world. So, you come to the school for free and then you teach students how to be world-class emcees while they're learning science. What is it that you teach them about being an emcee?

GZA: Well, for one, I teach them to make the rhyme "half short, twice strong." Be as visual as possible and really put time and thought into it. I mean, I can give certain rhymes to give an example. For instance, I may take a rhyme about dark matter. I may have a word like "light," right? And I may have a word like "bright." Now, those are simple words and a lot of emcees use those words. We use those words in everyday language. But it's about taking the word and making a sentence structure as strong as possible. Now, being that this is dealing with the universe, I'll start it by saying, "Before space and time, thought produced a speck of light. It was infinitely hot and so extremely bright." So it's just about showing them how to structure a convincing rhyme or taking the eight bars and making it four, but making it as tight as possible.

EMDIN: And what was dope about what he just described also is that—so when he spits a rhyme like that to the young people, they're like, "Oh, that's sick. But we can't bite GZA's rhyme," right? So they're like, "Well, how can we describe this same concept, lyrically differently?" So the kid might say, "Light," and say, "Well, light particles. So photons." So, the kid says, "Now, we're going to talk about the photons as it illuminates which makes me great." So they take the concept he describes and then layer that with scientific vocabulary and then attach rhyme to it. And so, it takes it up another notch. And he's understating what he does, by the way, immensely. Because this is important to state, so GZA goes into the classroom and the kids are around rhyming and he doesn't ever tell the kids this is dope or this is wack, right? Never does that. He just walks by and he just nods. Or he walks by and he nods more emphatically, right? [*Laughter*] So, by virtue of doing that the kid who gets the more emphatic nod, they're like, "Oh, what did that kid do?" And usually that kid is the one who's using a little bit more metaphor, a little bit more analogy, a little bit more wordplay. And so, these cues allow kids to be able to understand what is superficial and what's more complex. And when we talk about what's going on practically in classroom, GZA's presence also gives teachers those practical tools for pedagogy, right? The idea of a head nod is not necessarily a piece of what you learn in the teacher education program. And so, what he's doing through his presence, because he is a teacher, is giving teachers who don't have a key into the culture an understanding of what those subtle nuances are that get different results from students.

BROWN: What is the response that you're getting from the children?

GZA: It's a great response. Hip Hop is the voice of the youth. It has always been from day one. And it's easier to bring someone that's involved in Hip Hop into a classroom because all kids listen to Hip Hop, the majority of them. So by bringing the Hip Hop artist into the class, kids can relate more to that or they'll take time to listen to what this person has to say. Music is a universal language and music is in everything. That's why I think it's great to use music and involve it with science to teach children because music is part of our everyday lives. Everything is playing music, vibrating from day one. The heart and the pulse beat simultaneously in rhythm together. The first thing a baby hears is sound before vision is even in. So, music is a part of this. Music has healing properties. We can heal with music. We can heal with sound. Just with the voice, dependent on the frequency. That's why it's important for us as artists to really speak something that can raise the frequency of the vibration and keep things balanced. And by going into the classroom as a artist and speaking to the youth, there's some sort of connection. When I speak about music being part of everyday lives, as children we learn certain things through rhyme and reason. We learn our ABCs, the alphabets are a rhyme if you sing the alphabet. So certain things we learn through rhyming growing up, whether you're involved in Hip Hop as you get older or not. I mean, just like the saying, "i before e, except after c." So, it's part of our lives growing up.

EMDIN: Yeah, I couldn't have said it more brilliantly. Whenever this kind of question is asked, the first thing that comes to mind was like the ODB Grammy moment, rest in peace, ODB, right? When he gets on that stage and he's like, "Puffy's good, but Wu-Tang is great." And then he says that phrase, "Wu-Tang is for the children." And I think that a lot of folks at that time, and even now, didn't read that statement the way it should have been read. Because when he talks about Wu-Tang, I'm thinking he's saying Hip Hop. In many ways, he's saying that the music that's created is for the purpose of edifying the children. It's not a construct that's created outside of their existence. And so, if you think about what's the impact of Hip Hop on education, the purpose of Hip Hop is for edification of young people. And so, what it does for the children is allows them to realize that the largest cultural art form that has ever been created and consumed across the globe, has made people multimillionaires, etc., it's created for you. And so, when an educator understands that it's created for them and then the educator has a goal of having to want the kids to understand the content, then that means a chief mechanism through which the content is delivered has to be Hip Hop. And however way we play it out, whether it's Hip Hop music, whether it's Hip Hop dress, whether it's Hip Hop sensibilities. All the cultural forms of Hip Hop are created for the purpose of edifying young people. And when you think about it through that lens then, of course, that's why we have to do this work.

BROWN: I would just like the both of you to talk about how Hip Hop education addresses issues of race and culture and gender.

EMDIN: So, I think that when we talk about Hip Hop, especially when we talk about Hip Hop education, the first question I get when I go into these sanitized academic spaces where I work is, "But Hip Hop is grossly misogynistic. Hip Hop is overly commercial. What is it that you can use that can have any benefit in Hip Hop?" My response is always, "There are gradients to Hip Hop." To quote Meek Mill, "There's levels to this shit." [*Laughter*] So if there are levels to it, there are superficial renderings of Hip Hop, of course. Then there's commercial Hip Hop, then there's the core Hip Hop culture. And there are gradients. And so, why Hip Hop brings people together is because in these multiple levels of Hip Hop culture, there are people who tune into different parts. So certain people are going to be like, "Yo, I just want to hear that deep lyrical Hip Hop." So they get connected to that piece. Some people just want to party, so they connect to that piece. Some people want just to hear the bling because it helps them to escape an awful reality, so they connect to that piece. So Hip Hop is that one cultural artifact that can allow people from multiple levels of wherever they are to find a piece to connect them. And so that brings people together.

And then beyond that it's just the structure of Hip Hop. You ever seen a cipher and what it does? I mean, we did a research study where we actually took a bus to different hoods and we put two rappers on different street corners. And then we stood a block away and watched what happens. And in every instance, within 15 minutes, the two rappers that we implanted were joined by at least three other people, right? Because any time an emcee sees another emcee spittin, what happens? You start spittin. You want to be a part of it. And so, Hip Hop just in that structure also has this thing where it brings folks who have the same shared ideas to a common space. And I think that those kinds of spaces are the best teaching and learning spaces. And so, what we're doing through Science Genius or through Urban Science Education is just replicating the teaching and learning spaces already in Hip Hop and then bringing them into the traditional classroom.[2] And that brings people together.

GZA: I think music itself brings people together. And one of the other things I wanted to touch on was that in early Hip Hop, and you get a little bit of it now, in early Hip Hop artists were always speaking about social and political issues. And that was bringing people together, uniting them. If you take a song like "The Message" or even a Run DMC song, "It's like that, and that's the way it is!", they were speaking up because that's how rap started. It started from the youth in the hood, in the inner cities, that was using their voice to speak out rather than fight and hurt each other, using their voice to get the message out and let the world know what's going on. Because a lot of things that were happening were not being broadcasted through the news, you know what I mean?

BROWN: So, there are two common critiques about Hip Hop. The first of which is, How do we know that kids are actually learning when we use Hip Hop as a teaching tool? The second is that, "If I love country music, how does Hip Hop speak to me?" Can you address these?

GZA: I think regardless to what kind of music it is, it still speaks. I'm not a country artist but I listen to country music. It all depends. I mean, some people listen to beats, some people listen to words. Nowadays, a lot of people that listen to Hip Hop usually listen to the music and not the lyrics. I can listen to a country song because I'm always listening to what the artist has to say. But I think depending on what you say, your words will still speak to someone regardless to what kind of music it is; country, bluegrass, rock, rap, Hip Hop.

EMDIN: So, I take a more radical approach to why it's important for everyone to be able to engage in Hip Hop as opposed to teaching and learning the way a traditional educator would. What we're describing here is a phenomenon where the cultural artifact in itself is a teaching and learning tool, on par with whatever traditional teaching and learning tool that an educator has. We talk about Hip Hop as a brilliant teaching tool. You got a person who can stand on stage and command an audience, the same way you want a teacher to be able to command an audience. You teach students to be able to learn words, so they increase their vocabulary more than they'd have increased their vocabulary before. Once they've created these raps, they have to annotate those lyrics, so they have to understand multiple iterations to the lyrics they've just written. The common core learning standards have kids memorizing, and reading, and writing nonfiction texts. If they write in a rhyme, they're writing nonfiction text. You want kids to be metacognitive—thinking about what they're thinking. If they're performing their rhyme and rewriting and rethinking their rhymes, they're engaging in deep and complex metacognition. So, engaging in a Hip Hop–based pedagogical practice actually surpasses the expectations of the existing standards for education. So you can't critique Hip Hop education and say, "What if kids don't want to do it?" Well, this is what best practice is for who kids are. And if you don't like Hip Hop, it doesn't mean that you can't benefit from a Hip Hop–based approach to teaching and learning. That's the first thing.

And the second thing about the results, the attendance rates in this project tell a story. Friday is the Science Genius day in a school, for example. We have kids who won't show up to school Monday through Thursday and come to school on Friday because they know that they're gonna be doing Science Genius on Friday. We have kids who have not done homework all semester, whose parents are calling me like, "Dr. E, it's 2:00 a.m. and he's still working on his rhyme." We have students who are asking their friends if they can listen to their recording of their rap so they can understand the concept better. And this is not quite rolled out yet because we're working on expanding this project, but we've had indicators of increased test scores, surveys about increased engagement in classrooms.[3] So any traditional measure of success in education, we've met and surpassed. I mean, I reached a point where I'm not even gonna fight with you about justifying the approach to teaching and learning. It works. Not only does it work, it meets your standards for education and surpasses them, and what?! [*Laughter*]

The last thing is that we're switching the culture of Hip Hop from one where the young people in schools are just the consumers of the culture. See, if you have a population that's persistently just the consumer, the rhythm and the beats are so seductive that they want to consume anything that has those rhymes and beats. But if you change the consumer to a producer and you make them create more complex content, then you're balancing out the scales. Because now they're critiquing existing stuff and saying, "Well, this doesn't match up with what I have to offer." And so, that also sort of changes the scales a little bit and so that speaks to your point.

BROWN: So, as a world-class artist, when you go in and you participate in Science Genius, how do you make sure that the art is not compromised, that you're teaching them the art of Hip Hop while teaching them science at the same time?

GZA: Well, that has to be within you. I have this line where I say, "Music is a divine art." So, like the musician, I compose into the instrument, becomes my heart, which reflects back to what he was saying. When you become one with what you do, you may have a drummer, or a guitarist, they become one with the instrument to the point where the drummer may just be playing drums in the air because he's so connected to what he does with his music. We got into Hip Hop for the love of it. For the love. "It was just a hobby that I picked up in the lobby where my shoes was always muddy and my hair was always knotty." For the love. It become one with us. And of course we make money from it but if you're making music to try to make money or to get girls, if that's your reason for making music then it's not within you. Then it becomes compromised. So, I think you compromise it when you're not in it for the right reason.

EMDIN: I think that notion of oneness is so brilliant, man, because I think what Hip Hop has done is allow folks to become one with the art. And that's essentially what we're trying to do with Science Genius is that kids become one with the discipline also. So we have kids who, all of a sudden, because they're writing rhymes about science and they're listening to beats in their head and they're whispering lyrics to themselves, they start whispering scientific lyrics to themselves. And by virtue of experiencing something, every consistent pattern, action over time evolves to become a ritual. So, if I go through a practice of constructing a scientific rhyme one time and second time and third time, it becomes ritualized practice for me to be able to write rhymes about science. Then it becomes ritualized practice for me to be able to think about science. Then science becomes a piece of who I am as a person. And then when I confront science in academic spaces, I feel like I have the ability to be successful in it because I've done it already. So it's a pedagogy to create a oneness with the discipline, this idea of the universality of science and universality of Hip Hop combining to create a new type of human being.

And then lastly when you talk about the art being compromised, I remember our battle last year there was a young man who had the most Chief Keef down south bounce music possible. And the beat came on and everybody was turned up, everybody was boppin. And I'm not sure if they were listening to everything he was saying, but when he went off the stage, I went back and I read his lyrics on the screen behind him. And I said, "Man, this content is heavy." But they missed the content because they were so enamored by the beats and rhythms. And I think that for that young person though, his scientific content, he knew it had to be on point. And even though somebody might have perceived that brand of Hip Hop as being more anti-intellectual than, say, an East Coast brand of Hip Hop, whatever. He wasn't saying multiple syllables all at once. In that simplistic pattern of rhyme, it was complex scientifically. So it's all in one's expression of what they are tuned to. So if he was into a Chief Keef–type rhythm but his science was on point, he's still good. And if he had lyrics intricately woven and it was more complex lyrics and more of an East Coast style, he was still good. As long as the science is on point, we don't really care that much about the iterations of Hip Hop that are expressed.

BROWN: We've had a number of failed reforms in science education. What are your thoughts about why using Hip Hop for science education reform is a game-changer, in terms of the ways that we teach and learn science?

EMDIN: The use of Hip Hop as an approach to teaching and learning more broadly, it benefits all forms of education. I think that there are things about Hip Hop to me that are inherently scientific. But the use of Hip Hop also represents the use of youth culture. So you guys have heard before Gloria Ladson-Billings,[4] my academic mama was talking to you guys about culturally relevant pedagogy (see chapter 10). So, I could go into every teacher education program and say, "How many of you guys have heard about culturally relevant pedagogy?" And hands are raised. Then I can go to those same teachers' classrooms and say, "This don't look like culturally relevant pedagogy." And so, what Hip Hop does, it gives the educators who get the sensibility an opportunity to have practical tools for the implementation of the practice, you know what I mean? So it's more about culture, but the culture of young people in these spaces is Hip Hop. So it gets played out as Hip Hop.

GZA: Like I said before, sound has an effect on everything; it's the effect of sound on matter. Being that music is universal and Hip Hop is the voice of the youth, science is a way of getting an understanding of yourself and your surroundings and understanding the world. And the more you dig into science, the more the world seems to open to you. So it's a great thing to add science to music because the youth are listening to Hip Hop. You can't stop them from listening to it. Some students or some kids know more songs than they know schoolwork because it's easier to remember if you're remembering a song and you're singing it over and over. It's repetitive. And science is so beautiful in many different ways. And then you see other things—you see art, you see creativity. If you ever seen a water crystal, it's this hexagonal, six-sided crystal that looks like a snowflake. That's art but that's in water, you understand? So it's a way of just opening up yourself to the world. It's important for students to get involved in science and it's important to bring music to it.

EMDIN: You know what's ill about that is if we think about the most brilliant, most prolific, most iconic scientists of our time, let's think about what the traits, the dispositions, the attributes of those scientists are. So when you say scientists, first folks think about the Albert Einsteins of the world, for example. So, what is it about Albert Einstein that makes Einstein, right? It wasn't that he was a memorizing genius, right? Einstein was a person who was creative. He was imaginative. He spoke in metaphor and analogy. His quotes that relate to music and philosophy are actually more popular and more well-known than his quotes that are related to science. He was inquisitive. He was anti-authoritarian. He described information in different ways. He engaged in imagination—that's science.

See, he developed the theory of relativity by imagining himself in outer space, riding on top of a light beam and looking down at Earth. And so, the skills of the most prolific and brilliant scientists of our time, there's no other population that encompasses those same skills as the emcee. Every emcee thinks in metaphor and analogy and thinks in rhymes and is a skeptic and—this idea of keepin it 100—you're anti-authoritarian, it's evidence-based. You can't make a claim in the world of science without it being backed up by folks who are also within your discipline. You can't make a claim within Hip Hop about how nice or dope you are without you backing it up. You have to keep it real, keep it 100. So the same characteristics and tenets of the most brilliant and prolific scientists of our time, whether it's a Einstein or a Marie Curie or a Niels Bohr.

I mean, the structure of aromatic compounds was developed by a guy who imagined a snake biting its own tail. This idea of engaging in an artistic process to be able to stumble upon a scientific discovery is the same thing that emcees do. And so, if the kids are emcees inherently, what we're doing inadvertently, in addition to memorizing the content, is also teaching them all the skills and traits and dispositions of the most prolific and brilliant scientists of our time.

BROWN: So, we didn't speak about teachers. How do we get teachers to use Hip Hop?

EMDIN: It has to do with basic skills, that magic that you need to engage an audience, to engage a student. So, I make the argument that we reframe teacher education. That we could focus on content and that's fine. And we can focus on theories and that's fine. But content and theories with the absence of the magic of teaching and learning means nothing. Now, people oftentimes say, "Well, magic is just magic." But I'm here to tell you that magic can be taught.

You see, the process of learning to become a pedagogue, to become a person who delivers information to an audience, it cannot be found in a book. It cannot be found in a theory. It can only be found in the application of that theory into transformative practice. And so, the argument I was making was that I've seen amazing teachers completely outside of classrooms. So GZA doesn't like when I say this, like, "He's iconic. The iconic GZA." But he doesn't describe himself as a science teacher. But dammit, if you ain't a science teacher, I don't know who the hell a science teacher is. And let me tell you why, right? Because when you walk into a classroom and the kids are like, "Oh!" and they're at the edge of the seats, just waiting for you to say something, that's what you want a teacher to be able to do. When you say, "My universe runs like clockwork forever," and a kid doesn't understand what that means. The first thing they're gonna say is, "Let me go Google the universe. How's the universe run? What does he mean by clockwork?" So, your presence alone forces them to start asking more profound questions. So, my argument for teacher training is teacher education has to include the theory and practice, but it also has to involve the study of the magicians. The study of the practice of those who do what you do.

I've had the blessing to be able to watch a GZA show. And I watched as a teacher educator saying, "So let me see how you rock this show, right?" So, he comes in there and he asks, "When I say 'Uh' you say, 'Uh'." And so, when he does that, that call and response, if a person was in the back of the audience and just didn't even know who GZA was, which is virtually impossible, then all of a sudden that person is keyed in. That call and response that emcees do. Then when he walks back and forth on that stage, not standing in the same position but walking around, the audience is following his eyes. So they want to see what he does, right? Then when he stops and he acts like he doesn't remember a lyric. He's like, "Yo, how that song start again?" Then the beat drops and the crowd goes crazy! You see, those things are perceived as an artist on stage. But what he's doing is modeling teaching. Could you imagine if a teacher walked into the classroom and engaged in a call and response and got that audience poppin, right? Then that teacher was trying to describe a construct and the teacher acted like he ain't know what he was talking about, just for the purpose of the kid who actually knows it to start saying something, right? When he stops the beat and he stops everything in the classroom for a moment, and then he just turns up all of a sudden, and then the audience starts putting their hand up. All those things, if they happen in the classroom, would engage an audience.

I mean, they did a research study recently where they had a bunch of freestyle rappers and they attached fMRIs to their brains and they wanted to see what was going on with these rappers.[5] They found out that the medial premotor cortex of the freestyle rappers, when they were engaged in the freestyle process, was firing. The part of the brain that activates learning, attention, focus, all those things are going on while they're emceeing. Could you imagine then if the teacher was an emcee? Could you imagine if the teacher brought out the inner emcee in the student? That means then that the part of the brain that focuses on learning would be activated with a teacher who can call that forth. And so, my argument is simply that all that stuff looks like magic, but if you study folks who are true teachers, the performers, the magicians, the emcees, that magic can be taught. [*Applause*]

QUESTION 1: As a scientist, as an emcee, and as an entrepreneur, I definitely see where the strengths are in teaching the kind of conceptual learning and understanding of science. But I want to know how is Hip Hop going to help engage in the method, which has a lot to do with just the process of reasoning, in terms of analyzing, conducting background research, getting people to engage in a process and create as well too?

EMDIN: That's what each student does in the process of creating a rhyme, they actually engage in a scientific practice, right? When GZA writes a rhyme, for example, he doesn't just wake up and say, "That's my rhyme." He goes and he researches the information. Then he makes sure the information is on point. Tell me if I'm wrong about how I'm describing your artistic process. [*Laughter*] But he goes back and gets that information down pat, then he writes it down. He writes down just the constructs and he finds out how to make it rhyme. And then after he does that, he says, "How does this sound?" The first version of the rhyme is never the last version of the rhyme, because you're rewriting so that you're re-analyzing. Then you're annotating your own lyrics. So that entire process is actually the kind of processes that you require to engage in any scientific practice.

The thing about this question—is that sometimes it's happening, but we just don't know how to name it. So, once you say, "Well, what about the scientific reasoning process?" I think back on what the kids are doing every day, I'm like, "That's the scientific reasoning process." Or, "What about how they make sense of their lyrics?" And I think back to a kid—so they're doing it already and we just don't have the name. Can I go here for a second? Listen. [*Laughter*] So, science is a discipline that is rooted in a very deep Western tradition and it is oftentimes a way of the expression of a White supremacist ideology in many respects, right? And so, you think about the history of science, for example. So, the scientific icons that we know are all White, male scientists. We have this idea of you think about Watson and Crick and so on. So, this leads to the exclusion of women from the scientific process, the exclusion of People of Color from the scientific process, the lack of validation of Indigenous sciences, even though they oftentimes inform Western science. So, the nature of the discipline in itself is very linear, and in its linearity it excludes certain populations, but it also excludes certain ways of thinking.

And so, if that's the case, you have to understand the complex and robust culture like Hip Hop, if you're viewing and analyzing that complex culture through a very linear, White, supremacist ideology, you're viewing it through the small lens, but you can't catch it all. You can't find the words to describe it all. And so, because of that you could say, "Well, what about the reasoning piece?" Well, the reasoning piece is inherently in there, but the lens that we're using to look at what reasoning is, it's so simple that it cannot capture the complexity of the reasoning that's going on every day. [*Applause*]

QUESTION 2: So, in regards to Hip Hop, I think of traditionally women and even queer people, that's not necessarily the safest space. How do you guys deal with that?

EMDIN: What we're doing through the creation of Science Genius is almost taking what the structure of Hip Hop is and then reforming and recreating it. So that you take what the core Hip Hop elements are and then you erase from it all the negative aspects of it and you let the kids reconstruct what it becomes. So that we've gone into classrooms where the first thing we say is, "We're going to have y'all write rhymes." And the girls are like, "Oh, I can't write rhymes." They view it as a boys' space. And so, in this space, all of a sudden, with this reformation and recreation of Hip Hop, we've been able to empower the woman voices in that classroom to say, "That's what that Hip Hop is." The authentic Hip Hop, as it is formed here, values and respects your voice, right? You saw a video earlier of a young man who was shocked when GZA walked in. The student who actually represented that school was not that young man. The student who represented that school was Victoria. And that young man, he was boisterous, he was loud, he was going to be an emcee. And Victoria was the girl and GZA walked in that first day and she was like, "I don't really write rhymes." [*Laughter*] And she was taking on this role, this gendered role. And then all of a sudden, when she's writing and crafting her rhymes, I remember she said, "Just remember Mother Nature said anybody can get it." When she said that line, everybody nodded, was like, "Hmm." [*Laughter*] And then all of a sudden, she takes on a new Hip Hop identity as a woman in Hip Hop with voice in that space. And that helps us to challenge the established commercialized notion that excludes women's voices.

We've had LGBTQ students who don't see a voice in Hip Hop. See, Hip Hop becomes a tool that oppresses these populations, but it becomes the only tool that can heal them. There are folks who love Hip Hop so much and are so hurt by what Hip Hop tells them they could become. And they're just looking for an opportunity to reclaim what speaks to them in their own voice. And so, with Science Genius, we've allowed youth who have a different voice that have been marginalized to become central again. We're reforming and recreating what Hip Hop becomes. Just like you're creating a new palette for a new complex Hip Hop, you're creating a new palette for a new gendered Hip Hop, a new palette for a more queer Hip Hop, all at the same time infusing science.

QUESTION 3: So, I completely agree, but I worry for that individual that says, "Okay, I'm going to do some research. I'm going to look up Grandmaster Flash, listen to his music a little bit," and then say, "Hey, students, I know Hip Hop." I mean, this requires a lot of training.

GZA: If you're a boxer, and you could be a great boxer, I don't think you need to know and study everything there is about the fighters that came before you. You can be a great emcee and not know who Grandmaster Flash and Melle Mel is. But I think that it has to be in your heart. I mean, I know some people that love Hip Hop. In my mind, they can't rhyme at all but they try it. [*Laughter*] Honestly, when we were growing up, when I first heard the Beastie Boys, I didn't like it. I was like, "Who are these dudes? Why are they shouting like that?" They didn't sound like anything I was used to listening to. [*Laughter*] They didn't have the flow. To me, they didn't have delivery, they didn't have the words. But as time went on, I began to like their music. But more importantly, these dudes loved Hip Hop. It was in them. It was in their heart. They respected it and they also knew the culture. Some of them were musicians. So, it all depends on what you feel inside.

EMDIN: So, look, I think it's very important for us all to recognize that everybody is an expert in their unique relationship with Hip Hop. And so, let's say, you just heard your first rap song yesterday and you loved it. Just because you came in yesterday don't mean you don't love it and are not passionate about it. And so, when we talk about educators who oftentimes may not know the culture and feel like they want to study the culture, what you say to them is, "You have to have the key word of *respect* for the culture." And understand that once you have that respect for the culture, you can have lessons on Hip Hop from everybody in that classroom because they're all experts in Hip Hop. You got to create the space as a teacher where you're learning about the culture from the young people in that classroom. Shoot, matter of fact, depending on where you are, the nature of the relationship with Hip Hop varies. We were in New York City. Science Genius in the Bronx and Science Genius in Harlem and Science Genius in Brooklyn were completely different. Science Genius in Houston and Science Genius in Atlanta would be completely different. The larger cultural art form is Hip Hop. The iterations of it are different. The role of the educator is to understand what the unique relationship with the young people in that classroom is with their version of Hip Hop and then utilize that as the tool through which they teach.

So, in my work on reality pedagogy, to understand the reality of youth experiences, there are actually different mechanisms and tools that you give teachers to be able to understand the culture of their young people. Like pick four young people, pull them outside of the classroom and engage in a conversation with them about how they feel about the classroom and what their music and culture is. Then they give you an insight to what the rest of the kids are thinking, then you use the information to improve your instruction. So, if you rarify Hip Hop and make it this "thing," then it's tough to connect back and use it differently. As an educator you're learning Hip Hop consistently with your students and they're consistently teaching you. I mean, I consider myself a Hip Hop head, right? I go into schools sometimes and I don't know what's poppin, right? So, I have to engage in a conversation with the students about the Hip Hop they're listening to and their relationship to it. Now, I could be a Hip Hop pedagogue and teach from my version of Hip Hop and I won't be as effective, unless I learn directly from the students what their relationship is with the culture. So it's a matter of creating a mechanism where the teacher becomes the student of the culture as the students see it, and then utilizing the information from the students to improve their instruction. I hope that addressed your question. I see you nodding, so that's a good sign. [*Laughter*]

QUESTION 4: I use beat making and DJing to teach students scientific concepts, math, fractions, decimals, ratios, etc. Do you see the utility of using nonverbal forms of Hip Hop, the elements other than emceeing, as an educational intervention?

EMDIN: So just like education more broadly looks to, say, the common core learning standards or the next generation science standards as what we all want to use or reach towards, Hip Hop has given us our own educational standards which are the elements. So, the Hip Hop elements of b-boying, graffiti, turntablism, emceeing, and knowledge of self, they are the academic standards of the Hip Hop educator. That means that if you're a Hip Hop educator, those are the five elements that you could utilize in your instruction. I teach and utilize the art of emceeing as a practice. But to be a fully robust Hip Hop educator, I have to also use graffiti as a conduit, as a tool beyond just the geometry. Man, spatial reasoning, ratio, analogy, the inverse square law on physics, the chlorofluorocarbons in the graffiti, knowing the surfaces of the wall so I can make sure that my paint doesn't drip, knowing the different tips of the paints so I can understand volume. Then in the DJing and turntablism, it all revolves around 360 degrees. You have to know the exact point, so that's ratio. For certain educators, they use the verbal piece, but the nonverbal pieces are just as significant. Oh my God, the science of b-boying, are you crazy? These folks who are defying gravity. Sometimes I wish I could freeze them in time and just be like, "Do you know what you just did? Do you know how you have just defied scientific and mathematical constructs?" And for a person who's a b-boy then you teach science and math through b-boying, you know what I mean? Just like the person who's curious about why rubber stopped this kid from electrocuting himself, there has to be a space where you teach science and math through that tool. So if that's the tool that kids are keyed in to and they're turned on to, then we have to use it.

QUESTION 5: I wanted to go back to what you said about teaching teachers, that magic, that ability to command an audience and to grab your students' attention. So, some teacher educators think that there are about 80% of teaching practices that the field can agree on that are effective teaching practices. How might your theory of teacher education be at odds with those 80% of teaching practices, or how might you reconcile the two?

EMDIN: I think that there are basic practices that we can all identify as just good teaching. Gloria Ladson-Billings wrote this amazing piece, "But That's Just Good Teaching!"[6] So if you see a teacher who captures the attention of an audience and does certain kinds of things that they say is good, that's fine. But I'm saying that can be done in addition to teaching magic. There's got to be another layer because anybody who just follows a script is not going to reach their students.

So I'll tell you a quick story, real quick. I was in graduate school, I was at RPI Rensselaer Polytechnic Institute, you know what I mean? So it was my first time leaving home and I'm sitting there and I'm the only Black dude in this class of scientists, right? And so, nobody wanted to be my friend, you know what I mean? [*Laughter*] And then there was this White girl named Jill and she was like, "Chris, let's be friends." And I was like, "You know what, Jill? You could be my friend." And she goes, "What are you into?" And I was like, "I'm into music, I'm into Hip Hop." "I'm a Hip Hop dancer." And I was like, "Jill, are you sure?" [*Laughter*] She was like, "Yeah, I've been doing it my whole life." So one weekend she said, "Chris, you know what we're going to do? I am going to show you how cool I am. I'm going to take you to a club." So I'm like, "Alright, Jill. We're going to the club," you know what I mean? So, we get in the whip, we got to the club at Albany. We get to the club [*laughter*] and then all of a sudden she's looking at me, I'm looking at her, and the song comes on and she looks at me and she goes, "Chris, it's about to go down, right." [*Laughter*]. So I'm like, "Jill, what are you about to do?" She was like, "I'm going to dance," because she's a Hip Hop dancer, right? So I'm like, "Oh shoot, you're about to dance." So I get there and I open up the circle, I'm like, "My homegirl Jill about to get it in." So Jill goes in and starts dancing and this is what Jill starts doing. One and two and three and four, five and six. So, she had studied Hip Hop dance and she'd known all the numbers. And one, and two, and three, and four. And so she was out there dancing this calculated dance, right?

Now, technically, Jill was a Hip Hop dancer. [*Laughter*] She knew all the things that she was supposed to do to be a great dancer. But it was one of the most embarrassing moments of my life [*laughter*] because I brought Jill into the cipher. And so, Jill could have utilized the magic. And you could know the steps, but the magic is when you get there you can flow. Then when you calling, "One, two, three, four, five, six, seven," at some point at six and a half do something crazy. And all those little things are the magic. Folks can have the script, and I'm not saying the script doesn't work, but the script without the magic has you out there lookin like Jill on the dance floor [*laughter*], and you don't want to do that as an educator. Shout-out to Jill. [*Laughter*] [*Applause*]

QUESTION 6: I was wondering if you feel like anything is lost when you have to translate personal experience and everyday interactions into academic terms for it to be respected?

GZA: No, I don't feel anything is lost. I mean, this is what I do: make music, write rhymes, translate. I mean, working with him, I'm just the artist. He's the translator. I'm not a scientist, but I am intrigued by science. I just write music, songs, and use things I've learned to put into the music so I can teach others and they can learn from my writings. But nothing is lost. I mean, if translation is for someone that doesn't understand the language, then that's when you need to translate it. But if they understand it, there's no translation at all.

EMDIN: I think that was just so brilliantly and eloquently stated. My goal is to be able to reach a point where the young people who come from these urban communities, who are developing their scientific sensibilities, are able to enter into these sanitized ivory tower spaces and express who they are authentically and academically without feeling like any of that compromises how people view their intelligence. So, the goal for me is not even translation necessarily. It's about developing the ability in a young person to create a hybridized identity where their Hip Hop self and their scientific self and their academic self don't have to be at odds, so they have to be translating consistently. It's the larger, more political goal of this work is that they can authentically be who they are and their words and their brilliance alone has value, without people viewing them or viewing the words as pejorative because they say it differently or speak it differently. When we had the Science Genius battle at the end, we had all these kids from the hood walking through the campus and their pants are sagging. It's not my thing because I like to stay fresh, but their pants were sagging. They were being who they were, they were giving each other pounds, they were freestyling in the hallways. And what was beautiful about it was they were doing that at Columbia University. And that, to me, was the moment where I said, "This is what I'd like. I'd like to create a space where the institution values their academic value, being authentically who they are without any compromise." That if somebody goes into that space and says, "Well, I don't understand what they're saying because they're using hood language or whatever," that that person feels uncomfortable rather than the young person feeling uncomfortable because they're not speaking in a way that that person wants, you know what I mean?

I think that our words and our presence oftentimes have to become political acts. I go into academic spaces, necessarily putting forth my academic and intellectual self and my Hip Hop self concurrently. And I mean, so if something is dope, I'm going to say it's dope. I'm not going to try to translate what dope means to somebody who's academic. And if you feel uncomfortable because I use "dope" at Stanford then the onus is on you, because you don't get it but I do. And if I don't use your complex language, I don't have to feel uncomfortable because I'm not using your language because I know what the hell I'm talking about. And so, the larger goal is not to have translation, it's for us all to be able to view the intelligence and the brilliance of a population, no matter how they present that intelligence. And the larger goal is a shift in how the world looks at young people and their language. That's the larger goal. And that means that you don't have to translate who you are, you could just be who you are.

QUESTION 7: So, I want you to speak explicitly about the decision to create a partnership with a master practitioner, The GZA.

EMDIN: It wasn't even a decision on my part. It was really a decision on his part. He doesn't like to say it, you know what I mean, because of who he is, his calm demeanor, his extreme humility, but this is just GZA saying, "Let's partner." It's GZA understanding the power and potential of science, the power and potential of education, wanting to do something differently. And him just saying, "I'm going to bless you and this work with this." So it's hard for me to describe what the process is like. I'm in awe of this dude every time he speaks. I learn something new all the time.

GZA: Being a emcee for so many years and being in the industry for quite some time now, I've become kind of disappointed with Hip Hop, what it is today in contents, the lyrics, the music, the whole vibe and persona that's given off in the videos and what we see as kind of dumbing it down. So, I would like to get what it used to be back, at least lyrically and the culture and raise up the consciousness of some of these artists, because it's going down lyrically. On the other hand, like I mentioned before several times, the youth listen to Hip Hop. They're consuming this garbage—some of it is garbage. It's becoming part of them. So, for him to be in the school and get the children involved in science, they start to think differently. They grow in a certain way. They respect certain things. To me, science allows you to see the beauty in all things because the more you dig into it, the more it opens up. So, the thing is to get the students on track and get Hip Hop back on track also. I mean, I have a reason for being a part of this because we need more scientists, we need more engineers, and we need better rap. [*Laughter*] [*Applause*]

NOTES

1. Bryan A. Brown, *Science in the City: Culturally Relevant STEM Education* (Harvard Education Press, 2019).
2. See Christopher Emdin, *Urban Science Education for the Hip-Hop Generation* (Brill Sense, 2010).

3. See Edmund S. Adjapong and Christopher Emdin, "Rethinking Pedagogy in Urban Spaces: Implementing Hip-Hop Pedagogy in the Urban Science Classroom," *Journal of Urban Learning, Teaching, and Research* 11 (2015): 66–77.

4. Gloria Ladson-Billings, "Toward a Theory of Culturally Relevant Pedagogy," *American Educational Research Journal* 32, no. 3 (1995): 465–91.

5. See Roger E. Beaty, "The Neuroscience of Musical Improvisation," *Neuroscience & Biobehavioral Reviews* 51 (2015): 108–17. For evidence of how freestyle rapping encourages the neuroplasticity of integrated linguistic and musical feature processing in freestyle rappers' brains, see Keith Cross and Takako Fujioka, "Auditory Rhyme Processing in Expert Freestyle Rap Lyricists and Novices: An ERP Study," *Neuropsychologia* 129 (2019): 223–35.

6. Gloria Ladson-Billings, "But That's Just Good Teaching! The Case for Culturally Relevant Pedagogy," *Theory into Practice* 34, no. 3 (1995): 159–65.

13 Hip Hop, Whiteness, and Critical Pedagogies in the Context of Black Lives Matter

A. J. Robinson

We are all teachers. We are all students.

Youth often enter our classrooms with a galaxy of experiences, cultures, and perspectives that are separate and distinct from our own. This is especially true if one is, as I am, a member of a dominant culture—bathed in the privilege of being a White cisgender male—working and living in a historically Black and Brown community. No matter the differences across the various communities I have served, each with its own strengths, needs, and necessary strategies, one of the points of connection we have always shared is Hip Hop. Hip Hop is not simply a tool that enters the curriculum occasionally to "hook" students. It is not a cheap attempt to be culturally responsive. It is the foundation that underlies the anti-racist community and culture of our classroom.

MY FOUNDATIONS

Marc Lamont Hill, during his lecture for the 5th Element course that gave birth to this book, posed a question to educators who ground their work in Hip Hop culture (see chapter 11). He urged us to ask ourselves: "Who am I to do this?" As a White man whose work is rooted in a culture created partly to fight back against dominant White Eurocentrism, this question is paramount. Throughout my life, I have asked myself this very question repeatedly, as I discovered Hip Hop to be a culture that freed me to understand, analyze, and then attack White supremacy, patriarchy, and structural inequity. In my teaching, I continue to develop curricular, instructional, and relational strategies that attempt to interrogate and transform the White supremacist systems that benefit me from cradle to the grave.

Before moving on to some of the nuts and bolts of my curriculum and corresponding instructional strategies, I want to share the foundations from which these pillars were built. My critical understanding of how to build a positive, productive, and transformative learning community has roots in many different spheres, both within, and especially outside of, formal educational institutions. My life was changed in high school through community activism and work with organizations like Youth Speaks,[1] the renowned youth literacy movement founded in the Bay Area, where I was first introduced to the liberatory, earth-shattering power of the word. They also taught me what a space that valued all voices and intentionally constructed an anti-oppressive community could look like. I was pushed to develop a rich understanding of my intersectional layers of privilege, and how others are profoundly affected by how this privilege functions. Similarly, leaders of student activist organizations, arts collectives, and student-initiated outreach efforts at the University of California, Santa Cruz (UCSC) also taught me many of the strategies that would later shape my classrooms. Importantly, all these organizations consistently challenged me to interrogate the impact of my Whiteness and other overlapping forms of privilege.

The point of discussing these personal foundations is twofold. First, it is to demonstrate that Hip Hop pedagogies, especially when thinking about curriculum and instruction in formal educational institutions, cannot be simply learned or taught in teacher education programs. Hip Hop pedagogies must be lived and learned through action, self-reflection, accountability, and genuine, humble participation; then each teacher must adapt them for their community as they design learning spaces within which all students they encounter can flourish and grow. In addition, naming some of these forces that guided my life and shaped my strategies illustrates that no Hip Hop educator truly creates their curriculum from scratch. We build on the foundation laid by past leaders and teachers, interlace this historical teaching with the lived conditions, persistent problems, joyful expressions, and models of positive movement we encounter as we grow, and renew a Hip Hop pedagogy that is ancestrally rooted, deeply liberatory, healing, and ever-evolving.

PAULO FREIRE AND *PEDAGOGY OF THE OPPRESSED*

> Education must begin with the solution of the teacher-student contradiction, by reconciling the poles of the contradiction so that both are simultaneously teachers and students.
>
> Paulo Freire[2]

My first instructional strategies were built from the teachings of Brazilian educator Paulo Freire. One of Freire's most important contributions to teaching philosophy was his on-point naming of the traditional dominant Western mode of education, which he coined "banking" education, a model that mirrors oppressive societal structures. He argued that this model—in which the teacher is the so-called "sage on the stage" making deposits of knowledge into students' brains as someone would money in a bank—is inherently oppressive as it dulls students' potential, creativity, and critical thinking skills. Students in this model are treated as objects, "merely in the world, not with the world or with others; the individual is spectator, not re-creator."[3] Rather, Freire outlined principles of liberatory education (which he also called problem-posing education) which view all participants in the learning environment as both student and teacher working to critically analyze problems while wrestling with both the words in front of them and the world around them. Liberatory education is achieved through dialogue that is grounded in a deep love for the world and its people.

Despite all its contradictions, Hip Hop taught so many of us about a history of resistance, about expressive healing through collective arts, about a community of shared voice, celebration, and struggle. Hip Hop

Culture can serve as a solid foundation for the liberatory model of education described by Freire. While the segments of Hip Hop Culture that reinforce some forms of oppression must be clearly and intentionally addressed through deep planning and skilled instruction, the underlying communal and justice-oriented ethos of Hip Hop allows us to create the kinds of liberatory educational experiences that Freire described.[4]

Freire also pushed back against "ready-to-wear" education.[5] The current education "reform" movement often argues for privatized, top-down curricula, especially targeted towards young People of Color, which often have little cultural relevance (let alone sustenance) and treat both students *and* teachers as objects. I've seen these top-down curricula in multiple test score–driven charter school networks strip the power from teachers to respond to the needs of students in culturally relevant and sustaining ways.[6] Never mind that the same companies that make the tests also make the curricula, and reap extraordinary profits from both. Now *that's* a hustle, a prime example of how privatized reform within a capitalist system harms students of color. When I interact with the amazing global network of educators, artists, and practitioners engaging in the production of Hip Hop pedagogies (many of whom are in this volume), it is evident that Hip Hop can be a foundation for a liberatory, anti-oppressive education in communities around the world. Like Freire, Hip Hop pushes us to imagine the heights of what's possible.

HIP HOP PEDAGOGY AND A PEDAGOGY OF THE OPPRESSED IN PUBLIC SCHOOLS

My career as a facilitator of learning started in the form of spoken word workshops with middle school students in 2002, when I was 17 years old, but began formally as a professional in 2008 when I began facilitating various writing and recording after-school programs focused on Hip Hop and spoken word, but open to all forms of expression. Getting this program into schools began with putting my vision on paper and articulating my goals for students, families, the school, and the community, which I recommend to all who seek to take Hip Hop pedagogies into K–12 school spaces.

I showed up the first day with my cheap USB microphone, an outdated Mac laptop, and passion to pitch the program to students. Starting with five or six regulars, we built week by week to a larger group. After a conversation with one young emcee I had been working with for a few months, the principal sought me out. "Your program's not just connecting with the 'easy' kids. You're connecting with those that are always kicked out, who are always in my office." Within a month, I was hired as the school's new performing arts and literacy teacher. From there, I began creating college preparatory interdisciplinary curricula, grounded in Hip Hop pedagogies. This experience reflects how hungry students are for Hip Hop–based programs, pedagogies of liberation, and spaces built upon the power and freedom of expression.

Transitioning to being a full-time classroom teacher is always difficult, because students are often randomly assigned to your classroom (they are no longer choosing to be there, as is the case with out-of-school programs). Many innovative approaches to education that are truly culturally sustaining must take place in after-school programs, community organizations, and social movements; it is rare to see Hip Hop pedagogies—as foundation, not gimmick—in the college preparatory state-approved high school curriculum. One of the most important considerations for any prospective teacher engaged in Hip Hop pedagogy is choosing a school culture and administration that will support innovation and understand the youth and communities they serve. I have seen both powerfully positive and recklessly destructive administrations in my years working in public high schools, and can't stress enough the importance of finding administrators who value innovative culturally sustaining approaches.

It is because of forward-thinking and supportive administrators like Larry Vilaubi, Daniel Poo, Dylan Smith, Victoria Tarumoto-Wallace, and others that I was first given the opportunity to develop a college-preparatory curriculum grounded in Hip Hop Culture, with an explicit social justice focus. There exists a hunger in youth-centered, professional, open-minded educational leaders for new pedagogical approaches that meet the academic and socioemotional needs of youth and their communities. They thirst for the students they serve—particularly those forgotten, ignored, or unfairly targeted—to see school as a place where they belong, a place where their voice is heard and valued; where their desire for self-expression and interpersonal connection is not only tolerated but celebrated; where a learning community can be simultaneously real, relevant, rigorous, and funny-as-hell. Find administrators who share this vision, then the real work can begin.

HIP HOP CULTURE AS COMMUNITY—WHAT THEY CALL "CLASSROOM CLIMATE"

One of the most powerful ways Hip Hop pedagogies can impact a learning environment is through their use as the foundation for classroom community, what is termed in educational jargon as "classroom management" or the creation of "classroom climate." Both terms are problematic in that they dehumanize and disempower students as objects in the classroom rather than empowering youth as co-creators of a vital community of learners and teachers.

One hallmark of our classroom is that music is always blasting. There are different playlists for when students arrive in class, when they are completing independent reading and writing, when they are working collaboratively, and when they are working on creative projects. These playlists are living and breathing, responsive to each group of young people, and are subject to additions and revisions by youth. They evolve based on the cultures of students, the sounds of the moment, and the social issues most relevant in students' lives. That being said, some classics stay the same and have lived on the lists from jump, like Tupac's timeless "Dear Mama," for example. The musical backdrop for any creative writing, student-selected reading, and visual arts expression is instrumental Hip Hop, so students can focus on their own words and ideas as they work.

After students write and create, there is an open space for students to share what they've written, read, or created in a sort of daily cypher or open mic. As Freire says, "Those who have been denied their primordial right to speak their word must first reclaim this right and prevent the continuation of this dehumanizing aggression."[7] The daily opportunity to speak—and listen—is one of the humanizing practices at the heart of my pedagogy. Students consistently rank this foundation of Hip Hop music and space for free daily creation in our community (which we call "Spill time") as one of the parts of our class that should never change.

Students periodically give me feedback on how I am doing as the facilitator of our classroom, with a focus on what is specifically working for them and how I can improve. In one feedback letter, an undocumented, 14-year-old Latinx girl who had recently attempted suicide wrote, "I really like having Spill time because for me it is a way to let all my emotions and feelings out. It then helps me concentrate during class because I have let my problems out on paper ... I would like it if you keep playing music in class." Some students develop their rhymes and poetry during this time. Some engage in graffiti art. Administrators and consultants on the school, district, national, and global level consistently appreciate music and free expression's power when they visit our classroom. If students are having difficulty focusing, I'll often pause the music and wait until all are on-task before it returns. In these ways music can help, in the words of teacher education, "manage behavior" in the classroom and "build rapport" with students. Truthfully, it's just another way we can join in joyful and healing communion around the beat, around the word, while we grow together. This need for belonging in a positive community motivated toward collective survival and growth is at the very core of our humanity. Centering this humanity, and designing experiences in which students can recognize their common humanity, is one of the highest purposes of education. We strive for this purpose daily. Further, we also work to sustain and celebrate the uniqueness of each of our identities and cultures. Hip Hop helps us get there.

Hip Hop has always been grounded in local community, and each community sets the expectations for powerful participation in their own way. Following in this tradition, another way we build the community of our classroom and maintain mutual accountability is through youth-generated norms we call Community Agreements, Family Agreements, or Practices of Unity, depending on the course or program. They ground norm-setting in a collective effort that has real meaning in the world beyond the school walls. Each student-teacher has the opportunity to think, write, discuss, and share their ideas and experiences of both healthy and unhealthy spaces that could help lead the group to collectively imagining what a positive, safe community where all feel simultaneously supported and challenged could become. These thoughts are then formalized and synthesized into agreements that live on the wall and become a part of call-and-response throughout the year.

I work daily, and especially during this norm-creation process, to minimize the negative impact of privilege on my own thinking, planning, and interactions with youth. This process also provides a space to engage in critical conversations about layers of privilege, including how some students (such as cisgender male students of color) may simultaneously reinforce and be victimized by oppression. One aspect of working with my privilege that I often struggle with and work hard to diminish is my tendency as a White man to suck up the air in the room, to take up too much space. Many of my instructional and curricular strategies are designed so that throughout the year I can take up less space as the facilitator and further empower youth to step up and lead the classroom.

One important consideration in every classroom based in Hip Hop pedagogies (and really in any shared space in the educational, communal, or business worlds) is the boundary of "appropriate" language. This is especially complicated in a high school classroom, where students often are legally required to attend. In our classroom, what some people call "vulgar language" is defined as either *expressive* or *oppressive*. Youth are taught about codes used in different forms of communication and various contexts, and the power of understanding and communicating, written and orally, in various codes. When discussing these codes, explicit emphasis is given to the fact that none are inherently more valuable than others.

We define oppressive language as words that refer to or are taken from a certain group of people, such as the "b-word" and "n-word." Though these words are not limited in students' personal journaling and creativity, ideas spoken aloud to the class are expected to not include oppressive language, unless present for a critical, artistic purpose (these boundaries are expanded in after-school programs, where students choose to participate). In creative and personal work, and when sharing this work aloud with the class, youth are free to express themselves with expressive language that includes words labeled out-of-bounds in most classrooms, such as "shit" and "fuck," which we define as expressive. Students are also taught "academic language" as a second (or third) language, which is directly discussed as a product of White supremacy that is not any more worthy or powerful than the languages of students and their families; it is emphasized that "academic language" is simply another code one can assume in order to access resources and some forms of power for themselves, their families, and their communities.

Another element of Hip Hop Culture that grounds the relationships in our classroom is accountability and the importance of settling problems between people directly. As a co-developer and facilitator of a yearlong Restorative Justice course, I employ these strategies in all our classrooms when conflicts inevitably arise. We are almost always able to settle conflicts without administrative support. I often see other teachers, both White folks and People of Color, who have class-based and racialized views of student behavior, making colossal issues out of small incidents that could be easily solved through listening, proactive relational connections, and humility. With Hip Hop pedagogies, we talk out our beef directly while acknowledging the harm we may cause, so that the community may be restored, move forward, and flourish. Students consistently include these ideas in our creation of Community Agreements. Accountability is not a one-way street; I focus on being accountable to my students, apologizing to them when necessary,[8] publicly owning my own room for growth, and taking responsibility for my mistakes.

Finally, the idea of a cypher is also at the heart of our classroom, as referenced earlier. Each day we start the class with Quote and Word of the Day discussions (in addition to discipline-specific vocabulary, these Words of the Day include key terms such as White supremacy, patriarchy, and misogyny). Quotes of the Day are often taken from Hip Hop songs. Discussions are guided by questions that gradually build up Bloom's revised Taxonomy of Learning Domains, beginning with basic identification questions and ending with questions of synthesis and creativity.[9] Youth first discuss the questions in partners and then are invited to speak with equity cards that have each student's name on them. Once a few students have voiced their perspective through the equity cards, any student can volunteer themselves to build, connect, question, or offer another view. Students who tend to dominate discussion are encouraged to leave space for others, and reflect upon the privilege that allows them to feel comfortable speaking up. These same instructional strategies are used to discuss articles, songs, and poems. All are free to build from the central theme, often sharing stories, experiences, and deeply held beliefs. Sometimes debate ensues. Even a battle or two. As one ninth grader said in her written feedback to me about our classroom:

> Talking about the word and quote of the day has worked for me because it helps me get a better understanding of what they mean or how this person is trying to change the world ... It helps kids have their voice heard and share what they believe ... One thing I have learned that sticks with me is that we all have our own opinions and we have to respect that.

This quote illustrates how blossoming social consciousness during the adolescent developmental stage can be powerfully leveraged through Hip Hop pedagogies.

In discussing the centrality of dialogue to liberatory education, Freire argues, "Dialogue cannot exist without humility."[10] Both dialogue and humility must be explicitly taught and actively instilled in a classroom built on Hip Hop pedagogies. The facilitator of learning must consistently model deep listening and humility, which is especially important for those from dominant cultures. In our collective norms we establish agreements that are grounded in love and encourage a humble approach in all members of the classroom community. When youth are given space to freely create during Spill time, they are offered prompts derived from the quote, encouraging a form of remixing prior work with current aesthetics, problems, and possibilities. In other lessons, youth respond to a specific set of questions (like those that inspire our Community Agreements),[11] which are based on texts and connections that are "intimate, lived, and liberatory."[12] A discussion follows where youth can share their expression, or can discuss their personal responses to the prompt in small, thoughtfully designed groups and as a whole class. In all cases, youth have a structured but free space to build collective wisdom, always grounded in the intergenerational, multiracial struggle for justice.

BLACK HISTORY, CURRICULUM DESIGN, AND THE COMMON CORE

For a program in California state public schools to be deemed college-preparatory (and thus give students credits needed to attend universities), it must be state-approved by the University of California Office of the President. This can be a torturous process for many reasons, but especially because the system generally does not recognize interdisciplinary courses. Every art course must be "Dance," "Band," "Drama," etc. In order to attain state approval, my course has always been labeled Drama, even though I teach interdisciplinary performing arts, ethnic studies, and literacy. In submitting my courses for approval, I must mold all my strategies into standards-based units and projects that meet both California state standards for Drama and the Common Core standards.

Although movements to standardize education are often exclusionary, built to suit the needs of the dominant culture, I find a glimmer of hope in the controversial Common Core standards (not the corresponding standardized tests). Speaking from a perspective where my career began wrestling the epically long California state standards in English / Language Arts, the Common Core is well suited for strategic practitioners to create Hip Hop–based curricula that can leverage its focus on skill development rather than a laundry list of content. This allows our explicitly anti-racist, anti-sexist, anti-homophobic, anti-transphobic, and anti-Islamophobic curricula—rooted in the building of active community leaders, dialogue-driven collaboration, and radical collective action—to clearly and directly align to the standards. Though there are many curricular examples that can illustrate this point, describing one unit can better illuminate the place of Hip Hop pedagogies in a rigorous, standards-aligned classroom and give texture and concrete practice to the ideas discussed above.

Since my first year teaching, I have been developing a unit on Black History and Art that consumes over a quarter of the school year. The Essential Questions for my introductory performing arts course are: (1) How have different cultures and communities used performance for healing, education, change, connection, and community? (2) How has performance been used as a tool to resist oppression? After spending much of the first semester focusing on the birth of Hip Hop Culture, Native American and Latinx history, culture, art, and gender studies, we transition into second semester studying songs by women resisting patriarchy and misogyny through Hip Hop.

On the week of Martin Luther King, Jr. Day, we study a documentary about Dr. King's last days in Memphis and the Mountaintop Speech, and analyze songs dedicated to Dr. King, such as John Legend and Common's "Glory." Students write and reflect on how they can continue the legacy of the leaders of the Civil Rights and Black Power movements. We then study the role of music—specifically Stevie Wonder's "Happy Birthday"—in creating a national holiday honoring Dr. King after initial congressional efforts faltered. We frontload the study of key vocabulary that will arise throughout the unit, such as White supremacy and de facto segregation, which is especially crucial when teaching a majority of English language learners.

After beginning with accessible starting points, we move deeper into history. We study the Griot tradition in West Africa and African dance, and the ways in which these traditions are being remade in modern times, both in Africa and across the Atlantic in the Americas, with a focus on how these traditions are building blocks of modern Hip Hop Culture. We study the Middle Passage through art and Hip Hop created about it, before studying the central role of music in surviving, resisting, and creating love and community within the horrors of slavery. Students learn about the development of spirituals and work songs into Blues and Gospel, and how they provide a basis for all modern American music, including Hip Hop.

We study the Great Migration as context for diving into the foundational role of music in the Civil Rights Movement, beginning with Billie Holiday's "Strange Fruit." Through studying the music, we also learn about SNCC, the Freedom Rides, the March on Washington, sit-ins, voting rights, and the countless everyday people who sacrificed their lives in service of freedom. We read August Wilson's classic and groundbreaking play *Fences,* and explore how the history we have studied was experienced through families like the Maxsons. Youth creatively explore one character's experiences and motivations, which meets English / Language Arts and Drama standards while also explicitly teaching empathy.

Students study de facto segregation, redlining, and restrictive covenants in northern and western cities, in addition to the southern Jim Crow laws most often taught in schools. They study how these forms of segregation helped define the history of our community in East Palo Alto, and how they continue to affect us today. After studying the music of the Civil Rights Movement, I explicitly teach the history and music of the Black Lives Matter Movement, beginning with the cases of Trayvon Martin and Oscar Grant. Throughout the school year, and especially this unit, we focus on analyzing lyrics so youth are able to, in the words of the standards, "demonstrate understanding of figurative language, word relationships, and nuances in word meanings."[13]

Finally, students study the documentary *Rize*[14] about the originators of the krumping and clowning dance movements in Los Angeles, focusing on the ways in which all the history we studied is manifested in our modern day, in the oppressions faced, and the creative resistance that continues to build joyful community and motivate change. Special attention is given to how young people continue to be at the forefront of sparking social transformation and the creation of new forms of expressions. This unit consumes the third and beginning of the fourth quarter, transitioning to our final unit on the study, writing, and revision of Hip Hop and spoken word, where youth are empowered with the historical knowledge, concrete skills, and supportive structures to speak and tell untold stories.

All throughout, students read, analyze, and produce expository as well as creative writing. They are taught to make focused annotations (sharing these annotations later in discussions), and determine central ideas in each text, as well as how these ideas develop over the course of the piece. In addition to primarily project-based assessment, formal written assessments require youth to synthesize information they have studied and demonstrate their comprehension. Youth "participate effectively in a range of collaborative discussions (one-on-one, in groups, and teacher-led) with diverse partners, building on others' ideas and expressing their own clearly and persuasively,"[15] which takes place every day in our cyphers, open mics, and throughout this unit as each culture, artifact, and connection to Hip Hop is studied. Explicit connections are made to the other cultures we study in depth throughout the year, such as the Maya, Aztecs, Pacific Islanders, and Native Americans.

One 16-year-old Chicana student communicated her comprehension in a test by writing the following after being asked to draw connections between different cultures we have studied while answering our essential questions:

> The cultures I connect are African Americans and Chicanos. I find these two cultures' use of theater/performance similar because both are shaped around the suffering of their own people. Both cultures worked in fields,

were discriminated, had unfair working conditions, and unequal rights. African Americans ... as a result of them being oppressed, they fought back through "Work Songs" with hidden messages. Chicanos were forced to work for low pay in unfair working conditions. Chicanos were also victims of racial discrimination. To fight back against their oppressors, they used theatre to try and cause social change (El Teatro Campesino / Culture Clash). Both cultures used performance to fight for equal rights ...

This was written by a young woman struggling to make it through school. Due to a mosaic of struggles in her life, it was often a challenge just to show up. She is one of the young people most directly connected to Hip Hop, and she said many days she wouldn't come to school if it weren't for our class together and the music that always welcomed her. After almost dropping out, she won the most prestigious award bestowed at our school as a senior.

Countless other youth stories could be shared here. Many other examples of Hip Hop pedagogies that meet various standards could be enumerated. Standards aside, seeing growth, inspiration, and leadership blossom in young people previously alienated from education shows Hip Hop pedagogies are working.

EXTENDING THE SPACE: HIP HOP THEATRE OF
THE OPPRESSED

In theatre there is a phrase for the strategy that actors use to allow the audience to imagine a world beyond what is on stage—"extending the space." Similarly, Hip Hop pedagogies often have their greatest transformative possibilities in after-school, extracurricular spaces. It is no accident that I began my career as a creator and facilitator of these spaces. I continued facilitating these after-school programs and productions once I became a full-time classroom teacher, and many of the most powerful moments I've experienced as an educator took place in these spaces.

Inspired by Freire, Brazilian theatre director, educator, and activist Augusto Boal[16] first defined the principles for "Theatre of the Oppressed" during the 1970s.[17] Boal took the principles of Freire and ancestral legacies of performance as community, dialogue, joy, and resistance, and created the pillars from which a liberatory theatre could be constructed. He emphasized theatre as participatory, freeing, improvisational, dialogic, and grounded in lived reality. Theatre is not a spectacle, but a language that all can access to connect, express, and dream. Through dialogue, improvisation, and this participatory process, joy and community is both developed and sustained, and social change can take place; participants learn and create strategies to resist oppression in their daily lives, as well as the broader society. These principles are tailor-made for Hip Hop Culture and are deeply connected to the Hip Hop Theatre movement developing today. Boal's ideas could be describing the democratizing, communal, and anti-oppressive power of Hip Hop. It is these principles that form the foundation for how I teach, direct, and facilitate Hip Hop Theatre of the Oppressed with high school students.

One example is a collective process I have adapted for youth called Warrior Writers. This is based on a student activist and artist collective called Poets Corner at UCSC, a part of Rainbow Theatre, the African American Theatre Arts Troupe, and the Center for Cultural Arts & Diversity. As a member of these organizations during my undergraduate years, I adapted these processes for teenagers and renamed them Warrior Writers.

This involves facilitating and directing the collective writing, revision, and performance of full-length Hip Hop and performance poetry-based original plays. The process begins with focused community building between the group, working to build strong bonds between all members through authentic storytelling, and the breaking of bread [*laughter*]. Next, youth define all the problems and possibilities they see in their world. These brainstorms are synthesized before youth decide the issues on which they have the most to express. Once this process is complete, separate intensive writing workshops are conducted on each chosen theme. Students share and revise their work before creating the real-life scenes that ground their poetry and Hip Hop in lived experiences.

After seeing our most recent production, which climaxed with a young person dying at the hands of the police in a community suffering under violent gentrification, the White local school board president said, "The Warrior Writers was one of the most compelling, touching, and profound pieces of authentic, powerful, and professional grade theatre I have seen in years." We create these performances to facilitate healing and transformation in the youth involved, their families, and their communities. In fact, I used to feel like I had to hide our work from the "higher-ups," not thinking they would understand or value our work. Now I'm learning that sometimes they want (and need) to hear these stories as much as anyone.

In addition to completely original works, we have also produced other plays that marry Theatre of the Oppressed with Hip Hop pedagogies. One example was a play called *Freedom Dreams*. This play was an adaptation of several true stories about the justice system, all centered on people who were incarcerated (mostly on death row) for crimes they did not commit, including political prisoners. The main character was based on the autobiography of American Indian Movement political prisoner Leonard Peltier, still incarcerated for crimes that overwhelming evidence demonstrates he did not commit. Youth wrote or adapted songs and poems that connected to the themes of the play, and these were infused throughout.

Just as Hip Hop is built towards action, at each night of the play we had resource tables with information about students' rights with police and Immigration and Customs Enforcement (ICE), criminal justice reform efforts, free legal aid information, and other relevant resources. These plays are always free and open to the community, contrary to most public high school performing arts programs. In these ways, the elevation of youth voice extends far beyond the classroom in the form of Hip Hop Theatre.

BAY REBELLION: FIELD TRIPS WITH HIP HOP PEDAGOGIES

Another strategy that can extend the impact of Hip Hop pedagogies in K–12 schools is field trips. With supportive administration and work to access resources from outside communities or giving partners, there really is no limit to how youth can be offered access to opportunities that expand their vision and empower them as creators of their world. As I previously mentioned, it was through one such trip to a Youth Speaks Open Mic that I was introduced to the world of performing spoken word and Hip Hop as a high school student myself. Working with Alvin Rosales, a Hip Hop educator and activist, and Dr. Bronwyn LaMay, an educational leader who has since written the groundbreaking work *Personal Narrative, Revised: Writing Love and Agency in the High School Classroom*,[18] we created a weeklong experiential learning opportunity that we coined *Bay Rebellion*.

Students studied social movements that began or were catalyzed in the Bay Area. We learned about the Farmworkers Movement (the largely forgotten history that acknowledges the central role of both Filipinx and Latinx workers in the movement) and the critical role of San Jose. Students then worked on a community farm in East San Jose that provides free produce for local families. They also studied gentrification, immigrant rights movements, and LGBT+ rights movements in San Francisco's Mission and Castro Districts. Youth discussed the Black Panther Party with a former member in Oakland, and they learned about the Free Speech and Anti-War movements at UC Berkeley.

The entire experience was grounded in Hip Hop. All experiential lessons included Hip Hop songs that related to the movements. Students and teachers cyphered on public transportation and in the streets daily, including elements of the week's themes in rhymes. Rosales and I wrote a song with several of the young emcees in the group, putting on wax some lessons and inspiration from the week. This verse from a 16-year-old emcee captures some takeaways:

> I'm just another young rebel from the Bay/ Tryna get knowledge and educated in each and every way/ Day by day, I take it real slow/ But I know the real facts of San Jose that you don't even know/ Cuz propaganda got yo' mind like a prison/ You want a get-out-of-jail free card? Then stop and listen/ Cuz I'm about to kick some real facts: How Larry Itliong and Cesar Chavez got each other's backs/ Filipinos, Latinos and Blacks/ Chinese, Puerto Ricans unite and they all fight back . . .

This week of experiential learning was an indelible experience for all involved, and allowed the principles of social movement and Hip Hop Culture discussed daily in class to be seen and felt in the larger community. The impact of these experiences did not dissipate after that week; it contributed to large-scale youth protests the following year.

STUDENT PROTEST BORN OF HIP HOP PEDAGOGIES

Earlier I referenced oppressive districts and charter networks. *Bay Rebellion* took place at a school where much of the best work was done in opposition to the leadership at the charter network level (similar to the school district bureaucracy in a traditional public district). At the end of one year, several supportive administrators moved on or were replaced by a principal dedicated to towing the district line, which included a singular focus on standardized assessments, mandated prescribed curricula, and minimized student voice. Having tasted what education based on community, youth voice, and collective transformation could be, the youth of our school in East San Jose weren't having it.

Youth organized a student walkout in protest of administrative changes, including the unfair removal of remaining administrators who advocated for youth voice and liberatory, community-based pedagogies. Attended by almost the entire student population, youth walked out at the beginning of the day in silent protest. They gathered in the school quad with tape covering their mouths, symbolizing the lack of agency students had in their own educational community, and handmade pickets with messages such as, "Where is our voice?" and "What happened to our family?"

The leaders of this movement were students who had participated in *Bay Rebellion* and the classes that employed social justice and Hip Hop pedagogies. This effort led to weeks of student and parent-led organizing (with the strategic and organizational support of several teachers who risked their jobs in the process, including the *Bay Rebellion* squad, led by skilled community organizer Rosales), eventually forcing the CEO and board members of the charter network to face community members and answer for their corporate, privatized approach to education. Several of these student leaders continue to be active in community organizing and have entered the educational field.

This example illustrates how social justice–centered Hip Hop pedagogies in the classroom, combined with robust after-school efforts to deepen and strengthen these principles, can facilitate change and necessary dialogues in concrete ways. These pedagogies can also be at the heart of developing a new generation of community leaders and advocates who work against the dehumanizing, privatizing forces in public and social institutions (personified by former secretary of education Betsy DeVos).

Similar lessons can be taken from later protests born out of Hip Hop pedagogies that occurred when I transitioned out of this oppressive network to my home in East Palo Alto. In the summer and fall of 2014, during the early days of the modern Movement for Black Lives, students were studying the developments daily in our class. I threw out much of the planned curriculum to create new units responsive to the moment. This reflects how we cannot be content with a curriculum once it is created; it must be an evolving, living organism responsive to the youth that enter the classroom and the world as it is.

On the day of the non-indictment in the Eric Garner case (a Black man who was choked to death by police in New York in 2014) we were studying the unfolding events, and one young Black woman came to me after class and said, "I'm tired of this shit! I want to organize a protest." I responded, "I'm down to support you anyway I can." Thus began a sustained youth-led organizing campaign that joined with community organizations, elected leaders, and Stanford University student-activists to create dialogue around the criminalization of Black and Brown youth in East Palo Alto and beyond. It culminated in a youth-led march, with Hip Hop justice anthems blasting throughout, offering many students their first training in direct political action.

FINAL REFLECTIONS

In the days after the election of Donald Trump, my classroom was used as an organizing center for a mass student walkout. Older students who had spent years in our restorative community engaging with Hip Hop pedagogy stepped up as leaders. Protest signs created by our students in 2014 for their Black Lives Matter march were taken from my classroom and dusted off as Hip Hop bumped in the background. I changed the plan for producing the groundbreaking play *Real Women Have Curves* and instead produced an original Hip Hop theatre piece entitled *Letter to the President* with our students. The play was a collection of songs, poems, and stories, including both original Hip Hop and prewritten speeches and poems from events like the Women's March. More recently, just weeks before police murdered George Floyd, students were studying writing from the Movement for Black Lives, everything from the official platform to Jasiri X's[19] "A Song for Trayvon" and J. Cole's "Be Free" (see chapter 6 for more from Jasiri X). As the pandemic rages and the many faces of White

Figure 13.1 Left to right, Andy Robinson, Jasiri X, Casey Philip Wong, Remi Sobo, and H. Samy Alim at East Palo Alto Academy, East Palo Alto, California. Photo by Abdul Alim.

supremacy continue to be unmasked, I've struggled to process what is happening with students through Zoom. Without our shared classroom community, the ability to collectively mourn, heal, and organize has been handicapped. Layers of trauma are added daily. The work continues.

On a personal level, the 2016 election and ensuing intensification of hatred and violence toward immigrant, Black, LGBT+, Jewish, and Muslim communities have made me further question aspects of my own work. The school community I currently serve has exactly one White student. Though I know my current work has powerful impact, I also know I have a critical responsibility as a White man to educate those who look like me (while continually educating myself). I have engaged for years in work with my White family, friends, and colleagues to confront ignorance and privilege while encouraging action to dismantle the White supremacist systems that benefit us. However, our current crisis has deepened my resolve to work

Figure 13.2 Andy Robinson teaching about Hip Hop and social justice at East Palo Alto Academy, East Palo Alto, California. Photo by Abdul Alim.

with more White youth and adults in a professional capacity. In recent years, I have shifted the focus of my university lectures, professional development, and personal artwork to speak more directly to White America, and more explicitly, to educate about the all-encompassing, often invisible tentacles of White supremacy that have a chokehold on our educational institutions. This is not enough. So much more work needs to be done. I am still not sure what form this work will take, but I am sure of its necessity.

Stepping back, the urgent need for the liberatory Hip Hop pedagogies discussed in this book is clear and plain, and is magnified by our current crises. As the late, great Toni Morrison said as the Movement for Black Lives and the corresponding repression were building in 2015, "This is *precisely* the time artists go to work. There is no time for despair, no place for self-pity, no need for silence, no room for fear. We speak, we write, we do language. That is how civilizations heal."[20]

And that is exactly what we must do.

APPENDIX

Community Agreements: Writing and Discussion Prompts

QUOTE OF THE DAY

"I'm a reflection of the community."

—Tupac Amaru Shakur, Artist and Activist

DISCUSSION QUESTION

In what ways could someone reflect their community?

FREE-WRITE

Imagine the perfect community.

- How do people treat each other?
- What do people do so they get along?
- How do they handle fights or arguments that come up between people?

Imagine the worst possible community.

- How do people treat each other?
- What causes all the "drama" or problems?

OPTIONAL SENTENCE STARTERS

I imagine the perfect community would be ____

In the perfect community, people would treat each other ____

To get along, people would ____

When fights or arguments happen, people would ____

I imagine the worst community would be ____

All the drama and problems would be caused by ____

WITH YOUR TABLE:

After writing and discussing, come up with at least 5 SPECIFIC Agreements
(Show, don't tell. Don't just say, "be respectful", "be accepting," or "be nice." How can we SHOW that we are being respectful, accepting, or nice?)

Let these questions guide you:

What agreements could we make that would allow our small community here to be like the perfect community you imagine? How can we avoid the drama and problems of the unhealthy community?

Sample Community Agreements

- ONE MIC
  - Don't talk while someone else is talking
  - Listen deeply when others are speaking, especially when it's something real / personal

- RESPECT & ACCEPT
  - Make everyone feel like they have our respect
    - Don't share other people's business (don't start rumors)
  - Treat others how you want to be treated
  - Help people feel comfortable in the class
    - Don't judge them
    - Encourage each other

- PRACTICE POSITIVE COMMUNITY: LOYALTY MAKES US FAMILY
  - Be real with everyone, don't lie
  - Have fun
  - Sort problems out with people directly
  - Stand up for yourself, stand up for others
  - Be positive
    - Don't say rude things
    - Don't use violence
    - Keep the peace
  - Include everyone, ask others their opinion
  - Work to trust each other
  - Translate and help someone understand

- BE BRAVE
  - Have a growth mindset
  - Believe in yourself

- Never give up on yourself
- Work hard to achieve your goals
- Think outside the box
- Don't ever give up, don't doubt yourself
◦ Be yourself
  - Don't be fake because of other people; don't let people change you
  - Be real with yourself
◦ Speak up, speak from your heart

NOTES

1. See Michelle Lee's discussion on Youth Speaks in chapter 9 of this volume, "Beyond Trauma: Storytelling as Cultural Shift and Collective Healing."
2. Paulo Freire, *Pedagogy of the Oppressed, 30th Anniversary Edition* (Continuum International, 2005), 72.
3. Freire, *Pedagogy*, 75.
4. For the importance of "loving critique," see H. Samy Alim and Django Paris, "What Is Culturally Sustaining Pedagogy and Why Does It Matter," in *Culturally Sustaining Pedagogies: Teaching and Learning for Justice in a Changing World*, ed. Django Paris and H. Samy Alim, 1–24 (Teachers College Press, 2017).
5. Freire, *Pedagogy*, 76.
6. See chapter 10 with Gloria Ladson-Billings and Django Paris for more on culturally relevant and sustaining pedagogies, "'Where the Beat Drops': Culturally Relevant and Culturally Sustaining Hip Hop Pedagogies."
7. Freire, *Pedagogy*, 88.
8. Apologizing to students runs counter to many traditional teacher-training strategies (educational researchers like Cheryl Matias have explored how this is rooted in White male supremacy). Even in supposedly progressive public school districts, such as in the San Francisco Bay Area, I've seen new teachers instructed to "never apologize to your students, you lose your power." For more, see Cheryl E. Matias and Robin DiAngelo, "Beyond the Face of Race: Emo-Cognitive Explorations of White Neurosis and Racial Cray-Cray," *Educational Foundations* 27 (2013): 3–20.
9. David R. Krathwohl, "A Revision of Bloom's Taxonomy: An Overview," *Theory into Practice* 41, no. 4 (2002): 215.
10. Freire, *Pedagogy*, 89.
11. See the appendix to this chapter for an example of the quote, writing prompts, and discussion questions used in the creation of these collective agreements.

12. H. Samy Alim, "Global Ill-Literacies: Hip Hop Cultures, Youth Identities, and the Politics of Literacy," *Review of Research in Education* 35, no. 1 (2011): 120–46.

13. California State Board of Education, *California Common Core State Standards* (2013), 49.

14. David LaChapelle, *Rize* (Lions Gate Entertainment, 2005).

15. California State Board of Education, 68.

16. Augusto Boal, *Theatre of the Oppressed* (Theatre Communications Group, 1993).

17. For more on Boal and Freire, see Bryonn Bain's discussion in chapter 9 of this volume, "Beyond Trauma: Storytelling as Cultural Shift and Collective Healing."

18. Bronwyn Clare LaMay, *Personal Narrative, Revised: Writing Love and Agency in the High School Classroom* (Teachers College Press, 2016).

19. For more on Jasiri X, see his chapter 6 in this volume, "1Hood: Hip Hop Art, Activism, and Media Creation in Pittsburgh."

20. Toni Morrison, "No Place for Self-Pity, No Room for Fear," *The Nation*, April 6, 2015, https://www.thenation.com/article/no-place-self-pity-no-room-fear/.

PART IV Queer, Feminist, and Dis/ability Justice Hip Hop Futures

14 The Pleasure Principle

ARTICULATING A POST–HIP HOP FEMINIST
POLITICS OF PLEASURE

*Joan Morgan, Brittney Cooper, Treva Lindsey,
Kaila Adia Story, and Esther Armah*

H. SAMY ALIM: This is a special night for me personally because I feel like this has been a long time coming. Joan has been to campus a number of times now, but there was a moment in one of my courses that was really moving for me where we read Joan's book, *When Chickenheads Come Home to Roost*, on Hip Hop Feminism.[1] And my students were so moved by the text, Joan, that they actually stopped me in the middle of my lecturing and asked me to do an entire course solely on Joan Morgan's ideas and Hip Hop Feminism.[2] Those of you who know April Gregory and others, they really raised their voice in my class and demanded it to the point where I was like, "I don't know if I could teach that course, but I think I know who can." [*Laughter*] So conversations with Joan started then and a couple years later we're now incredibly happy and honored to have her here with us.

Throughout the entire quarter, I've been hearing a lot of amazing things about Joan's class from the students, so I just want to thank Joan publicly for creating that safe, critical, loving, caring space for us to engage these politics that are actually reframing Black feminist thought[3] and providing a new language, a new way of articulating pleasure,[4] especially in relation to Black women's bodies. What I think is so revolutionary and radical is that when you think about how Black women's bodies are usually portrayed and discussed, it's almost always—and this is in conversation with

Figure 14.1 Right to left, Joan Morgan, Brittney Cooper, Treva Lindsey, and Kaila Adia Story, affectionately known as the Pleasure Ninjas, discuss the politics of pleasure. Photo by John Liau.

Joan—it's almost always about Black women's bodies as sites of intersecting oppressions of race, class, and gender, misogyny, etc., that we sort of lose sight of the humanity. And the humanity is found through pleasure,[5] and love, and romance, and intimacy, etc. So it's revolutionary and it's pushing boundaries and it's reframing thought. And I can see this work transforming the students and this campus as well. So, just a warm, heartfelt thank you for that, Joan. Really happy to have all of you here. I'm going to turn it over to Joan Morgan. [*Applause*]

"THE LANGUAGE FOR THIS SIMPLY DID NOT EXIST":
ARTICULATING A POLITICS OF PLEASURE

JOAN MORGAN: I just briefly want to give a heartfelt thanks to IDA, to Samy Alim, Jeff Chang, and Ellen Oh. I do not know how this would've taken place without you. As always, the IDA Ridas and the Department of Feminist Studies. But my true appreciation in this moment has to go to my class.[6] Many of them are sitting here. I came to them with the wildly ambitious idea that we were going to find language to begin to articulate a politics of pleasure for Black feminism. I invited people to drop in on the first class because we had 10 weeks. We had a ridiculous amount of reading to do. I knew it was a ridiculous amount of reading. And class participation and discussion is not an option in my class. Because the language for this simply does not exist. And we were all charged with the responsibility of beginning to create it. So, they came and they made the commitment to work. And they have been absolutely incredible. I could not have had the space to workshop and refine and push—you guys have taught me as much as I could've possibly taught you. And so this is happening because *you* happened. And that shout-out is how we had to start this today. [*Applause*]

It's really sort of appropriate that this project would bring me back to Stanford, the intellectual journey started here. Samy invited me out to do a conversation with him in Harmony House and the Black House and it was a really nice conversation, and as Stanford students I've learned are wont to do, one of his students asked me a question that just stumped me. And [*laughter*] I actually wrote about it for a presentation I just did in Paris, and so I'm going to read you a little bit of what I said. He'd noticed that in *Chickenheads*, he said, there was a particular attention and commitment to the erotic in the writing. And he asked that, as a Caribbean-American woman, could I speak a bit about the ways that my Caribbean-ness played in shaping my theorizations of Hip Hop Feminism. And I was like, "It's a terrific question, and I have absolutely no idea." I mean the truth was, I'd never thought about it. And since questions of identity tend to emphasize the ways that the hyphen between Caribbean and American does not lend itself easily to responses that imply this nonproblematic sense of fluidity, the truth is that there is no neat answer to where the Caribbean-ness in my Hip Hop Feminist–self began, and ended.

Like the transnational imaginary that that hyphen would imply, the alleged margins of Caribbean-American, Hip Hop, and feminist constantly shift. And any attempt would require less of an answer, but a story, and one that does not easily recognize the geopolitical convenience of borders, processes of citizenship, or nationalities. So rather than delineating the specifics of those stops and starts, I started to believe that it was probably a more generative approach to start to approach my feminism as a *ting* that bends and leans, and intersects and divides, stops *h'an* drops *h'an* bubbles and wines. My feminism and its attention to pleasure, to safe erotic spaces, I realized, was mining what rhetorician Kevin A. Browne was describing as a space between the Caribbean and the American.[7] And it was after being at Stanford that I started to deliberately position my interrogative lens in the belief that its potential was plentiful and fruitful to a Black feminist politics of pleasure, and beyond.

So I started to play with this concept called *farin* feminism[8] that was placed specifically in Jamaican dancehall culture, which similar to Hip Hop, its US cousin, was often disparaged as hopelessly sexist and homophobic and violent, a space in which common roles for women to play were either as unwitting victims, or co-conspirators in some form of misogyny. But I've really felt that this generalization reveals a startlingly inaccurate understanding of women's erotic agency in both domains. So, my project here was to start to search for spaces for a Black female erotic, which are actually rooted in a politics of pleasure. And I argue that, within these complex spaces, that women are actually articulating complex economies of desire and pleasure, and have multiple strategies for achieving them that not only challenge respectability politics,[9] but also class and cultural biases that tend to circumscribe Black female sexuality.

However, this business of articulating a politics of pleasure for Black feminism, one that unapologetically centers women's rights to sexual pleasure, safe erotic spaces and beyond, actually requires some vehement commitments to going "post." This is a post-respectability politics conversation. That means that it acknowledges the way feminist discourse elucidates the internecine collusions between sexism and racism, how they culminate in a deeply racialized and sexual history that repeatedly violates and distorts Black female sexuality. Howsomever [*laughter*], it also understands that being able to wax eloquent about all the reasons why sex is a quagmire for Black women is not the same project as liberating us from the morass. On the contrary, a Black feminist politics of pleasure concerns itself with the hows. Integral to its methodology is this creation of language.

CARIBBEAN FEMINIST DISCOURSE AND HIP HOP FEMINISM: REFRAMING THE NARRATIVE AROUND BLACK FEMALE SEXUALITY AND PLEASURE

As a Black feminist writer deeply invested in Hip Hop Feminism, going "post" has necessarily meant the willingness to trouble my own theoretical frameworks. I came to Caribbean feminist discourse and *farin* feminism looking for theoretical affinities that could help do what Hip Hop Feminism had not yet been able to, which was to assist in the creation of safe, viable spaces to perform and explore Black female pleasure and the erotic,[10] recognizing that racialized gender oppression offers too limited a framework to adequately analyze multiple and complex erotic engagements that Black women have with Hip Hop. Hip Hop Feminism does hold the erotic dead front and center, and it does so with the explicit understanding that the very misogyny, sexism, and hypermasculinity it seeks to eradicate is also capable of producing contradictory, titillating, erotic pleasure and refuses to dismiss these impulses as a mere byproduct of patriarchal pathology. Feminist principle alone does not legislate desire.

But while the permission to acknowledge these desires without the threat of someone yanking away your feminist card is comforting, it also calls into question the usefulness in articulating a politics of pleasure. In other words, in Hip Hop Feminism, a declaration of desire might start, "I know this might not be particularly feminist, but all that in-your-face testosterone tends to make my nipples hard." I'm interested in a politics of pleasure that centers women's desires. One that recognizes that Black feminists' erotic composition may very well include attractions to non-heteronormative submissiveness, hypermasculinity, aggression, exhibitionism, voyeurism, queerness. Going post Hip Hop Feminism means accepting that there is theoretical utility in disarticulating Hip Hop from the conversation of pleasure. So this class was an exploration of all that. And like most smart feminists, when I'm about to do something wildly ambitious and outrageous, you call in your girls. [*Laughter*]

One of the things that we did in class was we started with, How is the narrative about Black female sexuality normally framed? And so we spent a lot of time really exploring the racial and sexual history. But we quickly came to a place, maybe after about four weeks, where we realized the liberating power in that was also beginning to develop a relationship with the history that didn't overdetermine our sexuality and our choices. And so this class was very much about what are the possibilities for reframing the narrative around Black female sexuality and pleasure. So to do that, I'm going to give you a very simple example of something that seems completely unrelated.

I actually have a pretty thriving business selling body butters, and one of the body butters that I make is called "Wench." The company's called Emily Jane, and it's been written about internationally and in several magazines and so I'm telling you this story for a reason. So I'm also on Facebook and people on Facebook can be very vocal about their opinions. [*Laughter*] And someone wrote on Emily Jane's page after someone actually posted something very nice about Emily Jane and they were responding to something they said. They said that, "I ought to be ashamed of myself." They wanted to know if I didn't know the history behind Black women and the word wench, and that all of my proceeds should be going to feminist causes and domestic violence shelters, and that I was absolutely just a dupe of commercialism and the market. I absolutely know the historical narrative around the word wench and Black female sexuality. But I also have another narrative. So I'm sitting in my house and my mother is playing with the scents, and all the scents in my house are unmarked because I sort of know what they are, so it's not necessary for me to label them. And my mother comes across this bottle and she puts this stuff on herself and she's like, "What is that?" And I was like, "Oh, Mom, that one's Wench." And she's slightly incredulous but not really because she knows her daughter. She goes, "You named a fragrance Wench?" I'm like, "Yeah, Ma, it's Wench." "There's a fragrance called Wench?" And I was like, "Yeah, it's kind of the bestseller." And she just burst out in this raucous laughter. And I said, "Well, what's going on?" And she goes, "I know that I have never told you his, but your great-grandmother who is the Jane of Emily Jane, whenever she got ready to cuss somebody out, she would call them a dirty wench." [*Laughter*] And so, I didn't know that wench had its own narrative within my particular family history.

So, then, there's a story done on Wench in the Jamaican newspapers. Wench is in *Essence*, it's in *Jet*, it's in *Ebony*, it's in all these places. And so now, the story of my great grandmother, The Jane, she was a daughter of an emancipated slave. So my great-great-grandmother was a slave in Jamaica. And she was emancipated when she was a child. My great-grandmother probably used "wench" in a way that was probably very hurtful to my mother, given her closeness to that historical period. But that act of putting this body butter on her body, and smelling it; I mean, she's wearing Wench now to church fairs. Right? Red dresses. I'm like, "Mom! What is going on?" It creates another narrative in our family about what "wench" can mean. And so here is my thing about the history, is that within the history there are multiple histories. Within the narrative there are multiple narratives. The archive is the archive is the archive. The narrative is the narrative is the narrative. But how we frame the narrative, in ways that can power or disempower us, is completely up to us.

And so, I became very interested in this idea of going back to how pleasure has existed historically among Black women. Because I believe that it always had to be there. I believe that it had to cross the Middle Passage. I believe that it had to exist during slavery. I believe that it had to exist in complicated ways that get buried in the service of justifiably reaffirming how horrible that history of slavery and racism and patriarchy has been to Black women. But in all that, I want to live, and I believe that the act of pleasure and a commitment to pleasure is our historical and ancestral legacy as Black women. And I believe that it's in our ancestral and historical legacy as Black feminists. And so, I want to unearth that history. And then I get these wild ideas, and I gotta always drag my crew along, which is kind of why they're here with me tonight. So just briefly, I want to end my little part of this talk with a statement from one of my students, Kiyan Williams. For class, we were reading Patricia Hill Collins's suggestions for erotic autonomy.[11] We were kind of like, "Okay, but we can probably do better." So we did. We really did. And I just want to read the beginning of what Kiyan wrote for the last response paper in my class, in terms of his investment.

"Let me begin this post by declaring my stake and investment in the project of rearticulating and reframing narratives around Black female sexuality. I was born to an Afro-Caribbean mother who birthed me at age 18. I was raised by my mother, grandmother, aunt, and my mother's friends who had children the same year I was born, and in a community of Black women who had children out of wedlock and raised us without the

Figure 14.2 Left to right, Kiyan Williams, Kaila Adia Story, Treva Lindsey, and Joan Morgan share a special moment. Photo by Abdul Alim.

constant presence of men. My mother and the mothers in my community, at times, were on government assistance to supplement their low paying jobs. Don't ever let my mother know I said that in public though." We won't tell, Kiyan. We promise. "My mother and the other single-parent, unwed Black women in my community also dated men who were not their babies' fathers. White supremacist and cisheteropatriarchal logics would have you and me believe that my mother, my grandmother, and the Black women in the community I was raised in are licentious, immoral, and abject. Reagan was likely referring to the women who I owe my very existence to during his diatribe about welfare queens. For a while, I internalized these sinister myths. I remember being called a bastard as a child and feeling so mad and betrayed by my mother for not being married to my absent father and for dating men who were not my father. But as I grew up, I realized that the love I was given by my mother was not compromised or tainted or flawed because she was an unwed single parent, that I was not somehow deprived of something because of the absence of a male parent. In fact, I would argue that I greatly benefited from being raised by and in a community of single women. They cultivated an affirming love that allowed a gender queer black boy like me to realize my full humanity and self-worth in ways that men in my community would not. They protected me from men who literally tried to beat the faggot out of me. In fact the community of single black women I was raised in created radical and subversive environments that challenged and averted, with all the spirit that only a mother wields, the types of heteronormative and patriarchal violences that a queer black boy in the hood like me would encounter. With that said, I am committed to articulating a new politics of Black female sexuality simply because my mother exists, my grandmother exists. And the love that they have for me and I for them exists. And I want to honor that love. Also, I believe the new articulations of Black female sexuality will have the possibility to liberate other bodies and desires rendered deviant within the White supremacist, cisheteropatriarchal capitalist project. And so my theorization of a new politics of Black female sexuality might also help me to rearticulate a politics of Black and queer desire. The ways we choose to love, who we choose to love, and how we choose to create family will not be obscured or erased or contested or pathologized by dominant narratives that seek to do exactly that. A new politics of Black female sexuality should be grounded in the histories and experiences of Black women, but should also have the potential to reframe the politics of desire of other marginalized folks. It should be embodied and expansive and engage the physical, psychic, and emotional dimensions of Black women's lives. I recognize that my attempt at articulating a politics of pleasure for Black female sexuality ultimately might be limited and flawed by the male privilege that I have access to, and whether consciously or not, exercise in my daily life. Ultimately, I believe that only Black women can rearticulate their politics of desire, but as a person who is deeply invested in the livelihood of Black women, I hope that these ideas and words might help us move closer to Black women's erotic liberation." [*Applause*]

When you have students like mine, you really don't have a choice but to bring it. [*Laughter*]

"CLOSER TO WHATEVER THEIR IDEA OF FREEDOM IS": FROM THE SPIRITUAL TO THE SEXUAL

H. SAMY ALIM: Beautiful, absolutely beautiful. I just want to ask all of you to take a minute and discuss why the politics of pleasure for Black women is so important.

TREVA LINDSEY: Well, for me, I think I had a conversation with Joan in New York at the Power of Women conference that we were both at when I heard her first say, "I'm really interested in this idea of a Black feminist praxis around politics of pleasure." And I said, "Yes. Oh, my God, yes." Right? And that comes into play because, one, when I was 19 and I first read Joan's book, *Chickenheads*. I mean, it completely changed my life. Because in a lot of ways it really helped me reconcile what I saw as contradictions and paradoxes in terms of the sexual life I was leading and the desire that I had sexually and intimately. And I used to see it as versus my feminist principles. And I think that there has been too long of a period of time where this idea of the singularity of truth for women's lives, particularly Black women, the very things that Joan was talking about, the very things that Kiyan said in that paper. That idea that the way that Black women's bodies are seen as infused with oppression and hypersexuality and degradation. And for me, growing up, I knew that that's how others saw my body. And I knew that that was others' projection of ideas of morality and politics and respectability onto my body. But that was not how I felt about my own body. And I know that that's not how my lovers felt about my body, either. And so, one, my investment has to do with erasing that. Trying to create multiple narratives and multiple scripts. Not just for me. Not necessarily, you know, how to do it, but just that it exists. That there are multiple sites of desire and attraction and sex and intimacy. And we as individual women, particularly individual women of color, are able to articulate for ourselves, through our music, through our movement, through our intimate partnerships, through our relationships. And these stories are things that never get told. So that's the first thing.

The second thing is I think that creating a Black feminist politics of pleasure would, in a lot of ways, allow Black women to reconcile the spiritual, the intimate, and the experiential knowledge that they carry with them and house with them that is not found in Black feminist theory and praxis, right? Typically, in Black feminist theory and praxis it only goes to a certain place. And that usually ends up with women of color and / or Black women's interactions with various institutions such as the police, or the law, or the welfare system, or the politics, or the government, right? And although those things are pertinent, important, and necessary to investigate, uncover, and dissect for the purposes of our empowerment and liberation, we also need to engage with those aspects of our humanity that are also necessary and fundamental to our liberation and empowerment. The spiritual, the intimate, and the experiential, the ways in which we create knowledge through our experiences, all of those need to be given voice in a variety of ways in order for us to move forward, and for Black women and other women of color to actualize their full humanity and full potential, and full lives, right?

And then the last thing is that it will also allow, particularly for me, who's interested in the actual carnal aspects, the actual sex, right—I'm really interested in that [*laughter*]—the ways in which we as Black women negotiate ideas of sex and intimacy, the things that we ask for, the things that we resist. Establishing an ideological and theoretical framework around pleasure, particularly when it pertains to sexuality and the actual act of sex would allow women to engage in their sexual limitations and also create alternative spaces of revolt and resistance within their personal and intimate relationships and sexual relationships. And this would be a force that in many ways to me would catapult Black women closer to whatever their idea of freedom is. [*Applause*]

I just want to say thank you for this space. This is incredibly moving on a number of levels and is giving me a certain level of emotional pleasure that we don't often get to have even in the academy as a space. And so I'm just very thankful for this, for you, and for all of you being here. My first investment comes from a very personal place. I'm kind of going to move personal and then move out. And it is as a survivor of sexual violence. And part of my work was saying, "How do I claim pleasure as my right?" As a right. As part of not a response to or reactionary to a normative space, but part of my survival is in the ability to seek, find, and articulate pleasure, right? So when we talk about the traumatic, of the violence, of our people, of Black women in general—I say in my work, I come from the question of

"What if we flip the lens?" When you were talking about the lens earlier. And then say, "What is the history of Black female exploitation and violence and trauma?" We do that work. I mean, that's so much of what the Black Feminist Project has done. And it's important work. But what if I start with the question of "What's the history of Black female pleasure?" Just fundamentally, what is that history? Because for me, recovering that history means that I can find my full humanity in an ancestral space, in a space that predates me, in a space that will exist after me. That the trauma that I encounter as a Black woman does not negate the possibility of pleasure. Not only does it not negate it, but it makes me fight even harder for what I think is rightfully mine and rightfully has been there.

So, when Joan mentioned earlier the possibility of saying if we look at the Middle Passage and see that as a site where pleasure is taking place, that is a really difficult and uncomfortable moment for a lot of people. Or to think about slavery as an institution, but saying, "Were there orgasms in slavery?"[12] Is that a legitimate archival question? And for me, it absolutely is because I need to know that my ancestors existed as human beings, as humans who found ways and strategies to survive such horrific circumstances. And I know that part of that survival, because part of mine is, is the experience and articulation of pleasure.

My investment comes from seeing pleasure as an emotional frontier for Black women to engage in, and to openly embrace. And that the move away from how you feel is one of the most devastating and potentially violent things that can be done to a body, to a person. And I say that when we ask in kind of emphatic language when we're walking past, you'll be like, "Hey girl, how you doing?" Right? You're not actually asking, you're not stopping to really interrogate that. But when you ask someone "How do you feel?", you actually have to wait, and you have to listen. And you have to give that space for that telling to happen, right? We have this practice in Black feminist studies of telling our stories, and engaging in storytelling.[13] And yet that storytelling has very much so been located in the space of trauma and pain, without necessarily thinking about the storytelling of those moments when you're laughing, when you're enjoying, when you're having an orgasm, when you are enjoying some good food. We've had that moment many times since we've been here. And mapping that terrain for me, that pleasure experience, yes it's sex, yes it's carnal, but yes it's the moments of intentional engagement with the beauty of the emotional selves of my sisters, right? And that is a really really important space for me to be able to invest in, not only as this Black feminist scholar but as me trying to navigate that space, right? To navigate a toxicity that can always tell you that pleasure is not my right. And I began to get very frustrated that in certain ways I felt like Black feminism was doing that because it's demanding that we acknowledge all of these systems without acknowledging the first kind of interior system that I'm negotiating of that level of what I feel and how I care, how I can touch it, how I can smell it, how I can taste it, right? So I want my language to do that kind of work as well.

So if I'm saying it's a frontier that we're approaching or negotiating, right, I think it's also about the interpretive communities that we're forming to be able to look at the very same archives we've looked at and mine different truths, right? That we mine those different spaces and mine the emotionality, mine the interiority of Black women to find that space where we can say, "I claim it, I own it, and it was never yours to take and you will not walk off with my shit." [*Applause*]

PLEASURE POLITICS AND THE POLITICAL-EPISTEMOLOGICAL PROJECT OF BLACK FEMINIST THEORIZING

BRITTNEY COOPER: I want to begin with a couple of short stories. The first is from a book that was published in 1940 by a famous Black feminist-activist and intellectual named Mary Church Terrell. She wrote a book called *A Colored Woman in a White World,* and this book is about 400 pages just recounting a life of service and activism on behalf of Black women.[14] She was the first Black female president of the National Association of Colored Women, which is the largest association of Black women in the country at the turn of the twentieth century. But in this narrative, there's an interesting moment both at the beginning and at the end where she talks about being a student at Oberlin College in the 1880s and sneaking out of her dorm room to go dancing. And she says, "People don't think respectable, intellectual girls go out and dance, but I do it." And then near the end of her life, she's in her 80s, and she writes that dancing is still one of her most favorite things to do, that she likes to "trip the light fantastic any time she gets the opportunity," which is just beautiful language. And I wondered how this woman, who was the paragon of Black racial respectability politics, why she would frame her autobiography of her life in terms of her love of dancing, structurally, and what kind of space she might be trying to make in that narrative for thinking about pleasure and thinking about eroticism in a moment in which Black women are largely not able to articulate that for all kinds of reasons.

Another story. When I was 22, I went to see my grandmother. I pulled up in her yard. She's a Black lady living in rural Louisiana, which is where I'm from, and I pull up in the yard in my car. She's sitting on the porch. I'm walking up on the porch, and she just looks at me, and she says, "It's time for you to start having sex," which is not a moment that you ever want to have with your grandmother. [*Laughter*] And she sees this incredulous look on my face like, "What's happening?" And she says, "No. I mean it. It's time for you to start doing that." And so then it began a long conversation that she and I sat on the porch and had that day, in which she said to me, "Don't ever let anyone make you believe them. My generation did do it, we did it. We went into the wood and did it—we did it!" [*Laughter*] And I just thought there's never going to be a moment when I'm grown enough to hear this story. [*Laughter*]

Third story. My first Black feminism course when I got to graduate school, my professor walks in. You know the first day that the professor walks into a course and you are trying to figure out who they are. And the first thing that she says out of her mouth is, "I am such and such, and I would just like to say that I like sex." And I thought, "What the hell?" [*Laughter*] Why would you begin a graduate seminar that way? And then she begins to talk about what it meant to be able to politically articulate as a Black woman that even though she was a professor and she did all of this work, that sex was an active part of her, an active part of her life, that she was doing it, she liked doing it, and she wanted to create the space for those of us to be able to see it. And all of these things really fucked my world up. [*Laughter*] Because I was a very repressed Christian good girl who had adopted a lot of religious respectability dictates in order to make it out of my working-class background. Good girls wanted to have sex but "Sex gets you pregnant," and this is not the thing you wanted because it could ruin your life, which leads to a lot of sexual repression. So, my grandmother said, "You made it now, girl, go get you sumthin." [*Laughter*] It's perhaps the most poignant moment, and why I think that pleasure politics matter for being a Black feminist is because my grandmother is perhaps the first Black feminist that I ever knew. And what she articulated for me was that pleasure was a part of her life, and that even in her whole life when she struggled with disability and poverty, and not being able to achieve many of the dreams that she had for herself, that never meant an abridgement of pleasure for her.

So, for me, pleasure politics matters for Black women on a few levels. First as a scholar, I really want to push Black feminism to suggest that pleasure politics is part of the political and epistemological project of Black feminist theorizing. That it is a natural outgrowth, that we're not pushing Black feminism to do anything that it is not capable of, or that is not in the legacy, the intellectual and political legacy, of that work to do. And part of what I mean when I say epistemological is real talk. There are some things that you do not know about yourself outside of intimate space. So when we offer and talk about Black women being permitted to articulate a sense of pleasure, we are also talking about Black women being able to fully embody an epistemological space. And the converse is if we do not have a pleasure politics, we are committing forms of epistemological violence against Black women. And that cannot be part of a justice project, right? If Black feminism asks us to buy into it on the grounds that we have to sacrifice pleasure, then that means that Black feminism's commitment to justice is in fact deeply called into question. There can be no justice without pleasure.

When we think about trying to create a just world, if the only thing that justice means is that you're free from oppression but not then free to build anything pleasurable, then what kind of justice is it really, and what have we been fighting for? So, for me, the last thing to say about this in this moment is that thinking about relationships between justice and pleasure is an acknowledgment that sex and pleasure and intimate space all map a space made of power. The same professor that rolled into my class and said, "I like sex." One of the things she said to me was, "Sex is a form of creative power. What are you creating?" And thinking of it in that way when I finally really reconciled all of those pieces allowed me to think about it as power, as pleasure, not as a thing that was being done to me destructively that I had no agency in, but as a real opportunity to participate in creative processes. So if the work of Black feminism is to create a different world, to spin the world anew to imagine what we have never seen before, then that means that we have to figure out where the spaces of creativity actually lie. And so, for me, recognizing that a pleasure politic articulates sex as one of those spaces wherein we create the world we want to see is really important to a Black feminist politic. [*Applause*]

"STRUGGLE HAS BEEN BLACK WOMEN'S LOVER FOR TOO LONG": TOWARD EMOTIONAL JUSTICE

ESTHER ARMAH: Wow, so this is a really emotional space for me. I just want to say thank you to Joan for making this possible. I am invested in a politics of pleasure because I feel struggle has been Black women's lover for too long. Struggle has been a commitment that is historical. It became a legacy that was inherited. It became this generational space that we made a commitment to, and it was a specific pleasure that was sanctioned. I am not a scholar. I don't self-ID as a feminist. I am British and Black and Ashanti and Ghanaian and all of those spaces for me are integrated. So my pleasure politics comes from wanting to give voice to a pleasure that is silenced. That inheritance comes from me—specifically from my mama—who is an Ashanti woman who in 1966 managed to get her four daughters out of a house where soldiers had broken in with rifle butts, broken and smashed everything, put a gun to her head, told her to get on her knees. And she said it was only incompetence that saved her life because they were child soldiers who were as terrified as she was. That was a story that was kept silent for 30-something years while men told the story of that night in February 1966 and how they rescued nations for a people. That was the story that was told. And it was 30 years of silence that was finally broken by my mother. And in the breaking of that, I understood the pieces. In all of this war is the presence of pleasure, but a pleasure that you have to craft and create because it is a pleasure that is rooted in power because it was my mother and women who got their children and themselves out safely of a space that was incredibly violent. The miracle that none of them died, and they could have absolutely died that night, was extraordinary.

And so I learned that my legacy is more than untreated trauma, and that I want to be in a place to create process and to give voice to the types of pleasure that are silenced. Because for me, for women, the pleasure that is sanctioned is one of service and sacrifice. And only those specific two spaces. We create intimate relationships with pleasure and violence and those spaces are problematic, but they seem to be the places that we are sanctioned to live in. But what if we created something different? So, for me, I'm invested in creating process, in wanting to literally build a path to introduce yourself to the idea of pleasure so that you can even define it, to be able to ask the question to young women in particular, like, "What does it mean?"; to offer an opportunity and space for older women to ask the question, "What does it mean to you? How do you define it? What does it look like?"

So, my point, it requires us to think much more carefully and with more respect around emotionality and its power. I crafted the term *emotional justice*,[15] because for me the absence of integrating emotionality into how we create identity means we are building incomplete selves. And then asking us to not just function with those incomplete selves, but to flourish. How do we thrive under that circumstance? What do you build when institutions keep falling down? How do they stand without the recognition that emotionality's something that literally shapes, not just your identity, but your relationship with the first institution, which is that of self? And so, you nurture an intellect and neglect an emotionality, and expect to create wholeness? But that's not what we create.

I understand intimately the power of my emotionality to free me from those spaces where my legacy's supposed to solely be defined as untreated trauma. There must be other things. Because I look into my mother's eyes and she's here. And she's more than here; she demands to be recognized, seen, and do more than exist. So we want to flourish, not simply function. [Applause]

BLACK FEMINIST THEORY, HOMOPHOBIA, AND
ENGAGING BLACK QUEER BODIES

KAILA ADIA STORY: Well, in my research and in my pedagogy, I attempt to elucidate the politics of pleasure by bridging different theoretical conceptions. So, I take from Feminist Theory, from Black Feminist Theory, from Black Queer Theory and also Queer Theory.[16] And I will merge all of those with one another, because I think that this kind of engagement across theoretical lines helps to articulate and give it a different type of reading, of not only Black female bodies but Black queer bodies, and ideas around pleasure and desire and sexuality. I actually think Black Queer Theory in a lot of ways opens up analysis for reading culture and our socialization in a different type of way than Feminist Theory does, in the ways in which Black Queer Theory utilizes new conceptions around language, identity, embodiment, desire.

And what I try to argue is that I want Black Feminist Theory to do away with a lot of its homophobia.[17] I think that that's something that's not really engaged in a lot of ways. Although it seems to me that Black Feminist Theory in a lot of ways is on point when it comes to analysis around racism and sexism and White patriarchal culture, it in a lot of ways perpetuates silence around Black queer identities. And therefore Black Queer Studies and Black Queer Theory had to be born itself, just like Black Feminist Theory had to be born out of an absence of Feminist Theory when it came to analysis of race. And I think that if Black Feminist Theory would utilize Black Queer Theory as more of a starting point and not necessarily a footnote to its main goals and objectives, it would be phenomenal, and I try to call attention to all those things in my writing.

And for the past seven months now, I have a podcast on WFPL, which is the local NPR station in Louisville, Kentucky, and I co-host a show called *Strange Fruit*, musings on politics, pop culture, and Black gay life with one of my comrades, Jaison Gardner. And on our show we talk about a variety of topics and engage with a variety of wonderful scholars and/or activists, and try to engage ideas around pleasure. We had Dr. Mireille Miller-Young on the show talking about Black women's participation in the porn industry, right, and reconceptualizing ideas around porn and/or pleasure for Black women and women of color.[18] And we had Darnell Moore on there.[19] I mean, we've had a tremendous amount of great guests who've really tried to unearth and refocus conversations around race, gender, and sexuality, and talk about these things in a way that is not always engaging the awfulness or the terror of these identities, but definitely trying to engage the full livelihood of people that occupy this community, including myself. A lot of my work is centered on my own experience, and my own struggles with reconciling all of these things for myself, for my students, and for people in my life. And I do think that as someone who is a Black girl lesbo, who's feminine performing, who intentionally performs high femininity every day with the exception of when I'm home I fall completely out of drag, okay. [*Laughter*] But you won't ever see that! [*Laughter*]

But again, I know that in a lot of ways, I know that my presentation and the way in which I walk through the world is completely misunderstood. And I live for the fact that it's misunderstood, and quite frankly I don't give a fuck. [*Laughter*] Because what's more important to me is the way in which I see myself. And in the ways in which I teach and the radio show, I try to give voice to those people who are living their lives with intentionality. And I think that one of the spaces where I have found the most intentionality in terms of embodiment performance, in terms of articulating a politics of pleasure, are black queer spaces. I feel like those spaces are revolutionary. They're untapped, they're consistently borrowed from and placed in pop culture, removed from any kind of root, and just seen as kind of histrionic and hyperbolic expressions of identity. So we laugh at them or we're excited by them but we don't necessarily take them seriously.

And in many ways, the ways in which Black queer people engage and move through the world is not only revolutionary and intentional, but it's using the body as a revolting weapon to make folks uncomfortable with ideas of what is normative—ideas of what is normative in terms of sexuality, in terms of gender, in terms of race. For me, who teaches around Black feminine embodiment especially, I go into my "Black Feminists in Action" class just like this. I wear this to school. And everybody lookin at me like, "Dr. Story, man, what you doing?! You're a professor!" And I'm like, "Well, I know. I can't be sexy, I can't be a sexy professor?" [*Laughter*] People are really offended by cleavage and the fact that this is Black cleavage—you know the idea of the Black body being any kind of nude or semi-nude produces such an uncomfortable reaction in people because it's consistently to me been socialized to be seen as something that should be hidden, something that shouldn't be discussed, something that is couched in terror, and White patriarchal racism.

And for me, the way in which I dress and perform is very liberatory for me and very freeing, not only because I consistently work on my body in terms of working out and try to eat right. Well, I don't got that down, but I work out, whatever, you know what I mean? But I'm trying with my own embodiment and in research to call attention to the fact that I am my own erotic, intellectual agent. The power is within me to change people's ideas, minds, and perceptions around the ways in which they're socialized to see Black women's bodies, to see what a Black female professor should be or look like. To me, it's bullshit. And even though we're in the academy and we talk about that we have to negotiate all these different things and we have a multitude of ideas and people and expressions—that really isn't the case. What really is the case is that we want to see everybody as the same way. We want to see everybody dress the same way, act the same way, in these types of ways, and I think it's extremely problematic because it removes one's agency and humanity. It's always making one have to conform to a certain idea. So, because enslavers in the 1800s saw Black female bodies as incredibly libidinous and hypersexual, is that how I should see my own? So should I have shame attached to my body and my breasts? Should I hide those things? And even if that's not your thing, even if you're like, "Girl, I don't like no cleavage, I don't like showing my body," that's fine, too. Do you, but don't shade me. Don't throw shade this way, and don't try and interpret the way in which I perform those types of things as problematic or somehow reductive or contradictory or paradoxical to my feminist politics and convictions.

And the only reason why I get so upset about it is because I was doing this to my own self. I was having the emotional battle with myself and saying that, "These are the things I like to do. These are the things that provide me freedom." The only things that I typically have access to is my students, my writing, and my body. And all those avenues that I have access to, I'm going to be damn sure to try and create a liberatory thing for myself. But it was so hard for me to reconcile that because there's so much pushback on all of the things I just talked about.

BRITTNEY COOPER: So I think one of the things you said I caught as really important, because I think that Black feminism has such a comfortable engagement with Audre Lorde, right? So basically, Audre Lorde wrote *Uses of the Erotic*,[20] and we never have to interrogate it again. And at that point, then it doesn't become feminism, right? It becomes religious dogma, like it's sacred text, and we're never supposed to retheorize it again, as if Lorde herself would have wanted us to do that, as if 1984 when she published that text is the same reality as today, as if Hip Hop never happened, as if the hypervisibility of hypersexual Black female bodies has never happened, and so in many ways, I do believe this is a post-Lorde conversation also, which you know, in feminism is like sacrilege.

TWERKING, THE BODY, AND HISTORICIZING PLEASURE

TREVA LINDSEY: My first point is, I brought up a little bit earlier that I'm a historian by training. I think in certain ways in terms of what I want to do, so I got to ask the question of the history of pleasure. So how do I get from being a trained nineteenth-century historian to talking about "ratchet feminism"?[21] That doesn't seem like the most natural jump, but for me, it seems absolutely plausible, and not only plausible but the right to demand that there were women who were existing in these marginal spaces who were asking questions in ways that made people very uncomfortable. We're asking things and living lives that made people very uncomfortable—that I believe a woman I studied, Lucy Diggs Slowe, the first dean of students at Howard University, had a wonderful and loving relationship with a brilliant playwright and poet, Mary Burrill, in Washington, DC.[22] And there's so much of her writing where she's *reading* folks about their politics, about African American gender ideology, and I'm just like, when I read her, all I can hear in my head is, "Who is going to check me?" [*laughter*], right?

And the mining of that tradition of pushing back even within our communities because I care about our community—I care about Black feminism, which is why I want to push back against it. I want to push back and say, "We already have the tools to do that." Brittney brought up Audre Lorde and Deborah King[23] about "establishing and reestablishing our priorities," right, that we have a constant responsibility to go back to our theories, to go back to our germinal texts, reimagine them, reenvision them, rearticulate them, and recognize moments as historically contingent moments. We have to own our moment and find ways to reestablish ourselves. So, for me, doing that work, mining from 1860 to today is so important because the tradition is there, right?[24] If we're looking at this kind of feminist epistemic, this kind of intellectual tradition, we need to look at the tradition of those marginal spaces that were already pushing back against the dominant ideologies of the day.

The second point is, I am a trained classical ballet dancer. One of the reasons I ballet is because I had no rhythm [*laughter*] growing up, absolutely none. But part of that was like, there was some kind of Black girl embodiment that I wanted to have, that I didn't have when I was little, right? I had an embodiment that allowed certain kinds of motions. And then suddenly I randomly got rhythm, I'm not quite sure how yet. But my other space is twerking. And the ability to do certain things with my body, which also goes back to my work of how I read Ciara, how I read Beyoncé, how I read their bodies and the texts that their bodies create, that gyration. I do a lot theorizing around gyrating and moving, and popping, and twerking, and clapping, and all of those things. And I also teach what I call kind of "sexy fitness classes," that has become the moniker, but particularly for women 50 and over. And what that means for them to discover their bodies in new ways. And they are always like, "We used to do it like this," meaning that pleasure had always been there for them. But the way they feel comfortable expressing that and how they express that—and seeing and teaching a 62-year-old woman how to make it clap has been one of the most dynamic feminist moments I've had, right? And the pride she took in being able to control her own body. Because as much as we think about control in terms of "reproductive justice," and "political agency," and all of these things—no. I want to be able to make my body move in certain ways that gives me a pleasure that ain't got nothing to do with anybody else. And that's a very important moment for me for articulating what autonomy can mean.

BRITTNEY COOPER: So, articulations for me, they happen in a couple of places. The first is the vignette that I told you at the beginning, which is about going back and rereading Black women's texts, and thinking about the very real ways in which they, in fact, do articulate pleasure in spaces that you are trained and conditioned not to see it, because what we've been trained and conditioned to see is that there's going to be a politics of respectability and a culture of dissemblance.[25] And Black women aren't talking about the body. So then what do I do when Ida B. Wells talks about how she doesn't know why this dude had her in the woods on the swing, trying to kiss on her, in her diary. And she shouldn't have let him do it. But she's not going to tell him that she loves him before he tells her that he loves her. [*Laughter*] And this is 22-year-old Ida B. So, those women come alive for me. One of the things that's intriguing about somebody like Ida B. Wells is, she had a real bad clothing habit, so she often couldn't make rent because she would go down to the local store and buy the latest fashion. I mean these are real problems and they're not new problems, you know? She really did take pleasure in looking fly to the point of not being able to pay her rent!

So making those women come alive, because here's the thing, that makes them more human, right. And so, she's not this deity. She's a person that was really real and human even as she fought for injustice and I think that we need models for that. And I think that that's for me part of a Black feminist intellectual history project. Also, when we were doing some of our work together over these last three days, we went back to look at definitions of feminism, Black feminism that would allow for what we're talking about because we talked about the fact that Black feminism more recently has become this kind of political project around articulating the oppression and structural issues. But there are other traditions. There's Ntozake Shange, and the kinds of pleasures that she articulates in *For Colored Girls*,[26] which is also at the start of Joan's book, too. So there are these multiple traditions.

The last thing I'll say is that my work with the Crunk Feminist Collective is the place that I actively try to articulate pleasure outside of academic space.[27] Our work with Crunk comes from the fact that when we were in school together working on PhDs, what we were doing was taking feminist classes and then going to the club and shaking our asses [*laughter*], right? And really enjoying it and not being willing to give it up because it was a way to cope. It was a way that you dealt with the bullshit. Grad school can be a space that actively tries to strip you of your confidence, of your sense of worth. It can be a very violent space. And so going back into Black cultural spaces and saying, "Right now, who can pop it, who can

Figure 14.3 The Pleasure Ninjas and the IDA Family. Photo by Casey Philip Wong.

move it?" whatever, is really important as a form of resistance and other things.

So, in that space, I do a lot of blogging and I've made a commitment to blog about my dating life in really vulnerable ways. I blog about dating, I blog about sex, I blog about what it means to be a big girl trying to get it in. Yes. [*Laughter*] And unapologetically so because there are moments that happen where sisters come over and say, "Thank you just for acknowledging the struggle, for naming it." It lets me know that sisters are looking for spaces where we are having a real set of conversations about the fact that, "Look, we have great politics but we want to fuck too sometimes," [*laughter*] and how we do that, right? And so one of the things I'm so thankful for, Joan, is that this work requires a certain vulnerability because it requires somebody to be willing to be honest and say that this matters in addition to everything else. And I think that's the way that I do it with the group of women who we have each other's back, so we ride for each other. [*Applause*]

TRANSFORMING TRAUMA TO TRIUMPH

ESTHER ARMAH: So, for me, as I said, process is just so crucial and I live in this space of giving emotionality the respect that it deserves and never gets. And so it's about creating safe spaces to have conversations that explore, for example, "Who have you become as a result of how you were loved? What legacy did that create for you? What lessons did you learn? How has all of that shaped the way you navigate the institutions that you move through? And that institution includes your body, your physical body. So, I created this thing called EJ, Emotional Justice conversations. And I wanted to build a space to have conversations about those points of vulnerability, that the space had to be sacred, that the conversations required an honesty about what people often saw as a space of contradiction.

So with EJ conversations, I do these live conversations in community and different spaces in New York and we do them with all men specifically exploring the way in which masculinity is shaped by how we were loved and the legacy that that created, but also talking about things like Black male privilege from a space that is personal and specific. So it is not simply about the articulation of the theory of Black male privilege but the way it manifests in your life. I want to make something live, stand up and breathe, so that we are able to interrogate it from a lived basis as opposed to this space of theory. So the other thing we've created is, we know March is International Women's History month, so I created something called International FlyGirls Day, which is March Ninth, and the intention of that specifically is to talk to young women and young girls specifically about power. To be able to ID your own power, to ID your brilliance, to ID your beauty as opposed to waiting for permission or being introduced to your beauty from outside worlds. Like what if you could turn to your girl and know for yourself, in your own voice, this is what is swag about me. Recognize. We are doing it with a middle school in Brooklyn and it's just been such a joy to watch girls navigate spaces where they're normally just waiting patiently to be given permission. But that they take that space and that you see when they take that space, that they know what they want, they don't require the permission that society tells them that they should wait for.

So what if you created spaces of sisterhood that were controlled by those young women as opposed to sanctioned by an older person who tells you what that is supposed to look like? What would that look like for you, what would you write in your "Diary of Fly" if you were 12? And so to watch girls be like, "Oh, I know exactly what I'm going to say!" And for them to literally take pleasure in the identification of their own power, that they control. You have a space to go to that you created, that you control, that is specifically about the power of your own pleasure. And so for me, that's what my pleasure practice is about, making the space sacred enough so that you can have the most difficult conversations but transform those legacies of untreated trauma, so that you have triumph. [*Applause*]

NOTES

1. Joan Morgan, *When Chickenheads Come Home to Roost: A Hip-Hop Feminist Breaks It Down* (Simon & Schuster, 1999).

2. Treva B. Lindsey, "Let Me Blow Your Mind: Hip Hop Feminist Futures in Theory and Praxis," *Urban Education* 50, no. 1 (2015): 52–77.

3. Patricia Hill Collins, *Black Feminist Thought: Knowledge, Consciousness, and the Politics of Empowerment* (Routledge, 2002).

4. Joan Morgan, "Why We Get Off: Moving towards a Black Feminist Politics of Pleasure," *Black Scholar* 45, no. 4 (2015): 36–46.

5. Brittney Cooper, "How Sarah Got Her Groove Back, or Notes toward a Black Feminist Theology of Pleasure," *Black Theology* 16, no. 3 (2018): 195–206.

6. In 2013 Joan Morgan taught a course at Stanford University, "The Pleasure Principle: A Post-Hip Hop Search for a Black Feminist Politics of Pleasure."

7. Kevin Adonis Browne, *Tropic Tendencies: Rhetoric, Popular Culture, and the Anglophone Caribbean* (University of Pittsburgh Press, 2013).

8. Joan references how Jamaican intellectuals have been theorizing around and thinking about Jamaican dancehall culture relative to feminism and a politics of pleasure. In *Sound Clash: Jamaican Dancehall Culture at Large* (Springer, 2004), Carolyn Cooper explores how Jamaican speakers have "reinterpreted borrowed English words via folks etymology," including "the English word 'foreign' pronounced 'farin' in Jamaican, consistent with a pattern of regular vowel change: from 'o' to 'a'." Cooper points out that "foreign" is "monomorphemic in English," and has been "reinterpreted as bimorphemic in Jamaican—'far' and 'in'." Thus, she argues that "there is perceived to be a clash between the meaning of the word and the meaning of the 'in' morpheme: 'Farin' is 'out,' not 'in'." (46). Morgan enters into conversation with scholars like Cooper.

9. Brittney C. Cooper, *Beyond Respectability: The Intellectual Thought of Race Women* (University of Illinois Press, 2017).

10. Audre Lorde, "Uses of the Erotic," in Lorde, *Sister Outsider: Essays and Speeches*, 53–59 (Crossing Press, 1978).

11. Patricia Hill Collins, *Black Sexual Politics: African Americans, Gender, and the New Racism* (Routledge, 2004).

12. Treva B. Lindsey and Jessica Marie Johnson, "Searching for Climax: Black Erotic Lives in Slavery and Freedom," *Meridians* 12, no. 2 (2014): 169–95.

13. For context of this tradition, see bell hooks, *Sisters of the Yam: Black Women and Self-Recovery* (South End Press, 1994); April Baker-Bell, "For Loretta: A Black Woman Literacy Scholar's Journey to Prioritizing Self-Preservation and Black Feminist-Womanist Storytelling," *Journal of Literacy Research* 49, no. 4 (2017): 526–43.

14. Mary Church Terrell, *A Colored Woman in a White World* (GK Hall, 1940).

15. See Armah Institute of Emotional Justice, "What Is Emotional Justice?", 2019, https://www.theaiej.com/emotional-justice.

16. Kaila Adia Story, "(Re)Presenting Shug Avery and Afrekete: The Search for a Black, Queer, and Feminist Pleasure Praxis," *Black Scholar* 45, no. 4 (2015): 22–35.

17. Kaila Adia Story, "Black Femme Menace: How Queer Battle Fatigue Intersects with Blackness and Gender," *GLQ: A Journal of Lesbian and Gay Studies* 26, no. 2 (2020): 233–36.

18. Mireille Miller-Young, *A Taste for Brown Sugar: Black Women in Pornography* (Duke University Press, 2014).

19. Darnell L. Moore, D., "Guilty of Sin: African-American Denominational Churches and Their Exclusion of SGL Sisters and Brothers," *Black Theology* 6, no. 1 (2008): 83–97.

20. Lorde, "Uses of the Erotic," in Lorde, *Sister Outsider*.

21. Treva B. Lindsey, "The Ratchet of the Earth: Black Women, Respectability, and Popular Culture," conference paper, presented at the Association for the Study of African American Life and History Convention, September 2012.

22. Treva B. Lindsey, *Colored No More: Reinventing Black Womanhood in Washington* (University of Illinois Press, 2017).

23. Deborah K. King, "Multiple Jeopardy, Multiple Consciousness: The Context of a Black Feminist Ideology," *Signs: Journal of Women in Culture and Society* 14, no. 1 (1988): 42–72.

24. Treva B. Lindsey, "Ula Y. Taylor's 'Making Waves: The Theory and Practice of Black Feminism': A Contemporary Observation," *Black Scholar* 44, no. 3 (2014): 48–51.

25. Cooper, *Beyond Respectability*.

26. Ntozake Shange, *For Colored Girls Who Have Considered Suicide / When the Rainbow Is Enuf* (Simon and Schuster, 1975).

27. Shange, *For Colored Girls*.

15 "When Can Black Disabled Folks Come Home?"

THE KRIP-HOP MOVEMENT, RACE, AND DISABILITY JUSTICE

Leroy F. Moore Jr. and Stephanie Keeney Parks

The Road to Krip-Hop

On my butt going down to the basement
Couldn't walk so I slid one stair at a time
Every time she turned her back I was gone
Get your brother from the basement
Surrounded by my father's records
It was like looking in the mirror
Blues and Soul musicians looked like me
No more searching I could not believe
Then one day I turned on the TV
And I saw another Black man who walked like me
Screaming, "Mommy mommy, I'm on TV!"
My mom laughed, "no baby that is Porgy!"
That was back in the late 70s
Then in the 80s two Black disabled boys and me
Did our own advocacy
Went upstairs to my bedroom to write letters to Black agencies
A few years later Hip Hop hit
1984 the movie *Breakin* kicked it

With Crazy Legs on crutches bustin a move in a cypher
Once again I found my mirror
Then hyphy in the Bay Area
That took it too far
The Black Kripple in the 90s blazed open mics
Told all of that ableist shit to go take a hike
Now 2020
Krip-Hop in every country
It is more than music
Going back to little Leroy in the basement

—Leroy F. Moore Jr.

STEPHANIE KEENEY PARKS: I have the pleasure of introducing Leroy F. Moore Jr., a co-founder of one of the most significant disability-related Hip Hop movements in the world, Krip-Hop Nation (KHN). Inspired by the Homohop scene, Leroy co-founded KHN in the Bay Area with Keith Jones and Rob Da Noize Temple in 2007. KHN is a global disability and Hip Hop movement that uses the art of rhyme to critique ableism and work towards disability justice. Krip-Hop as a movement centers the marginalization faced by those that experience the intersection of racism and ableism within the US and internationally.

According to Leroy, this collective of over 300 members across the globe has a mission to "educate the music, media industries, and general public about the talents, history, rights, and marketability of Hip Hop artists and other musicians with disabilities." KHN grew out of Moore's complex, sometimes ambivalent relationship with Hip Hop, his love of music, and his participation in activism. His work as a writer and poet spans from his column "Illin n' Chillin" for *POOR Magazine*, to published articles in the *New York Times*, and books such as *Black Disabled Art History 101*,[1] *The Black Kripple Delivers Poetry & Lyrics*,[2] and the *Krip-Hop Graphic Novel*.[3] As a Black disabled activist, Leroy also co-founded Sins Invalid, a disability arts justice performance project. On behalf of KHN and its global appeal, he has traveled extensively, including to the South Korea Paralympics, the 1995 Black Disabled Movement in London, and the DaDa Fest UK in 2014 (the biggest disability arts festival in Europe).

Leroy grew up learning to love Hip Hop on the street corners of New York City's boroughs. In those early ciphers, his Black/Brown able-bodied peers put him to work as a "lookout" for police, believing he was too "crippled" to enter the cipher. These moments laid the foundation for his love and critique of the genre (i.e., he wasn't too crippled for his able-bodied peers to use his disability to protect them from police brutality). The inherent ableism within Hip Hop precluded Leroy and those with disabilities from seeing their whole selves in the culture. However, as a Black disabled youth, he did see his full self mirrored in his father's record collection—a collection of Blues, Jazz, and Soul, where numerous Black disabled men like Blind Willie Johnson, Robert Winters, and Walter Jackson found their creative license. Leroy co-founded KHN aiming to push Hip Hop to accept and engage Black and disabled youth on their own terms and within this rich, musical tradition.

Collectively, Leroy and KHN have been a consistent voice on wrongful incarceration and police brutality against people with disabilities, including in his widely circulating 2014 documentary with Emmett Thrower, *Where Is Hope—The Art of Murder: Police Brutality against People with Disabilities*.[4] As we can see, Leroy is much more than just a Hip Hop poet and emcee, but an activist, community organizer, journalist, and filmmaker dedicated to representing for folks with disabilities around the world.

Now, Leroy, tell me a little bit about being a young, Black disabled boy growing up in the '70s and '80s in a White suburb of Connecticut, and how you fell in love with Hip Hop.

GROWING UP BLACK AND DISABLED IN A WHITE SUBURB

LEROY F. MOORE JR.: Yeah, you know, in the suburbs of East Hartford, Connecticut, I think we were the first Black family in that suburb. [*Laughter*] Looking back now I never saw myself as a Black disabled man until I went to school and I was in special education. I saw a lot of Black disabled boys until I was mainstreamed.[5] And I was like, "Ah, here's the White people." [*Laughter*] So that taught me how segregated special education was. This was in the '70s. I got mainstreamed because my mother took the school board to court. I think this is when the Individuals with Disabilities

Education Act (IDEA)[6] first passed in 1975. She used that and she sued the school board. So I was mainstreamed with a teacher's aide. My mom never really got into the disability rights movement though, because at that time she was going to a lot of support groups. And a lot of support groups had White parents. And the White parents are crying. My mom's like, "Why the fuck are you crying? You know, your son and daughter's *alive*. Why are you crying?" So, you know, because of that my mom just stopped going.

And not much has changed because just IDEA is not fully funded and not fully enforced. That's why anytime we have an IDEA celebration, like this year, I keep on saying, "Why are we celebrating?" It's not being enforced. It's so funny that now during the presidential elections this year, everybody had "fully funded IDEA" in their platform. And it's like, "Well, you guys have been in Congress how long?" You know, this should be nothing new. We should laugh at your platform. Why should we believe you now?

But like I said, I grew up in East Hartford, you know, White, White suburb. My father was an NFL football player and my mother was a nurse and worked in insurance. So I grew up like on Rock and Punk and Ozzy Osbourne. I had a mohawk. I was really punked out, you know. So I was listening to that. I was listening to The Jackson 5. And so when Hip Hop came around, I was like, "Whoa, what's this?" And I bought the Sugarhill Gang's "Rapper's Delight." I just played that sucker over and over and over again. Yeah! And, at that time, Rock was becoming kind of horrible. They had New Wave. I was like, "What the fuck is this New Wave, you know?" I think having New Wave just totally destroyed Rock. So, when that happened, I was like, "Okay, I'm going over there, Hip Hop." [*Laughter*] Being in New York and seeing the Hip Hop ciphers and, you know, in Connecticut, we were so close to New York—you had Eric B and Rakim back in the day. I used to go with my walker. I write about it in my graphic novel. I'd go in there with my walker, "Click, click." And because New York was hardcore back then. This was, you know, before gentrification. So, you know, all the boys was like, "Aw, you can't rap. So you look out for the cops." So that was my job, looking out for the cops. [*Laughter*] Because they thought, you know, "The cops won't mess with you because you're disabled." So I had one eye on the cipher and the other eye on the lookout for the cops.

Back then, I always chickened out, because the ciphers were so competitive. I mean, you got boys with muscles, you know, breakdancing. And

I was like, "Oh, no, I can't do that." I was totally intimidated. I always wrote poems, but I didn't perform them. I graduated in '95 and went to the UK. The UK had a Black disabled movement. And that's when things changed for me. It was like, "What the hell are these . . . ?!" So that's when I started to do open mic. I was like, "What the hell, I don't know nobody, so I might as well do it!" That was in '95, '96.

FROM THE BLUES, TO HIP HOP, TO THE KRIP-HOP MOVEMENT

PARKS: What is it about Hip Hop that moved you so much to love it like you do?

MOORE: I think it was the rawness and the politics of it, you know. KRS-One and Public Enemy, you know, just talking back to the system. I was always an activist. So, Hip Hop sparked that in me, just like Punk. Punk was totally going against the system. And just, just being a Black disabled man, I was going against the system anyway.

And Hip Hop was not the only thing I listened to, I always go back to the Blues. The Blues was like a mirror to my full being because I could look at the Blues and see myself, you know. And in Hip Hop, I couldn't. I didn't see my whole self. Because Blues had disabled Black men singing the Blues. One day I was looking through my father's record collection and saw like Robert Winters on crutches. I saw Curtis Mayfield after his accident, you know. I saw a lot of blind Blues artists. So I saw Black disabled men. It was like, "Wow, okay, this is my mirror, ain't it?" And I didn't see that in Hip Hop, especially in Hip Hop that was commercialized. It's more "macho." They see disability as a weakness. And the disability movement is so White that it's not even connected to Hip Hop. It's two different histories, and I brought them together when I started Krip-Hop Nation. The power of Hip Hop, though, is that it comes from the streets. It's not like opera where you have to do 20 years of school, you know? Anybody can do it, you know, it's accessible. It comes from street language, so it's more open to expressing what you're going through.

Now with Krip-Hop, we have more groups, with Krip-Hop being international and having many Hip Hop artists that come out in support. DMC supports Krip-Hop. He did a song on our album. I interviewed him twice. The late Rob Da Noize Temple, who was a co-founder of Krip-Hop, he was the DJ for the Sugarhill Gang. And he taught the Sugarhill Gang about Krip-Hop. The Sugarhill Gang was one of the first Hip Hop mainstream entities that supported Krip-Hop. So things like that keep us going.

PARKS: Can you talk about some of the challenges disabled Black folks face within Hip Hop?

MOORE: The challenge is just stupidity, from the record companies and from other Hip Hop artists. I mean, when Krip-Hop started we used to get hate emails from Hip Hop journalists, you know, saying that we are putting down Hip Hop because we are talking about disability. Our first conference was Krip-Hop and Homohop, bringing disabled Hip Hop artists with queer Hip Hop artists. And that stirred up *everything*. I mean, people were tearing down our posters. We got hate emails and hate calls. It was something else! I was like, "Are you serious, dude?" Even now with the latest blame that's going on in the media with Krip-Hop. You know, in my *New York Times* article, I put it out there. I put a challenge out there to Hip Hop. It's time for us to have a big conference to educate the Hip Hop industry about disability and to promote Krip-Hop artists and politics. I also said that I would like to see Krip-Hop taken seriously in Hip Hop Studies. And I haven't gotten anything yet so far. Krip-Hop hasn't been in a Hip Hop conference *ever*. You got Hip Hop Studies, and you have these major conferences going on, and nobody's inviting Krip-Hop. Nobody invites disability to the table.

I mean, the Hip Hop museums, they need to have Krip-Hop there. You know, the Blues museum in Mississippi has nothing around disability. The lynching museum has nothing about Jesse Washington who was lynched, nothing about disability that I know of. The erasure is constant. It's like we're always left out, even in our own museums. The sting is always harder when it comes from our own community. In fact, I can write beaucoup books about the White disabled community, but when it comes to the Black community, it's like, "Are you serious?" The story going back to my childhood is that me and two other Black disabled boys went up to my room for a whole month—this is like in the late '70s, early '80s—and we wrote letters. We wrote letters to *everybody*—NAACP, Urban League, Jesse Jackson, *everybody*—around not seeing us. And we got form letters back saying there's nothing out there. And these are even the people with PhDs, you know? And that was like 1980, 1979. Here we are in 2020 asking the same question.

There has to be a re-education, because like I say in my article, the Black community still has a slave mentality when it comes to disability. It's like, they don't see us, or it's all about services, or "You're gonna overcome it," you know? Come on! I think the Black community is still in the religious model of disability compared to the White society. They are in the cultural rights model of disability. We are like in the religious model of disability, and that's far behind.

PARKS: Can you tell me a little bit about your work with *POOR Magazine*?

MOORE: I got involved with *POOR Magazine* in, I think, '96, '97. And it's an organization that does advocacy and media and cultural work around poverty. And at that time I started to do my first online columns about race and disability called "Illin n' Chillin." I've been with them ever since. And now they're just kicking ass. They have a piece of land in Oakland. They're building homes. They have their own radio station. They have their own school and are building what they call Homefulness, a solution to homelessness. And they help feed the community, like, twice a month. They've been doing that way before Covid. They've been doing that the last 10 years in East Oakland. And then I co-produced and co-hosted a three-part series on Krip-Hop for a Berkeley radio station, which appeared on KPFA's *Pushing Limits*, which focused on news, arts, and culture for the disabled community.

PARKS: Can you give me a sense of the artists involved in Krip-Hop, their styles and themes?

MOORE: Well, Keith Jones is a co-founder, and he's been around since the birth of Hip Hop, like me. He's a Hip Hop artist, of course, but also a policy maker. He's running for president. He kicks ass. His style of music is more '80s and '90s. He's a kick-ass producer. He does everything with his feet. So he can produce beats with his feet. And he has stories of being so close to being signed, but you know, many record labels are like, "Oh no, we can't see a disabled person doing Hip Hop." And he even met, like, Chuck D and famous people, and they all said, "Nah." You know, "You're disabled. You can't do it." It's like, "Wow." But I'm pleased to sit now in H. Samy Alim and Chuck D's class and see how much it's changed. Talk about full circle! Rob Da Noize Temple, he just passed away. We called him our father of Krip-Hop, because he was the oldest, and he was down with the Sugarhill Gang as a DJ, keyboardist. And so when we used to travel he used to do all the tech, scratching and stuff. He's done everything from Soul to Gospel to Hip Hop. His whole family is like singers.

Toni Hickman is from Houston, and she's a Hip Hop artist. She's a stroke survivor. Her Hip Hop is more positive Hip Hop mixed with gangsta Hip Hop. She's dope. Kalyn Heffernan from Wheelchair Sports Camp in Denver. Oh my god, she kicks ass. She's a lead singer, and she's a small person. She does all kinds of Hip Hop. She really puts disability lyrics in her Hip Hop, which is really cool. One of her videos is called *It's Hard Out Here for a Gimp*. Her video takes the "stairway to heaven" line from Zeppelin and calls the ableism of that into question. Like, "What the fuck? A STAIRWAY to heaven? How's a gimp supposed to get there?" There's an autistic rapper in Russia as well.

Also, I hired disabled Black and Brown painters mostly. Ottis Smith has done like three pieces for Krip-Hop. He's working on another one, which I can't wait for. It's a blind Black woman down South on the corner, playing the Blues. She's in the middle of four corners. On every corner there's a Black church. So, I want to get that message out there because when the Blues started, the Black church didn't want anything to do with it. So they kicked the blind Blues singers out. So I wanted her to be in the middle of Black churches around that area.

Before the coronavirus, we were gonna have a Krip-Hop comicon gathering, like a comic book event, and we were gonna add Krip-Hop into it with all the paintings. But now one of our huge projects is to get a two-story house in Berkeley. And then have the lower level be a studio and a gallery. So we can put up the paintings. We can do our own music. We can open it to the public and, you know, show our stuff. We can have meetings

Figure 15.1 Krip-Hop Nation Painting. Art by Carina Lomeli.

there. We also do Black disabled men talk. We'd love to have a music day for Black disabled youth, an art day, you know? And have mentorship with Black men talk, and videos of our talks to Black disabled youth. The National Black Disability Coalition is gonna start something soon. I've been one of their founding members. And because of this time, where people are focused on anti-Blackness, a lot of support is coming our way. So we're gonna really do something big soon.

BLACK DISABILITY AND THE UPRISING AGAINST POLICE VIOLENCE

PARKS: Let's talk about what's going on now in the world and bring Black disability in conversation with these times of police violence and the uprisings against that.

MOORE: Yeah, well, I've done activities around police brutality since the '80s, so it's nothing new. The only thing that's new today is that *finally* the media's getting hold of Black and disabled people and police violence. Finally. So, that's good. To tell you the truth, I just don't trust the big movement, BLM. Because in the early goings, Krip-Hop and Sins Invalid, a disability justice–based performance project I was a founding member of, we tried to reach out to them, and we had, like, one meeting and that was it. And also Krip-Hop put out a CD and a movie, a documentary on police brutality and people with disabilities, and we got *no* kinda help from anywhere. And not only BLM, but October 22nd and other groups. Mothers Against Police Brutality. Nobody really stepped up to the plate.

And, again, beyond these organizations, "getting services" or "hush hush" are the two ways that disability is seen, especially in the Black community. So it's not seen as a political identity, a historical identity. It's not seen as a cultural identity. It's just seen as, "Okay, you gonna get services," or "Are you gonna overcome it?" [*Laughter*]

PARKS: That's brilliant. I think about this all the time, and I haven't thought about it in that manner at all. Like, I'll often have parents that refuse the labels. Do you know what I'm saying? They'll refuse to say that,

"My son Darryl has autism." They'll say some shit like, "Well, he's a little slow," right? But they won't use the biomedical label, and they do talk about overcoming it a lot or praying for it a lot.

BLACK ABLEISM

MOORE: Yeah, because they don't see it as a personal identity. They see it as something to overcome or "I'll send them to get services." Because the large White disability movement never did the job to educate the Black community. And they really can't, you know? It's really up to us to do that education. I have this term called "Black ableism." And it's so true. A lot of Black, disabled activists that are doing the work, can't come back home to the Black community because of the wounds, the open wounds. A lot of Black kick-ass activism is happening in disabled organizations, White disabled organizations. I haven't seen a lot of Black disabled people working in Black organizations. Now why is that, you know? Why doesn't the NAACP or Urban League or whatever have a disability component to it? I mean Harry Belafonte, he's an activist, you know, and he never talks about this, and he's disabled, you know what I'm saying? Because the education is not there. So when Black leaders, Black civil rights leaders get disabled, they want you to disappear or just go on with your work and not talk about disability. It's a big loss. It's a huge loss for the Black disabled community.

When can Black disabled folks come home? I was thinking about this yesterday. Can you imagine if all the Black disabled people that are working with these White disabled organizations just quit their job and came home? They would fold. They would fold big time. I was reading this article yesterday on Facebook, where this Black actress was doing a commercial for the Ruderman Foundation. They're a Jewish foundation that deals with disability, I could go on about them. But she does this commercial about disabled people in Hollywood. Now, she's Black, okay? She's doing it for a White Jewish organization, and she shows two clips of White disabled people. I'm like, could you imagine if she came to a Black disabled community and did that for us? It would be a game changer. Because a lot of White organizations use Black celebrities to do their PR. And for Black celebrities, it's a paycheck for them, and they feel that they've done something.

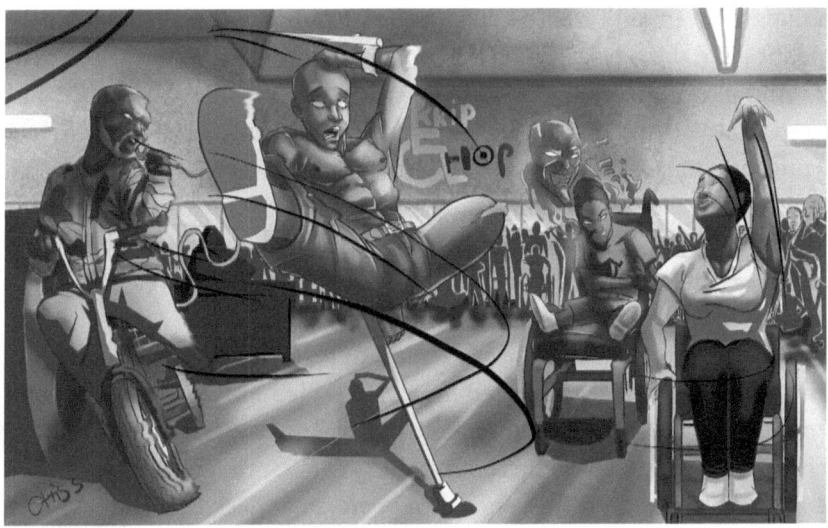

Figure 15.2 Once Abandoned Now Resurrected by Passion. Art depicting Krip-Hop Nation taking over an abandoned warehouse by Ottis Smith.

GENDER, SEXUALITY, AND DISABILITY: KRIP-HOP, HOMOHOP, GENDERKRIP COLLABORATIONS

PARKS: Tell me about your work with Peace Out and Homohop and how and why y'all collaborated?

MOORE: Yeah, Juba Kalamka did the Peace Out Festival in the '90s, and we got together and Juba also had chronic pain, you know, so he was just coming into his disability awareness. And I reached out to Juba when Krip-Hop started and he did an article in *Colorlines* about Krip-Hop. And he was like a music historian. He knows everything about music. So, he put the two together and since that time he performed at Sins Invalid, and that really shaped his education around disability. And so when we put together the conference on Homohop and Krip-Hop, I definitely wanted Juba to be on the panel, because Juba is a political thinker. That's one thing I notice is that you have two kinds of musicians. You have musicians that are just musicians, and you have musicians that are politically minded. So I really wanted Juba to be there because he came with the politics and the music at the same time.

And also it's so funny because I used to attend Juba's festivals. I just used to attend and just look around and just be educated about the queer Hip Hop scene. And this was before Krip-Hop. So when Krip-Hop started, it was like, "Oh, this has to be our first conference." Because we mainly have the same story about being on the outskirts of Hip Hop, you know? Both groups have been looked at as weak within Hip Hop and broader society, like we can't be masculine, etc.

To tell you the truth, when I first moved to the Bay Area back in '91, the only community that supported me and accepted me was the queer community in the Castro. I used to go to the Castro a lot. I was so welcomed there. They used to have this bookstore, A Different Light Bookstore, and that's where I sold my first published poem, in a Black lesbian magazine. I think that because they knew firsthand what it was like to be left behind, they could sympathize with what I might be going through as a Black disabled man.

It's so funny, can I tell you a story? Oh my God! I was interviewing Kurtis Blow and I told him about the conference. I didn't say the title. He's like, "Yeah, I'm down with Krip-Hop, I'll be there!" And I told him the title and he got all quiet. He's like, "Oh no, I can't, I can't, I can't support that." And I was like, "Okay, whatever." And that was Kurtis Blow. And I was thinking to myself, like, "You're an old man and you still can't, you know? You're not a teenager, you're 60-something years old." I don't know.

And you know, on the other side of things, Hip Hop is everywhere. It's international. I think that's why Krip-Hop blew up so easily. We blew up outside the US before we blew up here. And even our first major news article was in Italy. It was a five-page cover article with photos and everything! It came from Italy, not the US. We get more love internationally, even today. It is so amazing how international media gets it, you know? So, Liverpool was the DaDafest, one of the biggest disabled arts festivals in Europe. So, for two or three years, they had Krip-Hop, and the last year they had us do a tour around England. So we were there for two weeks doing the tour. And that was just amazing!

And South Africa, we were there in 2016, and this was from our own pocket, because it wasn't a festival. I got in contact with Simon Manda, who has a disability newspaper called *Thisability*. And he's not disabled, but he knows the politics. That's what I like about Simon. So we talked online for a year. And he wanted to do something like a concert or something but it just didn't happen. And he was like, "Fuck it, let's do a tour around South Africa." Because I've always wanted to go to South Africa, you know. I think since high school I was thinking about South Africa and people with disabilities under apartheid, you know? So I've always wanted to go to South Africa. So, at that point, on social networks, a lot of the African and disabled musicians were in Krip-Hop, not only South Africa but Zimbabwe, Congo, etc. So, I was like, "Yeah, let's do it!" So we raised funds, I think we raised like $4,000, $5,000, and my ticket at the time was so cheap, I think it was only $900. Can you believe that? So, yeah, so I got there and we did six cities in like one week. It was nuts. I mean Simon had it all planned out.

We went and interviewed Black disabled artists. So, a lot of artists we were talking to over Facebook, I got a chance to meet them, you know? So yeah, we have videos, interviewing people and have people doing their artwork. What I really want to do—and I was talking to Keith about it—is a documentary on Krip-Hop because it's international. I got footage from London, Germany, South Africa. I was going through my library a couple days ago and I still have an interview with the Blind Boys of Alabama. I gotta get it transferred to digital because I did it back in the '90s so it's like on little disks or something.

PARKS: That is just incredible! That can't stay in the library! This is Hip Hop knowledge. Now, how does the disability lens make us think differently about Hip Hop? What does it add to Hip Hop's 5th element?

MOORE: Oh my God! It adds so much. As KRS-One says, the knowledge! I mean, can you imagine viewing Hip Hop through a disability lens going back to the Blues? That's another project that I want to do before I can't do it, I want to go back to Mississippi. The first Black folk singer, Josh White, when he was like an early teenager, his job was to escort all the blind Blues artists all through the South. It's totally fascinating. I got a chance to interview his son, it was amazing. So I would love to go back down South and walk through his pathway. I know most of it's not there, you know. It's probably Starbucks or something, you know, but still. I want to walk through some of it, you know. That story is moving. I wrote a song about it. I wrote a poem about it. Because he was like a 12-year-old boy just guiding all these blind Blues artists down South. It was like, "I can't believe that's not in a book somewhere." I mean, like a Blues textbook or a Hip Hop textbook.

So, in terms of a disability lens on Hip Hop culture, first I would show people *Breaking*, the movie. It had a kid on crutches. And can you imagine in 1984, if they were open to having that kid in that role in Hip Hop today, it would be a totally different Hip Hop. But even at that time, because if you turn over the video, his name is not there. Can you imagine? I was shocked! I didn't believe it when my friend said it, but yeah, you turn it over and his name is not there. So even back then, they erased his name. He's the guy that's on crutches and breaking in the cipher.

Those are the kinds of things I would say about knowledge, you know? I mean, KRS-One has a statement about why they called it "the dozens," the history of the dozens. That story was that they would have Black disabled separated into dozens. So, those slaves like would compete with one another, you know, destroy each other. That's playing the dozens. So, I'm saying that disability started in Hip Hop back in the slave ships. Isn't that something else?! It just blows me away.

I have a song about Jim Crow. Jim Crow was a disabled Black man! I mean all, all these stories blow me away. And Krip-Hop takes these stories and we do songs about it. Me and Keith did the song about the dozens. I think it's called "It Started in a Cage." So, really, our songs can be in Hip Hop classes because they are educational. They are historical.

PARKS: I know you've called yourself a feminist. How do you think about race, gender, class, together with disability, the intersectional dynamics?

MOORE: Yeah, well you know, Krip-Hop has six things we live by. And one of them is not to put down other people. So we try not to do that, but it's Hip Hop, especially for the next generation, you know? It's hard to do that. You know, when Krip-Hop first started, it was male-dominated. I tried so hard to get women involved. Matter of fact, I just found another woman disabled Hip Hop artist last night. She had an article somewhere, and her album was coming out, so I reached out to her on Instagram. But from my Krip-Hop experience, I don't know why but women sometimes are hard to recruit. I mean, we have Kalyn, Toni Hickman, Lady MJ. In the beginning, we had Lady MJ, and she was from the UK, and she was White. Toni Hickman came in later, you know, she's Black.

PARKS: Do you think you have different gender dynamics within Krip-Hop than the larger project of Hip Hop does?

MOORE: No and yes. I mean, two years ago we put together an event called GenderKrip. I hired two people to do it. One was a gender nonconforming person, Lisa Ganser, and the other one was a queer woman. After organizing the event, we also did a Hip Hop CD with women and femme artists like AJ420, Irkalla Lustre, Kimya Dawson, Chrysalisamidst, Rowan Katz, Sol Patches, Earth Rituals, Young Ant, Shazz Williams, Imani Atlantic, Vita E & Kat So Poetic, Be Steadwell, Collander, Fire Officer Donald, Maya Songbird, Vita E Clevelant, Nomy Lamm's The Beauty, and others. I think, not to pop my collar, that Krip-Hop CDs are the first of their time. I mean, go back to the police brutality CD, that was the first of its time. The GenderKrip CD, that was the first of its time, you know.

RECLAIMING LANGUAGE, RECLAIMING POWER

PARKS: You know, one of the things about Hip Hop is that it's language play, right? And I've been reading your column, "Illin n' Chillin," there was a shit-ton of language play. And in your poem, "The 5th Element," there's a line that I want you to unpack, "From hyphy to mumble, I have CP but I'm more stable." That was funny *and* brilliant! [*Laughter*]

MOORE: I mean, that's the thing about Krip-Hop. It's about advocacy, education, and overcoming oppression. We reclaim negative terms associated with the disabled, like "crazy," "lame," "retarded," and "cripple," for example, and use them to shock people into understanding and respecting the disabled Black community. You know, Hip Hop, we reclaim language all the time. The "n-word." The "b-word." So, it's like that with disability. And also I think disability is not only reclaiming, but taking power away from nondisabled people, and pushing it and making it hip, and also making it political at the same time. I've always had my battle with hyphy, because hyphy uses disabled language but without disabled artists doing it. Phrases like "riding the yellow bus" "and "acting retarded" and all of that are ableist. So I always want to put that out. And mumble rap, you know, I did that when I was younger. It's called CP (cerebral palsy), you know? Nothing new. I've been doing mumble rap since I was eight years old, without needing to get drunk or high or wear gold teeth! [*Laughter*]

In terms of language play, a lot of people think that Krip came from the gangs, you know, the Crips and the Bloods, but they don't know about the history of, when a gang member was disabled, it was just like, "Oh, we'll just call you crip or crippled," you know? It's in Tookie Williams' book.[7] So the root of that word comes from people with disabilities. It's just a negative way of looking at it. So we wanted to take it back and flip it on its head like Hip Hop always does, you know? Flip it on its head, make it political, make it educational, and use it to tell our stories about oppression, to tell our stories about our art and our way of living, you know? Do the Crips and Bloods have a copyright on the word? No. You know, like did they discover the word? No. Once again it's alright, though, it's a lack of disability education. Way before gangs, you had doctors and professionals and psychologists using that word. You had slave masters using that word.

"THERE'S A LOT OF WORK TO DO": PUSHING HIP HOP TOWARD DISABILITY JUSTICE

PARKS: Do you know about Snoop Dog's disability football league?

MOORE: Yeah, I heard about it. And also, he has a daughter with a disability. And also, he partnered with 4 Wheel City that I know that was disabled in New York. Oh, he is also working with Rox the Fox in LA, a Black disabled female rapper. See, the thing about Snoop and the thing about many Hip Hop artists, they don't want to go deep. They love the surface stuff. And I love their music, but they don't go deep, you know. So they're glad when Snoop Dog does a deal with them. And I'm saying fuck the video, let's go deep. Let's get into Krip-Hop politics. If you want to do something for Krip-Hop, bring Krip-Hop to the main stage, engage Krip-Hop's politics, read our articles, read our mission statement, listen to our songs, and have us on your platform. Have Keith Jones on your platform. He's running for president! Things like that would change the whole conversation. A video and song is great but this is serious. We're in COVID-19, you know? I mean, things are about to change, totally. People are dying, and you're glad about a video? It's totally out of sync with what's going on. But getting serious means giving up a piece of your power. And you know people don't do that. We saw that during Nelson Mandela and apartheid in South Africa. They don't want to give up that power, you know?

And another example is Ice Cube. And just hurts me to the T. A lot of Hip Hop artists do charities for people with disabilities, I can't stand that. So, Ice Cube did a T-shirt charity for Autism Speaks. I was like, "Are you serious, Ice Cube? Are you serious?" I mean, Autism Speaks is an organization that is not controlled by people with autism; they don't listen to self-advocates. They are only about the cure. They get so much money, even Hip Hop artists donate to them which upsets me. How can Ice Cube be hard as fuck, and you're doing a charity for Autism Speaks? I mean, like, God, man. That tells it all. It's like, you're doing movies, you're doing football, you're doing all this stuff and your disability politics is weak as fuck. I mean, it's not only Ice Cube, of course. Drake has a long history, you know, of appropriating disability. And I was like, "Come on, Drake!" You know? I mean, his career started by playing a disabled character. Then, he went out doing the Wheelchair Jimmy dance! I'm like, "Oh my God." [*Laughter*] I was like, any other group of people in society, if people did that, it would be an uproar. That's why I laugh when people say it displays solidarity. I just laugh. It's like there is no solidarity. There is no solidarity when 50 Cent can make fun of autistic people three times in a row and still get an acting gig, you know? I mean, he got nailed three times for verbally abusing an autistic youth. Three times in a row. Then he gets called out, and gives Autism Speaks $100,000. That's like, "Oh God." [*Laughter*] It's something else. No moral standard for this, at all. And they keep on getting away with it.

Since the beginning of Krip-Hop Nation I only saw two rappers that spit about mental health and depression in ways that really resonated with me. One was Invincible. On her debut album *ShapeShifters*, she rhymed about the complexities of mental health on her groundbreaking song "Ropes." The video was accepted then rejected by MTV due to their fears about the issue. Invincible has always been a strong supporter of Krip-Hop Nation. The second rapper I never had a chance to meet, but Pharoahe Monch's album *PTSD: Post Traumatic Stress Disorder* (2014) blew me away! I was so impressed by his raw interviews on depression, and how that played out in his music, like even on the song and video for "Still Standing" with Jill Scott (2012). That video has a little Black boy playing, running and climbing a tree, dealing with asthma and being out of breath, and then visually comes back as Monch is in the recording studio having an asthma attack. Invincible and Monch gave me hope in the early days of Krip-Hop Nation when it felt like we were being attacked on all sides because we dared to bring up disability and ableism in Hip Hop. I still watch these videos and follow their careers.

But, more recently, I gotta shout out Kendrick! The music he's been doing is fucking amazing. I mean, that man, I want to meet that man. Because, almost like every video he does he touches on disability, and in a political way. And it's like, "Wow. What the hell?" Like, a couple years ago, the first track on *DAMN.* was a blind woman. Kendrick, Lord. What does that say? I love this because it takes disability and flips it. Is it negative? Is it positive? What is it? Kendrick leaves that question in your lap to figure out. So, that and the song "King Kunta." I mean, we all know that Kunta Kinte lost his foot, right? So, that's another disability focus. It just woke me way up. Like, what is Kendrick's relationship to disability, because, it's there, you know? And no one really talks about it. If I had a chance to interview Kendrick, oh my God, it would be a totally different interview. I saw in one interview when the journalist asked about that song from *DAMN.*, "BLOOD." He's like, "No, I don't want to explain it." I was like, "You can't say 'no'." I mean, that first skit is loaded. It's loaded. Is the White woman the devil? Or is she White? It's loaded with questions. So, why isn't that in disability studies and Hip Hop studies?

As we approach the 30th anniversary of the Americans with Disabilities Act, as I wrote in my *New York Times* article in July of 2020, I would like to challenge Hip Hop to do better. I would like to see a major conference to educate the industry about disability and promote Krip-Hop artists and politics. I would like to see a recognition of Krip-Hop as an official subculture of Hip Hop from the music arena. And, of course, I would like to see Krip-Hop in Hip Hop Studies. I would like to see more books on how disability has existed throughout Hip Hop history, as well as the inclusion of Krip-Hop in the Hip Hop museum in New York. There's a lot of work to do.

NOTES

1. Leroy F. Moore Jr., *Black Disabled Art History 101* (Xochitl Justice Press, 2017).

2. Leroy F. Moore Jr., *The Black Kripple Delivers Poetry & Lyrics* (Poetic Matrix Press, 2015).

3. Leroy F. Moore Jr., *Krip-Hop Graphic Novel* (Poor Press, 2019).

4. Emmitt H. Thrower (dir.), *Where Is Hope—The Art of Murder: Police Brutality against People with Disabilities* (Wabi Sabi Productions, 2015).

5. Mainstreaming is a term used to refer to disabled students who are placed in general education courses.

6. The Individuals with Disabilities Education Act (IDEA), previously known as the Education for All Handicapped Children Act (EHA), was passed in 1975 and reauthorized in 1990. IDEA was enacted by Congress to require states to provide all students with disabilities a free appropriate public education (FAPE), with allocated federal funds. For more, see Roy Carleton Howell, "The Individuals with Disabilities Education Act (IDEA): Reaching the Black Legal Community to Inform Black People of Their IDEA Rights," *Southern University Law Review* 31 (2003): 85.

7. Stanley Tookie Williams, *Blue Rage, Black Redemption: A Memoir* (Simon and Schuster, 2007).

16 Queering Hip Hop Feminist Pedagogies in the New South

Bettina Love, Regina N. Bradley, and Mark Anthony Neal

BETTINA LOVE: Before I was ever a researcher, or college professor, I was an elementary school teacher, and I say that with pride. I was an elementary school teacher. And I was teaching in what many would call an underperforming school filled with Black and Brown faces. And I had a connection to my students, a rich connection, and I thought that connection had everything to do with skin color. Until I realized and dug a little bit deeper to find found out that that connection was Hip Hop. And this connection that I had with my students was not just the music of Hip Hop, it was the culture of Hip Hop. And I saw my students do amazing and incredible things in the classroom, strictly bringing their culture into the classroom. And to many people, the outside person will look at the classroom and say, "There's no learning going on there." It is loud. [*Laughter*] And I saw it as organized noise. I saw it as kids using everything that they had to learn.

So what do I mean by that? I'm sure many of you, if you're a teacher, you have walked into a classroom, especially with students who identify with Hip Hop culture, and they are banging away on a table, just bangin. And you ask a child, "Could you please stop?" And they look at you like, "I'm not banging on the table." [*Laughter*] And so then you're having this moment to yourself saying, "I just saw you banging on the table." And then five seconds later, they're banging on the table again. But what they're doing, they're drumming. They are honing in on their African and African American spirit. Or you have seen a child walking down the street with no headphones on, bobbin like this talking to themselves. And you're thinking to yourself, "Is this child crazy?" But what they're actually doing is there's a soundtrack playing in their bodies, and they are responding to that soundtrack.

So when I was in my classroom, I saw students construct masterful narratives using rap, using poetry. I saw young girls use their entire body to learn and see knowledge as an embodied practice. And so what I was seeing in the classroom was that, yes, my students were learning differently, and there are many, many educators who have said this. "Yes, these students learn differently, but that does not mean they are deficient." And these experiences brought me out of the classroom into a PhD program. Because I was thinking to myself, "Okay, how can I do this over and over again?" [*Laughter*] "How could I make this happen? How can I scale this? How can I have students be in Hip Hop culture, identify with Hip Hop, and they are in every classroom everywhere?" So I had big goals: Hip Hop *everywhere*. [*Laughter*]

But what I learned is that my students weren't just doing Hip Hop, they were actually participating in their cultural DNA, and what Malcolm Gladwell would call their cultural legacy.[1] That the traditions and the customs of Hip Hop are actually African and African American customs. And that when you see Hip Hop, it is the latest iteration of Black genius. It is the newest thing of what you see of people creating a culture out of nothing—but it isn't nothing. It goes back generations and generations. So my students, they don't even know it, but they are tapping into their cultural legacy to learn. And so if they have a cultural legacy, if this is Black genius, and if they have what scholar Regina Bradley calls Hip Hop sensibilities,[2] then that is a way of knowing, a way of being, and a way of thinking. And I want to argue today that those Hip Hop sensibilities are directly linked to predictors of success.

So there's fascinating work right now from people like Angela Duckworth, Tony Wagner, Paul Tough, about what they call character strengths or mindsets. And I think this research is really fascinating about kids who have social emotional intelligence and how they're able to achieve. And these are some of these predictors of success. And when I look at this list, social and emotional intelligence, the ability to improv, curiosity, optimism, grit, I look at this list and I say, "Oh, that's Hip Hop." Is that how we're gonna measure success? Because if that's how we're going to measure success, oh, I got some kids for you! [*Laughter*]

Let's think about this. Let me back up a little bit, because I'm not just talking about kids who listen to the radio, right, because the radio plays the same 25 songs over and over again. So we all know if we get in our car at 8:00, 3:00, 5:00, and 11:00, the same song is on. I'm not talking about that Hip Hop. I am talking about the Hip Hop that is ingenious. I am talking about the students with no formal musical training, no computer programming, and they make unbelievable music. I am talking about the kids who will find the latest song from somebody that is so underground and make it the best thing since sliced bread. I am talking about the kids whose movements today will become mainstream tomorrow. Those are the kids who identify with Hip Hop. They live it, they breathe it. This is how they see the world. And if that is true, and if they see the world through Hip Hop, that means they have Hip Hop sensibilities. And I wanna argue today that those Hip Hop sensibilities are directly linked to character strength.

So I like to call them cultural strengths. So let's start with the first one, social and emotional intelligence. If you've ever gone to a Hip Hop cipher, you have kids all in a circle, and they could be freestyle rapping, they could be battling, they could be dancing, and when do they know when to go? Nobody raises their hand, "Um, it's my turn to rap?" [*Laughter*] Nobody does that. Nobody says, "Um, can I dance next?" How do these kids know when to go? And then, you could have rappers or dancers who don't know each other, and they just know who is next. How do they know that? That is social and emotional intelligence. And then you have to listen. You can't just go into the rap and you're wack, or you can't go into the rap and repeat what the last person said, and it not be a better iteration of what they just said. So you have to listen. This is drawing on social and emotional intelligence.

Or traditional schools, the morning meetings. We have kids in a circle, and we say to a child, "What did you do last night?" Before you even say, "What did" . . . All the hands go up and you're saying, "I didn't ask you a question yet." [*Laughter*] So the hands are up and the kids, you know, might just can't wait to be next. And then you call on them and they forget. And then they look at you like you gave them a hard question. They're not listening. They're not invested in that activity. So that is not social and emotional learning. A cipher is social and emotional learning. I am feeding off you, I am listening to you, I am engaging with you, and then I go.

Let's take the next, grit. That's funny. Grit, you wanna talk about grit? Hip Hop is grit. African and African American genius, resiliency, resolve, that is grit. I am standing here today because people were gritty. So when you wanna talk about grit, you cannot talk about grit without talking about African and African Americans and Hip Hop. Think about what Hip Hop is 40 years ago. We have Reaganomics, post-industrial New York, and they take something and make a cultural phenomenon that has lasted the last 40 years and become a billion-dollar global industry. I think that's grit.

Let's take the last one, the notion to improv. So in 2012, the Institute for Deafness and Other Communication Disorders they hooked up 12 freestyle rappers.[3] And freestyling is the ability to just spontaneously create rhymes in real time. So they hooked these rappers up, and they wanted to understand their brain activity. And what they found was amazing. These freestyle rappers' prefrontal cortex was moving at amazing speeds. And what is your prefrontal cortex? It's where emotion, motivation, and language is developed. So when you wanna talk about the ability to be creative, the crux of that is the ability to improv, to come up with real thoughts on the spot. That's Hip Hop.

And so we have kids sitting in classrooms every single day with the ability to do this. And because we don't identify with Hip Hop, we don't like Hip Hop, Hip Hop has been co-opted and commercialized as something that's so watered-down now, and the rich and robust history of Hip Hop is lost, we say, "That's not academic." But you think about the root of it. We have kids in our classrooms who have the very things that we say are predictors of success, and we ask them to turn it off. You have students sitting in ciphers, learning from each other, understanding each other, listening to each other, and we ask them to turn it off.

Now there's a school in Atlanta, Georgia, called The Kindezi School. Last year, The Kindezi School had the highest-performing fifth grade class on the standardized tests. Now I'm not one for standardized tests, but they're the highest-performing fifth grade class. And what makes this school so innovative is that at this school, we put students' culture first—the ways in which they wanna learn, their identities. Their Hip Hop identity is first and we are seeing nothing but results. Also, we believe in small classes. And then, the principles of this school are love. That's our first principle. When do you hear that in a school? Love, integrity, perseverance. These are the principles of a school that gets results because you gotta put these things first, love. And our students are succeeding.

And this is also where I teach my Hip Hop class. And so for my Hip Hop class, we bring DJs in to talk about sound energy. We bring b-boys and b-girls, breakdancers, in to talk about physics and kinetic energy. And I am watching my students understand that who they are, their Hip Hop identities, are directly linked to schooling. And if students understand that who I am is academic, and I don't have to take my academics away when I enter the school doors, that I can still be who I am and academic, we can see success.

But we can only go so far. Grit, optimism, zest, the ability to improv, social emotional intelligence, these are all predictors of success, that I argue, kids who identify with Hip Hop have. But it's not enough. February 25, 2012, Trayvon Martin showed grit, he showed resolve, social and emotional intelligence, and it wasn't enough. That night, he fought for his life, it wasn't enough. He fled George Zimmerman, it wasn't enough. So when we have kids in our classroom who have it, we have to talk about racism, discrimination, bigotry, and hate. We can't just say, "Hey, you're gritty. Alright, you're gonna make it," and not talk to that student about how that door may close, and not have a conversation with society about why we're closing that door.

Now, I don't think any teacher is George Zimmerman, but I do think when we deny students the opportunity to express their culture in classrooms, we are spirit murdering them. When I am asking you every day to walk through that door and be something that you are not, I am murdering your spirit. When I am asking you to stop being who you are so I can do my job, I am taking away something from you and I am murdering your spirit piece by piece. And if you don't think this is right, and you say, "Oh, that's, that's a little much, Dr. Love." And yet we have the school-to-prison pipeline. We have students who are not dropping out of school; they're being pushed out of school. We have a disproportionate amount of African American boys in special education. Something is going on, and each one of those kids that is pushed into the criminal justice system, each one of those kids that is pushed into special education, each one of those kids that is pushed out of school, we have murdered their spirits. And until we take the knee off their necks that is holding them down called racism, bigotry, and hate, they will not be able to rise. [*Applause*]

AN ETHNOGRAPHY OF URBAN, BLACK GIRLHOOD

MARK ANTHONY NEAL: Bettina L. Love is author of *Hip Hop's Li'l Sistas Speak: Negotiating Hip Hop Identities and Politics in the New South*.[4] Of the book noted sociolinguist Elaine Richardson says, "With the unflinching bravery of a Hip Hop feminist, Bettina L. Love confronts the damaging effects of Hip Hop on young Black girls, while loving Hip Hop and articulating how it reflects the racism, capitalism, sexism, and patriarchy of America." Talk a little bit about your interest in doing an ethnography of urban Black girlhood, an underexplored area in the academy.

LOVE: I think that's exactly why I chose to do it. In my classes I'm talking a lot about Black girlhood, but there's not a lot of texts on Black girlhood. Then also, as a Hip Hop feminist, I really wanted to bring the stories of young Black girls to the forefront. And to get a fuller picture—I could never tell the full picture—but I think it's important that we start to talk about how African American girls negotiate Hip Hop music in very honest ways. And then to also think about how they do that in a particular city, because I think it's not monolithic. So I really wanted to bring Black girls' voices, their stories, to the forefront in a more complex way than just say like, "They like Hip Hop music, they interact with Hip Hop music." But what about the structures that they interact with Hip Hop in?

NEAL: Right, when we think about Hip Hop, we don't expect to hear a female voice there. You know, we don't expect to hear, as Ntozake Shange would say, "a Black girl song" in Hip Hop. But part of the genius of your book is that you tease out where there is in fact a Black girl song in this broader culture of Hip Hop.

LOVE: Yeah, and I'm part of that song. So that's why it was so important to me not only to tell the story of these six young girls but also to tell my story, as Joan Morgan would say (see chapter 14). You know, I'm a feminist, a daughter of privilege, and so here I am with this opportunity not only to tell their story, but to tell my story. And then also to make the story more complex. And so even though we may not be in the mainstream, we may not be the face of Hip Hop, we are shouting from the sidelines that you're gonna hear us. And so a lot of it was about saying young Black girls are listening to this music, they are engaging with this music in very complex ways, and this is just how they're doing it in Atlanta, Georgia. And they could be doing it very differently in other places, but in "the A," this is what is happening, these are the politics, the race relations, the gentrification, these are the things on the ground that the young girls have on one side—this local context—and then Hip Hop on the other side. And they're in the middle, and they're trying to negotiate all of these complex spaces.

NEGOTIATING GENDER AND QUEER IDENTITY IN "THE NEW SOUTH"

NEAL: This book is also, in part, an ethnography of "the New South." Being from Rochester, New York, what does it mean for you in terms of your own positionality? You know, you mentioned privilege, and you're queer. To go in "the Dirty South" and all that that means in terms of Black life, and be able to negotiate this and have a viable space within this context, was that challenging?

LOVE: Number one, I had to do a lot of internal work. I tell the story in the book about my father was from Jacksonville, Florida, and my mother was from upstate New York. Her family was from South Carolina—and so that Black migration—and my mother hated traveling to the south every summer. So my father would get into his baby blue Cadillac, it was leather and he would shine it up and he would drive down to the south, and my mother would just say egregious things about southerners. "Oh, they are so country, they are slow," and all of these things played on me when I moved to the south, and I did this research with these young girls. So a lot of it had to do with my own internalized work to understand how these stereotypes played on me. And then also southern Hip Hop. You know, I love Outkast, right, I love the southern twang of Andre 3000, but I didn't like to hear that southern twang with my students. And so dealing with these internalized feelings and stereotypes we have about other Black folks, and I had to do a lot of that work to understand Dirty South music, to appreciate it, and then to understand the context in which it exists.

And then also being someone who is openly queer and so dealing with homophobia in the south and how that gave me a space to really take up some of my own issues that I had around that. I thought I was openly gay, until I got with these young girls and they really put my sexuality on the forefront. And I couldn't do research with them. I internalized this homophobia and recognized that I had it, and they provided space for me to research with them. And so it was a lot going on within this space that I was trying to work through, along with these young girls.

NEAL: What's refreshing about your work and, say, the work of someone like David Stovall is that you take seriously how these young folks are consuming Hip Hop culture, Hip Hop visuals, and you sit down with them. As you mentioned, this is as much your culture as it is their culture. What was it like to sit down with these girls, these young teenagers, and watch these Hip Hop visuals, to have them talk about what it was like to see certain kinds of body types come up over and over again, right? Why don't we ever see White women in these situations, in these music videos? Why is it always Black women, and why Black women that look a certain kind of way? What surprised you in sitting down and talking with these young girls about these issues?

LOVE: First, it was how candid they were, how blunt, how in tune, how keen they were, and they picked up on so much. And I knew that these girls were critical thinkers, but for me to sit back and say, "Wow, they're consuming all of this and they're being critical of all of this." But then also to paint a fuller picture to say, "Okay, they don't have a real space to be critical. They don't have a space to have these conversations. They can't have these conversations in their AP English classes. They can't have these conversations in their math classes."

So for them, they wanted to engage in these conversations, and what made it so difficult for me at times is because of my queerness, they didn't see me as a role model. They didn't see me as another Black woman that they were talking to. So I really got an in-depth look at what they thought about Black women, because when they were talking about Black women, they weren't talking about me. And so it became this really awkward space where they're talking about not having role models, or this person is a role model, and I'm sitting across wondering like, "Hey, hey, I'm here, guys. I'm with you every day in the trenches. Do you think I'm a role model?" You know, so it was really difficult, I think, at times to hear them and to not know what to do with that, not knowing how to engage them differently. You know, if there was another gender performance, maybe the book would have been totally different, maybe the data would have been totally different. But I think my embodiment of gender really played a role, in terms of the research findings.

NEAL: You talk about growing up and playing ball very often with uncles and cousins, you know, and how they kind of gave you insight into performances of Black masculinity and also Hip Hop. How has that kind of knowledge helped you in talking to young Black girls about how they navigate the world that they're in?

LOVE: For me, at first I was very uncomfortable doing that work. That was one of the reasons why the girls put me on front street the first day I met them. You know, one of the questions they asked me as soon as I met them, maybe we've known each other maybe three minutes, the girls came up to me and said, "You gay?" I said, "Whoa." You know, me being a witty kid growing up with males, my first response back was, "You're in my business." And so we started this relationship that was built on these tensions. I think at a certain point it helped and it hindered, because I was at a place where I wasn't ready to talk about my experiences being a lesbian. And I thought I was openly gay! But I also think having an upbringing of playing basketball, being around a lot of males, it does have this confidence, it does invoke, you know, what we would call Hip Hop swag for a queer woman. And I think the kids oftentimes really relate to that. I do a lot of workshops with schools. I just left one actually, and the kids eat it up. And I think it's because not only is it this swag, but it's also an authenticity. And when the girls realized that I was there truly just to learn from them, it opened up.

REFRAMING HIP HOP PEDAGOGIES FROM THE SOUTH

NEAL: You talked towards the end of the book about rethinking what we might term Hip Hop pedagogy.

LOVE: For me, I was thinking about reframing Hip Hop pedagogies, and also about my regrets. I have a lot of regrets with the work that I did in the book. Number one, because I sat there. I listened to those young girls, but I'm also an educator and I forgot that I was an educator. I forgot that I was there also to teach. And so right now, a lot of my work is really about Hip Hop pedagogy, more than rap. And I think a lot of our youth understand Hip Hop as only rap. And when they do that, they don't understand that rap is actually culture. And we minimize Hip Hop when we only see it as rap. So I think about embracing the elements of Hip Hop, and then also embracing the 5th Element of Hip Hop in teaching kids about Knowledge of Self, and Knowledge of Community, and how we engage in that. So a lot of my work now is really about the 5th Element of Hip Hop. A lot of that has to do with my regrets in the research field, being a young researcher, being someone who wanted to have doctor behind their name, and I got really caught up in that. I should have been there for those girls first as an educator. So as they were telling me those stories and dealing with how they were constructing notions of identity by not seeing Black women, I should have been stepping in. But I was more concerned with, "Oh, I got this rich data." And so a lot of that has to do with me trying to right my wrongs.

A lot of my work right now is really taking Hip Hop pedagogy to elementary classrooms. You know, my work that I did with the girls in the book is high school, and I've learned that I have to start younger. So right now I'm working with fifth graders in Atlanta, Georgia, and the program that I created is called "Real Talk: Hip Hop Education for Social Justice." And we're not only linking Hip Hop to school, we're linking Hip Hop to issues of social justice.

So the kids, for their final project, they did a movie on the death of Trayvon Martin. The movie is just very powerful. They actually have the ghost of Trayvon watching in the back, watching everything that we're doing. And kids came up with this! They storyboarded the movie, wrote the movie, directed the movie, shot the camera angles for the movie. So, I'm trying to use multiple literacies that get kids not only engaged in education, but also education being meaningful. And we can still hit common core standards. We can still teach kids, but it can be meaningful. It can be done in culturally relevant ways, and it also can have a social justice aspect. And that has a lot to do with me saying, "You know what? My failures in that book, I'm trying to right those wrongs."

REGINA BRADLEY: Why is it important to include the south in conversations about Hip Hop pedagogy?[5]

LOVE: Well, I think first and foremost, it's about location and understanding the youth that you're dealing with. You know, I'm gonna say that there wasn't a time in my life where I thought teaching Hip Hop in the south was the thing to do. Like, I have evolved and I understand that it's about students' location. And so, as I mentioned, when I hear that southern twang in Andre's voice, I gotta make sure my students hear it in the classroom as well. And so they know and understand their greatness and their potential is here where they're from.

So I've really been intentional about all of the work that I do to not only talk about southern rap but southern history, so students can locate themselves in their present history. And that we got to understand that Hip Hop can't be something that it's just always about the north, because if that happens, kids can't locate themselves. They don't understand it. Their stories are not real. So for me, it's always about, "How do I reach kids where they are?" And if I'm in the south, I'm using southern music. If I was in LA working, I'd be using West Coast music. So I want to make sure that I am bringing the realities of students' lives in real time with the music that they're engaged in and listening to.

Figure 16.1 Regina Bradley and Bettina Love pose for the *Bottom of the Map* podcast. Photo by Floyd Hall.

OUTKAST AS PEDAGOGY: CENTERING ATLANTA

BRADLEY: With your Real Talk project over at The Kindezi School in Atlanta, why is it important to document how students are navigating through these ideas of struggle and triumph using southern Hip Hop like OutKast?

LOVE: I think, first and foremost, is what OutKast was able to do. As I said, I'm a big OutKast fan. I'm a fanatic. And I think for two major reasons. One, personal narratives. Right, this is something that everybody could relate to, and it was daily stories. And number two, they made these personal narratives relatable. And so no matter who you were, your ethnicity, your race, your sexual orientation, your class, all of those things, you can find yourself within an OutKast song, album, or video. And so to think about that and think about southern Hip Hop in general, about how relatable it is to the everyday struggle of oppressed people. And that's why I think students gravitate to it so much. I think that's why as a generation, as a globe, we gravitate to Hip Hop so much because it's deeply rooted in our experiences.

BRADLEY: Can you tell us a little bit more about your book *Hip Hop's Li'l Sistas Speak* and the ways in which you're trying to renegotiate what these ideas of gender and race mean?

LOVE: Well, I think first and foremost, I wanted to center Atlanta as part of the book. You know, I just didn't want to talk about young girls without talking about the space that they consume and they live in and they exist in. So since my study was in Atlanta, Georgia, it is so much about Atlanta. And for me as an outsider, Atlanta's a very interesting place. So you have Civil Rights Movement, right? This is the birthplace to King. Then in the same breath, you have strip club culture. In the same breath, you have Chick-fil-A, which is not open on Sundays, right? So the social conservative movement throughout the city. Then in the same breath, you have Coca-Cola, and not as in the drink, but as a metaphor for capitalism. And then the fifth thing, you have gentrification taking place, where you take a district like where King grew up, which in 2004 was about 94% African American. 2014, it's about 74% African American. And you have a city that is being turned upside down because of the economy, because of jobs, because of strip club culture. All of these things happening at one time with this unbelievable history. This local identity that's taking place, and then how do young girls see themselves within such an unbelievable site? And I think, for me, I wanted the book to be as messy as possible. I did not want it to be an easy-to-find narrative. I wanted to talk about where girls have agency and where girls don't have agency.

I really wanted it to be something that was as "gray" as possible, you know, thinking about Joan Morgan's notion of Hip Hop feminism.[6] I wanted all of that to really explain how these young girls interact and engage with Hip Hop. They're listening to Hip Hop trying to locate themselves and they're walking past neighborhoods that used to be burgeoning neighborhoods of Black folks, and now they're gone. And what does that mean for my local identity? And so I wanted all that to speak to how messy it is to consume Hip Hop. It's not just this, "Oh, I dance because I like this song." No, it's much more at play than that.

BRADLEY: I'm all about the messy, you know what I'm saying? And I'm especially all about making this idea of a contemporary southern Black identity messy. That's what I really like about the Real Talk project: it's almost like it's an archival project. OutKast was documenting what was going on and what was important to them and to the hood in the early '90s in the same way that you're using the Real Talk project to document what's going on, what's important to these kids that are coming up now, and putting them in conversation with each other is extremely important. So could you talk a little bit about what you feel the significance of OutKast is as a pedagogical tool of understanding local identity?

LOVE: I think as a pedagogical tool, it's just an unbelievable space. And so, as I mentioned, when you think about grit, when you think about struggle, when you think of the notion of improvisation, when you think about all the things kids need to be successful, to be able to write complex narratives, to be able to speak and engage in critical thought, you see all of that in the work of OutKast. And so for me, it's how do I take that ingenuity that is OutKast and then bring it to kids in their everyday lives and make it real? And I think one thing as a Hip Hop person who does work in Hip Hop but also thinks about the lives of kids, you really don't have to do much when you give kids the space. When you bring in authentic stories, when you let them understand that these authentic stories will be what you use to tell your story, they will start to do the work. They will start to engage.

And so, you know, it's funny because when I started Real Talk, the goal of the project was to do a historical piece on OutKast. I wanted these kids to understand how important OutKast was, not only to the world but to Atlanta. I wanted them to look at where Big Boi and Andre went to school, right, so we can go there. We can go to cities and understand where they went to school. But then every time we got to a final project, a Black boy was killed. And so, when we got to the final project two years ago, and I'm thinking about what the final project could be, the kids are saying, "I think it should be Trayvon Martin." As someone who understands that the crux of Hip Hop's creativity is improvisation, these kids got to be able to improv. And that means I got to be able to improv too. So the last three years, I have not been able to get my OutKast unit done. But we've done incredible things that are inspired by the work of OutKast. The storytelling, the talking back and forth, the imagination, understanding the struggle, talking about the struggle, are all the things that we've done in the work without ever saying the word OutKast. And I think that's the beauty of OutKast and the beauty of southern Hip Hop.

BEYOND SPIRIT MURDER: CREATING SPACES FOR HEALING THE SPIRIT

BRADLEY: Earlier you brought up this concept of spirit murder, the murdering of the spirit of these kids in these classrooms when we take away any type of language or creativity that they have because it doesn't fulfill a specific type of academic obligation. I just think that's so important, especially not just to southern Hip Hop, but just to Hip Hop in general, as a space in order to make yourself visible, to make yourself known.

LOVE: The concept comes actually from legal studies, thinking about critical race theory. And so it's a scholar by the name of Patricia Williams.[7] And she coined the term spirit murdering. And so she used it as more of a legal reference, the taking away of your liberty and your rights. And I kind of thought about it more in terms of education the same way. So if I'm sitting in the classroom and you're not letting me be myself, you're not letting me learn in the ways that I want to learn, and you say that I can't learn, you're murdering my spirit and who I am in the classroom. And so for me, you know, spirit murdering takes place when students have to sit there and be something that they're not. They have to learn in ways that they don't want to learn in. And so I'm rhythmic. I move a lot. I'm loud. This is just who I am. And you tell me to sit in the classroom, and I can't be that, you're murdering my spirit, and then you expect me to learn.

To bring it back to OutKast, I see it as a space of healing the spirit. And so through their narratives, you know, I remember growing up listening to

OutKast and it was a place of healing for me, because my spirit had been murdered so much. You know, teachers telling me that I was not college material. You know, walking in my community and seeing it dilapidated by drugs and by crime. And so when I turned on, "I remember her number like the summer," that was healing for me in "Da Art of Storytellin.'" There was a place I could go to understand why I was feeling the way I was feeling. It was a place to go to understand what I was seeing. And it was also a place where these people were telling me how to navigate this. Like, I'm gonna stumble. I'm gonna fail. But you got to get back up. And so I also see it as a place to tell those real stories of the spirit being murdered, but also see it as a place of healing for young kids to go, for older folks to go. I still go there when I need a little something. I still can turn on "In Due Time" when I need a little something, because it is a space of healing. And I think that's, for me, what OutKast has always been.

In terms of healing, the youth in Real Talk put out an amazing project, which is really focused on and centers on the work of the Dream Defenders. Philip Agnew actually came to our class and met with my Real Talk students. They had a unbelievable conversation with him, asked him some important and amazing questions. And then they dissected his two-minute speech. Each student took a section of his speech. They wrote their speeches right away. They really speak back to the Dream Defenders, speak back to Philip, because in the speech, he asks you to speak back to him. And so they are truly excited to think about what change they can make in their local community. So we're talking about queer folks, we're talking about CeCe McDonald. We're talking about Vietnam vets and homelessness, of course Ferguson, Mike Brown, all those topics are important. So I'm really excited for the kids.

NOTES

1. Malcolm Gladwell, *Outliers: The Story of Success* (Back Bay Books, 2008).
2. Bettina L. Love and Regina N. Bradley, "Teaching Trayvon: Teaching about Racism through Public Pedagogy, Hip Hop, Black Trauma, and Social Media," in *Racial Battle Fatigue: Instances from the Front Line of Social Justice*, ed. Jennifer L. Martin, 255–68 (Praeger, 2015).

3. Siyuan Liu, Ho Ming Chow, Yisheng Xu, Michael G. Erkkinen, Katherine E. Swett, Micheal W. Eagle, Daniel A. Rizik-Baer, and Allen R. Braun, "Neural Correlates of Lyrical Improvisation: An fMRI Study of Freestyle Rap," *Scientific Reports* 2 (2012): 834.

4. Bettina L. Love, *Hip Hop's Li'l Sistas Speak: Negotiating Hip Hop Identities and Politics in the New South* (Peter Lang, 2012).

5. This section of the discussion between Drs. Bradley and Love originally aired on an episode of the *Bottom of the Map* podcast episode titled "Study Hall: Hip-Hop from the Schoolhouse to the Ivy League" (August 5, 2019).

6. Joan Morgan, *When Chickenheads Come Home to Roost: My Life as a Hip Hop Feminist* (Simon & Schuster, 1999).

7. Patricia Williams, "Spirit-Murdering the Messenger: The Discourse of Fingerpointing as the Law's Response to Racism," 42 *University of Miami Law Review* 127 (1987).

17 "These Are Not Sonnet Times"

BUILDING TOWARD LIBERATORY FUTURES

Maisha T. Winn

H. SAMY ALIM: To deliver the final word, we welcome—last but most *definitely* not least—Maisha Winn. If you recall in chapter 8 of this volume, we mentioned Maisha Fisher's (now Maisha Winn's) seminal work, *Writing in Rhythm: Spoken Word Poetry in Urban Classrooms*, as a foundational, forward-looking case study of spoken word poetry.[1] Maisha has done work on girls, literacies, Black literate lives, Black independent institutions, the prison industrial complex, and transformative justice. Here, she will work through the relationships between Hip Hop, knowledges, pedagogies, and futures as we navigate, together, a possible way forward.

Winn's ethnography of spoken word poetry with a diverse group of Latinx and African American youth in the Bronx, taught by an extremely talented and caring teacher (Joe), met two to three days per week and collectively "(re)defined literacy and what it meant to be literate using the medium of spoken word poetry."[2] Through using an "open mic" tradition characterized by acts of reciprocity, Winn described the processes by which teacher and students together built a *literocracy*, an "intersection of literacy and democracy" that engages multiple literacies "while emphasizing that language processes exist in partnership with action in order to guide young people to develop a passion for words and language."[3] For Winn, literacy is a critical, social practice to mobilize students toward freedom.

In the opening of chapter 8 of this book, Jeff discussed the "complex dance" that happens when the line between teacher and student is blurred. The master pedagogue, Joe, let his "students," at critical moments, lead the dance. As he did this, he moved, as Jeff noted, from "being an agent of *transmission* to an agent of *transformation*." What happens when we let students lead in their own learning? What happens when we let youth lead movements for social justice and transformation? Well, if today's movements for racial justice are any indication, they're not waiting for us to "let" them do anything. They're already leading.

SISTA SONIA SANCHEZ STEPS INTO THE CIPHER

I want to share one anecdote that I think illustrates the possibilities of an intergenerational future, one where we move freedom forward together. I remember interviewing the legendary Black Arts Movement poet Sonia Sanchez almost 20 years ago to this day, in Philly at the International Association for African American Music Festival.[4] I asked her about the first time she heard Hip Hop music and she replied with characteristic energy, "Yeah, you heard that, and you said, 'Woooooh!' And then I said, out loud, 'They gon get in trouble!'" [*Laughter*] "Because that's what we did . . . Once you tell the truth about this country, about what's going on, you get in trouble." Sanchez continued, "And when I heard initially with the Hip Hop artists, when I saw the brothas dancing, doing all that, spinnin on their derrières, on their heads, on their elbows, on their knees, etc., I said, 'Go on! Resist!' Because that's what it's about, you see." Sanchez, who has been known to step up into the cipher with the next generation of Hip Hop poets, explained, "Well, it's not an alien circle . . . I heard everyone before I got up in that circle. And, initially, I stood and watched it. And I watched not only the energy, but I watched the respect that people had for each other. And then I watched the young brothas and sistas, you know, rapping. And the sistas coming up saying, 'It's my turn now! Let me go ahead and do this,' whatever. And it reminded me a great deal of when we also got up on the stages."

What would our pedagogies and our movements look like if, like Sonia Sanchez, we first "stood and watched," and listened to youth as they expressed themselves in their own unique ways? What possibilities would be opened up?

MAISHA WINN: I want to take up these questions by talking a little bit about what I'm calling a *pedagogy of possibility*, and put that in conversation with Hip Hop pedagogies, justice, and the futures of this work. To continue the Sonia Sanchez narrative, Sanchez once said that when Hip Hop and a new generation of poets came into the picture, the elders had to retrain their ears. And the older the elders were, the more they considered you "loud." Elders were like, "I don't know about this. This is too much, you know, you're spitting. You're talking really loud. You're moving your hands, you're moving around!" And instead of backing off, the younger poets and writers of the time said, "You have to readjust your ears. You know, we want you to readjust your ears in the way that you've been accustomed to hearing this thing that we call poetry. We've got a different kind of poetry. These are not sonnet times."

GWENDOLYN BROOKS AND A PEDAGOGY OF POSSIBILITY

Based on these intergenerational conversations, another poet, Gwendolyn Brooks, went on to work with Oscar Brown, who was a jazz musician. Oscar Brown started the Opportunity Please Knock youth ensemble in Chicago, Illinois, which included members of the Blackstone Rangers, a notorious street gang in Chicago. And Gwendolyn Brooks partnered with Oscar Brown and started creating writers workshops for young people. She also started doing writers workshops in prison. She did some work in New York prisons, like the Green Haven Correctional Facility in Stormville, New York. The poet Etheridge Knight became one of her mentees. She worked with him to help him publish his book *Poems from Prison*.[5] They worked together very closely to develop other kinds of workshop strategies for other incarcerated folks. She also launched a poetry workshop for teenagers called THEM, which stood for "Trying Hard to Express Myself." And these young people met in her home. She fed them, she gave them feedback on their work. And I love what she says about how she imagined this work that she was doing with them. I think we can learn a lot from this: "We were friends that talked about poetry and read our poetry to each other." And she talks a lot about being a "friend in writing" as opposed to being a teacher. What does it mean to be a friend in writing? She talks about adults and their relationship to young people in writing workshops as the adult initiators. She didn't believe that adults should be in the forefront for long, even if they were established. Adults needed to figure out how to put systems in place, and then move out of the way. So she refers to adults as adult initiators.

And then Gwendolyn Brooks talks about presenting poetry as a living thing, right? As something that's all around us. And she said, "Students enjoy it when it's that way." She talks about the model that it's all in the doing. So a big part of her writing workshop was she really believed in doing a lot of writing. She said sometimes the students got a little impatient with her, but what she said was, "You gotta keep practicing. You gotta keep working on it." So that was something that she was a big stickler for. But then the more that you produce, the more you were likely to get at this sweet spot that you were trying to achieve. And she was trying to show them that building that body of work, having a body of work, was going to really help them figure out and find their voice.

I love how she just really humbled herself. I mean, she knew that in one place she was this really famous poet. But the young people didn't care about all those bells and whistles. They cared about who was in front of them. They cared about how organic she was with them, about how honest she was when she showed up with them. And she said, "You know, they didn't care who in the world I was, and why should they? But we worked, we did our work together." And so again, this idea of a pedagogy of possibility is also I think about writing for and with young people. So when I think about some of my later work, where I follow the work of teacher poets who worked in English classrooms, I made an argument that English teachers should be practitioners of the craft. English teachers shouldn't just be assigning books and assigning writing. What are you reading? What are teachers reading? What are teachers writing?

And when I follow the work of teachers who were also poets and writers, and I saw how they were writing to and about their students and bringing in their work and sharing their work with their students and seeing that exchange, that was so powerful. These young people could see themselves in that. Then they saw the work that they were doing in the class. They were developing a body of work that was for themselves, as opposed to it being an assignment that's for school, something that's for the teacher, "I'm turning this into the teacher." No, "I'm doing this for me. This is to grow my body of work," right?

FRIENDS IN WRITING

And I've been thinking a lot about the future, about the work of poets like Gwendolyn Brooks and how they come into conversation with a new generation of Hip Hop artists, rappers, and spoken word poets. What does it mean to be a friend in writing? What does it mean to support young people to build out their future trajectories as writers and as thinkers and as readers and as doers, to use the words of Carla Peterson. I've been thinking about this for a long time, as many of you know. I'm referencing my work, *Writing in Rhythm*,[6] where the poet teacher, Papa Joe, worked with his young people. He wanted them to become "Jedis of words." He wanted them to not see or hear any word and feel intimidated by it. He encouraged students to look words up or what he called "catching words." And one of the things that Papa Joe did for his students was he wanted them to think about the larger tapestry of how they would approach writing in the future, not just for now, but what did it mean to build a body of work and have access to that work?

I would say that he was a friend in writing. I thought about this work also in a Brooklyn classroom with a teacher named Mama C, which is in my book *Black Literate Lives*,[7] another teacher poet who worked with her students, especially around activism, police brutality. There were quite a few incidents when I was doing this work with her class in 2003, or 2004, where students were trying to process injustices that they were witnessing in their community in their borough and larger New York and in the United States. They went on radio stations together. They had community events together where the teacher, side by side with her students, was sharing poetry and writing about the incidents and the events that were happening. So she was modeling that work. She wasn't just telling them what to do, teaching the writing, but she was actually modeling and embodying the work.

Reflecting on my *Girl Time* work,[8] which I did in the Atlanta area, it was a six-year ethnography with a woman-focused theater company that worked with incarcerated and formerly incarcerated girls. Most of them were African American in youth detention centers and regional youth detention centers in the Atlanta area. And this team of teaching artists was committed to supporting these girls in teaching them playwriting and using playwriting and performance as tools to really think beyond the monolithic labels that had been given to them, especially as they were entangled in the juvenile detention process. So what did it mean to have girls become poets, playwrights, actresses, artists, and have them replace words like delinquent, at risk, promiscuous—the labels that they had heard all their lives—with this idea of how important it was for them to be seen as *writers*. What's interesting to me is in some ways we've come back to this place where some of the young people are using writing again to have to prove their humanity when we thought we had gotten away from that.

CENTERING JUSTICE, THEORIZING FUTURES

In thinking about my work with these girls, and these youth, I also want to ask: Are we thinking about their futures? How can we get back to this place where it's about your own self-reliance and not about having to prove to somebody else that you matter? In my most recent book, *Justice on Both Sides*,[9] I've been thinking a lot about how to approach justice work in all classrooms. I've written elsewhere that I'm really sorry that I said "Restorative English Education" in an earlier article. I'm sorry that I omitted the word justice, and didn't call for a Restorative *Justice* English Education. Because when you take justice out of it, you take away the reason why we have do this work in the first place. And so after spending lots of time immersed in restorative justice theory and spending a year on a William T. Grant fellowship with restorative justice practitioners and attorneys, I realized that I was wrong to omit that word.

So in future writings, I've been thinking a lot about: What does it means to keep justice centered and central to this work? And so *Justice on Both Sides* is about how we think about justice projects across disciplines and how we think about this justice work. Not just in the English Language Arts classroom, which is obviously where my heart is, having been an English teacher and a language, literacy, and culture scholar, but our colleagues in math need to know how to do this. And our colleagues in science need to know how to do this and our colleagues in social studies and history need to know how to do this. And so, in the last chapter of the book, I talk about a transformative justice teacher education and what justice projects look like across disciplines. Because sometimes I think, in the humanities, we have a little more wiggle room to explore and think about this work, but we need to make sure that we're doing this work in the sciences as well (see chapter 12).

I've been thinking a lot about these four pedagogical stances for justice work. And these four pedagogical stances are history matters, race matters, justice matters, and language matters. I've written about them extensively. As you see, history is the outer circle. History is important in all of our work. I teach a graduate seminar called "Humanizing Research" and we had class in the special collections and my students were thinking, "Well, I'm not doing historiography. I'm having history, I'm not doing history." And I had given the special collections librarian everyone's topic, and the librarian found materials that were related to everybody's topic. And we spent time thinking about how we historicize our research questions, our queries, all of our projects, all of the things that we're doing as part of something else and something larger.

And I don't think social studies, history teachers, or even history as a field should be doing all the heavy lifting on historicizing the life and the work. I think that it's something that's really important for all of us. And I created these stances because I think sometimes we're not sure how to even approach doing justice work. And I argue that it's a mindset, and that we actually have to really take on a stance. Like we have to take a position that all these things matter. And then most recently I've been thinking about this fifth pedagogical stance, which is actually not in *Justice on Both Sides*. It's been incubating really from a wonderful study group that I was a part of at the Literacy Research Association and conversations with my dear colleague Anna Stetsenko. I was trying to provide language for where I thought this work should be going.

And part of this work is about thinking about young people's futures and thinking about what's next for young people in the ways in which we interrupt and disrupt futures, and make sure they have access to these critical literacies, these critical encounters with really experienced writers. What's next for Hip Hop pedagogies? And so, I just want to leave you with, again, what I've learned from, and about, Black literate lives, across my career and life. Literacy is inextricably linked to community. Readers, writers, rappers, graffiti artists, DJs, Bgirls and Bboys, they have a sense of their historicized selves. They think about, and they understand that they are part of something bigger, even if they cannot name it, or they're not sure what it was exactly, that they have a sense that what they're doing is part and parcel of a larger movement. And I would say that we call on teachers to try to help close that circle so that we understand what we're a part of.

What is that feeling that we have, that we're a part of, and that's where we need our educators to help us name that thing that we're seeking. Youth and elders have mutual respect for each other and provide a foundation for youth to create and sustain literate identities. And then something that I think is so important is that there are no boundaries between the so-called Hip Hop artists, authors, performers, and the audience. So my being up here at this podium is no more important than you being there. The exchange that we're having, the head nods, the snaps or whatever it is, however you're feeling or are coming, or bringing to the work, but that there's no boundary here. The way that we're thinking together about this work is what's most important.

I also think this is really interesting, in terms of the larger work around independent Black institutions, which a lot of the participants do not consider "education" because they place the sole responsibility of education on schools and teachers in schools. What if we didn't need to seek out programs of study that would give us access to the culture of power and our own communities, or to ratify Hip Hop as important, right? What if those learning communities were outside the culture of power? Outside of schools? As Emile YX? (see chapter 2), Gloria Ladson-Billings, Django Paris, and H. Samy Alim (see chapter 10), and so many others in this volume raised, what would it really mean to build institutions for Hip Hop pedagogies, knowledges, and activism that would sustain our communities moving forward, on our terms?

In thinking about this future-oriented work, I want to close with some questions inspired by the words of Angela Davis, who argues that one of the consequences of racism and racist ideas, particularly in schooling, is that it has rendered a whole generation of people who do not see their future. What happens when we have generations of young people who do not see a future for themselves? How are we going to do the work of not only helping them see their future, but supporting them to really generate and think about a collective and expansive freedom? These are the questions that I hope we all carry with us as we continue to think about the intersection of Hip Hop knowledges, pedagogies, and futures, particularly in this moment where youth are leading a new racial justice movement in these decidedly "not sonnet times." But as Sonia Sanchez implied at the beginning of this piece, we cannot do this work if we do not retrain our ears. How will we be ready to think about liberatory futures, not just *for* our youth but *with* them? How will *you* show up for them? How will all of us show up for them?

NOTES

1. Maisha T. Fisher, *Writing in Rhythm: Spoken Word Poetry in Urban Classrooms* (Teachers College Press, 2007).
2. Fisher, *Writing in Rhythm*, 4.
3. Maisha T. Fisher, "Literocracy: Liberating Language and Creating Possibilities," *English Education* 73 (2005): 92–95.
4. H. Samy Alim, "Interview with Sonia Sanchez," International Association of African American Music Festival, Philadelphia, PA, June 9, 2000.
5. Etheridge Knight, *Poems from Prison* (Broadside Press, 1968).
6. Fisher, *Writing in Rhythm*. I am also referencing Carla L. Peterson, *"Doers of the Word": African-American Women Speakers and Writers in the North (1830-1880)* (Oxford University Press, 1995).
7. Maisha T. Fisher, *Black Literate Lives: Historical and Contemporary Perspectives* (Routledge, 2009).
8. Maisha T. Winn, *Girl Time: Literacy, Justice, and the School-to-Prison Pipeline* (Teachers College Press, 2019).
9. Maisha T. Winn, *Justice on Both Sides: Transforming Education through Restorative Justice* (Harvard Education Press, 2018).

Contributor Bios

A-LAN HOLT is the Director of the Institute for Diversity in the Arts at Stanford University. There she trains undergraduates in the areas of diversity and culture, arts leadership, and social justice. A-lan is a practicing playwright and filmmaker. She is a Sundance Fellow, a SF Film Screenwriting Fellow, and a frequent contributor on-air at KQED Arts.

A. J. ROBINSON, EdM, is a veteran high school teacher at East Palo Alto Academy in East Palo Alto, California. Beginning as an after-school educator, he has developed interdisciplinary curricula combining performing arts, literacy, creative writing, restorative justice, and ethnic studies. In Django Paris and H. Samy Alim's *Culturally Sustaining Pedagogies: Teaching and Learning for Justice in a Changing World*, his classroom is described as "giving students a place to engage and belong."

BETTINA LOVE, PhD, is an award-winning author and the William F. Russell Endowed Professor at Teachers College, Columbia University. Her writing, research, teaching, and educational advocacy work meet at the intersection of education reform, anti-racism, carceral studies, abolition, and Black joy. The aim of her scholarship is twofold: first, to advance how the field of education understands and critiques the systemic and structural racism of public education within the United States; and second, to advocate for abolitionist approaches in the field of education that seek new possibilities for educational justice. In 2020, Dr. Love co-founded the Abolitionist Teaching Network (ATN).

BRITTNEY COOPER, PhD, is an Associate Professor in the Department of Women's, Gender, and Sexuality Studies at Rutgers University. Dr. Cooper is co-editor of *The Crunk Feminist Collection* (The Feminist Press, 2017). She is the author of *Beyond Respectability: The Intellectual Thought of Race Women* (University of Illinois Press, 2017) and *Eloquent Rage: A Black Feminist Discovers Her Superpower* (St. Martin's Press, 2018). In particular, this work interrogates the manner in which public Black women have theorized racial identity and gender politics, and the methods they used to operationalize those theories for the uplift of Black communities.

BRYAN BROWN, PhD, is a Professor of Teacher Education at the Stanford University Graduate School of Education. His research interests explore the relationships among student identity, discourse, classroom culture, and academic achievement in science education. He is author of *Science in the City: Culturally Relevant STEM Education* (2019), which won the 2021 Outstanding Book Award, American Association of Colleges for Teacher Education (AACTE).

BRYONN BAIN is Brooklyn's own prison activist, actor, Hip Hop theater innovator, and spoken word poetry champion. Described by Cornel West as an artist who "speaks his truth with a power we desperately need to hear," his theater, film, and television work are critically acclaimed. Playing over 40 characters in his one-man theater production, *Lyrics from Lockdown*, executive-produced by Harry Belafonte, he tells the story of his wrongful imprisonment through Hip Hop theater, spoken word poetry, blues, calypso, comedy, and letters exchanged with fellow poet and friend Nanon Williams—who was wrongfully sentenced to Death Row at 17 years old. His most recent book is *Rebel Speak: A Justice Movement Mixtape* (2022), published in UC Press's Hip Hop Studies Series.

CASEY PHILIP WONG, PhD, is an Assistant Professor of Social Foundations of Education in the Georgia State University College of Education and Human Development. Dr. Wong's interdisciplinary research examines social justice in educational theory, policy, and practice. This involves interrogating processes of racialization and oppression in education through critical feminist, anti-colonial, and abolitionist frameworks, and by investigating and developing culturally sustaining and strength-based pedagogies to teach and learn otherwise. Hip Hop pedagogies, knowledges, and ways of knowing and being have been crucial to his educational work. Dr. Wong has been working inside and outside of schools to heal, cultivate critical thinking, and educate for collective freedom with K–16 youth and young adults, from Oakland to NYC, for over 15 years.

CHRISTOPHER EMDIN, PhD, is the Robert A. Naslund Endowed Chair in Curriculum Theory and Professor of Education at the University of Southern California, where he also serves as director of youth engagement and community partnerships at the USC Race and Equity Center. He is the author and editor of several books, including *For White Folks Who Teach in the Hood* (2016), *Between the World and the Urban Classroom* (2017), and *Ratchetdemic* (2021).

CHUCK D, rapper, producer, graphic artist, author, and political activist, rose to prominence through his groundbreaking, politically conscious hip hop recordings and performances. Chuck D assembled DJ Terminator X, Professor Griff, and Flava Flav, along with Hank Shocklee and Bill Stephney, and formed one of the most prominent and powerful hip hop groups of all time, Public Enemy, who was inducted into the Rock and Roll Hall of Fame in 2013. From *Yo! Bumrush the Show* to *It Takes a Nation of Millions* to *Hold Us Back* to *Fear of a Black Planet*, Chuck D's booming voice urged us not to believe the hype and always fight the power. As the UCLA Hip Hop Initiative's Inaugural Artist-in-Residence, he teaches undergraduate and graduate students about the history, evolution, and futures of Hip Hop Culture.

DAM (TAMER NAFAR, SUHELL NAFAR, AND MAHMOUD JRERI), meaning "everlasting" in Arabic, is the first Palestinian Hip Hop crew and among the first to rap in Arabic. DAM began working together in the late 1990s. Struck by the uncanny resemblance of the reality of the streets in a Tupac video to the streets in their own neighborhood in Lyd, Tamer Nafar, Suhell Nafar, and Mahmoud Jreri were inspired to tell their stories through Hip Hop. Martin Vennard from the BBC World Service described DAM's music as "the most entertaining, original and socially engaged music to come out of the Middle East."

DJANGO PARIS, PhD, is the inaugural James A. and Cherry A. Banks Professor of Multicultural Education and Director of the Banks Center for Educational Justice in the College of Education at the University of Washington on Coast Salish homelands. His teaching and research focus on understanding and sustaining languages, literacies, and lifeways among Indigenous, Black, Latinx, Asian, and Pacific Islander students in the context of ongoing resurgence, decolonization, liberation, and justice movements in and beyond schools. Having developed the concept of "culturally sustaining pedagogy" in his landmark 2012 piece in *Educational Researcher*, Paris is co-editor with H. Samy Alim of the best-selling volume *Culturally Sustaining Pedagogies: Teaching and Learning for Justice in a Changing World*.

EMILE YX? is a multiple-award-winning South African B-boy since 1982, MC with Black Noise, playwright, author, and teacher. Heal The Hood Project is a Hip Hop Cultural Education project he created in 1998, currently in 15 schools. He has recorded 35 albums. In 1992 he created *Da Juice*, South Africa's first Hip Hop magazine. Emile wrote and contributed to 25 books, including *My Hip Hop is African & Proud, Conscious Rhymes for Unconscious Times, Heal The Hood B-boying Grade 1 Manual, Barn och unga i sodra Afrika, Neva Again, Reconnect the String*, and *Hip Hop Cultural Education: We Live This*.

ESTHER ARMAH is a New York radio host, playwright, award-winning international journalist, and national best-selling author. Esther has been in the media in Europe, Africa, and now America for 15 years. As an international journalist she has written for *The Guardian* newspaper in London, *Essence* magazine in the US, and *West Africa* magazine in Africa. Her most recent writing is an essay on her life's work, Emotional Justice, entitled "The Posse," appearing in *Black Cool: One Thousand Streams of Blackness* (2012), edited by Rebecca Walker, daughter of the Pulitzer Prize winner Alice Walker.

GLORIA LADSON-BILLINGS, PhD, is the former Kellner Family Distinguished Professor of Urban Education in the Department of Curriculum and Instruction and faculty affiliate in the Department of Educational Policy Studies at the University of Wisconsin, Madison. She was the 2005–6 president of the American Educational Research Association (AERA). Ladson-Billings's research examines the pedagogical practices of teachers who are successful with African American students. She also investigates critical race theory applications to education. She is the author of the critically acclaimed *The Dreamkeepers: Successful Teachers of African American Children* and *Crossing Over to Canaan: The Journey of New Teachers in Diverse Classrooms*, as well as numerous journal articles and book chapters.

GUNNER JULES (SICANGU LAKOTA) is a talented independent Alternative R&B performing artist, singer, songwriter, and producer. He grew up on the Rosebud Sioux Rez in South Dakota. He is a founding member of the developing ALL-SZN artist collective and member of the Dream Warriors collective. Nammy nominee, Gunner Jules has traveled nationally and internationally, touring and providing workshops for aspiring Indigenous artists. He was a 2017 First Peoples Fund Artist in Business Leadership fellow and 2019 Cultural Capital fellow.

GZA AKA THE GENIUS is a founding member of the seminal Hip Hop group the Wu-Tang Clan. Within the group he is known as the "spiritual head," being both the oldest and the first to receive a record deal. Steve Huey of Allmusic has called him "one of the best lyricists of the 1990s," while the editors of About.com ranked him #17 on their list of the Top 50 MCs of Our Time. As a co-founder of the Science Genius program with Dr. Chris Emdin, GZA educates students about science through Hip Hop, one of today's most dominant cultural forces.

H. SAMY ALIM is the David O. Sears Presidential Endowed Chair in the Social Sciences, Associate Director of the Ralph J. Bunche Center for African American Studies, and Faculty Director of the Hip Hop Initiative at UCLA. His books include *Street Conscious Rap* (1999, with James G. Spady and Charles G. Lee), *Roc the Mic Right* (2006), *Tha Global Cipha* (2006, with James G. Spady and Samir Meghelli), *Global Linguistic Flows* (2009, with Awad Ibrahim and Alastair Pennycook), and *Neva Again: Hip Hop Art, Activism, and Education in Post-Apartheid South Africa* (2019, with Adam Haupt, Quentin Williams, and Emile Jansen).

CONTRIBUTOR BIOS   427

HODARI BLUE FKA ADORIE HOWARD (they/them, she/her) is an emerging performance artist/storyteller whose work utilizes dance, writing, photography, and soundscapes to externalize their inner space in an act of inviting others to encounter themselves more deeply. Their work is profoundly intimate and explores their own experiences and relationships as vessels to explore larger themes of race, gender, sexuality, mental illness, temporality, love, and spirituality. She believes that we cannot break out of oppressive systems until we meet them within ourselves and that as we do, we can begin to move into becoming something else—hopefully something more free.

JACINDA BULLIE AKA JAH DA AMP MOUTH is daughter of a Choctaw and a practicing mom of three. Jacinda is a sage-burning Muslim full of gratitude. Prior to rhymes, Jacinda was a natural critique of circumstances, interrogating the world through an Uptown upbringing. In 1996, alongside Jaquanda V. and Leida GM, Jacinda co-founded Kuumba Lynx, a performance collective developing culturally relevant work through a Critical Hip Hop Pedagogy, known as WE GET FREE. Jacinda is co-curator of the Chicago Hip Hop Theater Fest and contributed to the innovative BreakBeat Poets' *Halal If You Hear Me.*

JAQUANDA SAULTER-VILLEGAS is one of the three Founders of Kuumba Lynx. She has been instructing youth in various writing and theatre programs throughout the city since 1994. As the Co-Director of the Kuumba Lynx Performance Ensemble (KLPE) and Chicago KL Teen Slam team, Jaquanda championed six consecutive Chicago Slam wins. In 2017, Jaquanda was recognized by *Rolling Out* magazine as one of Chicago's Top 50 to watch for the Co-developing Half Pint Poetics (11-year-running citywide poetry slam for youth, ages 8–14). In 2018, Jaquanda received the Be Real Award from the Columbia College Dance Department in recognition of her 20-plus years of involvement in arts, activism, and the preservation of Hip Hop.

JASIRI X is the first independent Hip Hop artist to be awarded an Honorary Doctorate, which he received from Chicago Theological Seminary in 2016. This recognition grew out of the spiritual/political urgency and artistic vision he shared on songs like "Justice for Trayvon" and "Strange Fruit (Class of 2013)," which documented the unjust police killings of young Blacks in the millennial generation. Jasiri remains rooted in the Pittsburgh-based organizations he co-founded, the antiviolence group 1Hood, as well as the 1Hood Media Academy, which teaches youth of color how to analyze and create media for themselves.

JEFF CHANG writes on American history and culture, race, and the arts. He is the author of *Can't Stop Won't Stop: A History of the Hip-Hop Generation, Who We Be: A Cultural History of Race in Post–Civil Rights America, We Gon' Be Alright: Notes on Race and Resegregation, Water Mirror Echo: Bruce Lee and the Rise of Asian America,* and the editor of *Total Chaos: The Art and Aesthetics of Hip-Hop.*

JESSA CALDERON represents her Tongva, Chumash, and Yoemé lineages with love. Jessa is the Coordinator of Indigenous Oceans and Waters Protector Program for Sacred Places Institute. As a proud member of the Dream Warriors Society, Jessa is also a songwriter, poet, Hip Hop artist, performer, hypnotherapist, massage therapist, and energy worker, and she offers guided meditations. Jessa encourages our community and youth to find their healing mentally, physically, and spiritually through her words, music, and practices. Jessa has had the privilege to work with community and youth from many Nations, helping them to find themselves while helping them to feel good about themselves.

JOAN MORGAN, PhD, is an award-winning feminist author and journalist, and the Program Director for the Center for Black Visual Culture at the Institute of African American Affairs at New York University. Dr. Morgan coined the term "hip-hop feminism" in 1999, when her book was published, the groundbreaking *When Chickenheads Come Home to Roost*. Regarded internationally as an expert on the topics of Hip Hop, the Caribbean, and gender, Dr. Morgan has made numerous television, radio, and film appearances—among them on HBOMax, Netflix, and MSNBC. Her most recent book is *She Begat This: 20 Years of the Miseducation of Lauryn Hill*.

KAILA ADIA STORY, PhD, is an Associate Professor of Women's, Gender and Sexuality Studies, with a joint appointment in the Department of Pan-African Studies, at the University of Louisville. Dr. Story holds the Audre Lorde Chair in Race, Class, Gender, and Sexuality Studies. Dr. Story was a part of NBC's inaugural *#Pride30*, which featured LGBTQ community leaders and change makers. She co-hosts an award-winning podcast with longtime Louisville activist Jaison Gardner called *Strange Fruit: Musings on Politics, Pop Culture, and Black Gay Life* on WFPL (Louisville affiliate of NPR). Episodes of *Strange Fruit* can be found at https://www.npr.org/podcasts/440577316/strange-fruit.

LA LLAMA RAP COLECTIVO is a youth collective from the Raval neighborhood in Barcelona, Spain. The collective is an educational and community project. They produce Hip Hop that speaks to contemporary sociopolitical issues in their neighborhood such as police brutality, racism, sexism, religious discrimination, immigration, education, and the struggle for human rights.

LEYDA "LADY SOL" GARCIA is a proud Mexican American street dance professional, mother, and wife from Chicago who is globally recognized as a Teaching Artist, Creative Director, Manager, and Cultural Ambassador. She is a Co-Founder of Kuumba Lynx, Teaching Artist with Urban Gateways, and a Professional Development Trainer with Everybody Dance Now Chicago. Lady Sol is a self-proclaimed Professor of Practice who has taught fusions of Afro-Caribbean movement workshops at Columbia College, Stanford University, Northwestern University, and the University of Chicago. She has worked with major media networks including MTV, BET, NBC, TBS, and Hip Hop artists including Busta Rhymes, Wyclef Jean, and Lauryn Hill.

LEROY F. MOORE JR. is co-founder of Krip-Hop Nation. Since the 1990s, he has written the column "Illin n' Chillin" for *POOR Magazine*. Moore is one of the founding members of the National Black Disability Coalition and an activist dedicated to ending police brutality against people with disabilities. His cultural work includes the documentary film *Where Is Hope*, and spoken-word CDs, poetry books, and children's books including *Black Disabled Art History 101* (Xochitl Justice Press), as well as his graphic novel, *Krip-Hop Graphic Novel Issue 1: Brown Disabled Young Woman Superhero Brings Disability Justice to Hip-Hop* (Poor Press, 2019). Moore has traveled internationally, networking with other disabled activists and artists. He is currently pursuing his doctorate in Anthropology at UCLA.

LYLA JUNE is an Indigenous public speaker, artist, scholar, and community organizer of Diné (Navajo), Tsétsêhéstâhese (Cheyenne), and European lineages from Taos, New Mexico. Her messages focus on Indigenous rights, supporting youth, traditional land stewardship practices, and healing intergenerational and intercultural trauma. She blends undergraduate studies in human ecology at Stanford University, graduate work in Native American Pedagogy at the University of New Mexico, and the Indigenous worldview she grew up with to inform her perspectives and solutions. Her internationally acclaimed presentations are conveyed through the medium of poetry, music, and speech. She is currently pursuing a doctoral degree at the University of Alaska, Fairbanks, in Indigenous Studies with a focus on Indigenous Food Systems Revitalization.

MAISHA WINN, PhD, is the Chancellor's Leadership Professor and the Co-Founder and Co-Director (with Torry Winn) of the Transformative Justice in Education (TJE) Center in the School of Education at the University of California, Davis. Professor Winn's program of research examines the ways in which teachers and adult allies for youth in schools and in out-of-school contexts practice "justice" in the teaching of literacy. Professor Winn is the author of several books including *Writing in Rhythm: Spoken Word Poetry in Urban Schools* (published under maiden name "Fisher," Teachers College Press); and *Justice on Both Sides: Transforming Education through Restorative Justice* (Harvard Education Press).

MARC LAMONT HILL, PhD, is currently the host of BET News and the *Coffee & Books* podcast, and the Steve Charles Professor of Media, Cities, and Solutions at Temple University. He has worked in solidarity with human rights movements around the world. Dr. Hill is the founder and director of The People's Education Center in Philadelphia, as well as the owner of Uncle Bobbie's Coffee & Books. He is the author or co-author of six books, including the award-winning *Beats, Rhymes, and Classroom Life: Hip-Hop Pedagogy and the Politics of Identity*. He has received numerous prestigious awards from the National Association of Black Journalists, GLAAD, and the International Academy of Digital Arts and Sciences.

MARK ANTHONY NEAL, PhD, is the James B. Duke Distinguished Professor of African & African American Studies at Duke University. He offers courses on Black Masculinity, Popular Culture, and Digital Humanities, including The History of Hip-Hop, which he co-teaches with Grammy-award-winning producer 9th Wonder (Patrick Douthit). He is the author of several books, including *Looking for Leroy: Illegible Black Masculinities* and *New Black Man*. Additionally, Dr. Neal is the host of the video webcast *Left of Black*, which is produced in collaboration with the Franklin Humanities Institute at Duke.

MARK GONZALES is a father, futurist, and one of the most innovative storytellers of our time. Mark's work breaks borders to wage beauty across continents of language and culture, which has earned him respect for his creative approaches to suicide prevention, human rights, and human development. His creative portfolio spans 20 countries and includes three TED stages, HBO Def Poetry, Stanford University, and the United Nations. *Yo Soy Muslim* is his first venture into children's literature, a journey inspired by his daughter and the stories she'll grow up reading. Currently, Mark journeys between California and northern Africa with his family, seeding ways to excite the human imagination.

MEASHA FERGUSON SMITH is founder of Solidarity in Progress, where she counsels and accompanies individuals on their personal social justice journeys. She is also a student affairs professional, bridging the gap between where we learn and where we are loved. Measha's work aims to nurture the capacity for empathy and critical analysis that can transform ourselves and society toward a more just future. While attending Stanford University, Ferguson Smith was a researcher for the Institute for Diversity in the Arts' (IDA) Arts and Education Project.

MICHELLE "MUSH" LEE is a poet, narrative strategist, founder of Whole Story Group, and Executive Director of Youth Speaks. Mush engages story-based techniques and public narratives to infuse policy-making and organizational practice with creative, culturally competent thinking and problem-solving designed to promote cultural resilience and civic belonging. A Harvard University, Project Zero Fellow, Mush is frequently a featured speaker on cultural equity, racial justice, and women of color in leadership. Her writing is published in *All the Women in My Family Sing*, an anthology of essays by women of color at the dawn of the twenty-first century. Mush is the Vice-Chair of the City of Oakland's Cultural Affairs Commission, and serves on the city's Funding Advisory Committee.

OMAR OFFENDUM is a Syrian American rapper / spoken word artist. Known for his unique blend of Hip Hop and Arabic poetry, he has been featured on prominent world news outlets, lectured at a number of prestigious academic institutions, collaborated with major museums and cultural organizations, and helped raise millions of dollars for various humanitarian relief groups. Offendum was recently named a Kennedy Center Citizen Artist Fellow, an Arab America Foundation "40 Under 40" award recipient, and a member of both the Pillars Fund cohort for Muslim narrative change and the RaceForward Butterfly Lab cohort for immigrant narrative strategy. He currently resides in the great state of New York with his wife and two little children, while daydreaming about the jasmine tree–lined streets of Damascus.

RAKIM is widely acknowledged as one of hip hop's most transformative artists. Along with his partner Eric B, he recorded *Paid in Full* in 1987, a landmark recording. MTV named it the greatest hip hop album of all time. Rakim's brilliant, inimitable lyrical style, adding layers, depth, complexity, musicality, and soul to elevate the art of emceeing, has drawn comparisons to jazz icons, like Thelonious Monk and John Coltrane, and has been cited as an influence on a wide range of top selling musicians. Rakim is the recipient of the 2012 I Am Hip Hop Trophy, the 2013 BET Hip Hop Lifetime Achievement Award, as well as many others. His is also author of *Sweat the Technique: Revelations on Creativity from the Lyrics Genius* (2020).

RAMZI SALTI, PhD, is an award-winning Lecturer in Arabic at Stanford University. He is also a fully Certified ACTFL Oral and Written Proficiency Tester of Arabic. He authors his own *Arabology* blog at www.arabology.org. Dr. Salti hosts a radio program titled *Arabology*, which airs on KZSU Stanford 90.1 FM, as well as his own YouTube Channel featuring interviews and talks about Arabic language, literature, and music. Dr. Salti's collection of short stories, *The Native Informant & Other Stories: Six Tales of Defiance from the Arab World* (1994), received critical acclaim.

REAGAN NICOLE (they / them, she / her) is a PhD student in the Department of Communication and Vice President of the Black Graduate Student Association at Stanford University. She is an organizer and racial justice researcher who studies issues at the intersections of race, gender, and new media and technology. Nicole is also interested in understanding how new technology might be used to disrupt anti-Black racism.

REGINA N. BRADLEY, PhD, is an alumna Nasir Jones Hip Hop Fellow (Hutchins Center, Harvard University, Spring 2016), Associate Professor of English and African Diaspora Studies at Kennesaw State University, and co-host of the critically acclaimed southern Hip Hop podcast *Bottom of the Map* with music journalist Christina Lee. Dr. Bradley is one of the foremost authorities on contemporary Black culture in the American South. Her expertise and research interests include post–Civil Rights African American literature, Hip Hop culture, race and the contemporary US South, and sound studies. Dr. Bradley is author of *Chronocling Stankonia: The Rise of the Hip-Hop South* (2021), which was selected as a *Rolling Stone* best music book of 2021.

SHAHEEN ARIEFDIEN is a South African–born Hip Hop head, music producer, Child and Youth Worker, and an educator at The Humber College Institute of

Technology & Advanced Learning. As a founding member of the South African pioneering Hip Hop group, Prophets of da City (POC), he co-produced six albums and embarked on several educational tours around southern Africa, including a national voter campaign across South Africa leading up to the first democratically held election. He has worked on numerous community- and youth-based projects in regions as diverse as South Africa, Angola, Holland, Namibia, Denmark, Northern Ireland, and Canada.

SONYA CLARK-HERRERA is a painter, and the co-founder and current leader of the Mural Music and Arts Project ("MMAP"), a nonprofit youth development organization that educates, empowers, and inspires youth through engagement in the arts. Mentoring and teaching in after-school and community-based programs, including her own, and researching in the field of youth development, Ms. Clark-Herrera has dedicated herself to the positive development of traditionally disadvantaged youth with a particular emphasis on public art as a form of cultural empowerment and catalyst for social development and political activism.

STEPHANIE KEENEY PARKS is a doctoral student at the University of California, Los Angeles in the Department of Anthropology. She also possesses a master's degree in medical anthropology from Creighton University. Stephanie is a Robert Wood Johnson Health Policy Research Scholar and the recipient of the Eugene V. Cota-Robles Fellowship. Stephanie's research centers on the everyday lives of Black parents who have children with autism. The impetus for Stephanie's research is her lived experience as a Black woman and mother of an autistic child. Her dissertation research project, "The Struggle for Black Disability Justice: Advocacy and Inequality in the U. S.," brings together the fields of medical, linguistic, and psychological anthropology to consider how Black parents of disabled children are enacting advocacy efforts in their schools and communities.

TALIB KWELI is a Brooklyn-based MC who has been releasing Hip Hop for over 25 years. Whether working with Mos Def as one-half of Black Star, partnering with producer Hi-Tek for Reflection Eternal, releasing landmark solo material or collaborating with Kanye West, Pharrell Williams, Just Blaze, J Dilla, or Madlib, Kweli commands attention by delivering top-tier lyricism, crafting captivating stories and showing the ability to rhyme over virtually any type of instrumental. In 2011, Kweli founded Javotti Media, which is self-defined as "a platform for independent thinkers and doers." Kweli has set out to make Javotti Media into a media powerhouse that releases music, films, and books.

TALL PAUL is an Anishinaabe and Oneida Hip Hop artist enrolled on the Leech Lake reservation in Minnesota. Born and raised in Minneapolis, his music strongly reflects his inner-city upbringing. From personal expressions of self, to thought-provoking commentary on issues affecting Indigenous and diverse communities as a whole, Tall Paul's music evokes a wide variety of substance and soul.

TANAYA WINDER is an author, singer/songwriter, poet, and motivational speaker who comes from an intertribal lineage of Southern Ute, Pyramid Lake Paiute, and Duckwater Shoshone Nations, where she is an enrolled citizen. Winder's poetry collections include *Words Like Love* and *Why Storms Are Named after People and Bullets Remain Nameless*. In 2013, she was a featured TEDxABQ speaker and a 2016 National Center for American Indian Enterprise Development "40 Under 40" emerging American Indian leaders recipient. Winder's performances and talks blend storytelling, singing, and spoken word to teach about different expressions of love and "heartwork." Her specialties include youth and women empowerment, healing trauma through art, creative writing workshops, and mental wellness advocacy.

TREVA B. LINDSEY, PhD, is Professor of Women's, Gender, and Sexuality Studies and founder of the Transformative Black Feminisms Initiative at The Ohio State University. She is the author of *America, Goddam: Violence, Black Women, and the Struggle for Justice* (2022) and *Colored No More: Reinventing Black Womanhood in Washington D.C* (2017), which was a Choice 2017 "Outstanding Academic Title." Her research and teaching interests include African American women's history, Black feminisms, Hip Hop studies, and social movement history. She writes for and contributes to outlets such as *Time*, Al Jazeera, BNC News, BET, Complex, Vox, The Root, *Huffington Post*, PopSugar, *Teen Vogue*, CNN, NBC, The Grio, and *Cosmopolitan*.

Index

Page numbers *in italics* represent figures. Page numbers followed by n denote notes.

Abrahams, Nazli, 55
Abrica, Ruben, 201
Abu-Jamal, Mumia, 269
accountability in classroom, 328, 330
Achievement and Achievement Motives: Psychological and Sociological Approaches (Boykin), 251
achievement gap, 269–272
Adorno, Theodor, 276
affective labor in MMAP spaces, 210–212
African American Theatre Arts Troupe, 336
The African Hip Hop Indaba, 54
Afrocentricity influences, 65
after-school programs, 326, 329, 335
Age of Truth (album), 53–54
AJ420, 391
Alexander, Michelle, 206
Alim, H. Samy, Dr.: on culturally sustaining pedagogies (CSPs), 14–15, 245–247, 254; *Roc the Mic: The Language of Hip Hop Culture*, 29–30; *Street Conscious Rap*, 30; *Tha Global Cipha: Hip Hop Culture and Consciousness*, 30
ALKEMY, 68
All-American Girl, 222
Allhiphop.com, 164
"All Nations Rise" (song), 120
Alsalman, Yassin, 84
American Educational Research Journal, 247
American Indian Movement, 123
AmeriKKKa's Most Wanted, 50
Andre 3000, 403
Andrés, Juan, killing of, 138
apartheid regime and music ban, 62
Apollo, 179
"Arab Spring," 101n1
Ariefdien, Shaheen, 6–7; early life, 53–54; education, 53; on Knowledge of Self, 79–81; work, 53–54, 56; on young people voices, 78–79
Armah, Esther: on emotional justice, 364–365; Emotional Justice conversations, 373–374
Articulate While Black (Alim and Smitherman), 258
Ashanti woman, narrative of, 364
"A Song for Trayvon" (song), 340
Associació Joves TEB (a youth association), 132–133
authenticity of Hip Hop, 279–282
Autism Speaks, 393

Bahamadia, 30
Bain, Bryonn, 213; building curriculum in reverse at Rikers Island, 230–232, 235; on facing challenges, 240–241; on Hip Hop pedagogy, 229–230, 235; lyrics, 227–228; Ngũgĩ wa Thiong'o's *Decolonising the Mind*, 232–233; performance theatre in prisons, 229–230, 235; on spoken word pedagogies, 229–230, 234
Baker, Anita, 61
Banks, James, 272
Basin, Michael, 164
Bay Area Hip Hop, 65
Bay Rebellion, 337–339
b-boying, 13–14, 35, 56, 69, 76, 79, 296, 316–317, 400
BDS Campaign, raising consciousness, 61–63
Beastie Boys, 314
Beats, Rhymes, and Classroom Life: Hip Hop Pedagogy and the Politics of Identity (Hill), 269
The Beauty, Nomy Lamm, 391
BEES, the Black Economic Empowerment Strategy, 80
"Be Free" (song), 340
Begatz, 93
Belafonte, Harry, 218, 229
Bell, Dereck, 287
Ben Haana Wa Maana (album), 84
Bernal, Coral, 106
Be Steadwell, 391
Bey, Yasiin, 45
biases: class, 352; culture, 352
Big Daddy Kane, 42–43, 197
"Biggie Smalls (aka The Notorious B.I.G.)," 105, 275, 279, 280
Big Pun, 198
Big Quarters, 105
Biko influences, 65
Black: ableism, 377, 386; authors, 284; class, 281; cultural spaces, 371–372; desire, politics of, 357; disabled movement, UK, 380
Black Arts Movement, 22, 31
Black Disabled Art History 101 (Moore), 377
Blacked Out through Whitewash (Suzar), 72
Black female sexuality and pleasure, narrative around, 353–357
Black Feminist Project, 360
The Black Kripple Delivers Poetry & Lyrics (Moore), 377
Black Language (BL) and Hip Hop cultures, 258

Black Literate Lives (Winn), 417
Black Lives Matter march, 340
Blackness as political identity, 79–80, 281
Black Noise: Rap Music and Black Culture in Contemporary America (Rose), 54, 71, 73, 79, 274
Black Panther Party, Tanzania, 230–231, 267
Black queer theory, 366–367
Black Raw Medusa, 179
Black Spades, 61
Blackstar, 32, 45
Blackstone Rangers, 415
"Black Thing" (song), 64–65
Black Thought, 50, 51–52
Black Watch, 60
BLM (Black Lives Matter), 385
"BLOOD" (song), 394
Blow, Kurtis, 388
The Blues, 380, 389–390
Boal, Augusto, 231–232, 335–336
Bone Thugs-n-Harmony, 105, 108
Boogie Down Productions, 42
Botero, Fernando, 156n12
Bourdieu in '77, 275
Boyd-Pates, Tyree, 33
Boykin, Wade, 251
Bradley, Regina, 397
Brave New Voices program, 213
Brave space, 192n6
breakdance, 45, 107, 129, 379
Breaking (movie), 390
Brooks, Gwendolyn, 415–417
Brown, Oscar, 415
Browne, Kevin A., 352
Bullie, Jacinda: on activism and citywide movement in Chicago, 183–184; on getting funds, 189–190; on Kuumba Lynx, 181; on longitudinal excellence, 187–188; lyrics, 185–187; mandated curriculum for public schools, 184–185; on sustainability, 187–188
Burge, Jon, 184
Burrill, Mary, 369
Bush Radio, 79
"Butterflies Fly By" (music video), 4, 69–70

Calderon, Jessa: growing up Hip Hop, 107–108; healing and solidarities through Hip Hop, 119; portraying Indigenous communities and struggles, 115–117; raising awareness about Indigenous communities, 121–122; on sacredness of land, 126–127

Can't Stop Won't Stop: A History of the Hip-Hop Generation (Chang), 255
Cape Flats, 60–61
Carlos I, Juan, King, 2
Carter, Prudence, 270
Casual of Hieroglyphics, 65
50 Cent, 32, 279, 280, 393
Center for Cultural Arts & Diversity, 336
Chali 2na, 44, 51
Chamberlain, Wilt, 50
Chang, Jeff, 254, 255, 350
Chatah, 129
Check It While I Wreck It (Pough), 286
Chicanos, 334–335
Chickasaw, 129
Chief Keef, 308
The Child and the Curriculum (Dewey), 280
Cho, Margaret, 222
Chrysalisamidst, 391
Chuck D, 3, 30, 32, 33–35, 383; on female emcees, 46; on Hip Hop and politics for impact, 48–49; on Hip Hop as an educational tool, 43–45; on his personal favorites, 50–51; on Rakim, 36–40; on spiritual practices, 47–48
cipher, 13, 23, 44, 107, 181, 195, 210, 231, 293, 304, 318, 378–380, 398, 414–415
Clark-Herrera, Sonya: engagement with Hip Hop, 197–198; history through Hip Hop (HHH) program, 203–206; relationship to activism growing up, 198–199; starting MMAP, 199–203
class biases, 352
The Classroom and the Cell (Hill and Abu-Jamal), 269
classroom community, Hip Hop culture as, 327–331; accountability, 330; building classroom community, 328–329; creative writing and open space, 327–328; feedback by students, 328, 331; language, boundary of, 329
classroom life, relevance of Hip Hop in, 269–296; engaging class with Hip Hop stories, 282–283; Hip Hop lit, 277–279; overview, 269–270; politics of authenticity, 279–282; politics of identity and culture, 270–273, 274–277; ways forward, 287–296
Cole, J., 340
Collander, 391
collective healing, storytelling as; *see* storytelling
collective liberation and Indigenous futures, 124–130; *see also* Indigenous Hip Hop

collective survival and growth, 328
collective wisdom, 331
A Colored Woman in a White World (Terrell), 361
Colorlines, 387
Coltrane, Alice, 39
Coltrane, John, 32
Common, 30, 279
Common Core standards, 331
community building, 180, 328, 336; *see also* classroom community, Hip Hop culture as
community organizations, 210–212, 261, 266, 326, 340
Condry, Ian, 277
Cooper, Brittney: on Black female body, 371; on Black Feminism, 368–369; on pleasure politics of Black women, 361–364; vignette, 361–363
co-teaching, 278
counterstorytelling, 287
The Creative Habit (Tharp), 225
creative writing, 334
Crew Girl Order, 46
critical consciousness, 133, 264
critical pedagogy, 275–277; *see also* Hip Hop and critical pedagogies
Crocker, Frankie, 35
Crunk Feminist Collective, 371
Cubberley, Ellwood P., 262
cultural competence, 247–248
cultural dexterity, 262–264
cultural forms of Hip Hop, 303–304
cultural justice, 254–255, 260
cultural legacy, 397
culturally relevant education and teachers, 260–262, 265, 325; *see also* teacher education
culturally relevant pedagogy, 13–16, 247–249, 254, 256, 277, 283–284; *see also* Hip Hop pedagogies
culturally sustaining pedagogy (CSP), 14–15, 206, 254–257, 261, 265, 267; *see also* Hip Hop pedagogies
cultural pluralism, 256
cultural shifts, evolving, 257–259; *see also* storytelling
cultural studies, 15, 275–276
culture: biases, 352; politics of, 270–273
curriculum: curricular silencing, 255; design, 331–335; interdisciplinary, 326; on police torture in Chicago public schools, mandating, 184–187; top-down, 325
cypher, 327, 330, 334, 338

Dabke on the Moon (album), 84, 87, 102n4
DaDafest, 388
Daily Show, 249
DAMN, 394
DAM (Palestinian group), 83–84, 87–88; beginning of, 98; *Ben Haana Wa Maana* (album), 84; criticism, 87–89; *Dabke on the Moon* (album), 87; *Dedication* (album), 87; group formation, 98; meaning of, 84; "Meen Erhabi?—Who Is the Terrorist?" (song), 84; rejection on performing, 92–93; *Slingshot Hip Hop* (documentary film), 84; success of, 84, 90; and women, 88
Dangerous Minds (film), 276
Davis, Angela, 421
Dawson, Kimya, 391
Dead Poets Society (film), 276
"Dear Mama" (song), 327
Death Row Records, 107
"Death to the Borbones" (song), 147
Dedication (album), 84, 87
Def Jam, 169
De La Soul, 198, 270
Dewey, John, 280
Diallo, Amadou, 32
dialogue, 23, 180, 184, 190, 235, 278, 324, 331–332, 335–336, 339–340
Digable Planets, 279, 284
Digital Underground, 65
Dimensions (album), 111
Dimitriadis, Greg, 277
disability justice-based performance project, 385
DJing, 316
DMC, 381
"Don't Believe the Hype" (song), 35
"Do We Need to Start a Riot?" (music video), 175–178
Dream Defenders, 174, 411
Dreamkeepers: Successful Teachers of African American Children (Ladson-Billings), 247, 251
Dream Warriors, 5–6, 109–111, *113*, 125, 130
Du Bois, W. E. B., 264
Duckworth, Angela, 397
Duncan-Andrade, Jeff, 273
Dynasty (album), 283

Earth Rituals, 391
educational institutions and achievement gap, 271–272
educational justice, 260
Edward, Antoine, 111
The 18th Letter (album), 44
El Raval, Barcelona. *see* La Llama Rap Colectivo
emcee. *see* female emcees; *specific* entries
Emdin, Christopher, 289; on addressing race, culture, and gender issue through Hip Hop, 304–305; on balancing Hip Hop science education, 307–308; on benefits of Hip Hop for science education, 308–310; on children's involvement with music, 303–304; on children's response in classroom, 303–304; on consciousness shifting, 298; empowerment of woman and LGBTQ students, 313–314; on engagement with students, 305–307, 312–313; on experiential science knowledge, 300; on involving teachers, 310–312; on partnership with GZA, 320; on teacher education practice, 317–318; teaching about being an emcee, 302; teaching science in classrooms with Hip Hop, 300–301; translating personal experience and everyday interactions, 318–319; on uniqueness of relating with Hip Hop, 315–316; on using nonverbal forms of Hip Hop, 316–317
Emile YX?: family surname, 69; Kemoja Project, 75–76; making knowledge of self real, 70–75; mass rally, 69–70; Mixed Mense, 76–77; reaching out, 70–72; work, 54–55
Eminem, 32, 51, 279
emotional justice, 364–365
Emotional Justice conversations, 373–374
English Journal, 273
epigenetics, 218
EPMD, 197
Eric B, 31–32, 36, 39, 379
"Eric B Is President" (song), 37, 40
Estes, Nick, 125
Etheridge Knight, 415
ethnography of urban, Black girlhood, 401–402
Eve, 30
experiential knowledge, 358–359
experiential learning, 337–338

families of activists, targeting, 95
Family Stone, 43
farin feminism, 352, 353
Farmworkers Movement, 338

Fatback Band, 33
Fear of a Black Planet (album), 32, 38
feedback from students, 328
feminist discourse and Hip Hop feminism, Caribbean, 353–357; *see also* Hip Hop feminism; women
Fences (Wilson), 333
Ferguson Smith, Measha, 206; on relationship between individuals in Hip Hop space, 210; "Street Religion" (song), 208; on working with young people in MMAP, 208
field trips and Hip Hop pedagogies, 337–338
5 Elements Gallery, 266
5th Element of Hip Hop, 101–102, 406
"The 5th Element" (poem), 391
Fire Officer Donald, 391
First Peoples, 58, 77, 82
First Wave program, 253
Fisher, Maisha. *see* Winn, Maisha
Flava Flav, 32, 49
Flores, Paul, 219
Floyd, George, 340
"Follow the Leader" (song), 35, 39, 40
For Colored Girls (Shange), 371
41 Shots, 32
Franklin, Aretha, 277
El Franquismo, 1–2
Freedom Dreams (play), 337
Freedom Riders (film), 276
freestyling, 399
Freire, Paulo, 231, 324–325, 331, 335
From Brooklyn Beats 2 Beirut Streets, 84
The Fugees, 105
Furious Five, 62, 78

Ganser, Lisa, 391
Gardner, Jaison, 366
Garner, Eric, 340
Gay, Geneva, 272
gender: and Hip Hop education, 304–305; identity in "the New South," negotiating, 402–405
GenderKrip, 391
genetic memory, 218
Ghost Dance movement, 121
Gibran, Khalil, 100
Girl Time: Literacy, Justice, and the School-to-Prison Pipeline (Winn), 418
Giroux, Henry, 276
Gladwell, Michael, 397

Gladys Knight, 44
Global Faction, 99
Godessa, 46
Gonzales, Mark, 84; on collective and cumulative effect of trauma, 217–218; creating creative and youth development spaces, 236–238; on figuring out life, 239; on healing and growth, 219; on storytelling, 214, 216–217; *In Times of Terror, Wage Beauty*, 214
Gonzalez, Javier, 176
"Good Times" (song), 35
Grae, Jean, 46
graffiti art, 35, 44, 138, 153, 195, 196, 316, 328, 420
Grandmaster Caz, 51
Grandmaster Flash, 30, 62, 78, 314
grass dancing, 129
Grinberg, Benjy, 169
griot tradition, African, 43
Guinier, Lani, 231
GZA: on addressing race, culture, and gender issue through Hip Hop, 304–305; on balancing Hip Hop science education, 307; on children's involvement with music, 302–303; on Hip Hop *vs* country music, 305; on his interest in science, 299; on partnership with Emdin, 320; teaching about being an emcee, 301–302; teaching science in classrooms with Hip Hop, 301; translating personal experience and everyday interactions, 318

Harvey, Mariah, 256
Hasél, Pablo, 1–2, 147
HB 2281 program, 256, 268n10
healing through Hip Hop, 109–110, 282–287; and creativity, 238; Indigenous Hip Hop, 115–123; and knowledge of self, 68–69; queering Hip Hop feminist pedagogies, 410–411; and solidarities, 117–118; and storytelling, 219; *see also* Mural Music & Arts Project (MMAP); storytelling
Heal the Hood Project, 54, 75–82, 267
Heather B, 45
Heffernan, Kalyn, 383, 391
Hernández, Kelly Lytle, 30–31
Heron, Gil Scott, 3
Hickman, Toni, 383, 391
High School of the Recording Arts, 266
Hill, Lauryn, 46, 107, 278–279, 284, 287, 322–323

Hill, Marc Lamont: *Beats, Rhymes, and Classroom Life: Hip Hop Pedagogy and the Politics of Identity*, 269; *The Classroom and the Cell*, 269; early education and racial identity, 271–272; *Nobody: Casualties of America's War on the Vulnerable, from Ferguson to Flint and Beyond*, 269; *Schooling Hip-Hop*, 269; teach literary interpretation, 273

Hip Hop: British, in South Africa, 61–62; and Colouredness, 62–63; focus on education, 63–64, 220; and hypermasculinity, 63, 288, 353; Knowledge of Self element, 64–65; narratives, 282–283; politics of authenticity, 279–282; purist, 43; raising consciousness, 63–64; sensibilities, 261, 303–304, 309, 318–319, 397–398; *see also* healing through Hip Hop; identity

Hip Hop, sustaining revolution through, 83–101; acceptance in Arab world *vs* West, 91–94; *al-shaab yurid isqat al-nitham* (song), resistance for, 94; *Dabke on the Moon* (album), 87; DAM, starting, 85–87; *Dedication* (album), 87; "*Law Arjaa bil-Zaman*" (song), criticism and praise for, 87–89; music to sustain Syrian Revolution, 94–96; overview, 83–84; resistance literature/lyrics, 89–91; *see also* DAM (Palestinian group)

Hip Hop and critical pedagogies, 322–345; Black history, 331–335; common core, 331–335; curriculum design, 331–335; field trips, 337–338; final reflections, 340–342; Freire, Paulo, and *Pedagogy of the Oppressed*, 324–325; Hip Hop culture as community, 327–331; Hip Hop theatre of oppressed, 335–337; in public schools, 325–327; and student protest, 338–340; Whiteness, impact on, 322–324

Hip Hop and science education, 298–320; addressing issues, 304–305; balancing the art of Hip Hop with science, 307–308; classroom structure, 300–301; Hip Hop as a teaching tool, 305–307; inclusion of women and queer people, 313–314; nonverbal forms of Hip Hop, 316–317; overview, 298–300; Science Genius, 304–305; students' engagement, 301–302, 312–313; students' response, 302–304; teacher education practices, 317–318; and teachers, 310–312; teaching approach, 308–310; training, 314–316

Hip Hop art and activism, 159–179; Black Liberation Theology, 173–175; "Do We Need to Start a Riot?" (music video), 175–178; 1Hood, 167–168, 178–179; Jasiri X, early life, 160–163; Jena 6, 163–164; Jordan Miles, 170–173; lyrics about city, 165–167; Wiz Khalifa, 168–170

Hip Hop feminism, 349–374; articulating a politics of pleasure, 350–352; Black feminist theory, 365–369; Black queer bodies, engaging, 365–369; Caribbean feminist discourse, 353–357; homophobia, 365–369; overview, 349–350; pleasure politics, 361–364; political-epistemological project, 361–364; spiritual to sexual, idea of freedom, 358–361; toward emotional justice, 364–365; transforming trauma to triumph, 373–374; twerking, the body, and historicizing pleasure, 369–372; *see also* women

Hip-Hop (Hill), 269

Hip-Hop Japan (Condry), 277

Hip Hop lit, 277–279

Hip Hop pedagogies, 192n3, 207, 211, 213, 233, 245–267; culturally relevant pedagogy, 247–249; culturally sustaining pedagogies, 253–257; cultural shifts, evolving, 257–259; Hip Hop(e), 247–249; migrating inward from a place of love, 259–267; new century students, 249–253; overview, 245–247; politics of identity and culture, 269–270; from the South, reframing, 405–407

Hip Hop's Li'l Sistas Speak: Negotiating Hip Hop Identities and Politics in the New South (Love), 401, 408

Hip Hop theatre: movement, 336; of oppressed, 335–337; *see also* Kuumba Lynx in Chicago

historical identity, 385

History through Hip Hop (HHH) program, 203–206

Hi Tek, 32

Hlehel, Ala, 93

hodari blue (fka Adorie Howard), 206, 208–209

Holiday, Billie, 333

Holt, A-lan, 214; *8ball*, 226; envisioning safe, sustainable futures, 223–226; *Inamorata*, 226; writing impossible worlds into existence, 226

"Home of the Brave" (song), 116

1Hood media, 167-168, 178-179
Human Writes Project, 84
hypermasculinity, 63, 88, 288, 353

"I Ain't No Joke" (song), 35, 36, 40
Ice Cube, 30, 42, 50, 393
Ice-T, 50-51
IDA. *see* Institute for Diversity in the Arts (IDA)
identity: Blackness as political, 79-80; creating, 63-64, 420; expressions of, 367; formation, 63-64; gender, 402-405; historical, 385; hybridized, 319; local, for young Black girls, 408-409; politics of, 270-273; queer, negotiating, 402-405; racial, 80-81, 271-272; regaining, 124-125; sustaining, 420
IDL (I Depend on Life), 179
Ihda, 87
"I Know You Got Soul" (song), 38
Illadelph Halflife (album), 197
"Illin n' Chillin" (column), 377, 382, 391
Ill Lucidity, 179
Imani Atlantic, 391
Inamorata, 214
"Indian Step" (breakdance move), 129
Indigenous Hip Hop, 103-130; collective liberation and envisioning Indigenous futures, 124-130; growing up Hip Hop and Indigenous, 103-111; healing and solidarities through, 115-123; Indigenous music traditions, 111-113; pushing boundaries of Hip Hop, 111-113; resisting settler colonialism through, 115-123; and revitalization of Indigenous language and culture, 113-115
individualism, 251, 252
Individuals with Disabilities Education Act (IDEA), 378-379
"I Never Dreamed You'd Leave in Summer" (song), 284
"Injustice" (song), 117
Institute for Diversity in the Arts (IDA), 19, 20, 21, 22, 23-24, 350-351
intergenerational healing, 219
International Association for African American Music Festival, 414
International FlyGirls Day, 373
internationalization of Hip Hop, 264
inter-personal connection, 326-327
In Times of Terror, Wage Beauty (Gonzales), 214
Invincible, 394

Irkalla Lustre, 391
Islamophobia in Spain, 142-145
It's Hard Out Here for a Gimp (video), 383
"It Started in a Cage" (song), 390
It Takes a Nation of Millions to Fear of a Black Planet (album), 32, 38

Jackson, Michael, 61
Jackson, Philip, 275
Jackson, Walter, 378
Jadakiss, 49
#Jan25 (album), 83-84
Jandali, Malek, 95
Jane, Emily, 354
Jasiri X, 340; "America's Most Livable City" (song), 164-167; *Black Liberation Theology*, 173-175; "Do We Need to Start a Riot?" (song), 175-178; early life, 160-163; 1Hood, 167-168; Jordan Miles, lyrics on, 170-173; lyrics, 165-167, 170-172, 174-178; meeting Wiz Khalifa, 168-170; "#NeverLovedUs" (song), 174; on racism, 163-164; on starting Hip Hop clubs in schools, 168
Jay-Z, 32, 51, 279, 283-284
Jidenna, 205
"Jim Thorpe" (song), 115
Johnson, Blind Willie, 378
Jones, Dennis, 114
Jones, Keith, 377, 382-383, 389, 390, 393
Joseph, Marc Bamuthi, 219
journaling, 329
Jreri, Mahmoud, 84, 90-91
Juba, 387-388
Jules, Gunner: connecting with Indigenous music traditions, 111-113; on Ghost Dance, 122-123; growing up Hip Hop, 104; Indigenous background, 103-104; on regaining identity, 124-125; relating the history to a post-settler colonial future, 125-126; singing Lakota vocal inflections, 112-113; solidarity with Indigenous peoples, 124-125, 129-130
June, Lyla: finding connection between Black and Brown peoples, 128-129; growing up Hip Hop, 106-107; lyrics, 126; relating the history to a post-settler colonial future, 125; solidarity with Indigenous peoples, 120, 123
Justice on Both Sides (Winn), 418-420

Kass, James, 219
Katz, Rowan, 391

Kelley, Robin D. G., 22
Kemoja Project, 75
Kennedy, Dom, 206
K-12 ethnic studies ban, 256
Khoi-San movement groups, 77, 82
Kid Frost, 108
The Kindezi School, 399–400, 407–408
King, Deborah, 369
King, Rodney, 176
"King Kunta" (song), 394
"King Tim III" (song), 33–34
Kiss FM (radio), 35
Kitwana, Bakari, 30–31
knowledge: centering local, 195; of people of color, 253–257; *see also* Mural Music & Arts Project (MMAP)
knowledge of self, 47–48, 406
knowledge of self in "post"-apartheid South Africa, 53–82; apartheid, 69–70; BDS campaign and raising consciousness, 61–63; Black consciousness and the politics of race, 63–68; creating own schools, 75–82; Hip Hop and healing, 68–69; introduction, 53–56; knowledge of self, 70–73; so-called "coloured" people, 57–59; South African apartheid, brief history, 57–59; US Hip Hop context, 60–61; writing own stories, 73–75
"Knowledge of Self" (song), 47
Kool Herc, DJ, 30, 129, 197, 255
Kool Moe Dee, 50, 51
KQED Arts, 214
Krip-Hop Graphic Novel (Moore), 377
Krip-Hop movement, 376–395; adding to Hip Hop's 5th element, 389–390; Black ableism, 386; Black and disabled in a White suburb, 378–380; Black disability and the uprising against police violence, 385–386; from the Blues to Krip-Hop movement, 380–383, 385; gender dynamics within Krip-Hop, 391; Homohop and Krip-Hop, 387–389; introduction, 376–378; Krip Hop Nation Painting, *384*; lyrics, 376–377; pushing Hip Hop toward disability justice, 392–395; race, gender, class, together with disability, 390–391; reclaiming language, 391–392
KRS-One, 42, 380, 390
K-12 school spaces, Hip Hop pedagogies into. *see* Hip Hop and critical pedagogies
Kurupt, 30
Kuumba Lynx in Chicago, Hip Hop theatre and activism with, 180–192; mandating curriculum on police torture in Chicago public schools, 184–187; overview, 180–183, 192n1; program participants, 180; sustainability and longitudinal excellence, 187–192
Kweli, Talib, 3, 32, 51, 279; on female emcees, 45–46; on Hip Hop as an educational tool, 42–43; on his personal favorites, 49–50; on Rakim, 39–40; on spiritual practices, 47

Ladson-Billings, Gloria, 245–246, 272, 274, 277, 317; changing assessment protocol, 265–266; *Dreamkeepers: Successful Teachers of African American Children*, 247; High School of the Recording Arts, 266; on movement, verve, communalism, 249–253; on reinventing culturally relevant pedagogy, 247–249; on United Alliance Community Center, 266–267; on White dominant culture, 264
Lady Sol, 181, 187–188, 190
"La Femme Fetal" (Planets), 284
La Llama Rap Colectivo, 1–2, 131–155, 267; Andrés, Juan, responding to police murder of, 136–138, 141–142; El Raval: gentrification and struggle against neoliberalism, 149–152; misrepresentation of, 135–136; freedom of expression, 145–149; Hip Hop art, activism, and education, 152–155; Islamophobia in Spain, exposing, 142–145; overview, 131–133; racism, exposing, 142–145; resisting anti-Blackness in Barcelona, 133–134; state repression against rap, 145–149; xenophobia, exposing, 142–145
Lamar, Kendrick, 277, 394
LaMay, Bronwyn, 337
Lamm, Nomy, 391
"LANDBACK campaign," 123
language, 124; as carrier of culture, 232–233; classroom, 329; dexterity, 262–264; Indigenous, revitalization of, 113–115; Menominee, revitalization among, 253; orientations and curriculum, 277; power of, 391–392; sharing, 259
LA riots, 176
Last Poets, 3, 43
"Law Arjaa bil-Zaman" (song), 87–89
Lean on Me (film), 276
Led Zeppelin, 229
Lee, Carol, 272, 273, 274

Lee, Michelle Mush, 213; on creating safe space, 235–236; on creativity and healing, 238; on expansive love, 232–233; on forgiveness, 223; on Hip Hop pedagogy, 234–235; on misrepresentation of high schoolers, 238–239; Youth Speaks, 219–223
Lenape, Ramapough, 129
Lenapehoking, 129
Lenape people, 129
liberatory education, 324–325, 331
liberatory theatre, 335–336
Life in Classrooms (Jackson), 275
Lil' Kim lyrics, 275
Lil Wayne, 288
Lindsey, Treva: historicizing pleasure, 369–370; on idea of freedom, 358–361; on twerking, 370
literocracy, 413–414
LL Cool J. LL, 51, 78
Lorde, Audre, 368–369
Lost in Translation (album), *86*, 100
Love, Bettina: ethnography of urban Black girlhood, 401–402; on social emotional intelligence of children, 397–398; on students expressing their culture, 399–401; on students identifying with Hip Hop, 396–399
"Love Is the Message" (song), 35
The Luniz, 105
Lyrics from Lockdown, 213
Lyte, MC, 45
Lytle, Susan, 270

Mac Miller, 170
Manda, Simon, 388–389
Mandela, Nelson, 54, 57, 68
Mansour, Shadia, 84, 84, 99
marginalization, 210
Marl, Marley, 35
Martin, Trayvon, 400, 406, 410
Maya Songbird, 391
Mays, Kyle, 120–121
McDonald, CeCe, 411
media creation. *see* Hip Hop art and activism
Melle Mel, 50, 51, 314
Mer-Khamis, Juliano, 99
Mexican American Studies program, 256
MF Doom, 50
Michael: on bad naming of El Raval, 135–136; beginning Hip Hop, 133–134; on Catalonian independence, 148–149; on facing racism, 143–145; on gentrification of El Raval, 149–152; "la Ley Mordaza," 145–146; "Luchando Derechos," 136–137, 141–142; lyrics on king, 146–148; on multiculturality, 136; on police prejudice, 137; on relationship between Hip Hop and education, 152–153; "Tanquem on CIEs" campaign, 145–146; "Verdades Ocultas," 142–143; "Voces Mudas," 153–154
Mighty Sparrow, 229
Miles, Jordan, 61, 170–173
Minaj, Nicki, 286, 288
Miracle Spotted Bear, 111
The Miseducation of Lauryn Hill, 108
MJ, Lady, 391
Monch, Pharoahe, 394
Monie Love, 45
Monk, Thelonious, 32
Moonwork (poems), 214
Moore, Darnell, 366
Moore, Leroy F., Jr.: on artists involved in Krip-Hop, 382–383, 385; on Black ableism, 386; on Black disability and uprising against police violence, 385–386; from the Blues to Krip-Hop movement, 380–381; on challenges faced within Hip Hop, 381–382; co-founding Krip-Hop Nation (KHN), 377–378; on gender dynamics within Krip-Hop, 391; growing up Black and disabled, 378–380; on Homohop and Krip-Hop, 387–391; on Peace Out, 387; pushing Hip Hop toward disability justice, 392–395; on race, gender, class, together with disability, 390–391; on reclaiming language, 391–392; work with *POOR Magazine*, 382
Morgan, Joan, 408; articulating politics of pleasure for Black feminism, 350–352; Caribbean feminist discourse and Hip Hop feminism, 353–355
Morrell, Ernest, 273
Morrison, Toni, 255, 260, 342
Mos Def, 30, 32, 45, 50, 279
Mothers Against Police Brutality, 385
Mount Rushmore protest in 2020, 123
Movement for Black Lives, 340
Mural Music & Arts Project (MMAP), 193–212; beginning of, 196; care, affective labor, and sustaining community organizations, 210–212; History through Hip Hop (HHH) program, 203–206; impact on youth and communities, 206–210; local knowledge, centering, 195; Power Writer program, 193, 195; social justice arts ecosystem, creating, 197–203

Murkus, Amal, 87
musicking, 275
Mu'tamar Al-Udaba', 93
Mvskoke, 129
"My Radio" (song), 78
My Secret Affair with Carla Bruni (Hlehel), 93
Myspace, 163–164
"My Stone" (song), 121–122
MyVerse, 43

NAACP, 386
Nach, 155n3
Nafar, Suhell, 84–85, 97
Nafar, Tamer, 84–85; childhood, 97; discrimination faced, 91–92; prioritize issues across different spaces, 100–101; "Stop Selling Drugs" (album), 98
Naimy, Mikhail, 100
Nas, 32, 279, 280
Nasty Boy Klick, 108
Nate Dogg, 107
National Association of Colored Women, 361
National Black Disability Coalition, 385
Nation of Islam, 60, 65
Native Americans, 116, 252
Native Tongues, 270
NDN Collective, 125–126
neoliberalism, struggle against, 149–152; *see also* La Llama Rap Colectivo
Neva Again: Hip Hop Art, Activism Education in Post-Apartheid South Africa (Haupt, Williams, Alim and Jansen), 30
"Never Again" (song), 65–68
New Jim Crow (Alexander), 206
The New Medina (Tunisia), 214
New York Times, 377, 381, 394–396
The Next America (Taylor), 256
"Night of the Living Baseheads" (song), 40
Nikki D, 45
Nipsey Hussle, 45
Nobody: Casualties of America's War on the Vulnerable, from Ferguson to Flint and Beyond (Hill), 269
nonverbal forms of Hip Hop, using, 316–317
Notorious B.I.G., 32
NWA, 42, 107, 279

Oceti Sakowin, 125
Offendum, Omar: Arabic writing, 99; background, 85–86; *From Brooklyn Beats 2 Beirut Streets*, 84; facing rejection, 89–90; #Jan25 (album), 83; *Lost in Translation*, 86; restrictions faced on performances, 93–94; success in Qatar, 94; on Syria, 94–96, 99; #Syria (album), 94; *SyrianamericanA*, 83–84; on 5th element of, 101; "We Have to Change" (song), 99; work, 83–84
Oh, Ellen, 350
Ojibwe tribe, 114
Once Abandoned Now Resurrected by Passion (Art), 387
opportunity gap, 270
Opportunity Please Knock youth ensemble, 415
Our History Is Our Future: Standing Rock Versus the Dakota Access Pipeline, and the Long Tradition of Indigenous Resistance (Estes), 125
Our World, 53
Outkast, 403
Outkast as pedagogy, 407–410

2Pac. *see* Shakur, Tupac
Paid in Full (album), 31–32
Palestine, revolution in. *see* Hip Hop, sustaining revolution through
Papa Joe, 417
Paris, Django, 206, 246; on dream institution, 266; on evolving cultural shifts, 257–259; on knowledge, Hip Hop, and culturally sustaining pedagogies, 253–257; on migrating inward from a place of love, 259–262; on pre-service teachers, 265; on White dominant culture, 263–264
"Patience" (song), 111
Peace Out Festival, 387
Pebblee-Poo, 45
pedagogical silencing, 255
Peltier, Leonard, 116, 337
performance poetry-based original plays, 336
Performing Identity / Performing Culture (Dimitriadis), 277
Perkins, William Eric, 275
Perry, Imani, 31, 282
Personal Narrative, Revised: Writing Love and Agency in the High School Classroom (LaMay), 337
Peterson, Carla, 417
Pharoahe Monch, 30, 279
Pieterson, Hector, 71
Pips, 44
Pittsburgh. *see* Hip Hop art and activism
Plank, Thomas, 192n2

The Pleasure Ninjas, *372*
POC, 79
Poems from Prison (Knight), 415
police violence and uprisings, 385–386
political identity, Blackness as, 79–80
political movements and Hip Hop, 60–61, 78–79
Poo, Daniel, 326
POOR Magazine, 377, 382–383, 385
Pop Smoke, 45
Potter, Russell, 274
Pough, Gwendolyn, 286
"Prayers in a Song" (song), 113–114
Pride (film), 276
Professor Griff, 32
Project NIA, 184
Prophets of da City, 63–68
Prophets of the Hood (Perry), 31, 282
PTSD: Post Traumatic Stress Disorder (2014) (album), 394
public education, 278
Public Enemy, 32, 78, 197, 198, 380
Punk, 380
Pushing Limits (radio show), 382

Queen Latifah, 30, 45
queer desire, politics of, 357
queer Hip Hop artists, 381
queer identity in "the New South," negotiating, 402–405
queering Hip Hop feminist pedagogies, 396–411; creating spaces for healing the spirit, 410–411; ethnography of urban, Black girlhood, 401–402; negotiating gender and queer identity in "the New South," 402–405; Outkast as pedagogy, 407–410; reframing Hip Hop pedagogies from the South, 405–407; students identifying with Hip Hop, 396–401
queer people in Hip Hop and science education, 313–314

Al-Rabita Al-Qalamiya, 100
race and Hip Hop education, 304–305
Race Music, 275
racial authenticity, 280–281
racial identity and neo-apartheidism, 80–81
racial segregation, 205
racism in Spain, 142–145
Rainbow Theatre, 336
Rakim, 3, 30–32, 379; on being inspired, 41–42; on female emcees, 45; on his book, 41; on his personal favorites,

51–52; introduction to Hip Hop, 36–37; on spiritual practices, 47
Ramsey, Guthrie, 275
"Rapper's Delight" (song), 34–35, 379
Ras Kass, 275
"ready-to-wear" education, 325
"Real Talk: Hip Hop Education for Social Justice," 406
Real Talk project, 407, 409
Real Women Have Curves (play), 340
Reconnect the String: The African Origins of Hip Hop Culture and Its Ancestral Healing Power (Emile YX?), 78
Red Alert (radio show), 35
Reflection Eternal, 32
reggae, 255, 256
Reid, L. A., 169
Religious Freedom Act, 122
resistance literature and lyrics, 89–91
respectability politics, 352
restorative community engagement, 340
Restorative Justice course, 330
"Retrospect for Life" (song), 284
Richardson, Elaine, 401
Rihani, Amin, 100
Rize (documentary), 334
"Roar, Young Lions" (music video), 71
Roberts, Justice, 258
Robinson, A. J., 322–345; Black history, 331–335; common core, 331–335; curriculum design, 331–335; final reflections, 340–342; Freire, Paulo, and pedagogy of the oppressed, 324–325; Hip Hop culture as community, 327–331; Hip Hop pedagogies, field trips with, 337–338; Hip Hop theatre of the oppressed, 335–337; pedagogy of the oppressed in public schools, 325–327; student protest, 338–340; Whiteness, impact of his, 322–324
Robinson, Andy, 179n1
Roc the Mic: The Language of Hip Hop Culture (Alim), 29–30
The Roots, 51
"Ropes" (song), 394
Rosales, Alvin, 337, 338, 339
Rose, Tricia, 274
Ross, Reagan, 206, 210–212
Ross, Rick, 51
Rox the Fox, 392
Rozzano X, 79

Salloum, Jackie, 84
Salti, Ramzi, 87

INDEX

Salt-N-Pepa, 108
San (first people), 58, 82
Sanchez, Sista Sonia, 414–415
Saulter-villegas, Jaquanda: on Kuumba Lynx, 181, 183; on longitudinal excellence, 188–189; lyrics, 185–187
Scarface, 30
Schooling in Capitalist America (Bowles and Gintis), 275
Schoolly D, 42
Schultz, Kathy, 270
Science Genius, 304–305, 314, 315, 319
Scott, Jill, 394
Scott-Heron, Gil, 43
Secola, Keith, 123
segregation, racial, 205
self-expression, 210, 326–327
Seminole, 129
Seventh Generation prophecy, 126
The Seventh Seal (album), 44
Shakur, Assata, 230
Shakur, Tupac, 32, 105, 107, 108, 134, 230–231, 327
Shange, Ntozake, 371, 401
ShapeShifters (Album), 394
Sha-Rock, 45
Shawel, Tabia, 31
Shulman, Lee, 288–289
Sigel, Beanie, 283–284
silence, 285–286
Sinatra, Frank, 51–52
"Sing for Me, I'm Dying of Thirst"? (song), 277
Sins Invalid, 377, 385, 387
Slingshot Hip Hop (film), 84
Slowe, Lucy Diggs, 369
Sly, 43
Small, Christopher, 275
Smith, Dylan, 326
Smith, Ottis, 383
Smitherman, Geneva, Dr., 56
Snoop Dogg, 30, 105
social consciousness through Hip Hop pedagogies, 331
social emotional intelligence, 397–398
social justice arts ecosystem, creating, 197–203; *see also* Mural Music & Arts Project (MMAP)
social justice-centered Hip Hop pedagogy, 249–250, 339
social movement and Hip Hop culture, 326, 337–338
social transformation, 207, 256, 334
sociopolitical consciousness, 248
Sol Patches, 391
Sotomayor, Justice, 258
The Souls of Black Folk (Du Bois), 264
Souter, David, 284
South Africa, Hip Hop in. *see* knowledge of self in "post"-apartheid South Africa
Spady, James G., 30, 31
Spain. *see* La Llama Rap Colectivo
spirit murdering, 400–401, 410–411
spoken word, 229–230; pedagogies, 234, 253, 334, 337; workshops, 325
spoken word poetry, ethnography of, 413–421; Brooks, Gwendolyn, and a pedagogy of possibility, 415–417; centering justice, theorizing futures, 418–421; friends in writing, 417–418; introduction, 413–414; Sanchez, Sista Sonia, 414–415
Spur Pourier, 111
Stetsenko, Anna, 420
"Still Got Love for You" (song), 283
"Still Standing" (song), 394
Still Waters Run Deep, 179
Story, Kaila Adia, 17; on Black feminist theory, 365–369; on engaging Black queer bodies, 365–369; on homophobia, 365–369
storytelling, 213–241, 336, 360; beyond healing and toward growth, 219; concept of stories, 214, 216–217; decolonizing the mind, 232–241; envisioning safe, sustainable futures, 223–226; ethic and practice of radical love, 219–223; Hip Hop, spoken word, and performance theatre in prisons, 227–230; Rikers Island: building curriculum in reverse, 230–232; trauma as collective and cumulative, 217–218; writing impossible worlds into existence, 226
Stovall, David, 403
Strange Fruit (radio show), 366
"Strange Fruit" (song), 333
Street Conscious Rap (Alim and Spady), 30
"Street Religion" (song), 208–209
student protest and Hip Hop pedagogies, 338–340
Sugarhill Gang, 35, 379, 381, 383
Summer School (film), 276
Supaman, 123
sustaining community through Hip Hop. *see* Mural Music & Arts Project (MMAP)
sustaining revolution through Hip Hop. *see* Hip Hop, sustaining revolution through

Sweat the Technique: Revelations on Creativity from the Lyrical Genius (Rakim), 31
Syria, revolution in. *see* Hip Hop, sustaining revolution through
SyrianamericanA (album), 83–84
"#Syria" (song), 94

Tall Paul, 252–253; growing up Hip Hop, 104–106; indigenous language revitalization and culture, 113–115
Tarumoto-Wallace, Victoria, 326
Taylor, Paul, 256
teacher education, 290; and behavior management in class, 328; for culturally relevant pedagogies, 260–262, 265, 325; for culturally sustaining pedagogies, 260–261, 265–266; programs for updated curriculum, 323–324; for science education, 300–302, 309–311, 317–318; transformative justice, 419
teacher participation, 307–308, 323–324
teacher-student involvement, 260–261
Teen Mural Program (TMP), 200, 203–205
Temple, Rob Da Noize, 377, 383
Terman, Lewis, 262
Terminator X, DJ, 32
Terrell, Mary Church, 361
Tha Global Cipha: Hip Hop Culture and Consciousness (Alim and Spady), 30
Thanks Joey, *86*
Tharp, Twyla, 225
theatre, liberatory, 335–336
Theatre of the Oppressed, 335–337
Their Eyes Were Watching God, 273
THEM ("Trying Hard to Express Myself"), 415–416
Thiong'o, Ngũgĩ wa, 232
Thisability (disability newspaper), 389
Thomas, Clarence, 284
Thorpe, Jim, 113
Thriller (album), 61
Thrower, Emmett, 378
Toney, Alvin, 36
Tongva people, 116
Tough, Paul, 397
transitional youth in MMAP, 201–203
A Tribe Called Quest, 270
Trina, 30
Trudell, John, 116
Tuck, Eve, 261
turntablism, 316
Twilight Program, 278
Twista, 105

United Alliance Community Center, 266–267
Urban League, 386
Urban Science Education, 304–305
Uses of the Erotic (Lorde), 369
US Hip Hop in South Africa, 62
UVA guys, 198

verve, 252
Vilaubi, Larry, 326
Vita E Clevelant, 391
Vita E & Kat So Poetic, 391

Wagner, Tony, 397
Waln, Frank, 121–122, 123
Warrior Writers, 336–337
Watson, Henry Lewis, 176
Wattad, Nizar, 84
WBLS (radio), 35
Wells, Ida B., 371
West Coast Hip Hop, 65
WFPL (local NPR station), 366
Wheelchair Sports Camp, 383
When Chickenheads Come Home to Roost (Morgan), 349
Where Is Hope-The Art of Murder: Police Brutality against People with Disabilities (Thrower), 378
White: disability movement, 386; gaze, 255–256, 259, 264; patriarchal culture, 366; supremacist backlash, 258, 268n14
White, Josh, 389
Whiteness: impact on Hip Hop pedagogy, 322–324; in school, 281
Williams, Kiyan, 355–357
Williams, Patricia, 410
Williams, Shazz, 391
Wilson, August, 333
Winder, Tanaya, 103; Black and Brown peoples, connection between, 129; Dream Warriors, founding, 109–110; growing up Hip Hop, 108–109; healing and solidarities through Hip Hop, 117–118; Indigenous peoples, inclusion of, 128; Indigenous women and kids, working with, 118–119
Winn, Maisha (aka Maisha Fisher), 193–194, 195; literocracy, 413–414; on pedagogy of possibility, 415
Winters, Robert, 378
Wiz Khalifa, 168–170; *Deal or No Deal* (song), 170; *Kush and Orange Juice* (song), 170

women: Black, narrative around sexuality and pleasure, 353–357; emcees, 45–46; in Hip Hop and science education, 313–314; rappers, 102n3, 392; *see also* Hip Hop feminism
Wonder, Stevie, 284
Wong, Casey Philip, 197
Word Up! (magazine), 61, 71
World Islamic Economic Forum, 219
Writing in Rhythm: Spoken Word Poetry in Urban Classrooms (Fisher), 413, 417
Wu-Tang Clan, 252
Waqar: on bad naming of El Raval, 135; on being Muslim, 136; on Catalonian independence, 148–149; on facing racism, 143–144; on gentrification of El Raval, 149–152; "la Ley Mordaza," 145–146; "Luchando Derechos," 136–137, 141; lyrics on king, 146–148; "Protesto," 145; relating to Hip Hop, 134; on Rhyme Workshop, 133; "Verdades Ocultas," 142–143; "Voces Mudas," 153–154

X-Clan, 60
xenophobia in Spain, 142–145
Xhosa (angry looking man), 82

Yassin Alsalman, 84
Yo! Bumrush the Show (album), 32, 38
Young Ant, 391
Youth Speaks, 213, 219–223, 323, 337

Zimmerman, George, 400
Zulu Nation, 60, 82

Founded in 1893,
UNIVERSITY OF CALIFORNIA PRESS
publishes bold, progressive books and journals
on topics in the arts, humanities, social sciences,
and natural sciences—with a focus on social
justice issues—that inspire thought and action
among readers worldwide.

The UC PRESS FOUNDATION
raises funds to uphold the press's vital role
as an independent, nonprofit publisher, and
receives philanthropic support from a wide
range of individuals and institutions—and from
committed readers like you. To learn more, visit
ucpress.edu/supportus.

www.ingramcontent.com/pod-product-compliance
Lightning Source LLC
Chambersburg PA
CBHW032221230426
43666CB00033B/276